The Case for Poetry

PRENTICE-HALL ENGLISH LITERATURE SERIES

Maynard Mack, *Editor*

SECOND EDITION

The Case for Poetry
A Critical Anthology

Poems ◆ Cases ◆ Critiques

FREDERICK L. GWYNN
Trinity College

RALPH W. CONDEE
Pennsylvania State University

ARTHUR O. LEWIS, JR.
Pennsylvania State University

Prentice-Hall, Inc., Englewood Cliffs, New Jersey

PRENTICE-HALL INTERNATIONAL, INC., *London*
PRENTICE-HALL OF AUSTRALIA, PTY., LTD., *Sydney*
PRENTICE-HALL OF CANADA, LTD., *Toronto*
PRENTICE-HALL OF INDIA (PRIVATE), LTD., *New Delhi*
PRENTICE-HALL OF JAPAN, INC., *Tokyo*

Second printing........August, 1965

Library of Congress Catalog Card Number: 65-11029

Printed in the United States of America   11600-C

Acknowledgments

We are indebted to the poets, critics, and publishers listed below and in the later references,[1] and particularly grateful to the colleagues and students at the Pennsylvania State University, the University of Virginia, Yale University, Trinity College, and others who made suggestions or pointed out errors over the years. Actual compilation of the book was speeded by the (Arms and) Kuntz checklist, *Poetry Explication* (1950, 1962), in addition to the usual bibliographical sources. Behind this activity lies an indebtedness to the seminal critics, editors, and writers of texts and textbooks who have shaped our conceptions of poems, poetry, and poetics. Specifically, we thank Professor Priscilla Tyler and Mr. Kenneth Fish for material written especially for this volume; Professors Wentworth K. Brown and Sterling P. Olmsted for the emphasis on testing creative writing by paraphrase, in their *Language and Literature* (1962), Chap. 2; Professors Fredson T. Bowers, John C. Gerber, and Leonard F. Dean, and Mr. Paul E. O'Connell and Mrs. Barbara Conner of Prentice-Hall, for editorial advice; and Miss Barbara Barrett, for secretarial aid. We are most profoundly grateful to Professor Maynard Mack, Editor of the series, for his sensitive and sensible counsel on making books.

Aiken, "When Trout Swim Down Great Ormond Street," from *Collected Poems*, published by Oxford University Press, Copyright 1925, 1953 by Conrad Aiken. Anon., "Riddle #29: The Moon and the Sun" and "Deor," trans. Burton Raffel, *Poems from the Old English*, by permission of the author and the University of Nebraska Press. "Western Wind" Opinion 1: Donald A. Stauffer, *The Nature of Poetry*, by permission of W. W. Norton & Company, Inc., and Miss Ruth Stauffer. Opinion 2: Robert Penn Warren, by permission of *The Kenyon Review* and the author. Opinion 3: F. W. Bateson, *English Poetry: A Critical Introduction*, by permission of Longmans, Green & Co., Inc. Opinion 4: Richard R. Griffith, by permission of *The Explicator* and the author. "Humpty Dumpty" Opinion 1: Iona and Peter Opie, *The Oxford Dictionary of Nursery Rhymes*, by permission of the Clarendon Press, Oxford. Opinion 2: Bernard Knieger, "Humpty Dumpty & Symbolism," *College English*, Feb. 1959, reprinted with the permission of the National Council of Teachers of English. Auden, "Musée des Beaux Arts" and "Law Like Love," Copyright 1940 by W. H. Auden. Reprinted from *The Collected Poetry of W. H. Auden*, by permission of Random House, Inc., and Faber & Faber, Ltd. Betjeman, "In Westminster Abbey," from *Collected Poems* by John Betjeman, by permission of Houghton Mifflin Company and John Murray, Ltd. "The Sick Rose" Opinion 1: E. M. W. Tillyard, *Poetry Direct and Oblique*, Copyright 1934, 1945; by permission of The Macmillan Company and Chatto and Windus, Ltd. Opinion 2: Reprinted by permission of the publishers from C. M. Bowra, *The Romantic Imagination*, Cambridge, Mass.: Harvard University Press, Copyright 1949, by The President and Fellows of Harvard College. Opinion 3: Laurence Perrine, *The English Journal*, Sept. 1962, by permission of the National Council of Teachers of English and the author. Booth, "Siasconset Song," from *Letter from a Distant Land* by Philip Booth. Copyright 1951 by Philip Booth. First published in *The New Yorker*. Reprinted by permission of The Viking Press, Inc. Bridges, "A Passer-by," from *The Shorter Poems of Robert Bridges*, by permission of the Clarendon Press, Oxford. Ciardi, "Two Egrets" from *As If* and "In Place of a Curse" from *39 Poems*. Copyright by Rutgers, The State University of N. J., 1955, 1959. Reprinted by permission of the author. *The Rime of the Ancient Mariner* Opinion 3: Newton P. Stallknecht, *PMLA*, by permission of The Modern Language Association of America and the author; and in *Strange Seas of Thought*, 1945. Opinion 4: Elizabeth Nitchie, *PMLA*, by permission of The Modern Language Association of America and the author. Opinion 5: John Livingston Lowes, *The Road to Xanadu*, by permission of the Houghton Mifflin Company. Opinion 6: Reprinted by permission of the publishers from C. M. Bowra, *The Romantic Imagination*, Cambridge, Mass.: Harvard University Press, Copyright, 1949, by The President and Fellows of Harvard College.

1 The analysis of Frost's "The Draft Horse" was printed in the December 1964 issue of *College English*, and is reprinted by permission of the Editor and the National Council of Teachers of English.

Opinion 7: D. W. Harding, *Scrutiny*, 1941; by permission of Cambridge University Press and the author. Opinion 8: Frederick A. Pottle, "Modern Criticism of *The Ancient Mariner*," from *Essays on the Teaching of English* by Edward J. Gordon and Edward S. Noyes. Copyright © 1960, the National Council of Teachers of English. Reprinted by permission of Appleton-Century-Crofts and the author. Opinion 9: Lionel Stevenson, by permission of *The Personalist* and the author. Opinion 10: Charles A. Owen, *College English*, Jan. 1962; by permission of the National Council of Teachers of English and the author. Cummings, "anyone lived in a pretty how town" and "my father moved through dooms of love." Copyright, 1940, by E. E. Cummings. Reprinted from *Poems 1923-1954* by E. E. Cummings by permission of Harcourt, Brace & World, Inc. Opinion 1: Herbert C. Barrows and William R. Steinhoff, *The Explicator*, copyright 1950; by permission of *The Explicator* and the author. Opinion 2: Priscilla Tyler, who graciously wrote her analysis for this edition. De la Mare, "The Listeners," from *Collected Poems* by Walter de la Mare. Copyright, 1920, by Henry Holt and Company, Inc. Copyright, 1948, by Walter de la Mare. By permission of the publishers. Opinion 1: J. P. Kirby, *The Explicator*, copyright 1943; by permission of *The Explicator* and the author. Opinion 2: F. L. Lucas, *The Decline and Fall of the Romantic Ideal*, by permission of Cambridge University Press. Opinion 3: J. M. Purcell, *The Explicator*, copyright 1945. Opinion 4: DeLancey Ferguson, *The Explicator*, copyright 1945. By permission of *The Explicator* and the authors. De Suze, "Guitar Lament for a Mountain Boy," by permission of *The Saturday Review* and the author. Dickinson, Poems #130, 216, 303, 585, 632, 712, 1463, 1624. Reprinted by permission of the publishers and The Trustees of Amherst College from Thomas H. Johnson, Editor, *The Poems of Emily Dickinson*. Cambridge, Mass.: The Belknap Press of Harvard University Press. Copyright, 1951, 1955, by The President and Fellows of Harvard College. "Because I Could Not Stop for Death" Opinion 1: Allen Tate, *Reactionary Essays on Poetry and Ideas*, copyright 1936; by permission of Charles Scribner's Sons. Opinion 2: Yvor Winters, *In Defense of Reason*, by permission of the author and The Swallow Press and William Morrow and Company. Copyright 1938 by New Directions; copyright 1947 by Yvor Winters. Opinion 3: Richard Chase, *Emily Dickinson*, copyright 1951; by permission of William Sloane Associates, Inc. Opinion 4: Theodore C. Hoepfner, by permission of *American Literature* and the author. "A Route of Evanescence" Opinion 1: George F. Whicher, *This Was a Poet: A Critical Biography of Emily Dickinson*, copyright 1938; by permission of Charles Scribner's Sons. Opinion 2: Grover Smith, *The Explicator*, copyright 1949; by permission of *The Explicator* and the author. Opinion 3: Kenneth E. Fish, Jr., written for this edition, based on class discussion, Trinity College, Spring 1962. "The Canonization" Opinion 1: Pierre Legouis, *Donne the Craftsman*, by permission of Henri Didier and the author. Opinion 2: Cleanth Brooks, *The Well Wrought Urn*, by permission of the author. Dugan, "How We Heard the Name," reprinted from *Poems* (1961), Yale University Press, by permission of the author. Eberhart, " 'When Doris Danced' " and "The Horse Chestnut Tree," from *Collected Poems*, Copyright © 1960 by Richard Eberhart. Reprinted by permission of Oxford University Press, Inc., and Chatto & Windus, Ltd. Eliot, "The Love Song of J. Alfred Prufrock" and "Sweeney Among the Nightingales," from *Collected Poems of T. S. Eliot*, copyright, 1936, by Harcourt, Brace & World, Inc.; renewed ©, 1964, by T. S. Eliot and reprinted by permission of the publishers and Faber & Faber, Ltd. Opinion 1: George Williamson, *A Reader's Guide to T. S. Eliot*, by permission of The Noonday Press. Opinion 2 and Opinion A: Reprinted by permission of the publishers from Douglas Bush, *Mythology and the Romantic Tradition in English Poetry*, Cambridge, Mass.: Harvard University Press, Copyright, 1937, by The President and Fellows of Harvard College. Opinion 3 and Opinions B and C: Elizabeth Drew, *T. S. Eliot: The Design of His Poetry*, copyright 1949; by permission of Charles Scribner's Sons. Opinion 4 and Opinion C: Donald A. Stauffer, *The Nature of Poetry*, by permission of W. W. Norton & Company, Inc., and Miss Ruth Stauffer. "Journey of the Magi," from *Collected Poems 1909-1962* by T. S. Eliot, copyright, 1936, by Harcourt, Brace & World, Inc.; © 1963, 1964, by T. S. Eliot. Reprinted by permission of the publishers and Faber & Faber, Ltd. "Days" Opinion 2: Richard R. Kirk and Roger P. McCutcheon, *An Introduction to the Study of Poetry*, by permission of American Book Company. Opinion 3: Joseph Jones, *The Explicator*, copyright 1946. Opinion 4: George Arms, *The Explicator*, copyright 1945. By permission of *The Explicator* and the authors. Fearing, "Dirge," by permission of the author. Francis, "Pitcher," Copyright © 1953 by Robert Francis. Reprinted from *The Orb Weaver* by Robert Francis by permission of Wesleyan University Press. Frost, "Mending Wall," "After Apple-Picking," "Fire and Ice," "Stopping by Woods on a Snowy Evening," "The Most of It," from *Complete Poems of Robert Frost*. Copyright, 1930, 1949, by Henry Holt and Company, Inc. By permission of the publishers. "Design," from *Complete Poems of Robert Frost*. Copyright 1936, by Robert Frost. Copyright renewed © 1964 by Lesley Frost Ballantine. Reprinted by permission of Holt, Rinehart & Winston, Inc. Opinion 1: Reuben A. Brower, *The Poetry of Robert Frost: Constellations of Intention*, by permission of Oxford University Press, Inc. Opinion 2: Elizabeth Drew, *Poetry: A Modern Guide to Its Understanding*, by permission of Dell Publishing Co., Inc., and Holt, Rinehart and Winston, Inc. "It Bids Pretty Fair," from *Steeple Bush* by Robert Frost. Copyright, 1947, by Henry Holt & Company, Inc. By permission of the publishers. "The Draft Horse," from *In the Clearing* by Robert Frost. Copyright © 1962 by Robert

Frost. Reprinted by permission of Holt, Rinehart & Winston, Inc. "Elegy" Opinion 2: I. A. Richards, *Practical Criticism*, by permission of Harcourt, Brace & World, Inc. Opinion 3: William Empson, *English Pastoral Poetry*, by permission of W. W. Norton & Company, Inc. Opinion 4: Cleanth Brooks, *The Well Wrought Urn*, by permission of the author. Opinion 5: William Empson, by permission of *The Sewanee Review*. Opinion 6: Frank H. Ellis, *PMLA*, by permission of The Modern Language Association of America and the author. Gunn, "Jesus and His Mother," reprinted from *The Sense of Movement* of Thom Gunn by permission of The University of Chicago Press and Faber & Faber, Ltd. Copyright 1957 by Thomson William Gunn. Haiku, Moritake, trans. Deutsch, and Opinion 1: reprinted from Babette Deutsch, *Poetry Handbook: A Dictionary of Terms*, 1957, by permission of Funk & Wagnalls Company, Inc. Issa and Bashō, trans. Keene, and Opinion 2: reprinted from *Japanese Literature: An Introduction for Western Readers*, Copyright 1955 by Donald Keene, Published by Grove Press, by permission of Grove Press and John Murray, Ltd. Chiyo, trans. Henderson, and Opinion 3: from *An Introduction to Haiku* by Harold G. Henderson. Copyright © 1958 by Harold G. Henderson. Reprinted by permission of Doubleday & Company, Inc. Hall, "The Sleeping Giant," from *Exiles and Marriages* by Donald Hall. Copyright © 1955 by Donald Hall. First published in *The New Yorker*. Reprinted by permission of The Viking Press, Inc. Hardy, "The Darkling Thrush," "The Phantom Horsewoman," "The Oxen," Copyright 1925 by The Macmillan Company. By permission of The Macmillan Company, the Trustees of the Hardy Estate, and The Macmillan Company of Canada, Ltd. "In Time of 'The Breaking of Nations,'" from *The Collected Poems of Thomas Hardy* by permission of The Macmillan Company, the Trustees of the Hardy Estate, Macmillan & Co., Ltd., London, and The Macmillan Company of Canada Limited. "Upon Julia's Clothes" Opinion 1: E. M. W. Tillyard, *Essays and Studies by Members of the English Association for 1934*, by permission of Oxford University Press, Inc. Opinion 2: Elisabeth W. Schneider, *The Explicator*, Mar. 1955. Opinion 3: Nat. Henry, *The Explicator*, Dec. 1955. Opinion 4: William O. Harris, *The Explicator*, Dec. 1962. By permission of *The Explicator* and the authors. Hopkins, "Spring," "Spring and Fall: To a Young Child," "Thou Art Indeed Just, O Lord," "God's Grandeur," "Heaven-Haven," "Felix Randal," "Pied Beauty," "The Windhover," from *Poems of Gerard Manley Hopkins*, Third Edition, edited by W. H. Gardner. Copyright 1948 by Oxford University Press, Inc. Reprinted by permission. Housman, "Loveliest of Trees," To an Athlete Dying Young," "Terence, This Is Stupid Stuff," "Easter Hymn," "I to My Perils," from *The Collected Poems of A. E. Housman*, Copyright, 1922, 1940, by Henry Holt and Company, Inc. Copyright, 1936, 1950, by Barclays Bank Ltd. By permission of the publishers and The Society of Authors as the Literary Representative of the Trustees of the Estate of the late A. E. Housman, and Messrs. Jonathan Cape, Ltd., publishers of A. E. Housman's *Collected Poems*. Jarrell, "The Death of the Ball Turret Gunner," from *Little Friend, Little Friend* by Randall Jarrell, by permission of the author. "Ode on a Grecian Urn" Footnote: Robert M. Adams, by permission. Kennedy, "Little Elegy," copyright © 1960 by X. J. Kennedy; originally appeared in *The New Yorker*, June, 1960. From *Nude Descending a Staircase* by X. J. Kennedy. Reprinted by permission of Doubleday & Company, Inc. Kipling, "Danny Deever," from *Departmental Ditties and Barrack-Room Ballads*, by Rudyard Kipling, reprinted by permission of Mrs. George Bambridge, Doubleday & Company, Inc., and the Macmillan Company of Canada, Limited. Levertov, "The Jacob's Ladder," from *The Jacob's Ladder* by Denise Levertov. Copyright © 1961 by Denise Levertov Goodman. Reprinted by permission of New Directions. The selections from MacLeish, "The End of the World," "You, Andrew Marvell," "Ars Poetica" from *Collected Poems* by Archibald MacLeish are reprinted by permission of and arrangement with Houghton Mifflin Company, the authorized publishers. Meredith, "Lucifer in Starlight," reprinted from *Selected Poems* by George Meredith, Copyright 1897 by George Meredith, 1925 by William M. Meredith, used by permission of the publishers, Charles Scribner's Sons. "When I Consider How My Light Is Spent" Opinion 1: E. M. W. Tillyard, *Milton*, copyright 1930; by permission of The Macmillan Company and Chatto and Windus, Ltd. Opinion 2: E. G. Brown, *Milton's Blindness*, by permission of Columbia University Press. Opinion 3: Earl Daniels, *The Art of Reading Poetry*, by permission of Holt, Rinehart & Winston, Inc., and the author. Opinion 4: Donald C. Dorian, *The Explicator*, copyright 1951; by permission of *The Explicator* and the author. Opinion 5: Lysander Kemp, by permission of *The Hopkins Review*. Nash, "The Private Dining Room," reprinted by permission of the author. Copyright © 1951 by The New Yorker Magazine, Inc. Nemerov, "The Goose Fish," from *The Salt Garden*, reprinted by permission of the author. Pound, "Sestina: Altaforte," "In a Station of the Metro," "Envoi" are from *Personae* by Ezra Pound, Copyright 1926 by Ezra Pound, and are reprinted with the permission of the publisher, New Directions. Opinion 1: T. A. Hanzo, *The Explicator*, copyright 1953. Opinion 2: John J. Espey, *The Explicator*, copyright 1953. By permission of *The Explicator* and the authors. Ransom, "Winter Remembered," "Bells for John Whiteside's Daughter," reprinted from *Selected Poems* by John Crowe Ransom, by permission of Alfred A. Knopf, Inc. Copyright 1924, 1945 by Alfred A. Knopf, Inc. Opinion 1: Robert Penn Warren, by permission of *The Virginia Quarterly Review* and the author. Opinion 2: R. B. Heilman, by permission of *Pacific Specator* and the author. "The Equilibrists," Copyright, 1924, 1927 by Alfred A. Knopf, Inc. Renewed, 1952, 1955 by John Crowe Ransom. Reprinted from *Selected Poems* by John Crowe Ransom. Reed, "Naming of Parts," from *A Map of Verona and Other Poems*, by Henry Reed, copyright, 1947, by Henry Reed. Reprinted by permission of Harcourt, Brace & World, Inc., and Jonathan Cape, Ltd. "Luke Havergal" Opinion 1: Ellsworth Barnard, *Edwin Arlington Robinston: A Critical Study*, copyright 1952; by permission of The Macmillan Company. Opinion 2: Walter Gierasch, *The Explicator*, copyright 1944; by permission of *The Explicator* and the author. The selection from Robinson, "Miniver Cheevy," reprinted from *The Town Down the River*, Copyright 1910 by Charles Scribner's Sons, 1938 by Ruth Nivison; used by permission of the publishers; "Mr. Flood's Party," reprinted with permission of The Macmillan Company from *Collected Poems* by Edwin Arlington Robinson. Copyright 1921 by Edwin Arlington Robinson, Renewed 1949 by Ruth Nivison. Roethke, "My Papa's Waltz," "Elegy for Jane," copyright 1942 by Hearst Magazines, Inc., from *Words for the Wind* by Theodore Roethke. Reprinted by permission of Doubleday & Company, Inc. "When to the Sessions" Opinion 1: Reprinted by permission of the publishers from Stephen C. Pepper, *The Basis of Criticism in the Arts*, Cambridge, Mass.: Harvard University Press, Copyright, 1945, by The President and Fellows of Harvard College. Opinion 2: Samuel R. Levin, *Linguistic Structures in Poetry*, Mouton & Co., The Hague, The Netherlands; by permission of the publisher and the author. "Poor Soul, the Center" Opinion 1: Donald A. Stauffer, by permission of *The American Scholar* and Miss Ruth Stauffer. Opinion 2: Edward Hubler, *The Sense of Shakespeare's Sonnets*, by permission of Princeton University Press. Shapiro, "Buick," Copyright 1941 by Karl Shapiro. Reprinted from *Poems 1940-1953*, by Karl Shapiro, by permission of Random House, Inc. "As You Say: An Anti-Poem," © Copyright 1964 by Karl Shapiro. Reprinted from *The Bourgeois Poet*, by Karl Shapiro, by permission of Random House, Inc. "Ode to the West Wind" Opinion 1: Richard H. Fogle, by permission of *The Journal of English Literary History*, Johns Hopkins Press, and the author. Opinion 2: F. W. Bateson, *English Poetry: A Critical Introduction*, by permission of Longmans, Green & Co., Inc. Opinion 3: From *The Visionary Company* by Harold Bloom. Copyright © 1961 by Harold Bloom. Reprinted by permission of Doubleday & Company, Inc., and the author. Spender, "I Think Continually of Those," Copyright 1934 and renewed 1961 by Stephen Spender. Reprinted from *Collected Poems 1928-1953*, by Stephen Spender, by permission of Random House, Inc., and Faber & Faber, Ltd. Starbuck, "Fable for Blackboard," from *Bone Thoughts* by George Starbuck, reprinted by permission of Yale University Press. Stephens, "The Waste Places," from *Songs from the Clay* by James Stephens, reprinted by permission of The Macmillan Company, Macmillan & Co. of Canada, and Mrs. James Stephens. Stevens, "The Emperor of Ice-Cream," reprinted from *Harmonium* by Wallace Stevens, by permission of Alfred A. Knopf, Inc. Copyright 1923, 1931 by Alfred A. Knopf, Inc. Opinion 1: Copyright, 1932, by Richard P. Blackmur. Reprinted from his book, *Language as Gesture* by permission of Harcourt, Brace & World, Inc. Opinion 2: Richard Ellmann, *The Kenyon Review*, by permission of the author. Opinion 3: Max Herzberg and Wallace Stevens, *The Explicator*, copyright 1948; by permission of *The Explicator* and the authors. Opinion 4: M. L. Rosenthal, *The Modern Poets: A Critical Introduction*, by permission of Oxford University Press and the author. "Sunday Morning," "Anecdote of the Jar," "The Plot Against the Giant," Copyright, 1923 by Wallace Stevens. Renewed, 1951. Reprinted from *The Collected Poems of Wallace Stevens*, by permission of Alfred A. Knopf, Inc. "Tears, Idle Tears" Opinion 1: Fred H. Stocking, *The Explicator*, copyright 1947; by permission of *The Explicator* and the author. Opinion 2: Cleanth Brooks, *The Well Wrought Urn*, by permission of the author. Opinion 3: Graham Hough, by permission of *The Hopkins Review*. Thomas, "Poem in October," from *Selected Writings of Dylan Thomas*, Copyright 1946 by New Directions, reprinted with permission of New Directions, the Trustees of the Dylan Thomas Estate, and J. M. Dent & Sons, Ltd. "In My Craft or Sullen Art," from *The Collected Poems of Dylan Thomas*, © 1957 by New Directions. Reprinted by permission of New Directions and J. M. Dent & Sons, Ltd. Wilbur, "June Light," from *The Beautiful Changes and Other Poems*, copyright, 1947, by Richard Wilbur. Reprinted by permission of Harcourt, Brace & World, Inc. "The Death of a Toad," Copyright, 1950, by Richard Wilbur. Reprinted from his volume, *Ceremony and Other Poems* by permission of Harcourt, Brace & World, Inc. "Two Voices in a Meadow" and "Junk," © 1957 and 1961 by Richard Wilbur. Reprinted from his volume *Advice to a Prophet and Other Poems* by permission of Harcourt, Brace & World, Inc. Yeats, "The Magi," Copyright 1916 by The Macmillan Company, Renewed 1944 by Bertha Georgie Yeats; "Leda and the Swan," "Among School Children," Copyright 1928 by The Macmillan Company, Renewed 1956 by Georgie Yeats; "Long-Legged Fly," Copyright 1940 by Georgie Yeats; "The Scholars," "Sailing to Byzantium," Copyright 1928, 1933, 1950 by The Macmillan Company. Reprinted with permission of The Macmillan Company, A. P. Watt & Son, Mrs. W. B. Yeats, and The Macmillan Company of Canada, Ltd., from *Collected Poems* by W. B. Yeats. Opinion 1: Elder Olson, by permission of *The University of Kansas City Review* and the author. Opinion 2: Cleanth Brooks, *Modern Poetry and Tradition*, by permission of The University of North Carolina Press. Opinion 3: Donald A. Stauffer, *The Nature of Poetry*, by permission of W. W. Norton & Company, Inc., and Miss Ruth Stauffer. Robinson, "Luke Havergal," "Cliff Klingenhagen," "Richard Cory," reprinted with the permission of Charles Scribner's Sons from *Children of the Night* by Edwin Arlington Robinson (Charles Scribner's Sons, 1897).

Introduction to the Second Edition

When *The Case for Poetry: A New Anthology* was published in 1954, its subtitle indicated that it presumed to be another but different collection, whereas the main title was designed to signal its intellectual, critical, and even disputatious concern with the genre of lyric poetry. With one-third of its poems bearing explications, it was one of the many offspring of the New Criticism and of the Brooks and Warren school. But the details of its glossarial footnotes, dialectic cases and critiques, and reference bibliography attempted to provide something new—a substantial body of critical material from which understanding and appreciation could be inductively derived by students, especially those without a background of sophisticated reading. As the Introduction to the first edition stated,

> For each poem so treated, these opinions are selected and organized according to conflicting points of view, so as to present a case whose merits the reader may examine and judge, and in so doing, learn a great deal about the poem in particular and poetry in general.
> To speak genetically, we have crossed the reading of poems with the case method of learning that is now well established in the professional study of law, medicine, business administration, military science, diplomacy, social relations, and education. We have aimed at utilizing those features of the method that encourage close analysis of facts, judicious generalization, recognition of imponderables, critical decision, and respect for a total situation.

That the poems and the critical material satisfied the needs of some students and teachers seems demonstrated by the noiseless tenor of the book's life over a decade. Yet life means change, and there have been substantial additions to our textual and critical knowledge since the early 1950's. One is also happy to note that there has been a change in educational preparation, that young men and women know and expect more than they used to. And so another case for poetry may be made, with some new poems now available or better understood, some new critical opinions come to publication or to light, most of the original cases—now tested over a dozen years—newly tightened, condensed, or made more demanding by being simplified, and some that proved insufficiently challenging or persuasive excised. If the book can no longer accurately be called "A New Anthology," it is at least a newly changed one.

Figures will demonstrate the major changes between editions. In round numbers, there are now nearly 200 poems instead of 150, 25 having been dropped from the original selection, and 65 new choices added. Four of the 35 cases have gone, and one opinion each has been added to two cases. Two new critiques added to the original 22 make 24, with 10 opinions dropped and 18 added within 19 of the original critiques.

The poems are still arranged alphabetically by author to allow quick reference and individual sequence of class instruction, although there is of course an index and there is a pedagogical appendix that suggests patterns of assignment and discussion. An effort has been made to use the best text of each poem, with the original spelling and punctuation modernized only in poetry from the ballads to Dryden. Glossarial footnotes have been held to a reasonable minimum, and unless otherwise noted every gloss is based on the *Oxford English Dictionary* or the *Oxford Companion to Classical Literature*.

THE CASE FOR POETRY

The rationale of this textbook is that whereas good poems are autonomous works of art never to be translated fully into discursive language, most of them demand critical study to be appreciated, and such study must be highly organized to be effective. For teachers of poetry who have developed their own methods, this book offers 135 poems without any apparatus and another 58 whose cases and critiques can be ignored if necessary. For teachers and students who can make use of orientation and pressure toward resolution, the book offers suggestions for reading, together with the critical structures labeled cases and critiques. (See directions below.)

Critiques are comparatively sophisticated selections from published criticism, chosen to present varying general views of a poem or various particular points involved in understanding it. Many of these passages are necessarily abridged from much longer articles and chapters whose references are given for further consultation. Although chiefly explicatory, the critiques often introduce—or beg—general critical questions, allowing discussion of literary matters beyond the subject poems.

The cases comprise the basic educational aid, designed to lead the student step by step through the poems. Dialectical like most of the critiques, they usually represent simplifications of opinions about the poem, opinions and points invented by the editors or derived by them from some of the analyses listed after each case or occasionally from student argument, the whole having been summarized into opposing or overlapping thematic statements. (For most of the cases, the emphasis on a "primary theme" among several possibilities may be identified—in the later terms of Northrop Frye's *Anatomy of Criticism*, 1957—as an approach to *lyric* as *thematic mode* and *thematic form* and as an application of critical *formal commentary*.) As noted in the Introduction to the first edition, we feel that

> this method of poetic analysis, judiciously employed, is more effective than any other approach for bringing about understanding and appreciation. For one thing, it provides a critical vocabulary and atmosphere to be learned functionally and unobtrusively. For another, it makes inevitable the discussion of poems—and competitive discussion is the classroom's most powerful catalyst. But chiefly, it *forces* students to read carefully, to draw considered conclusions, to become aware of the mysterious effects of rhythm and symbol, to decide on the merits of poems, and to see poems as whole works of art. . . .

Suggestions for Using Poems, Cases, and Critiques

Poem Without Case or Critique

(For an example of this procedure, see the analysis of Frost's "The Draft Horse," page 131.)

1. Read the poem, preferably aloud, chiefly for the factual meaning. When reading aloud, observe appropriate pauses for normal phrasing and punctuation and for ends of lines, sections, and stanzas.

2. Paraphrase the poem, writing it out in literal prose if necessary, noting the words and phrases most difficult to translate and seeking reasons for the difficulty.

3. Note the structure of rhythm (recurring stresses), scanning each line if necessary, and trying to relate unusual metrical patterns to the meaning. (See appendix on Poetics.)

4. Note the structure of rhyme (recurring sounds), including alliteration, assonance, and end-rhyme, trying to discover any significant patterns. (See appendix.)

5. Note the structure of rhetoric, the recurring patterns of
   (a) syntax (grammatical relations of words, phrases, clauses, and sentences to each other),
   (b) sense-images (words addressed to the senses of seeing, hearing, smelling, tasting, touching, and moving) or their absence,
   (c) direct language or figurative (metaphorical) language,
   (d) symbols and archetypes, and
   (e) the speaker's tones. (See appendix.)

6. Try to summarize the preceding analysis in a phrase that indicates the primary theme of the poem, adding remarks that summarize the contribution of each structure to the theme.

7. Reread the poem, aloud if possible, trying to experience it as a whole.

Poem With Case or Critique

1. Read the whole poem, preferably aloud, chiefly for the factual meaning. When reading aloud, observe appropriate pauses for normal phrasing and punctuation and for ends of lines, sections, and stanzas.

2. Read the whole case or critique, observing the general differences among the opinions.

3. Make sure of the meaning of any technical terms in the case or critique, consulting the appendix on Poetics or a recent handbook or dictionary. (See Index.)

4. Consider the merits of the individual points in a case or critique, noting your agreement or comparative disagreement with each point by some comment or sign (e.g., "yes," "no," "partly"; plus, minus, plus-or-minus sign; plain, crossed, slashed number; uncircled, circled, parenthesized number).

5. As you work, note phrases or line-numbers that provide evidence for your reasoning.

6. Consider the merits of the opinions as wholes, noting your agreement or comparative disagreement by some comment or sign.

7. If no opinion seems satisfactory, note your own interpretation of the poem with several points as evidence.

8. Reread the poem, aloud if possible, and try to experience it as a totality of meaning, rhetoric, and sound.

Contents

When Trout Swim Down
Great Ormond Street

When trout swim down Great Ormond Street,
And sea-gulls cry above them lightly,
And hawthorns heave cold flagstones up
To blossom whitely,

Against odd walls of houses there,   5
Gustily shaking out in moonlight
Their country sweetness on sweet air;
And in the sunlight,

By the green margin of that water,   9
Children dip white feet and shout,
Casting nets in the braided water
To catch the trout:

Then I shall hold my breath and die,   13
Swearing I never loved you; no,
'You were not lovely!' I shall cry,
'I never loved you so.'

Riddle #29: The Moon and the Sun

I saw a silvery creature scurrying
Home, as lovely and light as heaven
Itself, running with stolen treasure
Between its horns. It hoped, by deceit
And daring and art, to set an arbor   5
There in that soaring castle. Then,
A shining creature, known to everyone
On earth, climbed the mountains and cliffs,
Rescued his prize, and drove the wily
Impostor back to darkness. It fled   10
To the west, swearing revenge. The morning
Dust scattered away, dew
Fell, and the night was gone. And no one
Knew where the soft-footed thief had vanished.

[1]

Deor

(Wayland, a legendary smith whom Nithad had crippled and enslaved,
forged himself metal wings, killed Nithad's sons, drugged and violated
Nithad's daughter, Beadhild, and flew to safety. Nithad's kingdom was
Wermland, now western Sweden.)

Wermland was misery's home for Wayland
The smith, stubborn even in suffering.
Enduring his exile alone, in longing
And wintry sadness, locked in the snows   4
Of that northern kingdom when Nithad slit
His sinews and trapped a wonderful slave.

That passed, and so may this.

Her brothers' death meant less to Beadhild   8
Than the tears she shed for herself, seeing
Her belly sprouting and knowing herself
With child, remembering nothing, never
Any man's bride but bearing fruit.

That passed, and so may this.

We've heard that rape in a thousand songs,   14
And the infinite love which left old Nithad
Tossing sleepless on a bed of regret.

That passed, and so may this.

And Theodoric, once thirty years   18
The Maerings' ruler, and now no more.

That passed, and so may this.

We've heard them sing the story of Ermric's   21
Fierceness, who ruled the Gothic folk
Like a savage wolf. His throne was set
In twisted hearts, and hundreds of warriors
Languished in futile dreams of his fall
While waiting, helpless, for what was sure to come.

That passed, and so may this.

They sat where Ermric chained them, empty   28
Of everything life had held, lost
In thoughts of their endless pain. And yet
They could have followed the silent footsteps

Of God, walking over the world,
Shedding mercy and grace to many   33
And dropping sorrow on a few lost souls.
Of myself I will say that once I sang
For the Héodénings, and held a place
In my master's heart. My name was Deor.
I sang in my good lord's service through many   38
Winters, until Heórrend won
My honors away, struck his harp
And stole my place with a poet's skill.

>   That passed, and so may this.

The Three Ravens

A Dirge

There were three Ravens sat on a tree,
>   Downe a downe, hey downe, hey downe.
There were three Ravens sat on a tree,
>   With a downe.
There were three Ravens sat on a tree,   5
They were as blacke as they might be.
>   With a downe derrie, derrie, derrie, downe, downe.

The one of them said to his mate,   8
>   Downe a downe, hey downe,
The one of them said to his mate,
>   With a downe.
The one of them said to his mate,   12
Where shall we our breakefast take?
>   With a downe derrie downe.

Downe in yonder greene field,   15
>   Downe a downe, hey downe,
Downe in yonder greene field,
>   With a downe.
Downe in yonder greene field   19
There lies a Knight slain under his shield,
>   With a downe.

His hounds they lie downe at his feete,   22
   Downe a downe, hey downe,
His hounds they lie downe at his feete,
   With a downe.
His hounds they lie downe at his feete,   26
So well they can their Master keepe,
   With a downe.

His Haukes they flie so eagerly,   29
   Downe a downe.
His Haukes they flie so eagerly,
   With a downe.
His Haukes they flie so eagerly,   33
There's no fowle dare him come nie,
   With a downe.

Downe there comes a fallow Doe,   36
   Downe a downe.
Downe there comes a fallow Doe,
   With a downe.
Downe there comes a fallow Doe,   40
As great with yong as she might goe,
   With a downe.

She lift up his bloudy hed,   43
   Downe a downe.
She lift up his bloudy hed,
   With a downe.
She lift up his bloudy hed,   47
And kist his wounds that were so red,
   With a downe.

She got him up upon her backe,   50
   Downe a downe.
She got him up upon her backe,
   With a downe.
She got him up upon her backe,   54
And carried him to earthen lake,
   With a downe.

She buried him before the prime,   57
   Downe a downe.

36 *fallow:* species of deer.   55 *lake:* pit.

She buried him before the prime,
   With a downe.
She buried him before the prime,   61
She was dead her selfe ere even-song time,
   With a downe.

God send every gentleman,   64
   Downe a downe.
God send every gentleman,
   With a downe.
God send every gentleman   68
Such haukes, such hounds, and such a Leman,
   With a downe.

Case

A

1. The poem is primarily a simple narrative of loyalty and devotion.

2. The greedy ravens who begin the ballad are effectively counteracted by the diligent hawks and hounds who hunted with the knight.

3. The loyalty of the hawks and hounds could be merely habit, but the doe's sympathy is that of a wild thing, owing no debt to the knight, influenced only by instinct and the atmosphere of devotion surrounding the body.

B

1. The poem is primarily a symbolic contrast between material and spiritual behavior.

2. The first five stanzas contrast the bestial, materialistic enemies of human dignity with the civilized followers who protect it.

3. In the last five stanzas, the emphasis on the values of family, love, respect for the dead, and self-sacrifice—embodied in the knight's "Leman," a woman as gentle and graceful as a deer—is climaxed by the reference to an appropriate relationship between God and man.

61 *prime:* first hour of day.   69 *Leman:* wife or sweetheart.

BIBLIOGRAPHY

Brooks, C., and R. P. Warren, *Understanding Poetry*, 1938, 1950 ed., pp. 44-46; Daniels, E., *The Art of Reading Poetry*, 1941, pp. 133-37; Hillway, T., *Explicator*, **5** (Mar. 1947), 36; Lainoff, S., *Explicator*, **17** (May 1959), 55; Locke, L. G., *Explicator*, **4** (June 1946), 54; Rosenthal, M. L., and A. J. M. Smith, *Exploring Poetry*, 1955, pp. 311-14

Edward

"Why dois your brand sae drap wi' bluid,
    Edward, Edward,
Why dois your brand sae drap wi' bluid,
  And why sae sad gang yee O?"
"O I hae killed my hauke sae guid,   5
    Mither, mither,
O I hae killed my hauke sae guid,
  And I had nae mair bot hee O."

"Your haukis bluid was nevir sae reid,   9
    Edward, Edward,
Your haukis bluid was nevir sae reid,
  My deir son I tell thee O."
"O I hae killed my reid-roan steid,   13
    Mither, mither,
O I hae killed my reid-roan steid,
  That erst was sae fair and frie O."

"Your steid was auld, and ye hae gat mair,   17
    Edward, Edward,
Your steid was auld, and ye hae gat mair,
  Sum other dule ye drie O."
"O I hae killed my fadir deir,   21
    Mither, mither,
O I hae killed my fadir deir,
  Alas, and wae is mee O!"

"And whatten penance wul ye drie for that,   25
    Edward, Edward?
And whatten penance will ye drie for that?
  My deir son, now tell me O."

1 *brand:* sword. 20 *dule:* grief. 20 *drie:* suffer.

"Ile set my feit in yonder boat,   29
    Mither, mither,
Ile set my feit in yonder boat,
   And Ile fare ovir the sea O."

"And what wul ye doe wi your towirs and your ha',   33
    Edward, Edward,
And what wul ye doe wi your towirs and your ha',
   That were sae fair to see O?"
"Ile let thame stand tul they doun fa',   37
    Mither, mither,
Ile let thame stand tul they doun fa',
   For here nevir mair maun I bee O."

"And what wul ye leive to your bairns and your wife,   41
    Edward, Edward?
And what wul ye leive to your bairns and your wife,
   Whan ye gang ovir the sea O?"
"The warldis room, late them beg thrae life,   45
    Mither, mither,
The warldis room, late them beg thrae life,
   For thame nevir mair wul I see O."

"And what wul ye leive to your ain mither deir,   49
    Edward, Edward?
And what wul ye leive to your ain mither deir?
   My deir son, now tell me O."
"The curse of hell frae me sall ye beir,   53
    Mither, mither,
The curse of hell frae me sall ye beir,
   Sic counseils ye gave to me O."

Sir Patrick Spence

The king sits in Dumferling toune,
   Drinking the blude-reid wine:
"O whar will I get guid sailor,
   To sail this schip of mine?"

Up and spak an eldern knicht,   5
   Sat at the kings richt kne:

This version (from Percy's *Reliques,* 1763) is the shortest and most compressed of several.

"Sir Patrick Spence is the best sailor,
    That sails upon the se."

The king has written a braid letter,   9
    And signd it wi' his hand,
And sent it to Sir Patrick Spence,
    Was walking on the sand.

The first line that Sir Patrick red,   13
    A loud lauch lauchèd he;
The next line that Sir Patrick red,
    The teir blinded his ee.

"O wha is this has don this deid,   17
    This ill deid don to me,
To send me out this time o' the yeir,
    To sail upon the se!

"Mak hast, mak hast, my mirry men all,   21
    Our guid schip sails the morne:"
"O say na sae, my master deir,
    For I feir a deadlie storme.

"Late late yestreen I saw the new moone,   25
    Wi' the auld moone in hir arme,
And I feir, I feir, my deir mastèr,
    That we will com to harme."

O our Scots nobles wer richt laith   29
    To weet their cork-heild schoone;
Bot lang owre a' the play wer playd,
    Thair hats they swam aboone.

O lang, lang, may their ladies sit,   33
    Wi' thair fans into their hand,
Or eir they se Sir Patrick Spence
    Cum sailing to the land.

O lang, lang, may the ladies stand,   37
    Wi' thair gold kems in their hair,
Waiting for thair ain deir lords,
    For they'll se thame na mair.

21 *mirry men:* followers, not gay men.   25 *yestreen:* yesterday evening.   29 *laith:* loath.   30 *schoone:* shoes.   31 *owre:* after.   32 *aboone:* above.   35 *Or eir:* before.

Have owre, have owre to Aberdour,   41
  It's fiftie fadom deip,
And thair lies guid Sir Patrick Spence,
  Wi' the Scots lords at his feit.

Western Wind, When Wilt Thou Blow

Western wind, when wilt thou blow,
  The small rain down can rain?
Christ, if my love were in my arms
  And I in my bed again!

Critique

1. . . . Two lines of description, two of emotion. And for description, the eliminating of everything but the wind and the rain. Then, for the sake of sharpness, the two adjectives—the "western" wind, the "small" rain. . . . The words are exactly chosen, even to the sound of the *w*'s in the first line and the droning *n*'s in the second. But more than that, the poem has been made intense by a rigorous narrowing down to two simple elements.   (DONALD A. STAUFFER)

2. The lover, grieving for the absent beloved, cries out for relief. Several kinds of relief are involved in the appeal to the wind. First there is the relief that would be had from the sympathetic manifestation of nature. . . . Second, there is the relief that would be had by the fulfillment of grief—the frost of grief, the drouth of grief broken, the full anguish expressed, then the violence allayed in the peace of tears. . . .

In the last two lines, the lover cries out for the specific solace of his case: reunion with his beloved. But there is a difference between the two lines. The first is general, and romantic. . . . But with the last line the perfectly literal meaning suddenly comes into sharp focus. . . . We can look straight at the words, which, we discover with a slight shock of surprise, do mean exactly what they say. . . .

41 *Have owre:* probably, halfway over.

All of this does not go to say that the realistic elements here are to be taken as cancelling, or negating, the romantic elements. There is no ironical leer. The poem is not a celebration of carnality. . . .

(ROBERT PENN WARREN)

3. . . . Here ll. 1-2, addressed to the west wind, are a prayer for rain for the growing crops, and ll. 3-4, addressed to Christ . . . , are a prayer for the return of the lover. And the parallelism of form overcomes the contrast of content. The effect is to suggest that the lover whose return is desired so passionately is also involved in the natural cycle of the seasons. In spite of appearances to the contrary spring will eventually come again, and the speaker tries to attribute a similar certainty to the return of the lover. By a blasphemous implication Christ is in effect assigned the rôle of a fertility spirit. The 'sides' in this poem are therefore (a) the non-human processes of growth, and (b) human self-fulfilment in sexual love. To define the content of the poem in more abstract terms would be to distort its meaning.   (F. W. BATESON)

4.   Westron wynde when wyll thow blow
          the smalle rayne downe can rayne.
          Cryst yf my love were in my Armys
          And I yn my bed A gayne

                              —*Royal MS.* App. 58, fol. 5ᵃ

All previous interpreters of this poem (EXP., Oct., 1955, xiv, 6; April, 1956, xiv, 43; Feb., 1957, xv, 28; Oct., 1957, xv, 28; *inter alia*) have depended on a corrupt text, in which the spelling is modernized (eliminating all warning that the language may not be equally up-to-date), the punctuation is entirely editorial, and an interpolated word, *that*, appears at the beginning of line 2. . . .

The original error, accountable also for the intruded *that*, lay in misreading *can* as its present-day equivalent, and accepting that the west wind would somehow *enable* it to rain. Our modern word *can*, stemming from *ken* in the sense of "know how to," was rarely used until recently without a sentient subject. However, in Middle English *can* is a familiar variant of *gan* (from *ginne*), usually meaning simply "did," and this is far more likely to be the intent of the sentence. For the British winter is so notoriously damp and unpleasant that a wish for additional drizzle in the spring could occur only to some improbable farmer-poet. And, if rain is sought, the west wind is hardly the proper one to call on. According to folk-rhyme, "When the wind is in the west, / Then it is the very best" (*The Week End Book*, ed. Vera Mendel and Francis Meynell, London, Nonesuch Press, 1928, p. 360); a manuscript from the same period as the poem (MS Digby 88, f. 12b) asserts, "yf the wynde be in the west it signyfyeth fayr wether"; and in the most familiar account of medieval spring the "shoures soote" of April unequivocally precede, not follow, sweet-breathed Zephyrus.

Thus the true meaning of the opening lines is the exact opposite of that usually suggested; the speaker, far from requesting rain, declares that showers—the first token of spring—have already appeared, and longs for the warm breezes and fair weather which should follow. . . .

Exactly why the lovers cannot be together cannot be inferred. It may be merely that they cannot meet except in garden or greenwood, which would explain neatly the plea for better weather. However, the intensity of the poem suggests something deeper, and something the speaker cannot affect any more than he can hasten the coming of spring. Perhaps she is dead, and he hopes to find spring a restorer of meaning to life, not a cruel reviver of old desires. However, the juxtaposition of the two wishes suggests that they are both possible of fulfillment, though her coming may be less certain than springtime. In any case, he does not desire her as petty compensation for the foul weather. Rather, his plaint at the tardiness of spring is the spontaneous surface outcry of a profoundly troubled heart finding even the weather against him. . . .

(RICHARD R. GRIFFITH)

BIBLIOGRAPHY

Bateson, F. W., *English Poetry: A Critical Introduction*, 1950, p. 81; Griffith, R. R., *Explicator*, 21 (May 1963), 69; Stauffer, D. A., *The Nature of Poetry*, 1946, p. 63; Warren, R. P., *Kenyon Review*, 5 (Spring 1943), 233-34.

Humpty Dumpty

Humpty Dumpty sat on a wall,
Humpty Dumpty had a great fall.
All the king's horses and all the king's men
Couldn't put Humpty together again.

Critique

1. Humpty Dumpty has become so popular a nursery figure and is pictured so frequently that few people today think of the verse as containing a riddle. The reason the king's men could not put him together again is known to everyone. 'It's very provoking to be called an egg—very', as Humpty admits in *Through the Looking-Glass*, but such common knowledge cannot be gainsaid. What is not so certain is for how long the riddle has been known. It does not appear in early riddle books, but this may be because it was already too well-known. Students of linguistics believe that it is one of those pieces the antiquity of which 'is to be measured in thousands of years, or rather it is so great that it cannot be measured at all' (Bett). Humpty Dumpty of England is elsewhere known as 'Boule, boule' (France), 'Thille Lille' (Sweden), 'Lille-Trille' (Denmark), 'Hillerin-Lillerin' (Finland), 'Annebadadeli' (Switzerland), and 'Trille Trölle', 'Etje-Papetje', 'Wirgele-Wargele', 'Gigele-Gagele', 'Rüntzelken-Püntzelken', and 'Hümpelken-Pümpelken' (different parts of Germany). The riddles have the same form and motif, and it seems undeniable that they are connected with the English rhyme. The word *Humpty-dumpty* is given in the *OED* for a boiled ale-and-brandy drink from the end of the seventeenth century. Its first use in the nursery sense, however, does not occur before 1785, 'a little humpty dumpty man or woman; a short clumsy person of either sex'. The earliest recording of the rhyme itself is in manuscript, a contemporary addition to a copy of *Mother Goose's Melody* published about 1803. . . . Perhaps the rhyme was not originally a riddle. Eggs do not sit on walls; but the verse becomes intelligible if it describes human beings who are personating eggs. E. G. Withycombe (*Oxford Dictionary of Christian Names*) also associates a human being with the name, suggesting that it echoes the pet forms of *Humphrey*, which were *Dumphry* and *Dump*, while Robert L. Ripley, 'Believe it or Not', has stated that the original Humpty was Richard III (1452-85). (IONA AND PETER OPIE)

2. Not only the concluding couplet, but also the poem as a whole dramatizes the limits of temporal power: certain actions cannot be done; others should not be. Thus eggs which sit on walls risk almost certain destruction. As an egg, Humpty Dumpty is a symbol of fragility; as an egg sitting on a wall, he is a symbol of aspiring

pride. Pride, however, is a human trait; so Humpty Dumpty emerges as a symbol of sinful man.

"Humpty Dumpty," in its fullest implications, is definitely a religious poem, an example of how folk wisdom, if you will, justifies the ways of God to man in four lines. Eggs have a seemingly hard exterior but a ridiculously flabby interior—they are not equipped to sit on walls. This prohibition is not arbitrary any more than God's prohibitions against a sinful action are arbitrary. Rather, these prohibitions are a manifestation of God's wisdom, of the infinite power of God contrasted with the finite powers of man, of a recognition that in an ordered universe there can be no trespassing beyond prescribed limits. And "a great fall" certainly has specific theological and mythic connotations: one thinks of the fall of Adam, of Satan, of Icarus, of Phaethon.   (BERNARD M. KNIEGER)

BIBLIOGRAPHY

Knieger, B. M., *College English*, **20** (Feb. 1959), 245; Opie, I., and P., *The Oxford Dictionary of Nursery Rhymes*, 1951, p. 215.

Shakespeare

Others abide our question. Thou art free.
We ask and ask—Thou smilest, and art still,
Out-topping knowledge. For the loftiest hill,
Who to the stars uncrowns his majesty,
Planting his steadfast footsteps in the sea,   5
Making the heaven of heavens his dwelling-place,
Spares but the cloudy border of his base
To the foiled searching of mortality;

And thou, who didst the stars and sunbeams know,   9
Self-school'd, self-scann'd, self-honour'd, self-secure,
Didst tread on earth unguess'd at.—Better so!

All pains the immortal spirit must endure,
All weakness which impairs, all griefs which bow,
Find their sole speech in that victorious brow.   14

1 *abide:* endure.   8 *mortality:* mortals.

To Marguerite—Continued

Yes! in the sea of life enisled,
With echoing straits between us thrown,
Dotting the shoreless watery wild,
We mortal millions live *alone*.
The islands feel the enclasping flow,
And then their endless bounds they know.

But when the moon their hollows lights, 7
And they are swept by balms of spring,
And in their glens, on starry nights,
The nightingales divinely sing;
And lovely notes, from shore to shore,
Across the sounds and channels pour—

Oh! then a longing like despair 13
Is to their farthest caverns sent;
For surely once, they feel, we were
Parts of a single continent!
Now round us spreads the watery plain—
Oh might our marges meet again!

Who order'd that their longing's fire 19
Should be, as soon as kindled, cool'd?
Who renders vain their deep desire?—
A God, a God their severance ruled!
And bade between their shores to be
The unplumb'd, salt, estranging sea.

Dover Beach

The sea is calm tonight.
The tide is full, the moon lies fair
Upon the straits;—on the French coast the light
Gleams and is gone; the cliffs of England stand,
Glimmering and vast, out in the tranquil bay. 5
Come to the window, sweet is the night-air!
Only, from the long line of spray
Where the sea meets the moon-blanch'd land,
Listen! you hear the grating roar

Of pebbles which the waves draw back, and fling,   10
At their return, up the high strand,
Begin, and cease, and then again begin,
With tremulous cadence slow, and bring
The eternal note of sadness in.

Sophocles long ago   15
Heard it on the Aegean, and it brought
Into his mind the turbid ebb and flow
Of human misery; we
Find also in the sound a thought,
Hearing it by this distant northern sea.

The Sea of Faith   21
Was once, too, at the full, and round earth's shore
Lay like the folds of a bright girdle furl'd.
But now I only hear
Its melancholy, long, withdrawing roar,
Retreating, to the breath
Of the night-wind, down the vast edges drear
And naked shingles of the world.

Ah, love, let us be true   29
To one another! for the world, which seems
To lie before us like a land of dreams,
So various, so beautiful, so new,
Hath really neither joy, nor love, nor light,
Nor certitude, nor peace, nor help for pain;
And we are here as on a darkling plain
Swept with confused alarms of struggle and flight,
Where ignorant armies clash by night.

Case

A

1. The primary theme is loss of faith.
2. The recollection of Sophocles is a link between the strictly personal experience of the first stanza and the comparative generalization of the third.

23 *girdle:* belt.   28 *shingles:* pebbled beaches.   35 *darkling:* in the dark.

3. The dominant "thought" (19) which Arnold finds in this contrast and comparison is that while religious faith was once at full tide and as universal as the sea, its tide is now ("Dover Beach" was published in 1867) sadly ebbing.

4. The imagery of the poem makes a strong appeal to the senses, primarily to the ear.

5. Arnold's agonized reaction to the insecurity of his times finds appropriate expression in the irregular meter, which ranges from dimeter to pentameter, and in the rhyme scheme, which follows no standard pattern.

B

1. The primary theme is reality versus appearance.

2. The speaker contrasts the bright, calm, full sea with the ceaseless sad motion of surf, corresponding to the "turbid ebb and flow / Of human misery."

3. Later, he states categorically that "the world, which seems" to be beautiful and certain and peaceful, "really" lacks these qualities.

4. Although the poem's central symbol is the sounding sea, its use of light and darkness is subtler and ultimately more emphatic, proceeding as it does from the open "moon-blanch'd" scene to the obscure "darkling plain."

5. Furthermore, the pattern of sound imagery is flawed by the fact that the sea, whose ceaseless waves are imitated in the rhythm of 9–14 and 25, disappears at the end of Stanza 3.

C

1. Although "Dover Beach" contains but one brief mention of personal affection, the primary theme is the power of love.

2. In line 6 the poet asks his lady to share the beauty of the calm, moonlit night with him, but he soon points out to her the ancient eternal sadness "Of human misery" which he implies is especially prevalent now that materialism has replaced faith.

3. Recognizing love as the only power that can prevail in such a situation, the poet exhorts his lady and himself to "be true / To one another" in the face of modern uncertainty.

4. One of the clues to the personal nature of the poem is the poet's use of exclamation points three times to emphasize direct dramatic speech, as opposed to description and meditation.

5. Although the reference to Sophocles creates an atmosphere of dignity and antiquity, it is not strictly relevant to the emotional progress of the poem. In fact, the poet might well have omitted the whole second stanza without harming the thematic pattern.

BIBLIOGRAPHY

Delasanta, R., *Explicator,* 18 (Oct. 1959), 7; Drew, E., *Poetry: A Modern Guide,* 1959, pp. 221-23; Gwynn, F. L., *Explicator,* 8 (Apr. 1950), 46; Kirby, J. P., *Explicator,* 1 (Apr. 1943), 42; Morrison, T., *Harper's,* 180 (Feb. 1940), 235-44; Pottle, F. A., *Explicator,* 2 (Apr. 1944), 45; Stageberg, N. C., *Explicator,* 9 (Mar. 1951), 34.

Musée des Beaux Arts

About suffering they were never wrong,
The Old Masters: how well they understood
Its human position; how it takes place
While someone else is eating or opening a window or just walking
    dully along;
How, when the aged are reverently, passionately waiting
For the miraculous birth, there always must be
Children who did not specially want it to happen, skating   7
On a pond at the edge of the wood:
They never forgot
That even the dreadful martyrdom must run its course
Anyhow in a corner, some untidy spot
Where the dogs go on with their doggy life and the torturer's
    horse
Scratches its innocent behind on a tree.

In Brueghel's *Icarus,* for instance: how everything turns away   14
Quite leisurely from the disaster; the ploughman may
Have heard the splash, the forsaken cry,
But for him it was not an important failure; the sun shone
As it had to on the white legs disappearing into the green
Water; and the expensive delicate ship that must have seen
Something amazing, a boy falling out of the sky,
Had somewhere to get to and sailed calmly on.

Law Like Love

Law, say the gardeners, is the sun,
Law is the one
All gardeners obey
Tomorrow, yesterday, today.

Law is the wisdom of the old   5
The impotent grandfathers shrilly scold;
The grandchildren put out a treble tongue.
Law is the senses of the young.

Law, says the priest with a priestly look,   9
Expounding to an unpriestly people,
Law is the words in my priestly book,
Law is my pulpit and my steeple.

Law, says the judge as he looks down his nose,   13
Speaking clearly and most severely,
Law is as I've told you before,
Law is as you know I suppose,
Law is but let me explain it once more,
Law is The Law.

Yet law-abiding scholars write: 19
Law is neither wrong nor right,
Law is only crimes
Punished by places and by times,
Law is the clothes men wear
Anytime, anywhere,
Law is Good-morning and Good-night.

Others say, Law is our Fate;   26
Others say, Law is our State;
Others say, others say
Law is no more
Law is gone away.

And always the loud angry crowd   31
Very angry and very loud
Law is We,
And always the soft idiot softly Me.

If we, dear, know we know no more   35
Than they about the law,
If I no more than you

Know what we should and should not do
Except that all agree
Gladly or miserably   40
That the law is
And that all know this,
If therefore thinking it absurd
To identify Law with some other word,
Unlike so many men   45
I cannot say Law is again,
No more than they can we suppress
The universal wish to guess
Or slip out of our own position
Into an unconcerned condition.   50
Although I can at least confine
Your vanity and mine
To stating timidly
A timid similarity,
We shall boast anyway: 55
Like love I say.

Like love we don't know where or why   57
Like love we can't compel or fly
Like love we often weep
Like love we seldom keep.

In Westminster Abbey

Let me take this other glove off
    As the *vox humana* swells,
And the beauteous fields of Eden
    Bask beneath the Abbey bells.   4
Here, where England's statesmen lie,
Listen to a lady's cry.

Gracious Lord, oh bomb the Germans.   7
    Spare their women for Thy Sake,
And if that is not too easy
    We will pardon Thy Mistake.   10
But, gracious Lord, whate'er shall be,
Don't let anyone bomb me.

Keep our Empire undismembered   13
   Guide our Forces by Thy Hand,
Gallant blacks from far Jamaica,
   Honduras and Togoland;   16
Protect them Lord in all their fights,
And, even more, protect the whites.

Think of what our Nation stands for,   19
   Books from Boots' and country lanes,
Free speech, free passes, class distinction,
   Democracy and proper drains.   22
Lord, put beneath Thy special care
One-eighty-nine Cadogan Square.

Although dear Lord I am a sinner,   25
   I have done no major crime;
Now I'll come to Evening Service
   Whensoever I have time.   28
So, Lord, reserve for me a crown,
And do not let my shares go down.

I will labour for Thy Kingdom,   31
   Help our lads to win the war,
Send white feathers to the cowards
   Join the Women's Army Corps.   34
Then wash the Steps around Thy Throne
In the Eternal Safety Zone.

Now I feel a little better,   37
   What a treat to hear Thy Word.
Where the bones of leading statesmen,
   Have so often been interr'd.   40
And now, dear Lord, I cannot wait
Because I have a luncheon date.

The Ecchoing Green

The Sun does arise,   1
And make happy the skies;
The merry bells ring
To welcome the Spring;
The skylark and thrush,

The birds of the bush, 6
Sing louder around
To the bells' chearful sound;
While our sports shall be seen
On the Ecchoing Green.

Old John, with white hair, 11
Does laugh away care,
Sitting under the oak,
Among the old folk.
They laugh at our play,
And soon they all say: 16
"Such, such were the joys
"When we all, girls & boys,
"In our youth time were seen
"On the Ecchoing Green."

Till the little ones, weary, 21
No more can be merry;
The sun does descend,
And our sports have an end.
Round the laps of their mothers
Many sisters and brothers, 26
Like birds in their nest,
Are ready for rest,
And sport no more seen
On the darkening Green.

The Lamb

Little Lamb, who made thee?
Dost thou know who made thee?
Gave thee life, & bid thee feed
By the stream & o'er the mead;
Gave thee clothing of delight,
Softest clothing, wooly, bright; 6
Gave thee such a tender voice,
Making all the vales rejoice?
Little Lamb, who made thee?
Dost thou know who made thee?

Little Lamb, I'll tell thee,   11
Little Lamb, I'll tell thee:
He is called by thy name,
For he calls himself a Lamb.
He is meek, & he is mild;
He became a little child.   16

I a child, & thou a lamb,
We are called by his name.
Little Lamb, God bless thee!
Little Lamb, God bless thee!

The Little Black Boy

My mother bore me in the southern wild,
And I am black, but O! my soul is white;
White as an angel is the English child,
But I am black, as if bereav'd of light.

My mother taught me underneath a tree,   5
And, sitting down before the heat of day,
She took me on her lap and kissed me,
And pointing to the east, began to say:

"Look on the rising sun: there God does live,   9
"And gives his light, and gives his heat away;
"And flowers and trees and beasts and men receive
"Comfort in morning, joy in the noonday.

"And we are put on earth a little space,   13
"That we may learn to bear the beams of love;
"And these black bodies and this sunburnt face
"Is but a cloud, and like a shady grove.

"For when our souls have learn'd the heat to bear,   17
"The cloud will vanish; we shall hear his voice,
"Saying: 'Come out from the grove, my love & care,
" 'And round my golden tent like lambs rejoice.' "

Thus did my mother say, and kissed me;   21
And thus I say to little English boy,
When I from black and he from white cloud free,
And round the tent of God like lambs we joy,

I'll shade him from the heat, till he can bear   25
To lean in joy upon our Father's knee;
And then I'll stand and stroke his silver hair,
And be like him, and he will then love me.

The Chimney Sweeper

When my mother died I was very young,
And my father sold me while yet my tongue
Could scarcely cry " 'weep! 'weep! 'weep! 'weep!"
So your chimneys I sweep, & in soot I sleep.

There's little Tom Dacre, who cried when his head,   5
That curl'd like a lamb's back, was shav'd: so I said
"Hush, Tom! never mind it, for when your head's bare
You know that the soot cannot spoil your white hair."

And so he was quiet, & that very night,   9
As Tom was a-sleeping, he had such a sight!
That thousands of sweepers, Dick, Joe, Ned, & Jack,
Were all of them lock'd up in coffins of black.

And by came an Angel who had a bright key,   13
And he open'd the coffins & set them all free;
Then down a green plain leaping, laughing, they run,
And wash in a river, and shine in the Sun.

Then naked & white, all their bags left behind,   17
They rise upon clouds and sport in the wind;
And the Angel told Tom, if he'd be a good boy,
He'd have God for his father, & never want joy.

And so Tom awoke; and we rose in the dark,   21
And got with our bags & our brushes to work.
Tho' the morning was cold, Tom was happy & warm
So if all do their duty they need not fear harm.

The Sick Rose

O rose, thou art sick!
The invisible worm

That flies in the night,
In the howling storm,

Has found out thy bed   5
Of crimson joy,
And his dark secret love
Does thy life destroy.

Critique

1. . . . The rose is earthly love (with its potentialities of innocent fulfillment), the worm is the wicked instinct to be possessive and predatory that battens on and corrupts earthly love. . . . The first line violently personifies the flower, forces the mind to seek something more than the mere physical rose. . . . And the rest of the poem, though it may solve the puzzle, fixes the attention even more firmly on the place where it was first directed. For though the rose is clearly a symbol, Blake vivifies it by keeping the physical existence of the rose in our imaginations. . . . He expresses in 'thy bed of crimson joy' the shape and the feel and the glow of the physical flower with incomparable felicity. The same phrase helps out the symbolic meaning, for it . . . refers to the bed where the joys of love are experienced. The trend of the poem then is to make us dwell on the sick rose as the symbol of innocent love corrupted. . . .

(E. M. W. TILLYARD)

2. . . . If we ask what the poem means, we can answer that it means what it says, and that this is perfectly clear. It conjures up the vision of a rose attacked in a stormy night by a destructive worm, and so Blake depicts it in his accompanying illustration. But, as in all symbolical poems, we can read other meanings into it. . . . We may say that it refers to the destruction of love by selfishness, of innocence by experience, of spiritual life by spiritual death. All these meanings it can bear, and it is legitimate to make it do so. But the actual poem presents something which is common and fundamental to all these themes. . . . And this Blake sees with so piercing and so concentrated a vision that the poem has its own independent life and needs nothing to supplement it. . . .   (C. M. BOWRA)

3. . . . But *if* the rose can mean love, innocence, humanity, imagina-

tion, and life; and *if* the worm can mean the flesh, jealousy, deceit, concealment, possessiveness, experience, Satan, rationalism, death (and more), *can* the two symbols therefore mean just anything? The answer is No. The rose must always represent something beautiful or desirable or good. The worm must always be some kind of corrupting agent. Both symbols define an area of meaning, and a viable interpretation must fall within that area. Blake's poem is not about the elimination of social injustice by an enlightened society; it is not about the eradication of sin by God; it is not about the triumph of freedom over tyranny. Any correct interpretation must satisfactorily explain the details of the poem without being contradicted by any detail; the best interpretations will rely on the fewest assumptions not grounded in the poem itself.

(LAURENCE PERRINE)

BIBLIOGRAPHY

Bowra, C. M., *The Romantic Imagination,* 1949, p. 44; Perrine, L., *English Journal,* **51** (Sept. 1962), 398; Tillyard, E. M. W., *Poetry Direct and Oblique,* 1934, pp. 169-70; 1945, pp. 64-65.

The Tyger

Tyger! Tyger! burning bright
In the forests of the night,
What immortal hand or eye
Could frame thy fearful symmetry?

In what distant deeps or skies   5
Burnt the fire of thine eyes?
On what wings dare he aspire?
What the hand dare sieze the fire?

And what shoulder, & what art,   9
Could twist the sinews of thy heart?
And when thy heart began to beat,
What dread hand? & what dread feet?

12: Blake may have emended this line, which began a sentence in the first draft, to the more logical "What dread hand forged [or "Formd"] thy dread feet?" (Nurmi).

What the hammer? what the chain?   13
In what furnace was thy brain?
What the anvil? what dread grasp
Dare its deadly terrors clasp?

When the stars threw down their spears,   17
And water'd heaven with their tears,
Did he smile his work to see?
Did he who made the Lamb make thee?

Tyger! Tyger! burning bright   21
In the forests of the night,
What immortal hand or eye
Dare frame thy fearful symmetry?

Case

A

1. The primary theme of the poem is the creation of evil.
2. The tiger is a symbol of evil, just as the Lamb is a symbol of good.
3. Although uncapitalized, the "he" of the poem is the Christian God, whose Son was "the Lamb of God, which taketh away the sin of the world" (John 1:29).
4. The evil of the tiger fills the poet with such terror that he wonders how God could have wanted to create it, let alone "smile his work to see."
5. The imagery of fire, traditionally associated with hell, permeates the poem.

B

1. The primary theme of the poem is natural energy, a force symbolized by the tiger.
2. The poet calls this force neither right nor wrong; he says in effect that it exists and that it is awesome.
3. It is characteristically active, in contrast to the principle of inertness in the universe, symbolized by the passive Lamb.
4. To embody the power of this force, the poet uses an appro-

priate extended metaphor, conceiving of the tiger as a living instrument forged by a powerful blacksmith.

5. The creator of the force was pleased with his work, for he knew that both energy and inertness are necessary to nature.

C

1. The primary theme is the physical beauty, strength, and destructiveness of the actual tiger.

2. Instead of presenting the reader with a photographic imitation of the animal, the poet suggests its nature by naming only a few vivid characteristics: the brilliant "burning" color, for example, that symbolizes the tiger's fiery destructiveness, and the difficulty of forging the heart, which implies the degree of strength.

3. The relevancy of the questions in 19-20 depends on the fact that in the balance of nature animals like tigers must prey on animals like sheep.

4. The last stanza, with its almost identical repetition of the first, comes as a kind of religious incantation expressing the poet's physical dread of, and esthetic admiration for, the tiger.

5. The vigorous rhythm of the piece owes something to the accent of the initial word "Tyger" and to the employment of masculine rhymes in every line.

BIBLIOGRAPHY

Drew, E., *Discovering Poetry*, 1933, p. 160; Eberly, R. D., *Explicator*, 8 (Nov. 1949), 12; Kazin, A., *The Portable Blake*, 1946, pp. 42-47; Nurmi, M. K., *PMLA*, 71 (Sept. 1956), 669-83; Rosenthal, M. L., and A. J. M. Smith, *Exploring Poetry*, 1955, pp. 185-87; Stone, G. W., *Explicator*, 1 (Dec. 1942), 19.

London

I wander thro' each charter'd street,
Near where the charter'd Thames does flow,
And mark in every face I meet
Marks of weakness, marks of woe.

In every cry of every Man,   5
In every Infant's cry of fear,

In every voice, in every ban,
The mind-forg'd manacles I hear.

How the Chimney-sweeper's cry   9
Every black'ning Church appalls;
And the hapless Soldier's sigh
Runs in blood down Palace walls.

But most thro' midnight streets I hear   13
How the youthful Harlot's curse
Blasts the new born Infant's tear,
And blights with plagues the Marriage hearse.

A Poison Tree

I was angry with my friend:
I told my wrath, my wrath did end.
I was angry with my foe:
I told it not, my wrath did grow.

And I water'd it in fears,   5
Night & morning with my tears;
And I sunned it with smiles,
And with soft deceitful wiles.

And it grew both day and night,   9
Till it bore an apple bright;
And my foe beheld it shine,
And he knew that it was mine,

And into my garden stole   13
When the night had veil'd the pole:
In the morning glad I see
My foe outstretch'd beneath the tree.

And Did Those Feet in Ancient Time

And did those feet in ancient time
Walk upon England's mountains green?
And was the holy Lamb of God
On England's pleasant pastures seen?

And did the Countenance Divine   5
Shine forth upon our clouded hills?

And was Jerusalem builded here
Among these dark Satanic Mills?

Bring me my Bow of burning gold!   9
Bring me my Arrows of desire!
Bring me my Spear: O clouds, unfold!
Bring me my Chariot of fire!

I will not cease from Mental Fight,   13
Nor shall my Sword sleep in my hand,
Till we have built Jerusalem
In England's green & pleasant Land.

Siasconset Song

The girls
of golden summers whirl
through sunsprung
bright Julys
with born right   5
sky-bright
star-night
eyes:

everywhere   9
their tennis-twirl
of young gold
legs and arms,
they singsong   13
summer-long
I-belong
charms;

and through   17
the summer sailing swirl
they cut like
shining knives
in sun-told   21
never old
ever gold
lives.

Siasconset: on Nantucket Island, Massachusetts.

A Passer-by

Whither, O splendid ship, thy white sails crowding,
    Leaning across the bosom of the urgent West.
That fearest nor sea rising nor sky clouding,
    Whither away, fair rover, and what thy quest?
    Ah! soon, when Winter has all our vales opprest,   5
When skies are cold and misty, and hail is hurling,
    Wilt thóu glíde on the blue Pacific, or rest
In a summer haven asleep, thy white sails furling.

I there before thee, in the country that well thou knowest,   9
    Already arrived am inhaling the odorous air:
I watch thee enter unerringly where thou goest,
    And anchor queen of the strange shipping there,
    Thy sails for awnings spread, thy masts bare;   13
Nor is aught from the foaming reef to the snow-capped, grandest
    Peak, that is over the feathery palms more fair
Than thou, so upright, so stately, and still thou standest.

And yet, O splendid ship, unhailed and nameless,   17
    I know not if, aiming a fancy, I rightly divine
That thou hast a purpose joyful, a courage blameless,
    Thy port assured in a happier land than mine.
    But for all I have given thee, beauty enough is thine,   21
As thou, aslant with trim tackle and shrouding,
    From the proud nostril curve of a prow's line
In the offing scatterest foam, thy white sails crowding.

My Last Duchess

Ferrara

That 's my last Duchess painted on the wall,
Looking as if she were alive. I call
That piece a wonder, now: Frà Pandolf's hands
Worked busily·a day, and there she stands.
Will 't please you sit and look at her? I said   5
"Frà Pandolf" by design, for never read

Ferrara: Italian city prominent in Renaissance.   3 Frà Pandolf: Brother Pandolf, imaginary artist-monk.

Strangers like you that pictured countenance,
The depth and passion of its earnest glance,
But to myself they turned (since none puts by
The curtain I have drawn for you, but I)   10
And seemed as they would ask me, if they durst,
How such a glance came there; so, not the first
Are you to turn and ask thus. Sir, 't was not
Her husband's presence only, called that spot
Of joy into the Duchess' cheek: perhaps   15
Frà Pandolf chanced to say "Her mantle laps
"Over my lady's wrist too much," or "Paint
"Must never hope to reproduce the faint
"Half-flush that dies along her throat": such stuff
Was courtesy, she thought, and cause enough   20
For calling up that spot of joy. She had
A heart—how shall I say?—too soon made glad,
Too easily impressed; she liked whate'er
She looked on, and her looks went everywhere.
Sir, 't was all one! My favour at her breast,   25
The dropping of the daylight in the West,
The bough of cherries some officious fool
Broke in the orchard for her, the white mule
She rode with round the terrace—all and each
Would draw from her alike the approving speech,   30
Or blush, at least. She thanked men,—good! but thanked
Somehow—I know not how—as if she ranked
My gift of a nine-hundred-years-old name
With anybody's gift. Who 'd stoop to blame
This sort of trifling? Even had you skill   35
In speech—(which I have not)—to make your will
Quite clear to such an one, and say, "Just this
"Or that in you disgusts me; here you miss,
"Or there exceed the mark"—and if she let
Herself be lessoned so, nor plainly set   40
Her wits to yours, forsooth, and made excuse,
—E'en then would be some stooping; and I choose
Never to stoop. Oh, sir, she smiled, no doubt,
Whene'er I passed her; but who passed without
Much the same smile? This grew; I gave commands;   45
Then all smiles stopped together. There she stands
As if alive. Will 't please you rise? We'll meet

25 *favour:* ornament.   41 *forsooth:* indeed.   45-47 *I gave . . . alive:* Did the
Duke have the Duchess murdered? Professor Hiram Corson of Cornell asked

The company below, then. I repeat,
The Count your master's known munificence
Is ample warrant that no just pretence   50
Of mine for dowry will be disallowed;
Though his fair daughter's self, as I avowed
At starting, is my object. Nay, we 'll go
Together down, sir. Notice Neptune, though,
Taming a sea-horse, thought a rarity,   55
Which Claus of Innsbruck cast in bronze for me!

Case

A

1. The focus of interest in the poem is the revelation of the Duke's aristocratic but easily misunderstood character.

2. The Duke of Ferrara's repeated deference to the emissary of a Count shows that he is a considerate and humane man.

3. The Duke is also a person of keen sensitivity to the beauty of painting and sculpture.

4. His disparagement of his "skill / In speech" (35-36) is polite modesty, since he demonstrates notable powers of expression.

5. Sometime in the past, despite these commendable qualities in her husband, the Duchess wronged him by her frivolous and rebellious behavior, justifying his proud action.

B

1. The focus of interest in the poem is the revelation of the inhumanity and villainy lying under the Duke's mask.

2. Actually, even his esthetic taste is superficial and his interest in art materialistic.

3. His last Duchess seems to have been a charming, spirited, and natural woman whose only fault was quickness to offer gracious

---

the question of Browning. "He made no reply, for a moment, and then said, meditatively, 'Yes, I meant that the commands were that she should be put to death.' And then, after a pause, he added, with a characteristic dash of expression, and as if the thought had just started in his mind. 'Or he might have had her shut up in a convent'" (*An Introduction to the Study of Robert Browning's Poetry*, 1886, viii). In short, the *specific* fate of the Duchess was as vague in her creator's mind as it must remain in a reader's.   50 *pretence:* claim.   56 *Claus of Innsbruck:* imaginary Austrian sculptor.

thanks for favors received, or possibly feminine pleasure in provoking a husband's jealousy.

4. The basic crudeness of the Duke manifests itself in his unblushing recital of intimate and possibly criminal events to a stranger (7).

5. The only explanation for this exposure is that it probably constitutes a clever man's instructions for his wife to be.

BIBLIOGRAPHY

Brooks, C., J. T. Purser, and R. P. Warren, *An Approach to Literature*, 1936, 1952, pp. 292-93; Jerman, B. R., *PMLA*, **72** (June 1957), 488-93; Kirk, R. R., and R. P. McCutcheon, *An Introduction to the Study of Poetry*, 1934, pp. 17-24; Langbaum, R., *The Poetry of Experience*, 1957, pp. 82-85; Perrine, L., *PMLA*, **74** (Mar. 1959), 157-59; Sessions, I. B., *PMLA*, **62** (June 1947), 508-10.

Soliloquy of the Spanish Cloister

Gr-r-r—there go, my heart's abhorrence!
   Water your damned flower-pots, do!
If hate killed men, Brother Lawrence,
   God's blood, would not mine kill you!
What? your myrtle-bush wants trimming?   5
   Oh, that rose has prior claims—
Needs its leaden vase filled brimming?
   Hell dry you up with its flames!

At the meal we sit together;   9
   Salve tibi! I must hear
Wise talk of the kind of weather,
   Sort of season, time of year:
Not a plenteous cork-crop: scarcely   13
   Dare we hope oak-galls, I doubt:
What's the Latin name for "parsley"?
   What's the Greek name for Swine's Snout?

Whew! We 'll have our platter burnished,   17
   Laid with care on our own shelf!
With a fire-new spoon we're furnished,
   And a goblet for ourself,

4 *God's blood:* strong oath referring to the Crucifixion. 10 *Salve tibi:* Hail to thee; greetings. Monks were supposed to speak Latin only. 14 *oak-galls:* growths used for making ink.

Rinsed like something sacrificial   21
  Ere 't is fit to touch our chaps—
Marked with L. for our initial!
  (He-he! There his lily snaps!)

Saint, forsooth! While brown Dolores   25
  Squats outside the Convent bank
With Sanchicha, telling stories,
  Steeping tresses in the tank,
Blue-black, lustrous, thick like horsehairs,   29
  —Can't I see his dead eye glow,
Bright as 't were a Barbary corsair's?
  (That is, if he'd let it show!)

When he finishes refection,   33
  Knife and fork he never lays
Cross-wise, to my recollection,
  As do I, in Jesu's praise.
I the Trinity illustrate,   37
  Drinking watered orange-pulp—
In three sips the Arian frustrate;
  While he drains his at one gulp.

Oh, those melons! If he's able   41
  We 're to have a feast! so nice!
One goes to the Abbot's table,
  All of us get each a slice.
How go on your flowers? None double?   45
  Not one fruit-sort can you spy?
Strange!—And I, too, at such trouble
  Keep them close-nipped on the sly!

There's a great text in Galatians,   49
  Once you trip on it, entails
Twenty-nine distinct damnations,
  One sure, if another fails;
If I trip him just a-dying,   53
  Sure of heaven as sure can be,
Spin him round and send him flying
  Off to hell, a Manichee?

Or, my scrofulous French novel   57
  On grey paper with blunt type!

22 *chaps:* jaws. 25 *forsooth:* indeed. 39 *Arian:* follower of Arius, the anti-Trinitarian heretic. 56 *Manichee:* follower of the heretic Manichaeus, 57 *French novel:* notoriously concerned with adultery. 58: i.e., cheaply printed.

Simply glance at it, you grovel
    Hand and foot in Belial's gripe:
If I double down its pages   61
    At the woeful sixteenth print,
When he gathers his greengages,
    Ope a sieve and slip it in 't?

Or, there's Satan!—one might venture   65
    Pledge one's soul to him, yet leave
Such a flaw in the indenture
    As he 'd miss, till, past retrieve,
Blasted lay that rose-acacia   69
    We're so proud of! *Hy, Zy, Hine* . . .
'St, there 's Vespers! *Plena gratiâ*
    Ave, Virgo! Gr-r-r—you swine!

The Bishop Orders His Tomb at
Saint Praxed's Church

Rome, 15—

Vanity, saith the preacher, vanity!
Draw round my bed: is Anselm keeping back?
Nephews—sons mine . . . ah God, I know not! Well
She, men would have to be your mother once,
Old Gandolf envied me, so fair she was!   5
What 's done is done, and she is dead beside,
Dead long ago, and I am Bishop since,
And as she died so must we die ourselves,
And thence ye may perceive the world 's a dream,
Life, how and what is it? As here I lie   10
In this state-chamber, dying by degrees,

60 *Belial's gripe:* devil's grip. 61 *double:* turn. 63 *greengages:* plums. 64 *sieve:* basket. 67 *indenture:* contract. 70 *Hy, Zy, Hine:* usually conjectured to be the sound of the Vespers (evening service) bells. 71-72 *Plena . . . Virgo:* Hail, Virgin, full of grace.

Saint Praxed: early virgin martyr. The church is real but the Bishop imaginary. 1 *Vanity:* worthlessness. The line adapts Ecclesiates 1:2, 12:8. 3 *Nephews-sons:* The offspring of celibate church officials were euphemistically referred to as nephews and nieces. 4 *would have:* rumored.

Hours and long hours in the dead night, I ask
"Do I live, am I dead?" Peace, peace seems all.
Saint Praxed's ever was the church for peace;
And so, about this tomb of mine. I fought   15
With tooth and nail to save my niche, ye know:
—Old Gandolf cozened me, despite my care;
Shrewd was that snatch from out the corner South
He graced his carrion with, God curse the same!
Yet still my niche is not so cramped but thence   20
One sees the pulpit o' the epistle-side,
And somewhat of the choir, those silent seats,
And up into the aery dome where live
The angels, and a sunbeam's sure to lurk:
And I shall fill my slab of basalt there,   25
And 'neath my tabernacle take my rest,
With those nine columns round me, two and two,
The odd one at my feet where Anselm stands:
Peach-blossom marble all, the rare, the ripe
As fresh-poured red wine of a mighty pulse.   30
—Old Gandolf with his paltry onion-stone,
Put me where I may look at him! True peach,
Rosy and flawless: how I earned the prize!
Draw close: that conflagration of my church
—What then? So much was saved if aught were missed!   35
My sons, ye would not be my death? Go dig
The white-grape vineyard where the oil-press stood,
Drop water gently till the surface sink,
And if ye find . . . Ah God, I know not, I! . . .
Bedded in store of rotten fig-leaves soft,   40
And corded up in a tight olive-frail,
Some lump, ah God, of *lapis lazuli,*
Big as a Jew's head cut off at the nape,
Blue as a vein o'er the Madonna's breast . . .
Sons, all have I bequeathed you, villas, all,   45
That brave Frascati villa with its bath,
So, let the blue lump poise between my knees,
Like God the Father's globe on both his hands
Ye worship in the Jesu Church so gay,
For Gandolf shall not choose but see and burst!   50

17 *cozened:* cheated.   21 *epistle-side:* where the New Testament epistle is read.
26 *tabernacle:* canopy.   27 *me:* as a carved stone effigy on the slab.   35 *if:*
even if.   41 *frail:* basket.   42 *lapis lazuli:* semiprecious stone.   46 *brave:*
splendid.   46 *Frascati:* resort near Rome.

Swift as a weaver's shuttle fleet our years:
Man goeth to the grave, and where is he?
Did I say basalt for my slab, sons? Black—
'T was ever antique-black I meant! How else
Shall ye contrast my frieze to come beneath?   55
The bas-relief in bronze ye promised me,
Those Pans and Nymphs ye wot of, and perchance
Some tripod, thyrsus, with a vase or so,
The Saviour at his sermon on the mount,
Saint Praxed in a glory, and one Pan   60
Ready to twitch the Nymph's last garment off,
And Moses with the tables . . . but I know
Ye mark me not! What do they whisper thee,
Child of my bowels, Anselm? Ah, ye hope
To revel down my villas while I gasp   65
Bricked o'er with beggar's moldy travertine
Which Gandolf from his tomb-top chuckles at!
Nay, boys, ye love me—all of jasper, then!
'T is jasper ye stand pledged to, lest I grieve
My bath must needs be left behind, alas!   70
One block, pure green as a pistachio-nut,
There's plenty jasper somewhere in the world—
And have I not Saint Praxed's ear to pray
Horses for ye, and brown Greek manuscripts,
And mistresses with great smooth marbly limbs?   75
—That 's if ye carve my epitaph aright,
Choice Latin, picked phrase, Tully's every word,
No gaudy ware like Gandolf's second line—
Tully, my masters? Ulpian serves his need!
And then how I shall lie through centuries,   80
And hear the blessed mutter of the mass,
And see God made and eaten all day long,
And feel the steady candle-flame, and taste
Good strong thick stupefying incense-smoke!
For as I lie here, hours of the dead night,   85
Dying in state and by such slow degrees,
I fold my arms as if they clasped a crook,
And stretch my feet forth straight as stone can point,
And let the bedclothes, for a mortcloth, drop

51: The line adapts Job 7:6.   57 *wot:* know.   58 *tripod:* stool of Apollo's
priest at the Delphic oracle.   58 *thyrsus:* staff of Bacchus.   60 *glory:* halo.
64 *bowels:* heart.   77 *Tully:* Cicero.   79 *Ulpian:* minor Roman writer.   87
crook: symbolic shepherd's staff carried by bishop.   89 *mortcloth:* funeral pall.

Into great laps and folds of sculptor's-work: 90
And as yon tapers dwindle, and strange thoughts
Grow, with a certain humming in my ears,
About the life before I lived this life,
And this life too, popes, cardinals and priests,
Saint Praxed at his sermon on the mount,   95
Your tall pale mother with her talking eyes,
And new-found agate urns as fresh as day,
And marble's language, Latin pure, discreet,
Aha, ELUCESCEBAT quoth our friend?
No Tully, said I, Ulpian at the best!   100
Evil and brief hath been my pilgrimage.
All *lapis*, all, sons! Else I give the Pope
My villas! Will ye ever eat my heart?
Ever your eyes were as a lizard's quick,
They glitter like your mother's for my soul,   105
Or ye would heighten my impoverished frieze,
Piece out its starved design, and fill my vase
With grapes, and add a visor and a Term,
And to the tripod ye would tie a lynx
That in his struggle throws the thyrsus down,   110
To comfort me on my entablature
Whereon I am to lie till I must ask
"Do I live, am I dead?" There, leave me, there!
For ye have stabbed me with ingratitude
To death—ye wish it—God, ye wish it! Stone—   115
Gritstone, a-crumble! Clammy squares which sweat
As if the corpse they keep were oozing through—
And no more *lapis* to delight the world!
Well, go! I bless ye. Fewer tapers there,
But in a row: and, going, turn your backs   120
—Ay, like departing altar-ministrants,
And leave me in my church, the church for peace,
That I may watch at leisure if he leers—
Old Gandolf—at me, from his onion-stone,
As still he envied me, so fair she was!   125

99 ELUCESCEBAT: he was beginning to shine, to be famous. 101: adapts
Genesis 47:9.   108 *visor*: mask.   108 *Term*: bust on pedestal.

Case

A

1. The Bishop is an unmitigated scoundrel.

2. He reveals himself as a hypocrite, a breaker of vows, a begetter of illegitimate children, a thief, and an attempted briber.

3. His feelings about immortality are materialistic and therefore un-Christian, and the dominant motive in a life supposedly devoted to pastoral care is a desire to outdo a rival.

4. Although his esthetic taste is vigorous, it is unclerically sensuous and even sensual.

5. Instead of facing death with spiritual composure, the Bishop allows his feelings to run erratically from concern (10-13, 111-13) through contentiousness (15-16), confusion (53-54, 68-69, 95, 102), suspicion (62ff., 103ff.), condescension (77-79, 99-100), religiosity (80-84, 120-22), and anger (113-17).

B

1. The Bishop is a Renaissance gentleman whose faults are minor when contrasted with the qualities of affection, piety, and esthetic sensitivity which he displays in his deathbed monologue.

2. One of his major characteristics is strong family feeling, in both concern for his sons and devotion to their mother.

3. The Bishop's lively esthetic sense is evidenced by his taste for beauty in woman, in stone, in classical scholarship, and in both Christian and pagan art.

4. He demonstrates ingrained religious piety by revealing a Christian belief in immortality, a Christian desire for peace, and an affinity for Biblical and moralistic patterns when his mind strays from connected discourse.

5. That a dying man should appear to be so vital a person is partly the result of the dramatic interplay between the speaker and his audience of sons.

BIBLIOGRAPHY

Daniels, E., *The Art of Reading Poetry*, 1941, pp. 99-101; Honan, P., *Browning's Characters*, 1961, pp. 134-35, 140-41, 149-50, 218-19, 237, 251.

Home-Thoughts, from the Sea

Nobly, nobly Cape Saint Vincent to the Northwest died away;
Sunset ran, one glorious blood-red, reeking into Cadiz Bay;
Bluish 'mid the burning water, full in face Trafalgar lay;
In the dimmest North-east distance dawned Gibraltar grand and gray;
"Here and here did England help me: how can I help England?"—say,   5
Whoso turns as I, this evening, turn to God to praise and pray,
While Jove's planet rises yonder, silent over Africa.

Case

A

1. The primary theme, partly indicated by the title, is the speaker's love for his country.
2. Foreign scenes of English victory remind him of the glory of empire and prompt him to offer God both praise for past help and prayer for future success in national affairs.
3. The long, end-stopped, single-rhyming lines reinforce the tone of reverence.

B

1. The primary theme, despite the title, is the speaker's feeling of inadequacy in the face of magnitude.
2. He expresses this feeling by implicitly contrasting immense and abiding items—capes, bay, rock, Nelson's fame, England, God, Jupiter, and Africa—with himself, the small and impotent individual.
3. The lines of the whole poem are linked together not only by the emphatic masculine rhyme but also by the overwhelming abundance of alliteration and assonance.

Meeting at Night—Parting at Morning

MEETING AT NIGHT

The gray sea and the long black land;   6
And the yellow half-moon large and low;

Cape Saint Vincent, Cadiz Bay, Trafalgar, Gibraltar: scenes of British military successes, the first three associated with Nelson.   7 Africa: rhymes with other lines.

And the startled little waves that leap
In fiery ringlets from their sleep,
As I gain the cove with pushing prow,
And quench its speed i' the slushy sand.

Then a mile of warm sea-scented beach;   7
Three fields to cross till a farm appears;
A tap at the pane, the quick sharp scratch
And blue spurt of a lighted match,
And a voice less loud, thro' its joys and fears,
Than the two hearts beating each to each!

PARTING AT MORNING

Round the cape of a sudden came the sea,   13
And the sun looked over the mountain's rim:
And straight was a path of gold for him,
And the need of a world of men for me.

Never the Time and the Place

Never the time and the place
    And the loved one all together!
    This path—how soft to pace!
    This May—what magic weather!
Where is the loved one's face?   5
In a dream that loved one's face meets mine,
    But the house is narrow, the place is bleak
Where, outside, rain and wind combine
    With a furtive ear, if I strive to speak,
    With a hostile eye at my flushing cheek,   10
With a malice that marks each word, each sign!
O enemy sly and serpentine,
    Uncoil thee from the waking man!
        Do I hold the Past
        Thus firm and fast   15
    Yet doubt if the Future hold I can?
This path so soft to pace shall lead
Thro' the magic of May to herself indeed!

15 *him:* the sun.

Or narrow if needs the house must be,
Outside are the storms and strangers: we—   20
Oh, close, safe, warm sleep I and she,
    —I and she!

John Anderson, My Jo

John Anderson my jo, John,
    When we were first acquent,
Your locks were like the raven,
    Your bonie brow was brent;
But now your brow is beld, John,   5
    Your locks are like the snaw;
But blessings on your frosty pow,
    John Anderson my jo.

John Anderson my jo, John,   9
    We clamb the hill thegither;
And mony a cantie day, John,
    We 've had wi' ane anither:
Now we maun totter down, John,   13
    And hand in hand we 'll go,
And sleep thegither at the foot.
    John Anderson my jo.

So We'll Go No More A-Roving

So we'll go no more a-roving
    So late into the night,
Though the heart be still as loving,
    And the moon be still as bright.

For the sword outwears its sheath,   5
    And the soul wears out the breast,
And the heart must pause to breathe,
    And love itself have rest.

1 *jo:* darling.   4 *brent:* smooth.   7 *pow:* head.   11 *cantie:* merry.   13 *maun:*
must.

Though the night was made for loving,   9
And the day returns too soon,
Yet we'll go no more a-roving
By the light of the moon.

Rose-Cheeked Laura, Come

Rose-cheeked Laura, come,
Sing thou smoothly with thy beauty's
Silent music, either other
   Sweetly gracing.

Lovely forms do flow   5
From concent divinely framed;
Heav'n is music, and thy beauty's
   Birth is heavenly.

These dull notes we sing   9
Discords need for helps to grace them;
Only beauty purely loving
   Knows no discord,

But still moves delight,   13
Like clear springs renewed by flowing,
Ever perfect, ever in them-
   Selves eternal.

The poem is in quantitative verse.   3 *either other:* each one the other.   6 *concent:* harmony.

Prologue to

The Canterbury Tales

(1) Introduction, (2) the Knight, (3) the Prioress,
(4) the Wife of Bath

Whan that Aprill with his shoures soote
The droghte of March hath perced to the roote
And bathed euery veyne in swich licour
Of which vertu engendred is the flour
Whan Zephirus eek with his sweete breeth   5
Inspired hath in euery holt and heeth
The tendre croppes and the yonge sonne
Hath in the Ram his half cours yronne
And smale foweles maken melodye
That slepen al the nyght with open eye   10
So priketh hem nature in hir corages
Than longen folk to goon on pilgrymages
And palmeres for to seken straunge strondes
To ferne halwes kouthe in sondry londes
And specially from euery shires ende   15
Of Engelond to Caunterbury they wende
The holy blisful martir for to seke
That hem hath holpen whan that they were seeke
    Bifel that in that sesoun on a day
In Southwerk at the Tabard as I lay   20
Redy to wenden on my pilgrymage
To Caunterbury with ful deuout corage
At nyght was come into that hostelrye
Wel nyne and twenty in a compaignye

When April with its sweet showers has pierced the drought of March to the root, and bathed every sap-vein in that liquid by virtue of which the flower is produced; when Zephyr [the West Wind] also with his sweet breath has quickened the tender shoots in every wood and heath, and the young sun [of Spring] has run halfway through the sign of the Ram [in the zodiac], and small birds that sleep all night with open eye make melody (so nature spurs them in their hearts)—then people long to go on pilgrimages, and pilgrims to seek strange strands, far-away shrines, famous in sundry lands. And especially, from every shire's end in England they go to Canterbury to seek the holy blissful martyr [St. Thomas à Becket] who has helped them when they were sick.

It befell that in that season on a certain day, as I lodged in Southwark at the Tabard, ready to go on my pilgrimage to Canterbury with very devout heart, at night there came into the hostelry nine and twenty in a company

Of sondry folk by auenture yfalle   25
In felaweshipe and pilgrymes were they alle
That toward Caunterbury wolden ryde
The chambres and the stables weren wyde
And wel we weren esed atte beste
And shortly whan the sonne was to reste   30
So hadde I spoken with hem euerichon
That I was of hir felaweshipe anon
And made forward erly for to ryse
To take oure wey ther as I yow deuyse
    But nathelees whil I haue tyme and space   35
Er that I ferther in this tale pace
Me thynketh it acordant to resoun
To telle yow al the condicioun
Of ech of hem so as it semed me
And whiche they weren and of what degree   40
And eek in what array that they were inne
And at a knyght than wol I first bigynne
    A KNYGHT ther was and that a worthy man
That fro the tyme that he first bigan
To riden out he loued chiualrye   45
Trouthe and honour fredom and curteisye
Ful worthy was he in his lordes werre
And ther to hadde he riden no man ferre
As wel in cristendom as in hethenesse
And euere honoured for his worthynesse   50

of sundry people, by chance fallen into fellowship, and pilgrims were they all, who intended to ride to Canterbury. The chambers and the stables were spacious, and we were entertained in the best style. And shortly, when the sun had gone to rest, I had so spoken to every one of them that I was immediately of their fellowship, and we made agreement to rise early and take our way there, as I will describe to you.

But nevertheless, while I have time and space, before I go further in this tale, it seems to me in accord with reason to tell you all the facts about each of them, as it seemed to me, and what sort they were, and of what social station, and also what array they were in. And with a knight then will I first begin.

A knight there was, and he was a worthy man, who, from the time he began to ride out, loved chivalry, truth and honor, generosity, and courtesy. Most worthy was he in his king's wars, and where he had ridden, no man went farther, in Christendom as in heathendom, and [he was] always honored for his worthiness.

At Alisaundre he was whan it was wonne
Ful ofte tyme he hadde the bord bigonne
Abouen alle nacions in Pruce
In Lettow hadde he reysed and in Ruce
No cristen man so ofte of his degree   55
In Gernade at the seege eek hadde he be
Of Algezir and riden in Belmarye
At Lyeys was he and at Satalye
Whan they were wonne and in the Grete See
At many a noble armee hadde he be   60
At mortal batailles hadde he been fiftene
And foghten for oure feith at Tramyssene
In lystes thries and ay slayn his foo
This ilke worthy knyght hadde been also
Som tyme with the lord of Palatye   65
Agayn another hethen in Turkye
    And euere moore he hadde a souereyn prys
And though that he were worthy he was wys
And of his port as meke as is a mayde
He neuere yet no vileynye ne sayde   70
In all his lyf vn to no maner wight
He was a verray parfit gentil knyght
    But for to tellen yow of his array
Hise hors were goode but he was nat gay
Of fustian he wered a gypoun   75
Al bismotered with his habergeoun

He was at Alexandria when it was won. Full ofttimes he had sat at the
head of the table above all nations in Prussia; in Lithuania he had served
and in Russia; no Christian man of his station had so often [done this].
In Granada he had also been at the siege of Algeciras, and he had ridden
at Benmarin [Morocco]. He was at Ayas [Armenia] and at Attalia
[Turkey] when they were won; and in the Great Sea [Mediterranean]
he had been in many a noble armada.

He had been in fifteen mortal battles, and fought for our faith at
Tlemcen [Algeria] in three tournaments, and had always slain his foe.
This same worthy knight had been also at one time with the lord of Balat
against another heathen in Turkey. And evermore he had a distinguished
reputation; and though he was worthy, he was wise, and in his bearing
as meek as is a maiden. He never yet had attempted any villainy in all his
life against any manner of person. He was a true, perfect, gentle knight.

But to tell you of his array, his horse was good, but he was not showy.
He wore a blouse of coarse cotton all besmutted by his coat of mail, for he

For he was late ycome from his viage
And wente for to doon his pilgrymage. . . .
      Ther was also a nonne a PRIORESSE
That of hir smylyng was ful symple and coy
Hir gretteste ooth was but by Seint Loy   120
And she was cleped Madame Eglentyne
      Ful wel she soong the seruyce dyuyne
Entuned in hir nose ful semely
And Frenssh she spak ful faire and fetisly
After the scole of Stratford atte Bowe   125
For Frenssh of Parys was to hire vnknowe
      At mete wel ytaught was she with alle
She leet no morsel from hir lippes falle
Ne wette hir fyngres in hir sauce depe
Wel koude she carie a morsel and wel kepe   130
That no drope ne fille vp on hir brest
In curteisie was set ful muchel hir lest
Hir ouer lippe wyped she so clene
That in hir coppe ther was no ferthynge sene
Of grece whan she dronken hadde hir draughte   135
Ful semely after hir mete she raughte
And sikerly she was of greet desport
And ful plesaunt and amyable of port
And peyned hire to countrefete cheere
Of court and to been estatlich of manere   140
And to been holden digne of reuerence

had lately come from his journey and was going to do his pilgrimage. . . .
    There was also a nun, a prioress, who was very simple and modest in
her smiling; her greatest oath was merely, "by Saint Loy." And she was
called Madame Eglantine. She sang the divine service very well, intoned
in her nose very properly; and she spoke French well and gracefully,
according to the school of Stratford-at-the-Bow, for the French of Paris
was unknown to her. At table she was well taught withal: she let no
morsel fall from her lips, nor wet her fingers deeply in her sauce; well
could she carry a morsel and keep it well so that no drop fell on her
breast. Her pleasure was to be courteous; she wiped her upper lip so clean
that on her cup there was no particle seen when she had drunk her
draught. She reached for her food very gracefully, and surely she was of
great good humor and very pleasant, and amiable in manner; and she took
pains to imitate a courtly appearance and to be stately in manner and to
be held worthy of reverence.

But for to speken of hir conscience
She was so charitable and so pitous
She wolde wepe if that she sawe a mous
Caught in a trappe if it were deed or bledde   145
Of smale houndes hadde she that she fedde
With rosted flessh or mylk and wastel breed
But soore wepte she if oon of hem were deed
Or if men smoot it with a yerde smerte
And al was conscience and tendre herte   150
   Ful semely hir wympel pynched was
Hir nose tretys hir eyen greye as glas
Hir mouth ful smal and ther to softe and reed
But sikerly she hadde a fair forheed
It was almoost a spanne brood I trowe   155
For hardily she was nat vndergrowe
Ful fetys was hir cloke as I was war
Of smal coral aboute hir arm she bar
A peyre of bedes gauded al with grene
And there on heng a brooch of gold ful shene   160
On which ther was first writen a crowned A
And after *Amor vincit omnia.* . . .
   A good WYF was ther of biside BATHE   445
But she was som del deef and that was scathe
   Of clooth makyng she hadde swich an haunt

But to speak of her conscience, she was so charitable and so full of pity that she would weep if she saw a mouse caught in a trap, if it were dead or bleeding. She had some small dogs that she fed on roasted meat or milk and white bread. She wept bitterly if one of them died or if anyone struck one of them smartly with a stick, and she was all pity and tender heart. Her head-dress was pleated very gracefully; her nose was well formed, her eyes were grey as glass, her mouth very small and also soft and red; and surely she had a fair forehead—it was almost a span broad, I think; for she certainly was not undersized. Very graceful was her cloak, as I was aware; about her arm she bore a rosary of small coral with green gauds [large beads], and thereon hung a bright gold ornament very shiny, on which was written first a crowned A, and after that, "Love conquers all." . . .

A good wife there was, from near Bath; she was somewhat deaf, and that was a pity. In cloth-making she had such a skill that she surpassed

She passed hem of Ypres and of Gaunt
In al the parisshe wyf ne was ther noon
That to the offrynge bifore hire sholde goon   450
And if ther dide certeyn so wrooth was she
That she was out of alle charitee
    Hir couerchiefs ful fyne were of ground
I dorste swere they weyeden ten pound
That on a Sonday weren vp on hir heed   455
Hir hosen weren of fyn scarlet reed
Ful streite yteyd and shoes ful moyste and newe
Boold was hir face and fair and reed of hewe
She was a worthy womman al hir lyue
Housbondes at chirche dore she hadde fyue   460
With outen oother compaignye in youthe
But ther of nedeth nat to speke as nouthe
    And thries hadde she been at Ierusalem
She hadde passed many a straunge strem
At Rome she hadde been and at Boloyne   465
In Galice at Seint Iame and at Coloyne
She koude muche of wandrynge by the weye
Gat tothed was she soothly for to seye
    Vpon an amblere esily she sat
Ywympled wel and on hir heed an hat   470
As brood as is a bokeler or a targe

those of Ypres and Ghent. In all the parish there was no wife who went before her to make an offering; and if anyone did, certainly, she was so angry that she lost all charity. Her head kerchiefs were of fine texture—I would dare swear they weighed ten pounds—that she had on her head of a Sunday. Her stockings were a fine scarlet red, very tightly tied, and her shoes very supple and new. Bold was her face, and fair, and red of hue. She was a worthy woman all her life; husbands at the church door she had five, not counting other company in her youth; but there is no need to speak of that just now. And thrice she had been to Jerusalem; she had crossed many a foreign stream; she had been at Rome and at Boulogne, in Galicia [in Spain] at [the shrine of] St. James, and at Cologne. She knew much from wandering by the way. Gap-toothed she was, to speak truly. Upon a pacer easily she sat; she had a good hood on,

A foot mantel aboute hir hipes large
And on hir feet a peyre of spores sharpe
    In felawshipe wel koude she laughe and carpe
Of remedies of loue she knew par chaunce   475
For she koude of that art the olde daunce. . . .

and on her head a hat as broad as is a buckler or a shield, a riding skirt
about her broad hips, and on her feet a pair of sharp spurs. In company
well could she laugh and talk. Probably, she knew remedies for love, for
she knew well the old dance of that art. . . .[1]

Two Egrets

On Easter morning two egrets
flew up the Shrewsbury River
between Highlands and Sea Bright

like two white hands   4
washing one another
in the prime of light.

Oh lemons and bells of light,   7
rails, rays, waterfalls, ices—
as high as the eye dizzies

into the whirled confetti   10
and rhinestones of the breaking blue
grain of lit heaven,

the white stroke of the egrets   13
turned the air—a prayer
and the idea of prayer.

[1] Translation based on glossary and notes of F. N. Robinson's edition, 1933.

2-3: on the New Jersey coast.

In Place of a Curse

At the next vacancy for God, if I am elected,
I shall forgive last the delicately wounded
who, having been slugged no harder than anyone else,
never got up again, neither to fight back,
nor to finger their jaws in painful admiration.

They who are wholly broken, and they in whom   6
mercy is understanding, I shall embrace at once
and lead to pillows in heaven. But they who are
the meek by trade, baiting the best of their betters
with the extortions of a mock-helplessness

I shall take last to love, and never wholly.   11
Let them all into Heaven—I abolish Hell—
but let it be read over them as they enter:
"Beware the calculations of the meek, who gambled nothing,
gave nothing, and could never receive enough."

The Latest Decalogue

Thou shalt have one God only; who
Would be at the expense of two?
No graven images may be
Worshipped, except the currency:
Swear not at all; for for thy curse   5
Thine enemy is none the worse:
At church on Sunday to attend
Will serve to keep the world thy friend:
Honour thy parents; that is, all
From whom advancement may befall: 10
Thou shalt not kill; but needst not strive
Officiously to keep alive:
Do not adultery commit;
Advantage rarely comes of it:
Thou shalt not steal; an empty feat,   15
When it's so lucrative to cheat:

Decalogue: Ten Commandments.

Bear not false witness; let the lie
Have time on its own wings to fly:
Thou shalt not covet; but tradition
Approves all forms of competition.   20

The sum of all is, thou shalt love,
If any body, God above:
At any rate shall never labour
More than thyself to love thy neighbour.

The Rime of the Ancient Mariner

In Seven Parts

PART I

An ancient
Mariner meet-
eth three Gal-
lants bidden
to a wedding-
feast, and de-
taineth one.

It is an ancient Mariner,
And he stoppeth one of three.
'By thy long grey beard and glittering eye,
Now wherefore stopp'st thou me?

The Bridegroom's doors are opened wide,   5
And I am next of kin;
The guests are met, the feast is set:
May'st hear the merry din.'

He holds him with his skinny hand,   9
'There was a ship,' quoth he.
'Hold off! unhand me, grey-beard loon!'
Eftsoons his hand dropt he.

The Wedding-
Guest is spell-
bound by the
eye of the old
seafaring man,
and constrained
to hear his tale.

He holds him with his glittering eye—   13
The Wedding-Guest stood still,
And listens like a three years' child:
The Mariner hath his will.

The Wedding-Guest sat on a stone: 17
He cannot choose but hear;
And thus spake on that ancient man,
The bright-eyed Mariner.

12 *Eftsoons:* soon.

'The ship was cheered, the harbour cleared,   21
Merrily did we drop

The Mariner
tells how the
ship sailed
southward
Below the kirk, below the hill,
Below the lighthouse top.

with a good
wind and fair
weather, till it
reached the
line.
The Sun came up upon the left,   25
Out of the sea came he!
And he shone bright, and on the right
Went down into the sea.

Higher and higher every day,   29
Till over the mast at noon—'
The Wedding-Guest here beat his breast,
For he heard the loud bassoon.

The Wedding-
Guest heareth
the bridal
music; but
the Mariner
continueth
his tale.
The bride hath paced into the hall,   33
Red as a rose is she;
Nodding their heads before her goes
The merry minstrelsy.

The Wedding-Guest he beat his breast,   37
Yet he cannot choose but hear;
And thus spake on that ancient man,
The bright-eyed Mariner.

The ship
driven by a
storm toward
the south pole.
'And now the STORM-BLAST came, and he   41
Was tyrannous and strong:
He struck with his o'ertaking wings
And chased us south along.

With sloping masts and dipping prow,   45
As who pursued with yell and blow
Still treads the shadow of his foe,
And forward bends his head,
The ship drove fast, loud roared the blast,
And southward aye we fled.

And now there came both mist and snow,   51
And it grew wondrous cold:
And ice, mast-high, came floating by,
As green as emerald.

The land of
ice, and of
fearful sounds
where no
living thing
was to be seen.
And through the drifts the snowy clifts   55
Did send a dismal sheen:
Nor shapes of men nor beasts we ken—
The ice was all between.

The ice was here, the ice was there,   59
The ice was all around:
It cracked and growled, and roared and howled,
Like noises in a swound!

Till a great sea-bird, called the Albatross, came through the snow-fog, and was received with great joy and hospitality.

At length did cross an Albatross,   63
Through the fog it came;
As if it had been a Christian soul,
We hailed it in God's name.

It ate the food it ne'er had eat,   67
And round and round it flew.
The ice did split with a thunder-fit;
The helmsman steered us through!

And lo! the Albatross proveth a bird of good omen, and followeth the ship as it returned northward through fog and floating ice.

And a good south wind sprung up behind;   71
The Albatross did follow,
And every day, for food or play,
Came to the mariners' hollo!

In mist or cloud, on mast or shroud,   75
It perched for vespers nine;
Whiles all the night, through fog-smoke white,
Glimmered the white Moon-shine.'

The ancient Mariner inhospitably killeth the pious bird of good omen.

'God save thee, ancient Mariner!   79
From the fiends, that plague thee thus!—
Why look'st thou so?'—With my cross-bow
I shot the ALBATROSS.

PART II

The Sun now rose upon the right: 83
Out of the sea came he,
Still hid in mist, and on the left
Went down into the sea.

And the good south wind still blew behind,   87
But no sweet bird did follow,
Nor any day for food or play
Came to the mariners' hollo!

His shipmates cry out against the ancient Mariner, for killing the bird of good luck.

And I had done a hellish thing,   91
And it would work 'em woe:
For all averred, I had killed the bird
That made the breeze to blow.
Ah wretch! said they, the bird to slay,
That made the breeze to blow!

62 *swound:* swoon.   76 *vespers:* evenings.

Nor dim nor red, like God's own head, 97
The glorious Sun uprist:
Then all averred, I had killed the bird
That brought the fog and mist.
'Twas right, said they, such birds to slay,
That bring the fog and mist.

But when the fog cleared off, they justify the same, and thus make themselves accomplices in the crime.

The fair breeze blew, the white foam flew, 103
The furrow followed free;
We were the first that ever burst
Into that silent sea.

The fair breeze continues; the ship enters the Pacific Ocean, and sails northward, even till it reaches the Line.

Down dropt the breeze, the sails dropt down, 107
'Twas sad as sad could be;
And we did speak only to break
The silence of the sea!

The ship hath been suddenly becalmed.

All in a hot and copper sky, 111
The bloody Sun, at noon,
Right up above the mast did stand,
No bigger than the Moon.

Day after day, day after day, 115
We stuck, nor breath nor motion;
As idle as a painted ship
Upon a painted ocean.

Water, water, every where, 119
And all the boards did shrink;
Water, water, every where,
Nor any drop to drink.

And the Albatross begins to be avenged.

The very deep did rot: O Christ! 123
That ever this should be!
Yea, slimy things did crawl with legs
Upon the slimy sea.

About, about, in reel and rout 127
The death-fires danced at night;
The water, like a witch's oils,
Burnt green, and blue and white.

And some in dreams assuréd were 131
Of the Spirit that plagued us so;
Nine fathom deep he had followed us
From the land of mist and snow.

A Spirit had followed them; one of the invisible inhabitants of this planet, neither departed souls nor angels; concerning whom the learned Jew, Josephus, and the Platonic Constantinopolitan, Michael Psellus, may be consulted. They are very numerous, and there is no climate or element without one or more.

And every tongue, through utter drought,   135
Was withered at the root;
We could not speak, no more than if
We had been choked with soot.

The shipmates,
in their sore
distress, would
fain throw the
whole guilt on
the ancient

Ah! well a-day! what evil looks   139
Had I from old and young!
Instead of the cross, the Albatross
About my neck was hung.

Mariner: in sign whereof they hang the dead sea-bird round his neck.

PART III

There passed a weary time. Each throat   143
Was parched, and glazed each eye.
A weary time! a weary time!
How glazed each weary eye,

The ancient
Mariner be-
holdeth a sign
in the element
afar off.

When looking westward, I beheld
A something in the sky.

At first it seemed a little speck,   149
And then it seemed a mist;
It moved and moved, and took at last
A certain shape, I wist.

A speck, a mist, a shape, I wist!   153
And still it neared and neared:
As if it dodged a water-sprite,
It plunged and tacked and veered.

At its nearer
approach, it
seemeth him
to be a ship;
and at a dear
ransom he
freeth his
speech from
the bonds of
thirst.

With throats unslaked, with black lips baked,   157
We could nor laugh nor wail;
Through utter drought all dumb we stood!
I bit my arm, I sucked the blood,
And cried, A sail! a sail!

A flash of joy;

With throats unslaked, with black lips baked,   162
Agape they heard me call:
Gramercy! they for joy did grin,
And all at once their breath drew in,
As they were drinking all.

And horror
follows. For
can it be a
ship that
comes onward
without wind
or tide?

See! see! (I cried) she tacks no more!   167
Hither to work us weal;
Without a breeze, without a tide,
She steadies with upright keel!

148 *element:* sky.   152 *wist:* knew.   166 *As:* as if.   168 *weal:* good.

The western wave was all a-flame.   171
The day was well nigh done!
Almost upon the western wave
Rested the broad bright Sun;
When that strange shape drove suddenly
Betwixt us and the Sun.

It seemeth   And straight the Sun was flecked with bars,   177
him but the
skeleton of   (Heaven's Mother send us grace!)
a ship.   As if through a dungeon-grate he peered
               With broad and burning face.

And its ribs   Alas! (thought I, and my heart beat loud)   181
are seen as   How fast she nears and nears!
bars on the
face of the   Are those *her* sails that glance in the Sun,
setting Sun.   Like restless gossameres?

The Spectre-   Are those *her* ribs through which the Sun   185
Woman and   Did peer, as through a grate?
her Death-
mate, and no   And is that Woman all her crew?
other on   Is that a DEATH? and are there two?
board the   Is DEATH that woman's mate?
skeleton ship.

Like vessel,   *Her* lips were red, *her* looks were free,   190
like crew!   Her locks were yellow as gold:
Death and
Life-in-Death Her skin was as white as leprosy,
have diced for The Night-mare LIFE-IN-DEATH was she,
the ship's   Who thicks man's blood with cold.
crew, and she
(the latter)
winneth the   The naked hulk alongside came,   195
ancient Mariner. And the twain were casting dice;
               'The game is done! I've won! I've won!'
               Quoth she, and whistles thrice.

No twilight   The Sun's rim dips; the stars rush out: 199
within the   At one stride comes the dark;
courts of the
Sun.   With far-heard whisper, o'er the sea,
               Off shot the spectre-bark.

At the rising We listened and looked sideways up!   203
of the Moon,   Fear at my heart, as at a cup,
               My life-blood seemed to sip!
               The stars were dim, and thick the night,
               The steersman's face by his lamp gleamed white;
               From the sails the dew did drip—
               Till clomb above the eastern bar

184 *gossameres:* cobwebs.

The hornéd Moon, with one bright star
Within the nether tip.

One after
another,

One after one, by the star-dogged Moon,   212
Too quick for groan or sigh,
Each turned his face with a ghastly pang,
And cursed me with his eye.

His shipmates
drop down
dead.

Four times fifty living men,   216
(And I heard nor sigh nor groan)
With heavy thump, a lifeless lump,
They dropped down one by one.

But Life-in-
Death begins
her work on
the ancient
Mariner.

The souls did from their bodies fly,—   220
They fled to bliss or woe!
And every soul, it passed me by,
Like the whizz of my cross-bow!

PART IV

The Wedding-
Guest feareth
that a Spirit
is talking to
him;

'I fear thee, ancient Mariner!   224
I fear thy skinny hand!
And thou art long, and lank, and brown,
As is the ribbed sea-sand.

I fear thee and thy glittering eye,   228
And thy skinny hand, so brown.'—

But the
ancient Ma-
riner assureth
him of his
bodily life, and
proceedeth to
relate his hor-
rible penance.

Fear not, fear not, thou Wedding-Guest!
This body dropt not down.

Alone, alone, all, all alone,   232
Alone on a wide wide sea!
And never a saint took pity on
My soul in agony.

He despiseth
the creatures
of the calm,

The many men, so beautiful!   236
And they all dead did lie:
And a thousand thousand slimy things
Lived on; and so did I.

And envieth
that *they*
should live,
and so many
lie dead.

I looked upon the rotting sea,   240
And drew my eyes away;
I looked upon the rotting deck,
And there the dead men lay.

I looked to heaven, and tried to pray;   244
But or ever a prayer had gusht.

245 *or:* before.

A wicked whisper came, and made
My heart as dry as dust.

I closed my lids, and kept them close,   248
And the balls like pulses beat;
For the sky and the sea, and the sea and the sky
Lay like a load on my weary eye,
And the dead were at my feet.

But the curse
liveth for him
in the eye of
the dead men.

The cold sweat melted from their limbs,   253
Nor rot nor reek did they:
The look with which they looked on me
Had never passed away.

An orphan's curse would drag to hell   257
A spirit from on high;
But oh! more horrible than that
Is the curse in a dead man's eye!
Seven days, seven nights, I saw that curse,
And yet I could not die.

In his lone-
liness and
fixedness he
yearneth to-
wards the
journeying
Moon, and the
stars that still
sojourn, yet
still move
onward; and
every where
the blue sky
belongs to

The moving Moon went up the sky,   263
And no where did abide:
Softly she was going up,
And a star or two beside—
Her beams bemocked the sultry main,   267
Like April hoar-frost spread;
But where the ship's huge shadow lay,
The charmèd water burnt alway
A still and awful red.

them, and is their appointed rest, and their native country and their own natural homes,
which they enter unannounced, as lords that are certainly expected and yet there is a silent
joy at their arrival.

By the light
of the Moon he
beholdeth
God's crea-
tures of the
great calm.

Beyond the shadow of the ship,   272
I watched the water-snakes:
They moved in tracks of shining white,
And when they reared, the elfish light
Fell off in hoary flakes.

Within the shadow of the ship   277
I watched their rich attire:
Blue, glossy green, and velvet black,
They coiled and swam; and every track
Was a flash of golden fire.

Their beauty
and their
happiness.

O happy living things! no tongue   282
Their beauty might declare:
A spring of love gushed from my heart,

*He blesseth
them in his
heart.*

And I blessed them unaware:
Sure my kind saint took pity on me,
And I blessed them unaware.

*The spell
begins to
break.*

The self-same moment I could pray;   288
And from my neck so free
The Albatross fell off, and sank
Like lead into the sea.

Part V

Oh sleep! it is a gentle thing,   292
Beloved from pole to pole!
To Mary Queen the praise be given!
She sent the gentle sleep from Heaven,
That slid into my soul.

*By grace of
the holy
Mother, the
ancient
Mariner is
refreshed with
rain.*

The silly buckets on the deck,   297
That had so long remained,
I dreamt that they were filled with dew;
And when I awoke, it rained.

My lips were wet, my throat was cold,   301
My garments all were dank;
Sure I had drunken in my dreams,
And still my body drank.

I moved, and could not feel my limbs: 305
I was so light—almost
I thought that I had died in sleep,
And was a blessèd ghost.

*He heareth
sounds and
seeth strange
sights and
commotions in
the sky and
the element.*

And soon I heard a roaring wind: 309
It did not come anear;
But with its sound it shook the sails,
That were so thin and sere.

The upper air burst into life!   313
And a hundred fire-flags sheen,
To and fro they were hurried about!
And to and fro, and in and out,
The wan stars danced between.

And the coming wind did roar more loud,   318
And the sails did sigh like sedge;

297 *silly:* simple.   319 *sedge:* grass-like plant.

And the rain poured down from one black cloud;
The Moon was at its edge.

The thick black cloud was cleft, and still   322
The Moon was at its side:
Like waters shot from some high crag,
The lightning fell with never a jag,
A river steep and wide.

The bodies of
the ship's crew
are inspired
and the
ship moves
on;

The loud wind never reached the ship,   327
Yet now the ship moved on!
Beneath the lightning and the Moon
The dead men gave a groan.

They groaned, they stirred, they all uprose,   331
Nor spake, nor moved their eyes;
It had been strange, even in a dream,
To have seen those dead men rise.

The helmsman steered, the ship moved on;   335
Yet never a breeze up-blew;
The mariners all 'gan work the ropes,
Where they were wont to do;
They raised their limbs like lifeless tools—
We were a ghastly crew.

The body of my brother's son   341
Stood by me, knee to knee:
The body and I pulled at one rope,
But he said nought to me.

'I fear thee, ancient Mariner!'   345

But not by the
souls of the
men, nor by
dæmons of
earth, or
middle air, but
by a blessed
troop of
angelic spirits,
sent down by
the invocation
of the guar-
dian saint.

Be calm, thou Wedding-Guest!
'Twas not those souls that fled in pain,
Which to their corses came again,
But a troop of spirits blest:

For when it dawned—they dropped their arms,   350
And clustered round the mast;
Sweet sounds rose slowly through their mouths,
And from their bodies passed.

Around, around, flew each sweet sound,   354
Then darted to the Sun;
Slowly the sounds came back again,
Now mixed, now one by one.

348 *corses:* corpses.

Sometimes a-dropping from the sky   358
I heard the sky-lark sing;
Sometimes all little birds that are,
How they seemed to fill the sea and air
With their sweet jargoning!

And now 'twas like all instruments,   363
Now like a lonely flute;
And now it is an angel's song,
That makes the heavens be mute.

It ceased; yet still the sails made on   367
A pleasant noise till noon,
A noise like of a hidden brook
In the leafy month of June,
That to the sleeping woods all night
Singeth a quiet tune.

Till noon we quietly sailed on,   373
Yet never a breeze did breathe:
Slowly and smoothly went the ship,
Moved onward from beneath.

The lonesome
Spirit from
the south-pole
carries on the
ship as far as
the Line, in
obedience to
the angelic
troop, but still
requireth
vengeance.

Under the keel nine fathom deep,   377
From the land of mist and snow,
The spirit slid: and it was he
That made the ship to go.
The sails at noon left off their tune,
And the ship stood still also.

The Sun, right up above the mast,   383
Had fixed her to the ocean:
But in a minute she 'gan stir,
With a short uneasy motion—
Backwards and forwards half her length
With a short uneasy motion.

Then like a pawing horse let go,   389
She made a sudden bound:
It flung the blood into my head,
And I fell down in a swound.

The Polar
Spirit's fellow-
dæmons, the
invisible in-
habitants of
the element,
take part in
his wrong;

How long in that same fit I lay,   393
I have not to declare;
But ere my living life returned,
I heard and in my soul discerned
Two voices in the air.

and two of
them relate,
one to the
other, that
penance long
and heavy for
the ancient
Mariner hath
been accorded
to the Polar
Spirit, who
returneth
southward.

'Is it he?' quoth one, 'Is this the man?   398
By him who died on cross,
With his cruel bow he laid full low
The harmless Albatross.

The spirit who bideth by himself   402
In the land of mist and snow,
He loved the bird that loved the man
Who shot him with his bow.'

The other was a softer voice,   406
As soft as honey-dew:
Quoth he, 'The man hath penance done,
And penance more will do.'

Part VI

FIRST VOICE

'But tell me, tell me! speak again,   410
Thy soft response renewing—
What makes that ship drive on so fast?
What is the ocean doing?'

SECOND VOICE

'Still as a slave before his lord,   414
The ocean hath no blast;
His great bright eye most silently
Up to the Moon is cast—

If he may know which way to go;   418
For she guides him smooth or grim.
See, brother, see! how graciously
She looketh down on him.'

FIRST VOICE

The Mariner
hath been
cast into a
trance; for the
angelic power
causeth the
vessel to drive
northward
faster than
human life
could endure.

'But why drives on that ship so fast,   422
Without or wave or wind?'

SECOND VOICE

'The air is cut away before,   424
And closes from behind.

Fly, brother, fly! more high, more high!   426
Or we shall be belated:

For slow and slow that ship will go,
When the Mariner's trance is abated.'

The super-
natural motion
is retarded;
the Mariner
awakes, and
his penance
begins anew.

I woke, and we were sailing on   430
As in a gentle weather:
'Twas night, calm night, the moon was high;
The dead men stood together.

All stood together on the deck,   434
For a charnel-dungeon fitter:
All fixed on me their stony eyes,
That in the Moon did glitter.

The pang, the curse, with which they died,   438
Had never passed away:
I could not draw my eyes from theirs,
Nor turn them up to pray.

The curse is
finally ex-
piated.

And now this spell was snapt: once more   442
I viewed the ocean green,
And looked far forth, yet little saw
Of what had else been seen—

Like one, that on a lonesome road   446
Doth walk in fear and dread,
And having once turned round walks on,
And turns no more his head;
Because he knows, a frightful fiend
Doth close behind him tread.

But soon there breathed a wind on me,   452
Nor sound nor motion made:
Its path was not upon the sea,
In ripple or in shade.

It raised my hair, it fanned my cheek   456
Like a meadow-gale of spring—
It mingled strangely with my fears,
Yet it felt like a welcoming.

Swiftly, swiftly flew the ship,   460
Yet she sailed softly too:
Sweetly, sweetly blew the breeze—
On me alone it blew.

435 *charnel:* bones.

And the
ancient
Mariner be-
holdeth his
native
country.

Oh! dream of joy! is this indeed   464
The light-house top I see?
Is this the hill? is this the kirk?
Is this mine own countree?

We drifted o'er the harbour-bar,   468
And I with sobs did pray—
O let me be awake, my God!
Or let me sleep alway.

The harbour-bay was clear as glass,   472
So smoothly it was strewn!
And on the bay the moonlight lay,
And the shadow of the Moon.

The rock shone bright, the kirk no less,   476
That stands above the rock:
The moonlight steeped in silentness
The steady weathercock.

And the bay was white with silent light,   480
Till rising from the same,

Full many shapes, that shadows were,
In crimson colours came.

And appear in
their own
forms of light.

A little distance from the prow   484
Those crimson shadows were:
I turned my eyes upon the deck—
Oh, Christ! what saw I there!

Each corse lay flat, lifeless and flat,   488
And, by the holy rood!
A man all light, a seraph-man,
On every corse there stood.

This seraph-band, each waved his hand: 492
It was a heavenly sight!
They stood as signals to the land,
Each one a lovely light;

This seraph-band, each waved his hand,   496
No voice did they impart—
No voice; but oh! the silence sank
Like music on my heart.

489 *rood:* Cross.

But soon I heard the dash of oars,   500
I heard the Pilot's cheer;
My head was turned perforce away
And I saw a boat appear.

The Pilot and the Pilot's boy,   504
I heard them coming fast:
Dear Lord in Heaven! it was a joy
The dead men could not blast.

I saw a third—I heard his voice: 508
It is the Hermit good!
He singeth loud his godly hymns
That he makes in the wood.
He'll shrieve my soul, he'll wash away
The Albatross's blood.

Part VII

The Hermit of
the Wood,

This Hermit good lives in that wood   514
Which slopes down to the sea.
How loudly his sweet voice he rears!
He loves to talk with marineres
That come from a far countree.

He kneels at morn, and noon, and eve—   519
He hath a cushion plump:
It is the moss that wholly hides
The rotted old oak-stump.

The skiff-boat neared: I heard them talk,   523
'Why, this is strange, I trow!
Where are those lights so many and fair,
That signal made but now?'

Approacheth
the ship with
wonder.

'Strange, by my faith!' the Hermit said—   527
'And they answered not our cheer!
The planks looked warped! and see those sails,
How thin they are and sere!
I never saw aught like to them,
Unless perchance it were

Brown skeletons of leaves that lag   533
My forest-brook along;
When the ivy-tod is heavy with snow,

524 *trow:* think.   535 *tod:* bush.

And the owlet whoops to the wolf below,
That eats the she-wolf's young.'

'Dear Lord! it hath a fiendish look—   538
(The Pilot made reply)
I am a-feared'—'Push on, push on!'
Said the Hermit cheerily.

The boat came closer to the ship,   542
But I nor spake nor stirred;
The boat came close beneath the ship,
And straight a sound was heard.

The ship
suddenly
sinketh.

Under the water it rumbled on,   546
Still louder and more dread:
It reached the ship, it split the bay;
The ship went down like lead.

The ancient
Mariner is
saved in the
Pilot's boat.

Stunned by that loud and dreadful sound,   550
Which sky and ocean smote,
Like one that hath been seven days drowned
My body lay afloat;
But swift as dreams, myself I found
Within the Pilot's boat.

Upon the whirl, where sank the ship,   556
The boat spun round and round;
And all was still, save that the hill
Was telling of the sound.

I moved my lips—the Pilot shrieked   560
And fell down in a fit;
The holy Hermit raised his eyes,
And prayed where he did sit.

I took the oars: the Pilot's boy,   564
Who now doth crazy go,
Laughed loud and long, and all the while
His eyes went to and fro.
'Ha! ha!' quoth he, 'full plain I see,
The Devil knows how to row.'

And now, all in my own countree,   570
I stood on the firm land!
The Hermit stepped forth from the boat,
And scarcely he could stand.

'O shrieve me, shrieve me, holy man!'   574
The Hermit crossed his brow.
'Say quick,' quoth he, 'I bid thee say—
What manner of man art thou?'

Forthwith this frame of mine was wrenched   578
With a woful agony,
Which forced me to begin my tale;
And then it left me free.

Since then, at an uncertain hour,   582
That agony returns:
And till my ghastly tale is told,
This heart within me burns.

I pass, like night, from land to land;   586
I have strange power of speech;
That moment that his face I see,
I know the man that must hear me:
To him my tale I teach.

What loud uproar bursts from that door!   591
The wedding-guests are there:
But in the garden-bower the bride
And bride-maids singing are:
And hark the little vesper bell,
Which biddeth me to prayer!

O Wedding-Guest! this soul hath been   597
Alone on a wide wide sea:
So lonely 'twas, that God himself
Scarce seeméd there to be.

O sweeter than the marriage-feast,   601
'Tis sweeter far to me,
To walk together to the kirk
With a goodly company!—

To walk together to the kirk,   605
And all together pray,
While each to his great Father bends,
Old men, and babes, and loving friends
And youths and maidens gay!

Farewell, farewell! but this I tell   610
To thee, thou Wedding-Guest!
He prayeth well, who loveth well
Both man and bird and beast.

He prayeth best, who loveth best   614
All things both great and small;
For the dear God who loveth us,
He made and loveth all.

The Mariner, whose eye is bright,   618
Whose beard with age is hoar,
Is gone: and now the Wedding-Guest
Turned from the bridegroom's door.

He went like one that hath been stunned,   622
And is of sense forlorn:
A sadder and a wiser man,
He rose the morrow morn.

Critique

1. During the first year that Mr. Wordsworth and I were neigh-
bours, our conversations turned frequently on the two cardinal
points of poetry, the power of exciting the sympathy of the reader
by a faithful adherence to the truth of nature, and the power of
giving the interest of novelty by the modifying colours of imagination. The sudden charm, which accidents of light and shade, which
moonlight or sunset diffused over a known and familiar landscape,
appeared to represent the practicability of combining both. These
are the poetry of nature. The thought suggested itself—(to which
of us I do not recollect)—that a series of poems might be composed
of two sorts. In the one, the incidents and agents were to be, in part
at least, supernatural; and the excellence aimed at was to consist
in the interesting of the affections by the dramatic truth of such
emotions, as would naturally accompany such situations, supposing
them real. And real in this sense they have been to every human
being who, from whatever source of delusion, has at any time be-
lieved himself under supernatural agency. For the second class,
subjects were to be chosen from ordinary life. . . .

In this idea originated the plan of the LYRICAL BALLADS; in which
it was agreed, that my endeavours should be directed to persons
and characters supernatural, or at least romantic; yet so as to
transfer from our inward nature a human interest and a semblance

623 *forlorn:* deprived.

of truth sufficient to procure for these shadows of imagination that willing suspension of disbelief for the moment, which constitutes poetic faith. . . .

With this view I wrote THE ANCIENT MARINER. . . .

(SAMUEL TAYLOR COLERIDGE)

2. Mrs. Barbauld once told me that she admired the *Ancient Mariner* very much, but that there were two faults in it—it was improbable, and had no moral. As for the probability, I owned that that might admit some question; but as to the want of a moral, I told her that in my own judgment the poem had too much; and that the only, or chief fault, if I might say so, was the obtrusion of the moral sentiment so openly on the reader as a principal or cause of action in a work of such pure imagination. . . .

(SAMUEL TAYLOR COLERIDGE)

3. . . . May we interpret this expression of Coleridge's regret as referring to the brief expression of piety at the close of the poem? ["He prayeth best," etc.] . . . Could Coleridge have considered this stanza as *too much* moral? He might well have thought so, if the lines in question were merely a pious recognition of the Mariner's sin in killing an albatross. But certainly Coleridge had a sense of the ridiculous which would have withheld him from writing a phantasy of some six hundred lines on the danger of cruelty to animals. . . .

(NEWTON P. STALLKNECHT)

4. . . . Mrs. Barbauld and Coleridge were speaking of two different things. She was certainly ignoring the stanza at the close of the poem and concentrating her attention upon the relation between the Mariner's crime and his punishment. . . . Is there any moral justification for the retribution which overtook the Mariner and his companions? . . . The case for the defense . . . has been put once and for all by Mr. Lowes in *The Road to Xanadu*. . . .

(ELIZABETH NITCHIE)

5. . . . The train of cause and consequence is more than a consolidating factor of the poem. It happens to be life, as every human being knows it. You do a foolish or an evil deed, and its results come home to you. And they are apt to fall on others too. You repent, and a load is lifted from your soul. But you have not thereby escaped your deed. You attain forgiveness, but cause and effect work on unmoved, and life to the end may be the continued reaping of the ·epented deed's results. (JOHN LIVINGSTON LOWES)

6. . . . To us the shooting of a bird may seem a matter of little moment, but Coleridge makes it significant in two ways. First, he

does not say why the Mariner kills the albatross. We might infer that it is in a mood of annoyance or anger or mere frivolity, but these are only guesses. What matters is precisely the uncertainty of the Mariner's motives; for this illustrates the essential irrationality of crime, which we may explain by motives but which is in many cases due to a simple perversity of the will. Secondly, this crime is against nature, against the sanctified relations of guest and host. . . . What matters is that the Mariner breaks a sacred law of life. In his action we see the essential frivolity of many crimes against humanity and the ordered system of the world, and we must accept the killing of the albatross as symbolical of them. (C. M. BOWRA)

7. The total pattern of experience in *The Ancient Mariner* includes partial recovery from the worst depression. The offence for which the dejection and isolation were punishment was the wanton rejection of a very simple social union. . . . In *The Ancient Mariner* his sufferings have first to reduce him to a dreadful listlessness and apathy. . . .
. . . Only when his individual striving has sunk to a low ebb does the recovery begin.

This naturally gives the impression, characteristic of such states of depression, that the recovery is fortuitous. It comes unpredictably and seemingly from some trivial accident. This part of the experience Coleridge has paralleled in the supernatural machinery of the tale by means of the dicing between Death and Life-in-Death. To the sufferer there seems no good reason why he shouldn't simply die, since he feels that he has thrown up the sponge. Instead, chance has it that he lives on.

The fact of its being Life-in-Death who wins the Mariner shows how incomplete his recovery is going to be. . . . Nevertheless, some degree of recovery from the nadir of dejection does unpredictably occur. It begins with the momentary rekindling of simple pleasure in the things around him, at the very moment when he has touched bottom in apathy. . . . It is the beginning of recovery because what is kindled is a recognition not only of their beauty but also the worth of their existence and, by implication of his own. . . .

In consistent development of the general theme, the Mariner's recovery leads on to reunion with the very simple and humble kinds of social life. He joins the villagers in the formal expression of atonement with each other, and with the source of love, which he sees in their religious worship. But it would be a mistake to think of this as anything like full recovery. For one thing, he never again belongs to a settled community, but has to pass from land to land. For another thing, there is the periodic "abreaction" and confession that he has to resort to. . . . (D. W. HARDING)

8. According to Miss [Maud] Bodkin [in *Archetypal Patterns in Poetry*, 1934], . . . His plot is a modification of the extended archetype which Jung calls The Night Journey Under the Sea, of which the most famous example is the Book of Jonah. Abstractly stated, it is a myth of Rebirth and Regeneration. This pattern is reinforced by other archetypes: wind and storm which symbolize creative force, stagnant calm which symbolizes dull inertia, slime from the depths which represents our disgust and guilt-feelings about matters of our experience that we fear, the color red which is primordially associated with guilt and punishment, the Wandering Jew who is the symbol par excellence of refusal or violation of fellowship. All these symbols carry great emotional charge, and in *The Ancient Mariner* they are exploited with deep artistic awareness of their tendency. The power of *The Ancient Mariner*, Miss Bodkin would say, derives from its use of an archetypal pattern as plot, and its building into the fabric at strategic points of so many more congruent primordial symbols. Her own allegorization is coolly psychological. She always uses the word *guilt*, never the word *sin*. For her the poem symbolizes no rare and spectacular crime, but matter of universal, everyday experience. At its symbolic level it is "about" frustration, depression, our horror of and revolt from elements in our experience that we consider primitive and sinister, our regeneration through acceptance of the disturbing elements. She reads the poem, in short, as a sort of symbol of psychoanalysis.

(FREDERICK A. POTTLE)

9. To one school of thought [the poem] is an elaborate allegory of Coleridge's theories. . . . To another group of critics it is an incoherent transcription of the poet's opium-inspired dreams. The new psychoanalytical critics interpret it as an unconscious revelation of his guilt complexes and sexual suppressions. . . .

They all ignore the third possibility—that it could have been intended as a realistic portrait of human behavior. . . .

Aside from three or four stanzas forming an expository "frame" —obviously made as brief as possible, to the verge of being perfunctory—"The Ancient Mariner" is a dramatic monologue . . . [that]

conforms . . . closely to all the conditions of the dramatic monologue as practiced by Browning. . . .

Browning . . . takes situations that occur from time to time in real life, and traces them to their springs of motive. *Question:* What happens when the wrong sort of man enters a monastic order? *Answer:* He becomes either a pervert ("Soliloquy of the Spanish Cloister") or an opportunist ("Fra Lippo Lippi"). . . . *Question:* How is a man affected by enduring the physical and mental tortures of thirst, exposure, and delirium, in which he alone is spared while his companions perish? *Answer:* He evolves a logical train of events to account for the occurrences, which would otherwise seem to be a cruel whim of fate, and he feels himself set apart forever as a man of apocalyptic vision, with an evangelical mission to save souls with the story of his miraculous conversion. . . .

The mariner's nursery-rhyme quatrain of "moral" is therefore an essential part of the poem; it is the stumbling effort of a man with no rudiment of intellectual training to formulate his sense of religious dedication to universal love and brotherhood. . . .

(LIONEL STEVENSON)

10. . . . But the Mariner's narrative, though it constitutes nearly all of the poem, is actually a part of the dialogue between the Mariner and the Wedding Guest; and the dialogue in turn is part of a narrative structure of encounter. These three structural elements, the Mariner's narrative, the dialogue, the narrative of encounter, nearly co-terminous and fitting like Chinese boxes one inside another, develop significant interrelationships which help to define the meaning of *The Ancient Mariner.* The narrative of encounter thus records a paradox in its action. The message that the universe is one in which the greatest power is the power of love turns the recipient from the marriage feast, the embodiment of love in the everyday world. Finally it makes him a sadder as well as a wiser man. What Coleridge is trying to convey here is the inadequacy of love as conventionalized and institutionalized. The neat moral tag the Mariner gives his tale is by no means its total message. Like the marriage feast it reduces to too pat a form what can only be fully experienced through some such pattern of suffering as the Mariner has lived:

He prayeth best who loveth best—

But the love that emerges from suffering has a quality not otherwise attained. The refinement comes from the fire. The testing to the limits of human endurance transforms the nature of the man. The Wedding Guest as witness of tragedy has thus both a glimpse of the potential meaning life can attain, a glimpse that illuminates and diminishes the trivialities we most of us live in, and at the same time a sense of what must be endured to attain such meaning, of the special circumstances, many of them not in the realm of choice, that form the necessary theatre for the tragic action. The conversion of the Wedding Guest reflects but in no sense repeats the conversion of the Mariner. (CHARLES A. OWEN, JR.)

BIBLIOGRAPHY

Bowra, C. M., *The Romantic Imagination*, 1949, p. 69; Coleridge, S. T., *Biographia Literaria*, 1817, Ch. 14; ———, *Table Talk*, 31 May 1830; Harding, D. W., *The Importance of Scrutiny*, 1948, pp. 177-80; Lowes, J. L., *The Road to Xanadu*, 1927, p. 298; Nitchie, E., *PMLA*, 48 (Sept. 1933), 868-69; Owen, C. A., Jr., *College English*, 23 (Jan. 1962), 261, 266; Pottle, F. A., in *Essays in the Teaching of English*, ed. Gordon, 1960, pp. 266-67; Stallknecht, N. P., *PMLA*, 47 (June 1932), 559-60; Stevenson, L., *Personalist*, 30 (Jan. 1949), 34-43.

Kubla Khan

Or, A Vision in a Dream. A Fragment.

In Xanadu did Kubla Khan
A stately pleasure-dome decree:
Where Alph, the sacred river, ran
Through caverns measureless to man
    Down to a sunless sea.   5
So twice five miles of fertile ground
With walls and towers were girdled round:
And here were gardens bright with sinuous rills
Where blossomed many an incense-bearing tree;

Title: Coleridge appended a note in which he said that after composing two or three hundred lines of proetry in a dream, and writing down fifty-odd lines on waking, he was interrupted by a visit that drove the rest from his memory. 1 *Kubla Khan:* Emperor Kubla, thirteenth-century Mongolian emperor of China. 2 *dome:* palace. 3 *Alph:* imaginary river based on Greek river that ran underground and rose in a fountain.

And here were forests ancient as the hills,   10
Enfolding sunny spots of greenery.

But oh! that deep romantic chasm which slanted   12
Down the green hill athwart a cedarn cover!
A savage place! as holy and enchanted
As e'er beneath a waning moon was haunted
By woman wailing for her demon-lover!   16
And from this chasm, with ceaseless turmoil seething,
As if this earth in fast thick pants were breathing,
A mighty fountain momently was forced:
Amid whose swift half-intermitted burst
Huge fragments vaulted like rebounding hail,   21
Or chaffy grain beneath the thresher's flail:
And 'mid these dancing rocks at once and ever
It flung up momently the sacred river.
Five miles meandering with a mazy motion
Through wood and dale the sacred river ran,   26
Then reached the caverns measureless to man,
And sank in tumult to a lifeless ocean;
And 'mid this tumult Kubla heard from far
Ancestral voices prophesying war!
    The shadow of the dome of pleasure   31
    Floated midway on the waves;
    Where was heard the mingled measure
    From the fountain and the caves.
It was a miracle of rare device,
A sunny pleasure-dome with caves of ice!

    A damsel with a dulcimer   37
    In a vision once I saw:
    It was an Abyssinian maid,
    And on her dulcimer she played,
    Singing of Mount Abora.   41
    Could I revive within me
    Her symphony and song,
    To such a deep delight 'twould win me,
That with music loud and long,
I would build that dome in air,   46
That sunny dome! those caves of ice!
And all who heard should see them there,
And all should cry, Beware! Beware!

13 *athwart a cedarn cover:* across the hill under a cedar grove. 35 *device:* invention. 37 *dulcimer:* stringed instrument played with hammers. 43 *symphony:* harmony.

His flashing eyes, his floating hair!
Weave a circle round him thrice,   51
And close your eyes with holy dread,
For he on honey-dew hath fed,
And drunk the milk of Paradise.

Case

A

1. The poem is purely a lyrical fragment, full of romantic suggestion and haunting beauty.

2. The fragmentary quality, appropriate to a dream, is a result of the colorful images and references that lead nowhere specific, the break in visions between Sections 2 and 3, and the inconclusive incantation of the final lines.

3. The musical beauty of the poem depends partly on the frequent use of alliteration and assonance in each section.

B

1. The poem is a structurally unified drama of profound conflict.

2. In the first two sections, the poet creates a relationship between natural and artificial beauty above ground and supernatural mystery below, resolved in Section 3 by the evocation of religious awe at this creation.

3. The bright beauty of the pleasure-park and the cold dark of the caverns beneath can symbolize the elemental forces of life and death, united by the "sacred river" that flows through both.

BIBLIOGRAPHY

Allen, N. B., *Modern Language Notes*, **57** (Feb. 1942), 108-13; Bewley, E. M., *Scrutiny*, **8** (Mar. 1940), 411-14; Bodkin, M., *Archetypal Patterns in Poetry*, 1934, pp. 90-115; Brooks, C., J. T. Purser, and R. P. Warren, *An Approach to Literature*, 1936, 1952, pp. 376-78; Fogle, R. H., *College English*, **13** (Oct. 1951), 13-18; House, H., *Coleridge*, 1953, pp. 114-22; Lowes, J. L., *The Road to Xanadu*, 1927, pp. 343, 355, 406-10; Mercer, D. F., *Journal of Aesthetics and Art Criticism*, **12** (Sept. 1953), 44-66; Meyerstein, E. H. W., *Times Literary Supplement*, **30** (Oct. 1937), 803; Schneider, E., *Coleridge, Opium, and Kubla Khan*, 1954, pp. 238-88; ——, *PMLA*, **60** (Sept. 1945), 784-801; Woodring, C. R., *Essays in Criticism*, **9** (Oct. 1959), 361-68.

On Donne's Poetry

With Donne, whose muse on dromedary trots,
Wreathe iron pokers into true-love knots;
Rhyme's sturdy cripple, fancy's maze and clue,
Wit's forge and fire-blast, meaning's press and screw.

Ode to Evening

If aught of oaten stop or pastoral song
May hope, chaste Eve, to soothe thy modest ear,
   Like thy own solemn springs,
   Thy springs, and dying gales,
O nymph reserv'd, while now the bright hair'd sun   5
Sits in yon western tent, whose cloudy skirts,
   With brede ethereal wove,
   O'erhang his wavy bed:
Now air is hush'd, save where the weak-ey'd bat,
With short shrill shrieks flits by on leathern wing,   10
   Or where the beetle winds
   His small but sullen horn,
As oft he rises 'midst the twilight path,
Against the pilgrim borne in heedless hum;
   Now teach me, maid compos'd,   15
   To breathe some soften'd strain,
Whose numbers, stealing through thy dark'ning vale,
May not unseemly with its stillness suit,
   As, musing slow, I hail
   Thy genial lov'd return!   20
For when thy folding star arising shews
His paly circlet, at his warning lamp
   The fragrant Hours, and elves
   Who slept in flow'rs the day,
And many a nymph who wreaths her brows with sedge,   25
And sheds the fresh'ning dew, and lovelier still,
   The pensive Pleasures sweet
   Prepare thy shadowy car.

1: if anything played on a rustic flute, or any shepherd's song.   7 *brede:* embroidery.   17 *numbers:* poetic meters.   20 *genial:* inspiring.   21 *folding star:* star appearing as shepherds drive sheep to fold.   25 *sedge:* grass-like plant.

Then lead, calm vot'ress, where some sheety lake
Cheers the lone heath, or some time hallow'd pile, 30
    Or up-land fallows grey
    Reflect its last cool gleam.
But when chill blust'ring winds or driving rain
Forbid my willing feet, be mine the hut,
    That from the mountain's side 35
    Views wilds, and swelling floods,
And hamlets brown, and dim-discover'd spires,
And hears their simple bell, and marks o'er all
    Thy dewy fingers draw
    The gradual dusky veil. 40
While Spring shall pour his show'rs, as oft he wont,
And bathe thy breathing tresses, meekest Eve;
    While Summer loves to sport
    Beneath thy ling'ring light:
While sallow Autumn fills thy lap with leaves, 45
Or Winter, yelling thro' the troublous air,
    Affrights thy shrinking train,
    And rudely rends thy robes.
So long, sure-found beneath the sylvan shed,
Shall Fancy, Friendship, Science, rose-lipp'd Health 50
    Thy gentlest influence own,
    And hymn thy fav'rite name!

anyone lived in a pretty how town

anyone lived in a pretty how town
(with up so floating many bells down)
spring summer autumn winter
he sang his didn't he danced his did.

Women and men (both little and small) 5
cared for anyone not at all
they sowed their isn't they reaped their same
sun moon stars rain

children guessed (but only a few 9
and down they forgot as up they grew

29 *vot'ress:* religious devotee. 29 *sheety:* broad. 30 *pile:* building. 31 *fallows:* unploughed field. 41 *wont:* is accustomed to do.

autumn winter spring summer)
that noone loved him more by more

when by now and tree by leaf   13
she laughed his joy she cried his grief
bird by snow and stir by still
anyone's any was all to her

someone's married their everyones   17
laughed their cryings and did their dance
(sleep wake hope and then) they
said their nevers they slept their dream

stars rain sun moon   21
(and only the snow can begin to explain
how children are apt to forget to remember
with up so floating many bells down)

one day anyone died i guess   25
(and noone stooped to kiss his face)
busy folk buried them side by side
little by little and was by was

all by all and deep by deep   29
and more by more they dream their sleep
noone and anyone earth by april
wish by spirit and if by yes.

Women and men (both dong and ding)   33
summer autumn winter spring
reaped their sowing and went their came
sun moon stars rain

Critique

1. Like many other poems by Cummings, "Anyone Lived in a
Pretty How Town" demands of the reader a radical reorientation
toward the uses of language. . . . In addition to their symbolic values,
his words function to create patterns of sound consonant with his
themes; they have further a special syntactical value. . . .

Examples of all these uses can be found in the first two lines
of the poem. The lightly accented words between the strongly

stressed ones have a carillon-like quality which effectively sets off the tolling measure of the refrain, "spring summer autumn winter." The imagery in the second line not only suggests the airy sound of the bells and their movement back and forth, but indicates how leisurely and harmonious is the passage of time in this particular town. An excellent example of syntax used to accent an otherwise commonplace statement is found in the word "how" in line one. It cannot be read as an adverb modifying "pretty" or any other single word. . . .

Even more important in the syntactical structure is the way in which "by" comes to stand for a variety of links between pairs of terms, the nature of the link being dictated in each case by what the reader recognizes as the significant relationship between the terms. . . .

It is by such handling of the language that the poem achieves its distinction, since the theme is simple and familiar. In substance it is an account of the lives of two people, "anyone" and "noone," and in theme it contrasts the response to life made by these two with the response made by the mass of people. The singularity of "anyone" and "noone" lies in their identification with a cycle of natural events rather than with routine and sterile human activities, and in their harmony with one another. . . .

(HERBERT C. BARROWS, JR. and WILLIAM R. STEINHOFF)

2. In "anyone lived in a pretty how town," cummings makes grammar a poetic device. He uses unexpected syntactic patterns as if they were metaphors to give special dimensions to the meaning of his words. He makes one sentence pattern tell the story of two contrasting ways of life. The contrast he develops by matched lexical opposites. The actor-noun + action-verb + object-noun pattern is a common one; every English speaker knows that this sequence means that the first noun acts somehow upon the second noun. cummings, however, gets a special counterpoint effect—between the lexical and syntactic meaning—by fitting into the pattern words not usually ordered this way in traditional English. For example, he adds special objects to "sing" and "dance," verbs which customarily take cognate objects, if any at all. His coined objects take on some of the meaning of cognates. When anyone "sang his didn't" and "danced his did," and someones "sowed their isn't," the meaning implied is that life for anyone flows strong and joyous— like singing a song or dancing a dance—but for someones the harvest

is doomed, the seed being sterile. cummings also replaces old words with new in two idioms having a verb-object pattern. Someones "said their nevers" when they might better have said their prayers. The common expression, "did their job" or "did their work" echoes in "did their dance." The antithesis set up in the poem between "danced his did" (anyone) and "did their dance" (someones) implies how extrinsic to the doers is the work of the someones and how much a part of his inner being and commitment is the work of anyone. cummings also forces some verbs and their objects into this pattern by omitting the particle which usually follows the verb. The impact of the action of the verb upon the object is stronger without the particle. "Laughed their cryings" is more forceful than "laughed about their cryings"; "cried his grief" stronger than "cried over his griefs." Verb follows verb in many of these sequences, with the second verb being given noun status by a preceding *his* or *their* ("his did," "their came"). A plural *s* suffix also accentuates the noun effect of some words ("nevers," "cryings"). . . . (PRISCILLA TYLER)

BIBLIOGRAPHY

Barrows, Jr., H. C. and W. R. Steinhoff, *Explicator*, 9 (Oct. 1950), 1; Tyler, P., written for this edition.

my father moved through dooms of love

my father moved through dooms of love
through sames of am through haves of give,
singing each morning out of each night
my father moved through depths of height

this motionless forgetful where   5
turned at his glance to shining here;
that if (so timid air is firm)
under his eyes would stir and squirm

newly as from unburied which   9
floats the first who, his april touch
drove sleeping selves to swarm their fates
woke dreamers to their ghostly roots

and should some why completely weep   13
my father's fingers brought her sleep:
vainly no smallest voice might cry
for he could feel the mountains grow.

Lifting the valleys of the sea   17
my father moved through griefs of joy;
praising a forehead called the moon
singing desire into begin

joy was his song and joy so pure   21
a heart of star by him could steer
and pure so now and now so yes
the wrists of twilight would rejoice

keen as midsummer's keen beyond   25
conceiving mind of sun will stand,
so strictly (over utmost him
so hugely) stood my father's dream

his flesh was flesh his blood was blood: 29
no hungry man but wished him food;
no cripple wouldn't creep one mile
uphill to only see him smile.

Scorning the pomp of must and shall   33
my father moved through dooms of feel;
his anger was as right as rain
his pity was as green as grain

septembering arms of year extend   37
less humbly wealth to foe and friend
than he to foolish and to wise
offered immeasurable is

proudly and (by octobering flame   41
beckoned) as earth will downward climb,
so naked for immortal work
his shoulders marched against the dark

his sorrow was as true as bread: 45
no liar looked him in the head;
if every friend became his foe
he'd laugh and build a world with snow.

My father moved through theys of we,   49
singing each new leaf out of each tree

(and every child was sure that spring
danced when she heard my father sing)

then let men kill which cannot share,   53
let blood and flesh be mud and mire,
scheming imagine,passion willed
freedom a drug that's bought and sold

giving to steal and cruel kind,   57
a heart to fear, to doubt a mind,
to differ a disease of same,
conform the pinnacle of am

though dull were all we taste as bright,   61
bitter all utterly things sweet,
maggoty minus and dumb death
all we inherit,all bequeath

and nothing quite so least as truth   65
—i say though hate were why men breathe—
because my father lived his soul
love is the whole and more than all

Care-Charmer Sleep, Son of the Sable Night

Care-charmer sleep, son of the sable night,
Brother to death, in silent darkness born,
Relieve my languish and restore the light;
With dark forgetting of my cares, return.
And let the day be time enough to mourn   5
The shipwreck of my ill-adventured youth;
Let waking eyes suffice to wail their scorn
Without the torment of the night's untruth.
Cease, dreams, th'imagery of our day-desires, 9
To model forth the passions of the morrow;
Never let rising sun approve you liars,
To add more grief to aggravate my sorrow.
Still let me sleep, embracing clouds in vain,
And never wake to feel the day's disdain.   14

11 *approve:* prove.

The Listeners

"Is there anybody there?" said the Traveller,
　　Knocking on the moonlit door;
And his horse in the silence champed the grasses
　　Of the forest's ferny floor:
And a bird flew up out of the turret,   5
　　Above the Traveller's head:
And he smote upon the door again a second time;
　　"Is there anybody there?" he said.
But no one descended to the Traveller;
　　No head from the leaf-fringed sill   10
Leaned over and looked into his gray eyes,
　　Where he stood perplexed and still.
But only a host of phantom listeners
　　That dwelt in the lone house then
Stood listening in the quiet of the moonlight   15
　　To that voice from the world of men:
Stood thronging the faint moonbeams on the dark stair
　　That goes down to the empty hall,
Harkening in an air stirred and shaken
　　By the lonely Traveller's call.   20
And he felt in his heart their strangeness,
　　Their stillness answering his cry,
While his horse moved, cropping the dark turf,
　　'Neath the starred and leafy sky;
For he suddenly smote on the door, even   25
　　Louder, and lifted his head:—
"Tell them I came, and no one answered,
　　That I kept my word," he said.
Never the least stir made the listeners,
　　Though every word he spake   30
Fell echoing through the shadowiness of the still house
　　From the one man left awake:
Aye, they heard his foot upon the stirrup,
　　And the sound of iron on stone,
And how the silence surged softly backward,   35
　　When the plunging hoofs were gone.

Critique

1. The conventional interpretation seems to indicate a living traveller knocking at the door of a house of death. Is it possible that the traveller is a revenant [ghost; returner from death] knocking vainly (since unheard) at the door of a living household? Lines 25-27 seem to support this latter interpretation. (J. P. KIRBY)

2. ... It should be remembered—I have it on the poet's authority —that the Traveller is himself the ghost. (F. L. LUCAS)

3. I have always taken, by no special warrant I know of, de la Mare's "Traveller" to be God, Christ, the Holy Spirit, or some supernatural messenger sent by God to communicate with the heart of man. But man, busy and distracted by the excitement of the Inn of Life, either does not hear or refuses to heed the evidence which tells him God wishes to speak to him. Only too late does he learn, through poets or other inspired persons (i.e. "the one man left awake") that he has had a chance to listen to the voice of God and that he has let the chance escape. ... (J. M. PURCELL)

4. ... The theme is not the voice of God speaking to man. It is ... a man keeping his pledged word in the face of all powers of darkness. (DeLANCEY FERGUSON)

5. It has been just recently reported to me—at about fourth hand —that de la Mare himself said that the occasion of "The Listeners" was a reunion that his class was to hold at some school he had attended. On the day set, only de la Mare appeared. The empty halls and corridors moved him to compose this poem. It has, therefore, none of the mysticism suggested by Mr. Ferguson and myself, much, I feel, to the poem's loss. ... (J. M. PURCELL)

6. The difficulty in "The Listeners" lies not in finding allegorical meanings for the figures, but in finding too many such meanings. One is tempted to suggest that since the Traveller knocks three times, and fruitlessly, he is really Casey at the Bat.

Most suggestions—including the comments attributed to de la Mare himself—have no basis in the poem. The Traveller is definitely a living human being, for he is "from the world of men" (16), he is "the one man left awake" (32), and even his horse is so alive and gross as to be seen—and heard—eating twice (3, 23). The listeners are specifically "phantom" (13).

What the poem does is to create a mysterious atmosphere by juxtaposing the flesh-and-blood Traveller with a nothingness that assumes a preternatural power by the vividness of its personification.

As for allegorical meanings, they are not in the poem. Since the Traveller does no traveling except away from the scene and since it is impossible to determine why he has kept his word (28), or what the word is, he is poor material for symbolism. And since the listeners do absolutely nothing in the poem but listen, their possible signification is severely limited. But there is a clue to their identity in the only repeated abstraction in the poem: the chief characteristic of the situation is *silence* (3, 12, 15, 22, 31, 35), and silence is the only thing left when the Traveller has gone (35-36). The listeners are not an allegorical symbol, but merely the poetic personification of the silence the non-symbolic Traveller finds and leaves at the house. (EDITORS)

BIBLIOGRAPHY

Kirby, J. P., *Explicator*, 1 (June 1943), Q40; Lucas, F. L., *The Decline and Fall of the Romantic Ideal*, 1936, 22n., quoted in *Explicator*, 3 (Nov. 1944), Announcements; Purcell, J. M., *Explicator*, 3 (Mar. 1945), 42; Ferguson, D., *Explicator*, 4 (Nov. 1945), 15; Purcell, J. M., *Explicator*, 4 (Feb. 1946), 31; Editors, expanded in *Explicator*, 12 (Feb. 1954), 26.

Guitar Lament for a Mountain Boy

They cut down the old pine tree in Tunisia
And the roar of her boughs makes eddies in the air
Though she's fallen, though she's gone, though she's gone.

The red Kentucky clay as Pappy used to say—   4
Soil with too much water, too much sun—
Has shuffled off the planet, and the mountain birds' song
Is stilled at the crack of a gun.

The well of lonely forest that drank the dewy night   8
Stands formless and shadowy and sad,
The bream never rises now at noon in the brook
One bullet in one second and that was all it took

1 *They cut down the old pine tree:* popular hill-billy ballad.   1 *Tunisia:* scene of fighting in World War II.   10 *bream:* sunfish.

For a world to wash away, purple hills far away
Drowned in the dust of dusty El Habad

The bay hound's call is stifled in her throat,   14
The senses she quickened once are stone,
No more the long mellow light will filter through these eyes,
The sunsets, the seasons are done.

They cut down the old pine trees in Tunisia   18
But the roar of her boughs makes eddies in the air
Though she's fallen, though she's gone, though she's gone.

These Are the Days When Birds Come Back (130)

These are the days when Birds come back—
A very few—a Bird or two—
To take a backward look.

These are the days when skies resume   4
The old—old sophistries of June—
A blue and gold mistake.

Oh fraud that cannot cheat the Bee—   7
Almost thy plausibility
Induces my belief.

Till ranks of seeds their witness bear—   10
And softly thro' the altered air
Hurries a timid leaf.

Oh Sacrament of summer days,   13
Oh Last Communion in the Haze—
Permit a child to join.

Thy sacred emblems to partake—   16
Thy consecrated bread to take
And thine immortal wine!

Safe in Their Alabaster Chambers (216)

Safe in their Alabaster Chambers—
Untouched by Morning
And untouched by Noon—

Sleep the meek members of the Resurrection—
Rafter of satin,
And Roof of stone.

Light laughs the breeze   7
In her Castle above them—
Babbles the Bee in a stolid Ear,
Pipe the Sweet Birds in ignorant cadence—
Ah, what sagacity perished here!

[version of 1859]

Safe in their Alabaster Chambers—
Untouched by Morning—
And untouched by Noon—
Lie the meek members of the Resurrection—
Rafter of Satin—and Roof of Stone!

Grand go the Years—in the Crescent—above them—   6
Worlds scoop their Arcs—
And Firmaments—row—
Diadems—drop—and Doges—surrender—
Soundless as dots—on a Disc of Snow—

[version of 1861]

The Soul Selects Her Own Society (303)

The Soul selects her own Society—
Then—shuts the Door—
To her divine Majority—
Present no more—

Unmoved—she notes the Chariots—pausing—   5
At her low Gate—
Unmoved—an Emperor be kneeling
Upon her Mat—

I've known her—from an ample nation—   9
Choose One—
Then—close the Valves of her attention—
Like Stone—

3 *Majority:* greatness.   11 *Valves:* folding doors, hinged shells, or closures in circulatory system.

I Like to See It Lap the Miles (585)

I like to see it lap the Miles—
And lick the Valleys up—
And stop to feed itself at Tanks—
And then—prodigious step

Around a Pile of Mountains— 5
And supercilious peer
In Shanties—by the sides of Roads—
And then a Quarry pare

To fit it's sides 9
And crawl between
Complaining all the while
In horrid—hooting stanza—
Then chase itself down Hill—

And neigh like Boanerges— 14
Then—prompter than a Star
Stop—docile and omnipotent
At it's own stable door—

The Brain Is Wider Than the Sky (632)

The Brain—is wider than the Sky—
For—put them side by side—
The one the other will contain
With ease—and You—beside—

The Brain is deeper than the sea— 5
For—hold them—Blue to Blue—
The one the other will absorb—
As Sponges—Buckets—do—

The Brain is just the weight of God— 9
For—Heft them—Pound for Pound—
And they will differ—if they do—
As Syllable from Sound—

14 *Boanerges:* "The sons of thunder" (Mark 3:17).

Because I Could Not Stop for Death (712)

Because I could not stop for Death—
He kindly stopped for me—
The Carriage held but just Ourselves—
And Immortality.

We slowly drove—He knew no haste   5
And I had put away
My labor and my leisure too,
For His Civility—

We passed the School, where Children strove   9
At Recess—in the Ring—
We passed the Fields of Gazing Grain—
We passed the Setting Sun—

Or rather—He passed Us—   13
The Dews drew quivering and chill—
For only Gossamer, my Gown—
My Tippet—only Tulle—

We paused before a House that seemed   17
A Swelling of the Ground—
The Roof was scarcely visible—
The Cornice—in the Ground—

Since then—'tis Centuries—and yet   21
Feels shorter than the Day
I first surmised the Horses Heads
Were toward Eternity—

Critique [1]

1. . . . If the word great means anything in poetry, this poem is
one of the greatest in the English language; it is flawless to the last
detail. . . . Every image is precise and, moreover, not merely beautiful, but inextricably fused with the central idea. . . . The content
of death in the poem eludes forever any explicit definition. He is

15 *Gossamer:* gauze.   16 *Tippet:* cape.   16 *Tulle:* light silk.

---

[1] The poem discussed here was an edited version in which "At wrestling" was
substituted for "At Recess" and from which Stanza 4 was omitted.

a gentleman taking a lady out for a drive. But note the restraint that keeps the poet from carrying this so far that it is ludicrous and incredible; and note the subtly interfused erotic motive, which the idea of death has prensented to every romantic poet, love being a symbol interchangeable with death. The terror of death is objectified through this figure of the genteel driver, who is made ironically to serve the end of Immortality. This is the heart of the poem: she has presented a typical Christian theme in all its final irresolution, without making any final statement about it. There is no solution to the problem. . . . The idea of immortality is confronted with the fact of physical disintegration. We are not told what to think; we are told to look at the situation. . . .   (ALLEN TATE)

2. . . . In the fourth line we find the familiar device of using a major abstraction in a somewhat loose and indefinable manner; in the last stanza there is the semi-playful pretence of familiarity with the posthumous experience of eternity, so that the poem ends unconvincingly though gracefully . . . ; for the rest the poem is a remarkably beautiful poem on the subject of the daily realization of the imminence of death—it is a poem of departure from life, an intensely conscious leave-taking. In so far as it concentrates on the life that is being left behind, it is wholly successful; in so far as it attempts to experience the death to come, it is fraudulent, however exquisitely. . . . Allen Tate, who appears to be unconcerned with this fraudulent element, praises the poem in the highest terms; he appears almost to praise it for its defects. . . .   (YVOR WINTERS)

3. . . . The only pressing technical objection to this poem is the remark that "Immortality" in the first stanza is a meretricious and unnecessary personification and that the common sense of the situation demands that Immortality ought to be the destination of the coach and not one of the passengers. The personification of death, however, is unassailable. In the literal meaning of the poem, he is apparently a successful citizen who has amorous but genteel intentions. He is also God. . . .

The word "labor" recalls Emily Dickinson's idea that life is to be understood as the slow labor of dying; now this labor is properly put away. So is the leisure, since a far more desirable leisure will be hers in "eternity." The third stanza is a symbolic recapitulation of life: the children playing, wrestling (more "labor") through the cycle of their existence, "in a ring"; the gazing grain signifies ripeness and the entranced and visionary gaze that first beholds the approach of death of which the setting sun is the felicitous symbol.

The last two stanzas are hardly surpassed in the whole range of lyric poetry. The visual images here are handled with perfect economy. All the poem needs is one or two concrete images—roof, cornice—to awake in our minds the appalling identification of house with grave. . . . There are progressively fewer visible objects in the last three stanzas, since the seen world must be made gradually to sink into the nervously sensed world. . . . (RICHARD CHASE)

4. The trouble with this remark [Chase's first sentence] is that it does not present the common sense of the situation. Emily Dickinson was taught Christian doctrine—not simply Christian morality but Christian theology—and she knew that the coach cannot head toward immortality, nor can one of the passengers. Dickinson here compresses two related but differing concepts: (1) at death the soul journeys to heaven (eternity), and thus the image of the carriage and driver is appropriate, and (2) the soul is immortal, and our immortality, therefore, "rides" always with us as a copassenger; it is with us because the soul is our immortal part and so may be thought of as journeying with us. The poet's language is compact and oblique, but there is no false personification in it. Since the soul is one's true person (essence, not mask), no personification is needed, except possibly what may be involved in the separable concept of the soul itself. Both immortality and death, however, need personification and are given it. The horses' heads are toward eternity, but not toward immortality. (THEODORE HOEPFNER)

BIBLIOGRAPHY

Chase, R., *Emily Dickinson*, 1951, pp. 249-51; Hoepfner, T., *American Literature*, **29** (Mar. 1957), 96; Tate, A., *Reactionary Essays on Poetry and Ideas*, 1936, pp. 14-15; Winters, Y., *In Defense of Reason*, 1947, p. 289.

A Route of Evanescence (1463)

A Route of Evanescence
With a revolving Wheel—
A Resonance of Emerald—

A Rush of Cochineal—
And every Blossom on the Bush   5
Adjusts it's tumbled Head—
The mail from Tunis, probably,
An easy Morning's Ride—

Critique

1. . . . Here is the whole *sensation* of hummingbird: first, a dazzle
of sudden sense impressions, movement, motion of wings, color, and
whir (in the reiterated *r's*), all at once; then (the bird's departure
taken for granted) the emptiness emphasized by the clear picture
of nodding blossoms; and finally the startled mind of the (assumed)
spectator regaining its poise with a whimsical comment. Nothing
could be spared and no more is needed. . . .   (GEORGE F. WHICHER)
2. In the final two lines the imagery is varied through the metaphors of "mail," which compel a second interpretation of the earlier
part. Beyond the image of the humming-bird is implicit that of
a speeding railway train, the mail and express, and also that of
the more common kind of mail—a letter. It is this which provides
the perhaps wistful irony of the concluding line. A train travels
upon a "route," it is borne along by many ["]a revolving wheel,"
its sound is a "resonance" and a "rush," and on it people "ride."
These words thus have a double value. . . . But the bird as pas-
senger train is also an ironic impossibility; no train crosses the sea
from Tunis, and no "easy morning's ride" will take us there. The
humming-bird is an envoy of curious lands ("Tunis"), of tropic
color ("cochineal"), of oriental opulence ("emerald"). These particular images transform the bird into remoteness invading the
familiar garden. . . .   (GROVER SMITH)
3. The first line refers to the seeming course of the sun around
the earth, Miss Dickinson's "revolving wheel." The next two lines
build color images, the first referring to the sun-bestowed verdure
of the earth, the second to the magnificence of the sunset as day
rushes out. Next, Miss Dickinson describes the obeisance of the
vegetable world to King Sol, a phenomenon modern scientists un-

4 *Cochineal:* red dye.

aesthetically call "phototropism." Finally, the authoress reinforces the theme of ephemerality introduced in the initial line of the poem by emphasizing the speed of Phaeton's chariot across the sky.

(KENNETH E. FISH, JR.)

[Although Emily Dickinson identified the subject of the poem as a hummingbird (see *The Poems of Emily Dickinson*, ed. Thomas H. Johnson, 1955, v. 3, 1011-13), there is no such assertion in the poem, as this student explication demonstrates.]

BIBLIOGRAPHY

Fish, K. E., Jr., written for this edition, based on class discussion, Trinity College, Spring 1962; Smith, G., *Explicator*, 7 (May 1949), 54; Whicher, G. F., *This Was a Poet: A Critical Biography of Emily Dickinson*, 1938, p. 262.

Apparently with No Surprise (1624)

Apparently with no surprise
To any happy Flower
The Frost beheads it at it's play—
In accidental power—
The blonde Assassin passes on—   5
The Sun proceeds unmoved
To measure off another Day
For an Approving God.

Jabberwocky

'Twas brillig, and the slithy toves
    Did gyre and gimble in the wabe:
All mimsy were the borogoves,
    And the mome raths outgrabe.

Jabberwocky: For meanings of these nonsense words, see Humpty-Dumpty's explanation in Lewis Carroll, *Through the Looking-Glass*, Ch. 6; Martin Gardner, ed., *The Annotated Alice*, 1960, pp. 191-97, 271-72.

"Beware the Jabberwock, my son!   5
    The jaws that bite, the claws that catch!
Beware the Jubjub bird, and shun
    The frumious Bandersnatch!"

He took his vorpal sword in hand;   9
    Long time the manxome foe he sought—
So rested he by the Tumtum tree,
    And stood awhile in thought.

And, as in uffish thought he stood,   13
    The Jabberwock, with eyes of flame,
Come whiffling through the tulgey wood,
    And burbled as it came!

One, two! One, two! And through and through   17
    The vorpal blade went snicker-snack!
He left it dead, and with its head
    He went galumphing back.

"And hast thou slain the Jabberwock?   21
    Come to my arms, my beamish boy!
O frabjous day! Callooh! Callay!
    He chortled in his joy.

'Twas brillig, and the slithy toves   25
    Did gyre and gimble in the wabe:
All mimsy were the borogoves,
    And the mome raths outgrabe.

Song

Go and catch a falling star,
    Get with child a mandrake root,
Tell me where all past years are,
    Or who cleft the devil's foot;
Teach me to hear mermaids singing,   5
Or to keep off envy's stinging,
        And find
        What wind
Serves to advance an honest mind.

2 *mandrake:* Its forked root resembles the human body.

If thou be'st born to strange sights,   10
   Things invisible to see,
Ride ten thousand days and nights
   Till Age snow white hairs on thee;
Thou, when thou return'st, wilt tell me   14
All strange wonders that befell thee,
     And swear
     No where
Lives a woman true and fair.

If thou find'st one, let me know;   19
   Such a pilgrimage were sweet.
Yet do not; I would not go,
   Though at next door we might meet.
Though she were true when you met her,   23
And last till you write your letter,
     Yet she
     Will be
False, ere I come, to two or three.

The Canonization

For God's sake hold your tongue and let me love,
   Or chide my palsy or my gout,
   My five gray hairs or ruined fortune flout;
With wealth your state, your mind with arts improve;
   Take you a course, get you a place,   5
   Observe his honor, or his grace;
Or the king's real or his stamped face
   Contemplate; what you will, approve—
   So you will let me love.

Alas, alas, who's injured by my love?   10
   What merchant's ships have my sighs drowned?
   Who says my tears have overflowed his ground?
When did my colds a forward spring remove?
   When did the heats which my veins fill   14
   Add one more to the plaguey bill?
Soldiers find wars, and lawyers find out still

5 *course:* of action.   7 *stamped:* on coins.   13 *forward:* early.   15 *plaguey bill:*
list of deaths from plague.

Litigious men which quarrels move,
Though she and I do love.

Call us what you will, we are made such by love;   19
   Call her one, me another fly,
   We're tapers too, and at our own cost die;
And we in us find the eagle and the dove.
   The phoenix riddle hath more wit   23
   By us: we two being one, are it.
So to one neutral thing both sexes fit,
   We die and rise the same, and prove
   Mysterious by this love.

We can die by it, if not live by love,   28
   And if unfit for tomb or hearse
   Our legend be, it will be fit for verse;
And if no piece of chronicle we prove,
   We'll build in sonnets pretty rooms;   32
   As well a well-wrought urn becomes
The greatest ashes, as half-acre tombs;
   And by these hymns all shall approve
   Us canonized for love,

And thus invoke us: "You, whom reverend love   37
   Made one another's hermitage;
   You, to whom love was peace, that now is rage;
Who did the whole world's soul contract, and drove
   Into the glasses of your eyes   41
   (So made such mirrors, and such spies,
That they did all to you epitomize)
   Countries, towns, courts: beg from above
   A pattern of your love."   45

Critique

1. "The Canonization" stands alone among the *Songs and Sonets* because the person addressed in it is a male friend, but love is still

17 *Litigious:* fond of bringing lawsuits.   22 *eagle and the dove:* traditional symbols of power and peace.   21 *die:* pun on a colloquial use of the verb, current in Donne's time, to refer to sexual intercourse.   23 *wit:* meaning.   30 *legend:* story of saint's life.   31 *chronicle:* history.   33 *becomes:* befits.   39 *now:* here on earth, for us.   41 *glasses:* eyeballs.   43 *epitomize:* concentrate.

the theme. The character who is speaking rejects the worldly-wise advice offered to him and vindicates his own abandonment to passion. . . .

The famous opening line . . . shows us Donne at his best in the brusque familiar style. In the rest of the stanza he makes fun of himself . . . and then of his friend. . . . The satirical note reappears in the second stanza. . . . The poet here parodies the hyperbolical metaphors of the Petrarchists. . . .

After this ironical outburst the lover pauses awhile to catch his breath, and the friend tries to get a word in. He upbraids the passionate couple with lack of sense: they are night-moths dazzled by a light. This speech, which takes place, if we may coin the word, in the inter-stanza, turns the lover's ardour from satire to self-glorification. . . . With the Phenix Donne openly reverts to the type of traditional hyperbole he has just ridiculed, but he wears the hackneyed symbol with a difference. . . .

Here the friend once more gets a chance and must be understood prosaically to object that . . . he is straying very far from the truth: their love may well destroy the lovers, but not call them back to this nether world. . . . The fourth stanza admits the hard fact, but answers defiantly: "Wee can dye by it, if not live by love." It then proceeds to improve upon a hint given in the last line of the third stanza: the love of the pair is a mystery; therefore they will have a "legend," . . . in "hymns." This last word, with its religious import, leads up naturally to the announcement that the poet and his mistress will be *"Canoniz'd* for love," on which the fourth stanza ends. The friend this time probably opens his mouth to remonstrate against pride amounting to blasphemy, . . . but no word of his can be even overheard, for the fourth stanza runs into the fifth, without a period. The new-made saints are already "invoked" by lovers who come after them. . . . The reader may well forget the friend who was the occasion of the piece. Yet without him, and unless we fill in his interruptions, we do not thoroughly realize why the lover-poet gradually warms himself up and passes from jesting impatience to an almost ecstatic vision.   (Pierre Legouis)

2. . . . The basic metaphor which underlies the poem (and which is reflected in the title) involves a sort of paradox. For the poet daringly treats profane love as if it were divine love. The canonization is not that of a pair of holy anchorites who have renounced

the world and the flesh. The hermitage of each is the other's body; but they do renounce the world, and so their title to sainthood is cunningly argued. The poem then is a parody of Christian sainthood; but it is an intensely serious parody of a sort that modern man, habituated as he is to an easy yes or no, can hardly understand. He refuses to accept the paradox as a serious rhetorical device; and since he is able to accept it only as a cheap trick, he is forced into this dilemma. Either: Donne does not take love seriously; here he is merely sharpening his wit as a sort of mechanical exercise. Or: Donne does not take sainthood seriously; here he is merely indulging in a cynical and bawdy parody.

Neither account is true; a reading of the poem will show that Donne takes both love and religion seriously; it will show, further, that the paradox is here his inevitable instrument. . . .

And how necessary are the paradoxes? Donne might have said directly, "Love in a cottage is enough." "The Canonization" contains this admirable thesis, but it contains a great deal more. . . .

I submit that the only way by which the poet could say what "The Canonization" says is by paradox. More direct methods may be tempting, but all of them enfeeble and distort what is to be said. . . . Deprived of the character of paradox with its twin concomitants of irony and wonder, the matter of Donne's poem unravels into "facts," biological, sociological, and economic. . . .

(CLEANTH BROOKS)

BIBLIOGRAPHY

Brooks, C., *The Well Wrought Urn*, 1947, pp. 10, 17-18; Legouis, P., *Donne the Craftsman*, 1928, pp. 55-61.

A Valediction: Forbidding Mourning

Love

Leaving mistress or wife

As virtuous men pass mildly away,
    And whisper to their souls to go,
Whilst some of their sad friends do say,
    The breath goes now, and some say, no:

Valediction: farewell.

Trying to tell him not to be sad about his parting

apposition —

So let us melt, and make no noise,   5
    No tear-floods, nor sigh-tempests move,
'Twere profanation of our joys
    To tell the laity our love.

Moving of the earth brings harms and fears,   9
    Men reckon what it did and meant,
But trepidation of the spheres,
    Though greater far, is innocent.

Dull sublunary lovers' love   13
    (Whose soul is sense) cannot admit
Absence, because it doth remove
    Those things which elemented it.

But we by a love so much refined   17
    That our selves know not what it is,
Inter-assurèd of the mind,
    Care less, eyes, lips, and hands to miss.

Our two souls, therefore, which are one,   21
    Though I must go, endure not yet
A breach, but an expansion,
    Like gold to airy thinness beat. — *gold leaf*

Explicit statement

If they be two, they are two so   25
    As stiff twin compasses are two,
Thy soul, the fixed foot, makes no show
    To move, but doth if the other do.

And though it in the center sit,   29
    Yet when the other far doth roam,
It leans and hearkens after it,
    And grows erect as that comes home.

parallel structure

Such wilt thou be to me, who must,   33
    Like the other foot, obliquely run;
Thy firmness makes my circle just,
    And makes me end where I begun.

---

8 *laity:* laymen, outsiders.   9 *Moving of the earth:* earthquakes.   11 *trepidation of the spheres:* vibration of globes surrounding the earth in Ptolemaic astronomy.   13 *sublunary:* under the moon, earthly.   14 *sense:* mere physical sensation.   16 *elemented it:* were its elements.

Death Be Not Proud, Though Some Have Called Thee

(Holy Sonnets, 6)

Death be not proud, though some have called thee
Mighty and dreadful, for, thou art not so,
For those whom thou think'st thou dost overthrow,
Die not, poor Death, nor yet canst thou kill me;
From rest and sleep, which but thy pictures be,   5
Much pleasure, then from thee, much more must flow,
And soonest our best men with thee do go,
Rest of their bones, and souls' delivery.
Thou art slave to Fate, chance, kings, and desperate men,   9
And dost with poison, war, and sickness dwell,
And poppy or charms can make us sleep as well
And better than thy stroke; why swell'st thou then?
One short sleep past, we wake eternally,
And death shall be no more, Death thou shalt die.   14

Batter My Heart, Three Person'd God

(Holy Sonnets, 10)

a plea to God to do something

Batter my heart, three person'd God; for, you
As yet but knock, breathe, shine, and seek to mend;
That I may rise, and stand, o'erthrow me, and bend
Your force, to break, blow, burn and make me new.
I, like an usurpt town, to another due,   5
Labour to admit you, but Oh, to no end,
Reason your viceroy in me, me should defend,
But is captiv'd, and proves weak or untrue,
Yet dearly I love you, and would be lov'd fain,   9
But am betroth'd unto your enemy,
Divorce me, untie, or break that knot again,
Take me to you, imprison me, for I
Except you enthrall me, never shall be free,
Nor ever chaste, except you ravish me.   14

wants to be divorced from his enemy and taken by God.

make me your slave.

david

A Hymn to God the Father

Wilt thou forgive that sin where I begun,
  Which was my sin, though it were done before?
Wilt thou forgive that sin through which I run,
  And do run still: though still I do deplore?
    When thou hast done, thou has not done,
      For, I have more.

Wilt thou forgive that sin which I won   7
  Others to sin? and, made my sin their door?
Wilt thou forgive that sin which I did shun
  A year, or two: but wallowed in, a score?
    When thou hast done, thou hast not done,
      For, I have more.

I have a sin of fear, that when I have spun   13
  My last thread, I shall perish on the shore;
But swear by thyself that at my death thy Sun
  Shall shine as it shines now, and heretofore;
    And having done that, Thou hast done;
      I fear no more.

A Lecture Upon the Shadow

Stand still, and I will read to thee
A lecture, love, in love's philosophy.
    These three hours that we have spent,
    Walking here, two shadows went
Along with us, which we ourselves produced;   5
But now the sun is just above our head,
    We do those shadows tread,
    And to brave clearness all things are reduced.
So whilst our infant loves did grow,
Disguises did, and shadows, flow
From us and our cares; but now 'tis not so.

That love hath not attained the high'st degree,   12
Which is still diligent lest others see.

2 *done:* pun on the poet's name.

8 *brave:* splendid.

Except our loves at this noon stay,   14
We shall new shadows make the other way.
   As the first were made to blind
   Others, these which come behind
Will work upon ourselves and blind our eyes.
If our loves faint, and westwardly decline,   19
   To me thou falsely thine,
   And I to thee, mine actions shall disguise.
The morning shadows wear away,
But these grow longer all the day;
But oh, love's day is short if love decay.

Love is a growing or full constant light,   25
And his first minute after noon is night.

Case

A

1. Although keenly aware of the danger of "shadows" to love, the speaker expresses to his mistress his conviction that he and she can control the progress of their love.

2. Calling his speech a "lecture," he addresses her in scientific tones, explaining (3, 11) how their love has developed.

3. After generalizing on the nature of love's integrity (12-13), he goes on to point out what will happen if (14, 19, 24) their loves begin to decline—the implication being that, if she heeds his "lecture," their love will remain constant.

B

1. Although naturally desirous of sustaining their love, the speaker expresses to his mistress the inevitability of its decline.

2. His analogy between love and the sun emphasizes their similarity in respect to rising and falling off.

3. In both the morning and the afternoon, the lovers produce "shadows," the earlier ones disguising their affection from the sight of others, and the later ones disguising their inevitable indifference to, and deception of, one another.

BIBLIOGRAPHY

Legouis, P., *Donne the Craftsman*, 1928, pp. 42-44; Van Doren, M., *Introduction to Poetry*, 1951, pp. 27-31.

14 *Except:* unless.   17 *behind:* later.

Since There's No Help, Come Let Us Kiss and Part

Since there's no help, come let us kiss and part;
Nay, I have done, you get no more of me;
And I am glad, yea, glad with all my heart
That thus so cleanly I myself can free.
Shake hands for ever, cancel all our vows,   5
And when we meet at any time again,
Be it not seen in either of our brows
That we one jot of former love retain.
Now at the last gasp of Love's latest breath,   9
When, his pulse failing, Passion speechless lies,
When Faith is kneeling by his bed of death
And Innocence is closing up his eyes,
    Now if thou would'st, when all have given him over,
    From death to life thou might'st him yet recover.   14

To the Memory of Mr. Oldham

Farewel, too little and too lately known,
Whom I began to think and call my own;
For sure our Souls were near ally'd; and thine
Cast in the same Poetick mould with mine.
One common Note on either Lyre did strike,   5
And Knaves and Fools we both abhorr'd alike:
To the same Goal did both our Studies drive
The last set out the soonest did arrive.
Thus *Nisus* fell upon the slippery place,
While his young Friend perform'd and won the Race.   10
O early ripe! to thy abundant store
What could advancing Age have added more?
It might (what Nature never gives the young)
Have taught the numbers of thy native Tongue.
But Satyr needs not those, and Wit will shine   15
Through the harsh cadence of a rugged line.
A noble Error, and but seldom made,
When Poets are by too much force betray'd.

Mr. Oldham: John Oldham, minor 17th-century satirist.   9-10: In the footrace
in Virgil's *Aeneid,* Nisus slips and loses, but trips up the second man so that
"his young friend" Euryalus wins.   14 *numbers:* poetic meters.   15 *Wit:* in-
genuity.

Thy generous fruits, though gather'd ere their prime ⎫
Still shew'd a quickness; and maturing time ⎬ 20
But mellows what we write to the dull sweets of Rime. ⎭
Once more, hail and farewel; farewel thou young,
But ah too short, *Marcellus* of our Tongue;
Thy Brows with Ivy, and with Laurels bound;
But Fate and gloomy Night encompass thee around. 25

Case

A

1. The poem is a graceful and stately expression of grief for the death of a fellow poet.

2. Twice comparing Oldham's work to the ripening of fruit, Dryden concludes that the only possible development for his friend might have been a more practised versification, which would, however, have led to a subduing of the vigorous verse best for satire.

3. Comforted by this knowledge, the poet once more bids his friend farewell, achieving a reserved but affectionate tone through an allusion prepared for earlier.

4. The rhythms of 16 and 21 imitiate the qualities which the lines describe.

B

1. The elegy is marred by faults so serious as to spoil its total effect.

2. The poet not only overburdens the reader by recondite allusions but also in the first reference actually fails to think through the comparison, with confusing results.

3. The regularity of the couplets (varied only by a triplet), the lack of variety in rhyming (almost half the rhyme-words use *n*, and *young / tongue* turns up twice), and the almost invariably end-stopped lines combine to give the poem a monotone incongruent with grief or praise.

20 *quickness:* vitality; speed in maturing; pungent taste. 23 *Marcellus:* Caesar Augustus' adopted son, a promising young man who died at 20; lamented by Virgil in the *Aeneid.* 24 *Ivy . . . Laurels:* symbols of learning and poetry.

4. The closing couplet, which we might expect to supply a poignant, pungent, or at least conclusive note, is conventional, anti-climactic, and vague.

BIBLIOGRAPHY

Brooks, C., and R. P. Warren, *Understanding Poetry*, 1950 ed., pp. 580-81; companion *Manual*, p. 45; Brown, W. C., *University of Kansas City Review*, 11 (Spring 1945), 182-84; Van Doren, M., *Introduction to Poetry*, 1951, pp. 94-98.

How We Heard the Name

The river brought down
dead horses, dead men
and military debris,
indicative of war
or official acts upstream,   5
but it went by, it all
goes by, that is the thing
about the river. Then
a soldier on a log
went by. He seemed drunk   10
and we asked him Why
had he and this junk
come down to us so
from the past upstream.
"Friends," he said, "the great   15
Battle of Granicus
has just been won
by all of the Greeks except
the Lacedaemonians and
myself: this is a joke   20
between me and a man
named Alexander, whom
all of you ba-bas
will hear of as a god."

19 *Lacedaemonians:* Spartans.   23 *ba-bas:* barbarian Persians.

'When Doris Danced'

When Doris danced under the oak tree
The sun himself might wish to see,
Might bend beneath those lovers, leaves,
While her her virgin steps she weaves   4
And envious cast his famous hue
To make her daft, yet win her too.

When Doris danced under the oak tree   7
Slow John, so stormed in heart, at sea
Gone all his store, a wreck he lay.
But on the ground the sun-beams play.   10
They lit his face in such degree
Doris lay down, all out of pity.

The Horse Chestnut Tree

Boys in sporadic but tenacious droves
Come with sticks, as certainly as Autumn,
To assault the great horse chestnut tree.

There is a law governs their lawlessness.   4
Desire is in them for a shining amulet
And the best are those that are highest up.

They will not pick them easily from the ground.   7
With shrill arms they fling to the higher branches,
To hurry the work of nature for their pleasure.

I have seen them trooping down the street   10
Their pockets stuffed with chestnuts shucked, unshucked.
It is only evening keeps them from their wish.

Sometimes I run out in a kind of rage   13
To chase the boys away: I catch an arm,
Maybe, and laugh to think of being the lawgiver.

I was once such a young sprout myself   16
And fingered in my pocket the prize and trophy.
But still I moralize upon the day

5 *amulet:* magic charm.

And see that we, outlaws on God's property,   19
Fling out imagination beyond the skies,
Wishing a tangible good from the unknown.

And likewise death will drive us from the scene   22
With the great flowering world unbroken yet,
Which we held in idea, a little handful.

The Love Song of J. Alfred Prufrock

S'io credesse che mia risposta fosse
A persona che mai tornasse al mondo,
Questa fiamma staria senza piu scosse.
Ma perciocche giammai di questo fondo
Non torno vivo alcun, s'i'odo il vero,
Senza tema d'infamia ti rispondo.

Let us go then, you and I,
When the evening is spread out against the sky
Like a patient etherized upon a table;
Let us go, through certain half-deserted streets,
The muttering retreats   5
Of restless nights in one-night cheap hotels
And sawdust restaurants with oyster-shells:
Streets that follow like a tedious argument
Of insidious intent
To lead you to an overwhelming question . . .   10
Oh, do not ask, "What is it?"
Let us go and make our visit.

    In the room the women come and go   13
Talking of Michelangelo.

    The yellow fog that rubs its back upon the windowpanes,   15
The yellow smoke that rubs its muzzle on the windowpanes,
Licked its tongue into the corners of the evening,
Lingered upon the pools that stand in drains,

Epigraph: "If I thought my answer were to one who ever could return to the world, this flame should shake no more; but since no one did ever return alive from this depth, if what I hear be true, without fear of infamy I answer you" (*Inferno* 27:61-66, trans. Carlyle and Oelsner).

Let fall upon its back the soot that falls from chimneys,
Slipped by the terrace, made a sudden leap, 20
And seeing that it was a soft October night,
Curled once about the house, and fell asleep.

And indeed there will be time 23
For the yellow smoke that slides along the street,
Rubbing its back upon the windowpanes;
There will be time, there will be time
To prepare a face to meet the faces that you meet;
There will be time to murder and create, 28
And time for all the works and days of hands
That lift and drop a question on your plate;
Time for you and time for me,
And time yet for a hundred indecisions,
And for a hundred visions and revisions, 32
Before the taking of a toast and tea.

In the room the women come and go 35
Talking of Michelangelo.

And indeed there will be time 37
To wonder, "Do I dare?" and, "Do I dare?"
Time to turn back and descend the stair,
With a bald spot in the middle of my hair—
[They will say: "How his hair is growing thin!"]
My morning coat, my collar mounting firmly to the chin, 42
My necktie rich and modest, but asserted by a simple pin—
[They will say: "But how his arms and legs are thin!"]
Do I dare
Disturb the universe?
In a minute there is time 47
For decisions and revisions which a minute will reverse.

For I have known them all already, known them all— 49
Have known the evenings, mornings, afternoons,
I have measured out my life with coffee spoons;
I know the voices dying with a dying fall
Beneath the music from a farther room.
So how should I presume?

And I have known the eyes already, known them all— 55
The eyes that fix you in a formulated phrase,
And when I am formulated, sprawling on a pin,
When I am pinned and wriggling on the wall,
Then how should I begin

To spit out all the butt-ends of my days and ways?   60
    And how should I presume?

    And I have known the arms already, known them all—   62
Arms that are braceleted and white and bare
[But in the lamplight, downed with light brown hair]
Is it perfume from a dress
That makes me so digress?
Arms that lie along a table, or wrap about a shawl.
    And should I then presume?
    And how should I begin?

            .   .   .   .   .

Shall I say, I have gone at dusk through narrow streets   70
And watched the smoke that rises from the pipes
Of lonely men in shirt-sleeves, leaning out of windows? . . .

    I should have been a pair of ragged claws   73
Scuttling across the floors of silent seas.

            .   .   .   .   .

And the afternoon, the evening, sleeps so peacefully!   75
Smoothed by long fingers,
Asleep . . . tired . . . or it malingers,
Stretched on the floor, here beside you and me.
Should I, after tea and cakes and ices,
Have the strength to force the moment to its crisis?   80
But though I have wept and fasted, wept and prayed,
Though I have seen my head [grown slightly bald] brought in
        upon a platter,
I am no prophet—and here's no great matter;
I have seen the moment of my greatness flicker,
And I have seen the eternal Footman hold my coat, and snicker,   85
And in short, I was afraid.

    And would it have been worth it, after all,   ·   87
After the cups, the marmalade, the tea,
Among the porcelain, among some talk of you and me,
Would it have been worth while,
To have bitten off the matter with a smile,
To have squeezed the universe into a ball   92
To roll it toward some overwhelming question,
To say: "I am Lazarus, come from the dead,
Come back to tell you all, I shall tell you all"—

82-83 *head . . . prophet:* cf. John the Baptist (Matthew 14:1-11).   92: cf.
Marvell's "To His Coy Mistress" (p. 207, ll. 41-42).   94 *Lazarus:* cf. John 11.

If one, settling a pillow by her head,
  Should say: "That is not what I meant at all.   97
  That is not it, at all."

And would it have been worth it, after all,   99
Would it have been worth while,
After the sunsets and the dooryards and the sprinkled streets,
After the novels, after the teacups, after the skirts that trail along
    the floor—
And this, and so much more?—   103
It is impossible to say just what I mean!
But as if a magic lantern threw the nerves in patterns on a screen:
Would it have been worth while
If one, settling a pillow or throwing off a shawl,
And turning toward the window, should say: 108
  "That is not it at all
  That is not what I meant, at all."

        .   .   .   .   .

No! I am not Prince Hamlet, nor was meant to be;   111
Am an attendant lord, one that will do
To swell a progress, start a scene or two,
Advise the prince; no doubt, an easy tool,
Deferential, glad to be of use,
Politic, cautious, and meticulous;   116
Full of high sentence, but a bit obtuse;
At times, indeed, almost ridiculous—
Almost, at times, the Fool.

  I grow old . . . I grow old . . .   120
I shall wear the bottoms of my trousers rolled.

  Shall I part my hair behind? Do I dare to eat a peach?   122
I shall wear white flannel trousers, and walk upon the beach.
I have heard the mermaids singing, each to each.

  I do not think that they will sing to me.   125

  I have seen them riding seaward on the waves   126
Combing the white hair of the waves blown back
When the wind blows the water white and black.

  We have lingered in the chambers of the sea   129
By sea-girls wreathed with seaweed red and brown
Till human voices wake us, and we drown.

105 *magic lantern:* photographic projector.   113 *progress:* royal procession.

Sweeney Among the Nightingales

ὤμοι, πέπληγμαι καιρίαν πληγὴν ἔσω.

Apeneck Sweeney spreads his knees
Letting his arms hang down to laugh,
The zebra stripes along his jaw
Swelling to maculate giraffe.

The circles of the stormy moon   5
Slide westward toward the River Plate,
Death and the Raven drift above
And Sweeney guards the hornèd gate.

Gloomy Orion and the Dog   9
Are veiled; and hushed the shrunken seas;
The person in the Spanish cape
Tries to sit on Sweeney's knees

Slips and pulls the table cloth   13
Overturns a coffee-cup,
Reorganised upon the floor
She yawns and draws a stocking up;

The silent man in mocha brown   17
Sprawls at the window-sill and gapes;
The waiter brings in oranges
Bananas figs and hothouse grapes;

The silent vertebrate in brown   21
Contracts and concentrates, withdraws;
Rachel *née* Rabinovitch
Tears at the grapes with murderous paws;

She and the lady in the cape   25
Are suspect, thought to be in league;
Therefore the man with heavy eyes
Declines the gambit, shows fatigue,

Leaves the room and reappears   29
Outside the window, leaning in,

Epigraph: "Oh! I am smitten deep with a mortal blow" (Fraenkel trans.): the
death-cry of King Agamemnon, murdered by his wife Clytemnestra, on his
victorious return from the Trojan War, in Aeschylus's play. 4 *maculate:*
spotted. 6 *River Plate:* in South America. 7 *the Raven, Orion and the Dog:*
constellations. 8 *guards the horned gate:* usually considered a reference to
the gate made of horn (*Odyssey* XIX, *Aeneid* VI), through which true dreams
come from the underworld.

Branches of wistaria
Circumscribe a golden grin;

The host with someone indistinct   33
Converses at the door apart,
The nightingales are singing near
The Convent of the Sacred Heart,

And sang within the bloody wood   37
When Agamemnon cried aloud,
And let their liquid siftings fall
To stain the stiff dishonoured shroud.

Critique

1. In this poem (1918) an attempt to seduce Sweeney in a café or public house is put into a framework that suggests the Agamemnon story . . . . Sweeney, at first neither alert nor collected, rouses to danger and departs, but does not escape the net, for he leaves in the shadow of Agamemnon. Whether inebriated or merely sleepy, Sweeney's emergence from this yawning, dangerously relaxed state describes the turn in the poem which ironically culminates in disaster. This irony is marked by his passage from uncollected laughter to the collected grin, circumscribed by wistaria. Sweeney sprawls, gapes, is silent and heavy-eyed, until the bait of the fruit makes him "contract" and become alert. His refusal to take this sacrificial pawn reveals the change in his state of mind. The actions of the lady in the Spanish cape and the "murderous paws" of Rachel together spell out his danger. The agent of his fate is of course the "someone indistinct" with whom the host converses apart.

(GEORGE WILLIAMSON)

2. . . . Then we come to the nightingales singing near the Convent of the Sacred Heart. Such is Mr. Eliot's power of concentrated suggestion that he can call up, in one apparently casual descriptive phrase, the two great traditions of civilization, the Christian and the classical. He makes us realize for ourselves that after two thousand years of Christianity this sordid intrigue is going on in

35 *nightingales:* Philomela was changed into a nightingale after being raped by her brother-in-law, King Tereus.

a brothel near a convent. . . . The allusion to the bird associated vith Greece in many Greek poets, and particularly in the *Agamemnon*, where it bewails Itys and the sensual crime of Tereus, leads up to the sensual crime of Clytemnestra. We feel a shock not merely of contrast but of elevation when we turn from the scheming of these idle wastrels to the death of the conqueror of Troy at the hands of a superhuman murderess.   (DOUGLAS BUSH)

3. These people have neither vitality nor order, and Eliot places them against a background which has both. The punctuation is significant here. After the introduction of Sweeney as a medley of animal shapes and markings, there are six lines of complete contrast which put him within a cosmic setting. There is no period at the end of these lines, just a semi-colon, and the sentence runs on to the end of the poem . . . . The contemporary scene, that is, fades in from the background of the great ordered rhythms of the natural world, and fades out into the reminders of the great ordered patterns of myth. . . . But their clarity and brightness is lost and their relationship with humanity. The stormy moon is blurred; it 'slides' to its setting towards the shallowest of rivers, with the ominous 'drift' of doom about it. All the myths linking man and the heavens . . . are 'veiled'; the sea itself, symbol of life, is 'hushed' and 'shrunken'. . . .

. . . Just as Sweeney blocks the hornèd gate, so that the messages from the shades—the human tradition—cannot get through, so the vertebrate in brown blocks the window on to the immediate realities. But the point is that outside in the dim night *are* the Convent and the nightingales and the wood and the memory of the dead Agamemnon, and all the associations they bring, about the relationships of man and nature and the gods, of mortality and immortality, death and resurrection, the temporal and the eternal, nature and spirit. . . .   (ELIZABETH DREW)

4. . . . Eliot will not set down his thought flatly. His method is comparable to *pointillisme* in painting, which proceeds on the theory that juxtaposed points of color on a canvas will coalesce *within the mind of the beholder* to give an effect of vibrancy impossible in monotone surfaces. Similarly, Eliot expects to keep his poem alive by compelling the reader to think *for himself* of possible relationships and connections between its parts. . . . Nor can he settle down with a complacent feeling that the poem is designed to contrast the sordid modern world with ancient splendor. For

there is *present* beauty in the branches of wistaria, and dignity and somber tragedy even today in such mysterious symbols as "Death and the Raven," "Gloomy Orion." And there is horror in the picture of the past: in the crucifixion of Christ, the murder of Agamemnon. Actually, the opposing poles, in Eliot's vision both of ancient and of modern times, are superficial beauty and underlying baseness. But the contrasts are not formally stated; they are implied by means of juxtaposed images. (DONALD A. STAUFFER)

BIBLIOGRAPHY

Bush, D., *Mythology and the Romantic Tradition*, 1937, pp. 513-14; Drew, E., *T. S. Eliot: The Design of His Poetry*, 1949, pp. 44-46; Stauffer, D. A., *The Nature of Poetry*, 1946, pp. 79-80; Williamson, G., *A Reader's Guide to T. S. Eliot*, 1953, pp. 97-98.

Case

A

1. The primary theme is the contrast between the nobility of ancient times and the sordidness of modern times.

2. The abstract contrast derives from the concrete juxtaposition of royal Greek figures with animalistic modern characters, of Christ's Sacred Heart and sacrifice with the cheap restaurant setting, and of Philomela's tragic suffering with modern vulgar and apathetic sexual play.

B

1. The primary theme is the similar depravity of past and present human activity when considered in the light of eternal beauty and truth.

2. The traditionally beautiful song of the nightingales, set against a background of religious truth both in past and present, is unconcerned with adjacent human activity, thus implying little difference between Agamemnon and Sweeney or between the conspirators around both men.

BIBLIOGRAPHY

Bush, D., *Mythology and the Romantic Tradition*, 1937, pp. 513-14; Drew, E., *T. S. Eliot: The Design of His Poetry*, 1949, pp. 133-35;

Hyman, S. E., *American Scholar*, **30** (Winter 1961), 43-55; Kerschbaum, L., and R. P. Basler, *Explicator*, **2** (Dec. 1943), 18; Matthiessen, F., *The Achievement of T. S. Eliot*, 1935, p. 129; Smith, G., *T. S. Eliot's Poetry and Plays*, 1956, pp. 45-47; Stauffer, D. A., *The Nature of Poetry*, 1946, pp. 78-80; Williamson, G., *A Reader's Guide to T. S. Eliot*, 1953, pp. 97-98.

Journey of the Magi

'A cold coming we had of it,
Just the worst time of the year
For a journey, and such a long journey:
The ways deep and the weather sharp,
The very dead of winter.'   5
And the camels galled, sore-footed, refractory,
Lying down in the melting snow.
There were times we regretted
The summer palaces on slopes, the terraces,
And the silken girls bringing sherbet.   10
Then the camel men cursing and grumbling
And running away, and wanting their liquor and women,
And the night-fires going out, and the lack of shelters,
And the cities hostile and the towns unfriendly
And the villages dirty and charging high prices: 15
A hard time we had of it.
At the end we preferred to travel all night,
Sleeping in snatches,
With the voices singing in our ears, saying
That this was all folly.

    Then at dawn we came down to a temperate valley,   21
Wet, below the snow line, smelling of vegetation;
With a running stream and a water-mill beating the darkness,
And three trees on the low sky,
And an old white horse galloped away in the meadow.
Then we came to a tavern with vine-leaves over the lintel,   26
Six hands at an open door dicing for pieces of silver,
And feet kicking the empty wine-skins.
But there was no information, and so we continued
And arrived at evening, not a moment too soon
Finding the place; it was (you may say) satisfactory.

The Magi: priests, the "wise men" at Christ's birth (Matthew 2).

All this was a long time ago, I remember,   32
And I would do it again, but set down
This set down
This: were we led all that way for
Birth or Death? There was a Birth, certainly,
We had evidence and no doubt. I had seen birth and death,   37
But had thought they were different; this Birth was
Hard and bitter agony for us, like Death, our death.
We returned to our places, these Kingdoms,
But no longer at ease here, in the old dispensation,
With an alien people clutching their gods.
I should be glad of another death.   43

Days

Daughters of Time, the hypocritic Days,
Muffled and dumb like barefoot dervishes,
And marching single in an endless file,
Bring diadems and fagots in their hands.
To each they offer gifts after his will,   5
Bread, kingdoms, stars, and sky that holds them all.
I, in my pleached garden, watched the pomp,
Forgot my morning wishes, hastily
Took a few herbs and apples, and the Day
Turned and departed silent. I, too late,   10
Under her solemn fillet saw the scorn.

Critique

1. Here is a prose sentence from Emerson's "Works and Days:"—

"The days are ever divine as to the first Aryans. They come and go
like muffled and veiled figures, sent from a distant friendly party; but
they say nothing, and if we do not use the gifts they bring, they carry
them as silently away."

7 *pleached:* interlaced (with branches).   14 *fillet:* headband.

Now see this thought in full dress [in the poem], and then ask what is the difference between prose and poetry . . . .

Cinderella at the fireside, and Cinderella at the prince's ball! The full dress version of the thought is glittering with new images . . . , and fringed with fresh adjectives . . . . That one word *pleached* . . . gives to the noble sonnet [lyric] an antique dignity and charm like the effect of an ancestral jewel. But mark that now the poet reveals himself as he could not in the prosaic form of the first extract. It is his own neglect of his great opportunity of which he now speaks, and not merely the indolent indifference of others. It is himself who is the object of scorn. . . . (OLIVER WENDELL HOLMES)

2. This poem is an extended metaphor in which Days, the daughters of Time, are pictured marching one by one endlessly. . . . The speaker . . . is so much interested in the pomp of the procession that he forgets his early ambitions, his plan to take only the best gifts, and hastily snatches a few trivial things as the Day is departing. The Day does not express audibly her opinion of this choice, but on her face, visible beneath her fillet, is written her scorn, her contempt for those who procrastinate. . . .

. . . In the sense that they are not what they seem to be, the Days are hypocritic. . . . They seem to pass slowly enough to give us every opportunity to choose wisely. But in reality they go both swiftly and silently. . . . (RICHARD R. KIRK and R. P. McCUTCHEON)

3. . . . Why "hypocritic"? . . . Emerson condemns himself at the end of the poem for not taking more of what one of the Days offered him . . . . But if the Day were tricking him, why should he blame himself? Nature as a deceiver is quite out of tone with Emerson's fundamental thought. . . .

A more acceptable interpretation is suggested by the original Greek meaning of "hypocritic": "acting out a part." Used in this sense, the word signals to the reader that days are to be personified—to be presented as actors in a processional pageant. . . . The Days come, then, as if they are actors on a stage and we the spectators . . . . No criticism is implied by the word; it is purely descriptive. . . . (JOSEPH JONES)

4. . . . There is no basis for seeking . . . a definition of hypocritic in its etymology; the days are hypocritic because they allow the poet to accept less than he ought . . . .

. . . Confusion arises only when we do not distinguish the poet as actor from the poet as narrator. In taking the herbs and apples the poet acts with clear conscience, though hastily. Too late he realizes his error, and it is in meditation upon that error that he gives us his poem. . . .   (GEORGE ARMS)

BIBLIOGRAPHY

Arms, G., *Explicator*, 4 (Nov. 1945), 8; Holmes, O. W., *Ralph Waldo Emerson*, 1886, pp. 312-13; Jones, J., *Explicator*, 4 (Apr. 1946), 47; Kirk, R. R., and R. P. McCutcheon, *An Introduction to the Study of Poetry*, 1934, pp. 35-36.

Dirge

1-2-3 was the number he played but today the number
    came 3-2-1;
    bought his Carbide at 30 and it went to 29; had the
    favorite at Bowie but the track was slow—

O, executive type, would you like to drive a floating   3
    power, knee-action, silk-upholstered six? Wed a Hol-
    lywood star? Shoot the course in 58? Draw to the
    ace, king, jack?
    O, fellow with a will who won't take no, watch out for
    three cigarettes on the same, single match; O, demo-
    cratic voter born in August under Mars, beware of
    liquidated rails—

Denouement to denouement, he took a personal pride in   5
    the certain, certain way he lived his own, private life,
    but nevertheless, they shut off his gas; nevertheless, the
    bank foreclosed; nevertheless, the landlord called;
    nevertheless, the radio broke,
And twelve o'clock arrived just once too often,   7
    just the same he wore one grey tweed suit, bought one
    straw hat, drank one straight Scotch, walked one
    short step, took one long look, drew one deep breath,
    just one too many,

2 *Carbide:* stock in Union Carbide and Carbon Corp.   2 *Bowie:* Maryland race-track.   4 *liquidated rails:* assets of bankrupt railroads distributed among creditors.   5 *Denouement:* unraveling of plot in a play.

And wow he died as wow he lived,   10
    going whop to the office and blooie home to sleep and
        biff got married and bam had children and oof got
        fired,
    zowie did he live and zowie did he die,

With who the hell are you at the corner of his casket, and   13
    where the hell we going on the right hand silver knob,
    and who the hell cares walking second from the end
    with an American Beauty wreath from why the hell
    not,

Very much missed by the circulation staff of the New   14
    York Evening Post; deeply, deeply mourned by the
    B.M.T.,

Wham, Mr. Roosevelt; pow, Sears Roebuck; awk, big   15
    dipper; bop, summer rain;
    bong, Mr., bong, Mr., bong, Mr., bong.

Pitcher

His art is eccentricity, his aim
How not to hit the mark he seems to aim at,

His passion how to avoid the obvious,   3
His technique how to vary the avoidance.

The others throw to be comprehended. He   5
Throws to be a moment misunderstood.

Yet not too much. Not errant, arrant, wild,   7
But every seeming aberration willed.

Not to, yet still, still to communicate   9
Making the batter understand too late.

14 *B.M.T.:* Brooklyn-Manhattan Transit, New York subway.
7 *arrant:* bad.

Mending Wall

Something there is that doesn't love a wall,
That sends the frozen-ground-swell under it,
And spills the upper boulders in the sun;
And makes gaps even two can pass abreast.
The work of hunters is another thing: 5
I have come after them and made repair
Where they have left not one stone on a stone,
But they would have the rabbit out of hiding,
To please the yelping dogs. The gaps I mean,
No one has seen them made or heard them made,   10
But at spring mending-time we find them there.
I let my neighbor know beyond the hill;
And on a day we meet to walk the line
And set the wall between us once again.
We keep the wall between us as we go.   15
To each the boulders that have fallen to each.
And some are loaves and some so nearly balls
We have to use a spell to make them balance:
'Stay where you are until our backs are turned!'
We wear our fingers rough with handling them.   20
Oh, just another kind of outdoor game,
One on a side. It comes to little more:
There where it is we do not need the wall:
He is all pine and I am apple orchard.
My apple trees will never get across   25
And eat the cones under his pines, I tell him.
He only says, 'Good fences make good neighbors.'
Spring is the mischief in me, and I wonder
If I could put a notion in his head:
'Why do they make good neighbors? Isn't it   30
Where there are cows? But here there are no cows.
Before I built a wall I'd ask to know
What I was walling in or walling out,
And to whom I was like to give offense.
Something there is that doesn't love a wall,   35
That wants it down.' I could say 'Elves' to him,
But it's not elves exactly, and I'd rather
He said it for himself. I see him there
Bringing a stone grasped firmly by the top

In each hand, like an old-stone savage armed.   40
He moves in darkness as it seems to me,
Not of woods only and the shade of trees.
He will not go behind his father's saying,
And he likes having thought of it so well
He says again, 'Good fences make good neighbors.'   45

After Apple-Picking

My long two-pointed ladder's sticking through a tree
Toward heaven still,
And there's a barrel that I didn't fill
Beside it, and there may be two or three
Apples I didn't pick upon some bough.   5
But I am done with apple-picking now.
Essence of winter sleep is on the night,
The scent of apples: I am drowsing off.
I cannot rub the strangeness from my sight
I got from looking through a pane of glass   10
I skimmed this morning from the drinking trough
And held against the world of hoary grass.
It melted, and I let it fall and break.
But I was well
Upon my way to sleep before it fell   15
And I could tell
What form my dreaming was about to take.
Magnified apples appear and disappear,
Stem end and blossom end,
And every fleck of russet showing clear.   20
My instep arch not only keeps the ache,
It keeps the pressure of a ladder-round.
I feel the ladder sway as the boughs bend.
And I keep hearing from the cellar bin
The rumbling sound   25
Of load on load of apples coming in.
For I have had too much
Of apple-picking: I am overtired
Of the great harvest I myself desired.
There were ten thousand thousand fruit to touch,   30

12 *hoary:* greyish white.   20 *russet:* reddish brown.   22 *round:* rung.

Cherish in hand, lift down, and not let fall.
For all
That struck the earth,
No matter if not bruised or spiked with stubble,
Went surely to the cider-apple heap   35
As of no worth.
One can see what will trouble
This sleep of mine, whatever sleep it is.
Were he not gone,
The woodchuck could say whether it's like his   40
Long sleep, as I describe its coming on,
Or just some human sleep.

Case

A

1. Although the poem may be read symbolically, it is more re-warding when considered simply as the expression of a sensitive man's weariness at the end of a late, good harvest.

2. With constant reference to his weariness, the speaker experiences again the physical sensations of the day.

3. His character is subtly revealed in the playfulness of the action with the ice and in the ironic suggestion that his sleep might be like the woodchuck's hibernation.

4. The irregular pattern of meter and rhyme effectively fits the dreamy, drowsy mood, especially the employment of an unusually long interval in the final rhyme and an almost hypnotic repetition of "sleep" as an internal rhyme at the end.

B

1. Although the poem may be read profitably on a literal level, it is more rewarding when considered as symbolically embodying a man's awareness of death.

2. To begin with the symbolic hints, "heaven" suggests both the literal sky and the symbolic Heaven; "Essence" suggests both "The scent of apples" and the indefinably essential nature of "winter sleep"; and the wintry ice suggests an end of things in nature.

3. Lines 1-6, 30-36 express the speaker's recollection of the tasks of life, and 7-15, 27-29 his premonition of death (symbolized by winter and night).

4. The last half-dozen lines are highly significant, for they represent the speaker's detached but ambiguous view of his previous observations: Is it death (compared to the hibernation of an animal) that is coming on, or is it just the ordinary overnight sleep of a human being?

BIBLIOGRAPHY

Brooks, C., *Modern Poetry and the Tradition*, 1939, pp. 114-16; ————, and R. P. Warren, *Understanding Poetry*, 1950 ed., pp. 90, 389-97; companion *Manual*, p. 5; 1960 ed., pp. 363-69; Heiney, D., *Recent American Literature*, 1958, pp. 445-46.

Fire and Ice

Some say the world will end in fire,
Some say in ice.
From what I've tasted of desire
I hold with those who favor fire.
But if it had to perish twice,   5
I think I know enough of hate
To say that for destruction ice
Is also great
And would suffice.

Stopping by Woods on a Snowy Evening

Whose woods these are I think I know.
His house is in the village though;
He will not see me stopping here
To watch his woods fill up with snow.

My little horse must think it queer   5
To stop without a farmhouse near
Between the woods and frozen lake
The darkest evening of the year.

He gives his harness bells a shake   9
To ask if there is some mistake.
The only other sound's the sweep
Of easy wind and downy flake.

The woods are lovely, dark and deep,   13
But I have promises to keep,
And miles to go before I sleep,
And miles to go before I sleep.

Case

A

1. The primary theme of the poem is the beauty of a winter scene.

2. The first two stanzas give the reader clear visual images of the woods, the ice-covered lake, the man and his horse stopping between them, the uninhabited terrain, the snow, and the night, while the third stanza centers on the auditory images of harness bells, wind, and snow.

3. Stanza 4 contrasts with the other three in being less factual and more suggestive, less brisk and more somnolent, especially in the drowsy repetition of long vowels in 15-16.

4. The ingenious use of each stanza's third-line rhyme as the dominant rhyme for the next stanza helps to unify the poem.

B

1. The primary theme of the poem is the conflict between a man's sensitivity to beauty and his sense of responsibility.

2. The conflict emerges in the speaker's concern for appearances in Stanza 1 and for human and animal differences in Stanzas 2 and 3.

3. The "promises" of Stanza 4 are representative of the surrounding human responsibilities that give poignancy to the brief experience of beauty.

4. The repetition of line 15 as line 16 perhaps symbolizes an acceptance (albeit a temporarily grudging one) of the transience of a beautiful experience, thus resolving the conflict.

BIBLIOGRAPHY

Blair, W., and J. C. Gerber, *Better Reading 2: Literature*, 1948, pp. 156-57; Ciardi, J., *How Does a Poem Mean?* 1959, pp. 671-76; ———, *Saturday Review*, **41** (12 Apr. 1958), 13-15; Cooper, C. W., and J. Holmes, *Preface to Poetry*, 1946, pp. 605-7; Cox, J. M., *Virginia Quarterly Review*, **35** (Winter 1959), 82-84; Thompson, L., *Fire and Ice*, 1942, pp. 25-27; Unger, L., and W. V. O'Connor, *Poems for Study*, 1953, pp. 597-600; Walcutt, C. C., *College English*, **14** (May 1953), 450.

Design

I found a dimpled spider, fat and white,
On a white heal-all, holding up a moth
Like a white piece of rigid satin cloth—
Assorted characters of death and blight
Mixed ready to begin the morning right,   5
Like the ingredients of a witches' broth—
A snow-drop spider, a flower like a froth,
And dead wings carried like a paper kite.

What had that flower to do with being white,   9
The wayside blue and innocent heal-all?
What brought the kindred spider to that height,
Then steered the white moth thither in the night?
What but design of darkness to appall?—
If design govern in a thing so small.   14

Critique

1. This is a poem of finding evil in innocence, a song of experience, though the voice is hardly that of Blake's child-like singer. At first we hear the cheerfully observant walker on back-country roads: 'I found a dimpled . . .' The iambic lilt adds a tone of pleasant surprise: 'I found a dimpled darling'—'Little Miss Muffet sat on a tuffet!' But in 'spider' the voice betrays itself, and in 'fat' and 'white' the dimpled creature appears less charming. On a small

scale the first line, like the whole poem, builds up a joke in tone, rhythm, and image that grows into a 'joke' of another sort.

In the octet [sic] the joking discovery develops gradually through a series of contradictory pictures. 'A white heal-all' suggests purity and safety, though the color echoes the white of the swollen spider. A satin-white moth has its charm, too, a party-going creature poised like Wordsworth's butterfly on its flower; but 'rigid' is too frozen, too easily remininscent of *rigor mortis* or the stiff shining satin of a coffin. In the aside of the next three lines, the speaker gives away his joke, but he does it *jokingly*, again partly by tricks of rhythm. First there is the very correct iambic of line 4,

> Assorted characters of death and blight . . .

in exactly ten syllables, every other one of which must be stressed, a little as in doggerel. The plain truth of the statement takes on a cheerful sing-song quality, an effect increased in the next line by reversing the stress and omitting the short in 'Mixed ready.' The tone now becomes quite jaunty, but 'right' hovers on a pun for 'rite,' as the poet mixes a brew worthy of the Weird Sisters, Shakespeare's most evil images of evil. The adding of unstressed syllables speeds up and lightens the next line to soften the ugliness of what is being said:

> Like the ingredients of a witches' broth . . .

And with

> A snow-drop spider, a flower like a froth,

more oblique joking is resumed in images of springtime freshness ('snow drop,' 'flower-like,' we hear). But the spider is there, and the fragility of 'froth' hardly conceals the link with venom. A surface of elegant gaiety is kept up, however, through symmetry of sound, as o's and i's, alliterated syllables, and apparent compounds are balanced in each half of the verse. Again we are brought up short with '*dead* wings,' and if kites are fun, a 'kite' is also a bird of prey, and 'a *paper* kite' is another image of death-like rigidity.

(REUBEN A. BROWER)

2. The factual material has been presented in vivid description. Now comes the questioning. What directive has brought these things together in the night? If we believe that some design operates in the universe, doesn't this prove that such cosmic laws are as

much evil as good, as much destructive as creative? What is this whiteness but "design of darkness" to appall us, and also to put a pall of death and blight over our easy assumptions of a divine providence?

Frost gives the poem a final sardonic twist in the last lines with the apparently offhand remark, "If design govern in a thing so small." At first he seems to be dismissing the matter, as if such a trifling catastrophe as a repulsive spider and an anemic flower and a dead moth were hardly worth mentioning at all. But the dismissal opens up a further dark possibility. We may be willing to accept that destructive forces exist, as part of a larger creative design that is beyond human comprehension. Supposing, though, there's no design at all, either in nature or in human fate? . . .

(ELIZABETH DREW)

BIBLIOGRAPHY

Brower, R. A., *The Poetry of Robert Frost: Constellations of Intention,* 1963, pp. 105-6; Drew, E., *Poetry: A Modern Guide to Its Understanding and Enjoyment,* 1959, pp. 187-88.

The Most of It

He thought he kept the universe alone;
For all the voice in answer he could wake
Was but the mocking echo of his own
From some tree-hidden cliff across the lake.
Some morning from the boulder-broken beach   5
He would cry out on life, that what it wants
Is not its own love back in copy speech,
But counter-love, original response.
And nothing ever came of what he cried
Unless it was the embodiment that crashed   10
In the cliff's talus on the other side,
And then in the far distant water splashed,
But after a time allowed for it to swim,
Instead of proving human when it neared
And someone else additional to him,   15

11 *talus:* debris.

As a great buck it powerfully appeared,
Pushing the crumpled water up ahead,
And landed pouring like a waterfall,
And stumbled through the rocks with horny tread,
And forced the underbrush—and that was all.   20

Case

A

1. The primary theme is the loneliness of an unloved man.

2. The "he" of the poem complains that in this life one must love, and be loved by, someone different from himself.

3. His need is not fulfilled, although the coincidental appearance of something that turns out to be merely a noisy wild animal gives him momentary hope.

4. In the title, "It" refers to the man's desire—the whole title ironically commenting on the small response that he gets.

B

1. The primary theme is nature's complete lack of concern with man.

2. When the "he" of the poem calls out, he raises only an empty echo of his own voice.

3. The indifference of nature is emphasized by its concrete "embodiment" in the form of a powerful but purposeless, nonhuman creature that is not even aware of the man's existence.

4. In the title, "It" refers to nature; the animal is "The Most of" active nature that the man ever comes in contact with.

C

1. The primary theme is the meaninglessness of the "universe."

2. When the "he" of the poem calls out, he is answered, but incomprehensibly and mockingly.

3. The ambiguity of 9-10 reflects the unfathomable quality of nonhuman force: Although the buck is an "embodiment," there is no indication as to what it embodies, nor if it comes in answer to the cry, nor what effect it has on "him."

4. In the title, "It" refers to nature—the whole title ironically commenting on "The Most" that man ever understands "of It."

BIBLIOGRAPHY

Winters, Y., *Sewanee Review*, 56 (Autumn 1948), 591-92; Jarrell, R., *Kenyon Review*, 14 (Autumn 1952), 545.

It Bids Pretty Fair

The play seems out for an almost infinite run.
Don't mind a little thing like the actors fighting.
The only thing I worry about is the sun.
We'll be all right if nothing goes wrong with the lighting.

The Draft Horse

With a lantern that wouldn't burn
In too frail a buggy we drove
Behind too heavy a horse
Through a pitch-dark limitless grove.

And a man came out of the trees   5
And took our horse by the head
And reaching back to his ribs
Deliberately stabbed him dead.

The ponderous beast went down   9
With a crack of a broken shaft.
And the night drew through the trees
In one long invidious draft.

The most unquestioning pair   13
That ever accepted fate
And the least disposed to ascribe
Any more than we had to to hate,

We assumed that the man himself   17
Or someone he had to obey
Wanted us to get down
And walk the rest of the way.

Analysis and Synthesis of "The Draft Horse"

(See procedure, pp. xi-xii.)

1. *Reading aloud.* Because the meter at first seems mechanical and the matching of sentences to stanzas almost inevitable, the reader must give special attention to the concluding sentence, which is fitted to two stanzas, demanding a transition of rising instead of falling pitch at the end of line 16.

2. *Paraphrase.* (Stanza 1) Without illumination—the lantern would not work—in a very light buggy, we were driving with a very weighty horse, through a very dark endless wood. (Stanza 2) Suddenly a man emerged from the woods, held the horse's head, and by putting a knife between his ribs, carefully killed him. (Stanza 3) The big animal dropped to the ground, breaking one of the buggy shafts, while the wind blew through the woods in a single, lengthy, terrible flow. (Stanza 4) The two of us, uninterested more than others in asking questions (but still) believing in fate, and more than others not particularly believing in the power of hatred, (Stanza 5) simply accepted the possibility that either the killer or a person ruling him desired us to descend to walk from there on.

The following words and phrases cannot adequately be paraphrased: lines 11-12, where the wind (a) is called "night," (b) seems to start up unaccountably, and (c) blows with a certain unity but without distinction of length in time; and lines 15-16, where the compressed phrasing places "us" at an extreme of naiveté at the same time that it implies a judicious flexibility in recognizing the exact need for coping with human hate.

✗ 3. *Rhythm.* Although the uniform trimeter seems jingly when it is read aloud, it is actually so varied in two kinds of feet as to barely allow a traditional foot label. With an almost equal number of anapests (31) and iambs (28, plus one truncated iamb beginning line 19), and with an exactly equal number of lines dominated by anapests or iambs, we must label the pattern mixed anapestic-iambic trimeter. The only "perfect" line is 16, with three anapests, and line 11's anapest-iamb-iamb structure is not repeated elsewhere— a fact that will have some meaning later.

⨉. 4. *Rhyme.* Beyond identifying the obvious ballad end-rhyme pattern (*abxb*), one can discover emphatic systems of alliteration and assonance ("emphatic" used here arbitrarily to designate sounds that bind together at least three lines of a stanza). The alliterative phonemes operate in all stanzas except the middle one as follows:

Stanza 1: /b/, Stanza 2: /t/, Stanza 4: / ð /, Stanza 5: /w/. For assonance, the colorless / ə / works in the odd stanzas (1, 3, 5) and the broad /æ/ in the three middle stanzas (2, 3, 4).[1] It may be significant that Stanza 3, which contains the difficult-to-paraphrase images and metaphor of lines 11-12, is the only stanza without "emphatic" alliteration and the only stanza with both / ə / and /æ/ assonance.

✕   5a. *Rhetoric of syntax.*[2] Sentence 1 (Stanza 1) almost buries the simple subject and verb under preceding and succeeding negative modifiers. Sentence 2 (Stanza 2) sets up one subject with three verbs coupled by "and," but with the climactic third verb delayed by two modifiers. Stanza 3 is composed of two sentences coupled by subjects and verbs ("The . . . beast went down" and "the night drew") and by modifiers describing sound ("with a crack of a broken shaft" and "In one long invidious draft"). Stanza 4 opposes structural and semantic superlatives in its first and third lines, and monosyllabic abstractions in the rhyme-words of the second and fourth lines. The last stanza has a minor coupling with the first stanza in its use of simple subject and verb ("we drove" and "We assumed"), but it is immensely more complicated by its having the entire Stanza 4 constituting the appositive subject, with an adjective clause and an infinitive phrase, and by its having the complement of Stanza 5's main verb ("assumed") a subordinate clause whose own compound subject and complement surround a simple verb somewhat as the modifiers surround the verb in the opening stanza-sentence.

To recapitulate, we may note that the declarative sentence pattern of the poem begins with a simple statement almost hidden in modifiers, proceeds to a polysyndetic (repeated conjunction) sentence with three predicates (the last climactic), moves in the center of the poem to two parallel statements, and then concludes with a long sentence whose appositive subject is marked by syntactic balance and semantic contrast. The effect of this variety is to increase the complexity of the poem's conclusion, contrasting with the simpler statements ending "Stopping by Woods on a Snowy Evening," Frost's other lyric about a horse in dark woods.

[1] In the International Phonetic Alphabet, / ð / is voiced *th*, / ə / is neutral *uh*, /æ/ is *a* as in *man*.
[2] This analysis owes to Samuel R. Levin's description of "coupling," the matching in poetry of equivalent meanings and/or sounds by their being placed in equivalent syntactical, metrical, or rhyming positions. (See pp. 250-252.)

✕ 5b. ·*Rhetoric of Sense Images.* The title and the first three stanzas are chiefly visual and kinesthetic, with usually one visual-kinesthetic image to the line, but with aural imagery taking over the last three lines of these stanzas. From there to the end there is no sense imagery (unless the reader can visualize "us" and "the man" or can feel any motion in "get down" and "walk"), only abstraction.

✕ 5c. *Rhetoric of Figurative Language.* The comparative lack of figurative language in the first three stanzas follows the same pattern as the sense imagery, with only the dead metaphor "pitch-dark" mildly interrupting the literal statements until the complex metaphor of "night" for wind is introduced. From then on, the language is abstract and more general until the concrete and specific "get down / And walk" of the final lines. With so few nouns, verbs, and adjectives in the poem, the use of "draft" and "drew" in the title and in lines 11-12 must be a deliberate pun in which the big drawing horse gets translated into a spiritual wind.

5d. *Rhetoric of Symbols and Archetypes.* Symbolically, the images and statements of Stanza 1 all point to a lack of preparation and lack of caution on the part of the subject couple, and after the unexplained act of Stanza 2, Stanza 3 gives us the results of incaution and unpreparedness. The metaphor in lines 11-12 symbolizes the awful power of some superhuman force involved in the killing and the translation of the horse. Finally, the abstract complexities of the long last statement in the poem symbolically define a fatalistic and morally relativistic unwillingness to try to explain the violent act of Stanza 2.

These symbols have some archetypal roots. In Stanza 1 the protagonists are in the woods, in the midst of mysterious nature and unable to escape—like Dante in the dark wood on Good Friday, or like Odysseus with Poseidon or Adam with God. Although the killing in Stanza 2 may at first seem like pointless human evil, we have only to associate the stabbing of an animal with primitive sacrificial rites (see Frazer's *The Golden Bough*) to understand the following points. (1) The role of the horse is that of a scapegoat for the human pair. (2) The role of the "man . . . out of the trees" is that of an initiated priest, like Frazer's King of the Woods. (3) The significance of "took our horse by the head" lies in the ritual act of the priest's putting his hand on the head of the sacrificial animal, as specified a dozen times in God's instructions to Moses on sacrifice (Leviticus 1-8). (4) The significance of the pun on "draft" in the title and lines 11-12 is that of the spirit of the animal as part of the mysterious transcendental element of ritual. The "someone he had to obey" is therefore a god or fate, something omnipotent and divine dwelling in a mysterious grove (lines 4, 5, 11), like the sacred groves described by Frazer (see also "Trees and Plants," Hastings's *Encyclopaedia of Religion and Ethics*) or referred to in the Old Testament (albeit in a KJV mistranslation; see "Asherah," *Interpreter's Dictionary of the Bible*).

As a matter of corroboration, if one turns to Northrop Frye's *Anatomy of Criticism* (1957, pp. 147-50), he will find that Frost's poem, as far as it goes, is almost a paradigm of Frye's demonic archetypal imagery, the imagery of hell and the undesirable. The *vegetable* world of "The Draft Horse" is "a sinister forest," and the *animal* world is that of "monsters" in that the horse—ordinarily a creature of romance and superiority—is pointedly monstrous in being "too heavy" and "ponderous," a wagon horse harnessed to a "frail . . . buggy." The *human* world is that of the "tyrant-leader" (the man of the woods) and the "sacrificed victim," with the animal sacrifice substituting for the victimized human pair. This all helps to identify Frost's "someone he had to obey" as of Frye's *divine* world, the domain of "inscrutable fate or external necessity." [3]

5e. *Rhetoric of Tones*. The speaker is explanatory in Stanza 1, he reduces himself to straight narrative in lines 5-10, and he then mentions the phenomenon of 11-12 in a tone of appreciative awe. The seeming ingenuousness of the last two stanzas, which produces a comic anticlimax at first reading, should eventually be recognized as disingenuous understatement in which the speaker reluctantly accepts a power greater than man's.

6. *Primary Theme*. On the basis of all the preceding analysis, we may synthesize the reading of Frost's "The Draft Horse" by stating the primary theme as the ironic acceptance of superhuman power. Caught without adequate means of protection or escape, the protagonists witness a primitive religious ritual attesting to power, in which their horse is sacrificed instead of them. Refusing on the one hand to attribute the act to mere human weakness, they also decline to fall down and worship the revealed power as purposeful

[3] This demonic "world of nightmare and the scapegoat" ironically parodies Frye's "apocalyptic world, the heaven of religion" (p. 141), whose animal component can be "at the opening of the Brihadaranyaka Upanishad, for instance, the sacrificial horse, whose body contains the whole universe . . ." (p. 143).

providence, preferring to oversimplify both the superhuman power and their own grudging reaction of acceptance. All the formal structures of the poem contribute to this primary theme, foreshadowed by the initial difficulty of paraphrasing the metaphor of mystery in lines 11-12 and the complex syntax of lines 15-16. The unique meter involved in these crucial passages, the assonance versus alliteration in Stanza 3, the aural imagery and the pun of Stanza 3 as opposed to the logical abstractions of Stanzas 4 and 5, the relationship of the archetypes of ritual sacrifice, and the tone of awe at mystery and power opposed to the tone of understated acceptance (the last being set in complex syntax)—all these elements center on the primary theme.

Elegy Written in a Country Church-yard

The Curfew tolls the knell of parting day,
The lowing herd wind slowly o'er the lea,
The plowman homeward plods his weary way.
And leaves the world to darkness and to me.

Now fades the glimmering landscape on the sight,   5
And all the air a solemn stillness holds,
Save where the beetle wheels his droning flight,
And drowsy tinklings lull the distant folds;

Save that from yonder ivy-mantled tow'r   9
The mopeing owl does to the moon complain
Of such, as wand'ring near her secret bow'r,
Molest her ancient solitary reign.

Beneath those rugged elms, that yew-tree's shade,   13
Where heaves the turf in many a mould'ring heap,
Each in his narrow cell for ever laid,
The rude Forefathers of the hamlet sleep.

The breezy call of incense-breathing Morn,   17
The swallow twitt'ring from the straw-built shed,
The cock's shrill clarion, or the echoing horn,
No more shall rouse them from their lowly bed.

For them no more the blazing hearth shall burn,   21
Or busy housewife ply her evening care:

2 *lea:* pasture.   11 *bow'r:* dwelling.

No children run to lisp their sire's return,
Or climb his knees the envied kiss to share.

Oft did the harvest to their sickle yield,   25
Their furrow oft the stubborn glebe has broke;
How jocund did they drive their team afield!
How bow'd the woods beneath their sturdy stroke!

Let not Ambition mock their useful toil,   29
Their homely joys, and destiny obscure;
Nor Grandeur hear with a disdainful smile
The short and simple annals of the poor.

The boast of heraldry, the pomp of pow'r,   33
And all that beauty, all that wealth e'er gave,
Await alike th' inevitable hour.
The paths of glory lead but to the grave.

Nor you, ye Proud, impute to These the fault,   37
If Mem'ry o'er their Tomb no Trophies raise,
Where thro' the long-drawn aisle and fretted vault
The pealing anthem swells the note of praise.

Can storied urn or animated bust   41
Back to its mansion call the fleeting breath?
Can Honour's voice provoke the silent dust,
Or Flatt'ry soothe the dull cold ear of Death?

Perhaps in this neglected spot is laid   45
Some heart once pregnant with celestial fire;
Hands, that rod of empire might have sway'd,
Or wak'd to exstasy the living lyre.

But Knowledge to their eyes her ample page   49
Rich with the spoils of time did ne'er unroll;
Chill Penury repress'd their noble Rage,
And froze the genial current of the soul.

Full many a gem of purest ray serene,   53
The dark unfathom'd caves of ocean bear:
Full many a flower is born to blush unseen,
And waste its sweetness on the desert air.

Some village-Hampden, that with dauntless breast   57
The little Tyrant of his fields withstood;

27 *jocund:* cheerfully.   39 *fretted vault:* ornamental arched ceiling.   43 *provoke:* call forth.   52 *genial:* animating.   57 *Hampden:* hero of England's Civil War, on the Parliamentary side, who "withstood" the collection of unfair taxes by the "tyrant" Charles I.

Some mute inglorious Milton here may rest,
Some Cromwell guiltless of his country's blood.

Th' applause of list'ning senates to command,   61
The threats of pain and ruin to despise,
To scatter plenty o'er a smiling land,
And read their hist'ry in a nation's eyes,

Their lot forbad: nor circumscrib'd alone   65
Their growing virtues, but their crimes confin'd;
Forbad to wade through slaughter to a throne,
And shut the gates of mercy on mankind,

The struggling pangs of conscious truth to hide,   69
To quench the blushes of ingenuous shame,
Or heap the shrine of Luxury and Pride
With incense kindled at the Muse's flame.

Far from the madding crowd's ignoble strife,   73
Their sober wishes never learn'd to stray;
Along the cool sequester'd vale of life
They kept the noiseless tenor of their way.

Yet ev'n these bones from insult to protect,   77
Some frail memorial still erected nigh,
With uncouth rhimes and shapeless sculpture deck'd,
Implores the passing tribute of a sigh.

Their name, their years, spelt by th' unletter'd muse,   81
The place of fame and elegy supply:
And many a holy text around she strews,
That teach the rustic moralist to die.

For who to dumb Forgetfulness a prey,   85
This pleasing anxious being e'er resign'd,
Left the warm precincts of the chearful day,
Nor cast one longing ling'ring look behind?

On some fond breast the parting soul relies,   89
Some pious drops the closing eye requires;
Ev'n from the tomb the voice of Nature cries,
Ev'n in our Ashes live their wonted Fires.

For thee, who mindful of th' unhonour'd Dead   93
Dost in these lines their artless tale relate;

73 *madding:* mad, wild.   81 *unletter'd muse:* spirit of folk art.   84 *moralist:* moral man.   92 *wonted:* customary.   93 *thee:* the stonecutter-poet of this graveyard? the speaker of the poem? Gray himself?

If chance, by lonely contemplation led,
Some kindred Spirit shall inquire thy fate,

Haply some hoary-headed Swain may say,   97
'Oft have we seen him at the peep of dawn
'Brushing with hasty steps the dews away
'To meet the sun upon the upland lawn.

'There at the foot of yonder nodding beech   101
'That wreathes its old fantastic roots so high,
His listless length at noontide would he stretch,
'And pore upon the brook that babbles by.

'Hard by yon wood, now smiling as in scorn,   105
'Mutt'ring his wayward fancies he would rove,
'Now drooping, woeful wan, like one forlorn,
'Or craz'd with care, or cross'd in hopeless love.

'One morn I missed him on the custom'd hill,   109
'Along the heath and near his fav'rite tree;
'Another came; nor yet beside the rill,
'Nor up the lawn, nor at the wood was he;

'The next with dirges due in sad array   113
'Slow thro' the church-way path we saw him born.
'Approach and read (for thou can'st read) the lay,
'Grav'd on the stone beneath yon aged thorn.'

The Epitaph

Here rests his head upon the lap of Earth   117
A Youth to Fortune and to Fame unknown.
Fair Science frown'd not on his humble birth,
And Melancholy mark'd him for her own.

Large was his bounty, and his soul sincere,   121
Heav'n did a recompence as largely send:
He gave to Mis'ry all he had, a tear,
He gain'd from Heav'n ('twas all he wish'd) a friend.

No farther seek his merits to disclose,   125
Or draw his frailties from their dread abode
(There they alike in trembling hope repose,)
The bosom of his Father and his God.

97 *Haply:* perhaps.   97 *Swain:* rustic.   116 *thorn:* probably, hawthorn tree.
119 *Science:* knowledge.   121 *bounty:* bounteousness.

Critique

1. In the character of his Elegy I rejoice to concur with the common reader; for by the common sense of readers uncorrupted with literary prejudices, after all the refinements of subtility and the dogmatism of learning, must be finally decided all claim to poetical honours. The *Church-yard* abounds with images which find a mirrour in every mind, and with sentiments to which every bosom returns an echo. The four stanzas beginning *Yet even these bones*, are to me original: I have never seen the notions in any other place; yet he that reads them here, persuades himself that he has often felt them. . . . (SAMUEL JOHNSON)

2. . . . Gray's *Elegy*, indeed, might stand as a supreme instance to show how powerful an exquisitely adjusted tone may be. . . . Gray . . . without overstressing any point, composes a long address, perfectly accommodating his familiar feelings towards the subject and his awareness of the inevitable triteness of the only possible reflections, to the discriminating attention of his audience. And this is the source of his triumph . . . . (I. A. RICHARDS)

3. Gray's *Elegy* is an odd case of poetry with latent political ideas. . . .

What this [Stanza 14] means, as the context makes clear, is that eighteenth-century England had no scholarship system. . . . This is stated as pathetic, but the reader is put into a mood in which one would not try to alter it. . . . By comparing the social arrangement to Nature he makes it seem inevitable, which it was not, and gives it a dignity which was undeserved. Furthermore, a gem does not mind being in a cave and a flower prefers not to be picked; we feel that the man is like the flower, as short-lived, natural, and valuable, and this tricks us into feeling that he is better off without opportunities. . . . (WILLIAM EMPSON)

4. . . . Empson, in his anxiety to establish the "latent political ideas," has extended the implications a little further than the total context of the whole poem warrants. . . .

. . . The paths of glory lead but to the grave, but so does the path along which the "plowman homeward plods his weary way." The graves are different . . . . But both are graves . . . .

. . . The general commentary on death (which ends with line ninety-two) has thus brought the proud and the humble together in a common humanity. . . .

The poet, it seems to me, carries very fairly here between both groups. To press, with Empson, the poet's complacency in seeming to accept the fate of the humble is to ignore these elements in the poem. . . .

Any doubt as to this last point should be dissipated by a consideration of the resolution of the poem. For what is the *speaker's* choice? After all, if the rude Forefathers of the village could not choose, . . . *he* at least can choose. "Fair Science frown'd not on his humble birth.". . .

. . . With line ninety-three the speaker comes to apply the situation to himself. . . . He is willing to see himself as he shall be, merely one with the others in the country churchyard.

(CLEANTH BROOKS)

5. . . . Mr. Brooks says that I ignored the rest of the poem, which brings "the proud and humble together in a common humanity" . . . . If the rustics are so much better off without opportunities that the speaker will leave the wicked world to join them, surely that is very near to saying that they *ought* not to have opportunities. What is more important, the paradox in the final epitaph of the speaker: "Large was his bounty. . . . He gave to Mis'ry all he had, a tear," seems to me more disagreeable than Mr. Brooks allows. Presumably he was poor by the standard of the great world but still rich compared to the rustics. . . . The poem takes for granted that he does not have to work. No doubt he really did give them a little money. But they ought to be much more grateful because he gave them a tear; that is what counts on the epitaph; the sympathy of a gentleman is enough, and ought to make them contented. All this seems to me much worse than, not any kind of justification for, the verse about the flower born to blush unseen. . . . I am quite prepared to agree with Mr. Brooks that Gray set out to express good feeling about the matter; I only claim that he failed to. . . .

(WILLIAM EMPSON)

6. . . . The central figure in the poem, the village Stonecutter. . . .
. . . A rustic artist, who . . . composes some "uncouth rhyme" or chooses some "text" from the Bible to decorate the gravemarker. . . . But who was there among the illiterate peasantry . . . [who] would write the epitaph-writer's epitaph?

Gray assigns this role to a literate outlander, the Spokesman of the poem, the "me" of line 4. But in order to introduce the

Epitaph into the poem, a further dramatic complication had to be invented. Gray imagines that after the village Stonecutter is dead and buried, another melancholy wayfarer ("Some kindred Spirit,") will enter the churchyard seeking to learn of the Stonecutter's fate. Still another peasant ("some hoary-headed Swain,") will be able to tell the Enquirer something of the irregular life of the Stonecutter and point to the *Epitaph* written by the Spokesman and now fixed over the Stonecutter's grave. . . .

. . . The poem is not destitute of plan. . . . [An] alternation of description and reflection sets a pattern which is repeated throughout the poem and which constitutes its basic structure . . . .

The theme of these reflections may best be approached by isolating the basic contrast of the poem. This, of course, is primarily a class distinction. The ruling classes are contrasted with the rural proletariat. This contrast is developed mainly in terms of the differing burial customs of the two classes . . . . Attitudes toward the two classes are developed through the Spokesman, who . . . identifies himself with neither class. . . .

. . . His melancholy contemplation of the unrealized virtues buried in the village churchyard is balanced by his ironic recognition of the buried vices. In fact this "balance" is one of the outstanding features of the poem. . . .

. . . But this balance is easily upset, particularly when the poem is interpreted as a political tract. And it has been interpreted *both* as rightist and as leftist propaganda. Actually the poem is concerned neither with amelioration nor with acceptance of the condition of the rural worker. It is concerned with Fame . . . .

It is here that the full significance of the Stonecutter may be seen. The imagined death of the peasant-poet supplies the dramatic example which illustrates and makes cogent the large generalities of the previous argument. The case-history of the village Stonecutter should make the reader *feel* what previously the poem simply *stated*, namely, what it is to be a poet *manqué*, a "mute inglorious Milton" possessed of a "noble Rage" which is drowned in poverty, ignorance, lack of sympathy and scope. . . .

But in the *Epitaph* he achieves a measure of remembrance. . . . So far from being an extraneous tin-kettle tied to the tail of a "stately" but rather "complacent" poem, the *Epitaph* is actually the conclusion of a very tightly-organized rhetorical structure. . . .

(FRANK H. ELLIS)

BIBLIOGRAPHY

Brooks, C., *The Well Wrought Urn*, pp. 103, 104, 106-7; Ellis, F. H., *PMLA*, **66** (Dec. 1951), 992, 984-85, 998-99; Empson, W., *English Pastoral Poetry [Some Versions of Pastoral]*, 1938, p. 4; ————, *Sewanee Review*, **55** (Oct.-Dec. 1947), 692; Johnson, S., in *Lives of the Poets*, 1779-81, last paragraph on Gray; Richards, I. A., *Practical Criticism*, 1929, pp. 206-7.

Jesus and His Mother

My only son, more God's than mine,
Stay in this garden ripe with pears.
The yielding of their substance wears
A modest and contented shine: 4
And when they weep with age, not brine
But lazy syrup are their tears.
'I am my own and not my own.'

He seemed much like another man,   8
That silent foreigner who trod
Outside my door with lily rod:
How could I know what I began   11
Meeting the eyes more furious than
The eyes of Joseph, those of God?
I was my own and not my own.

And who are these twelve labouring men?   15
I do not understand your words:
I taught you speech, we named the birds,
You marked their big migrations then   18
Like any child. So turn again
To silence from the place of crowds.
'I am my own and not my own.'

Why are you sullen when I speak?   22
Here are your tools, the saw and knife
And hammer on your bench. Your life
Is measured here in week and week   25
Planed as the furniture you make,
And I will teach you like a wife
To be my own and all my own.

Who like an arrogant wind blown   29
Where he may please, needs no content?
Yet I remember how you went
To speak with scholars in furred gown.   32
I hear an outcry in the town;
Who carried that dark instrument?
'One all his own and not his own.'

Treading the green and nimble sward   36
I stare at a strange shadow thrown.
Are you the boy I bore alone,
No doctor near to cut the cord?   39
I cannot reach to call you Lord,
Answer me as my only son.
'I am my own and not my own.'

Critique

1. **haiku**   A Japanese poem in three lines, of 5, 7, and 5 syllables
respectively, which presents a clear picture so as at once to rouse
emotion and suggest a spiritual insight. The strict rules governing
the form cannot be followed in translation, especially since Japanese is unstressed. This version by Babette Deutsch of a haiku by
the sixteenth-century poet Moritake may hint at the structure:

> The falling flower
> I saw drift back to the branch
> Was a butterfly.

The poem refers to the Buddhist proverb that the fallen flower
never returns to the branch; the broken mirror never again reflects. . . . (BABETTE DEUTSCH)

2. . . . Certainly no modern poet has managed to suggest more
with so few words than did Issa (1763-1828) after the death of his
only surviving child. We may imagine that his friends attempted to
console him with the usual remarks on the evanescence of the
things of this world, and the meaninglessness of this existence as
compared to the eternal life in Buddha's Western Paradise. Issa
wrote:

Tsuyu no yo wa	The world of dew
Tsuyu no yo nagara	Is a world of dew and yet,
Sarinagara	And yet.

(DONALD KEENE)

3. ... For Bashō [seventeenth century] both change and permanence had to be present in his *haiku*. In some of his greatest poems we find these elements present . . . but also, if we may state the terms geometrically, as an expression of the point where the momentary intersects the constant and eternal. We find it, for example, in what was perhaps his most famous *haiku:*

furuike ya	The ancient pond
kawazu tobikomu	A frog leaps in
mizu no oto	The sound of the water.

In the first line, Bashō gives us the eternal component of the poem, the timeless, motionless waters of the pond. The next line gives us the momentary, personified by the movement of the frog. Their intersection is the splash of the water. Formally interpreted, the eternal component is the perception of truth, the subject of countless Japanese poems; the fresh contribution of Bashō is the use of the frog for its movement, instead of its pleasing cries, the hackneyed poetical image of his predecessors. (DONALD KEENE)

4. Here it will be considered that both estimates of Chiyo are correct: that she was a true poet, but not a haiku master. Her finest poem is probably the one she wrote after the death of her little son. A fairly literal translation is:

> The dragonfly hunter—
> today, what place has he
> got to, I wonder. . . .

This has been beautifully rendered by Curtis Hidden Page as:

> I wonder in what fields today
> He chases dragonflies in play,
> My little boy—who ran away. . . .

(HAROLD G. HENDERSON)

BIBLIOGRAPHY

Deutsch, B., *Poetry Handbook: A Dictionary of Terms*, 1957, pp. 59-60; Henderson, H. G., *An Introduction to Haiku: An Anthology of Poems and Poets from Bashō to Shiki*, 1958, p. 82; Keene, D., *Japanese Literature: An Introduction for Western Readers*, 1955, pp. 21, 39.

The Sleeping Giant

(A Hill, so Named, in Hamden, Connecticut)

The whole day long, under the walking sun
That poised an eye on me from its high floor,
Holding my toy beside the clapboard house
I looked for him, the summer I was four.

I was afraid the waking arm would break   5
From the loose earth and rub against his eyes
A fist of trees, and the whole country tremble
In the exultant labor of his rise;

Then he with giant steps in the small streets   9
Would stagger, cutting off the sky, to seize
The roofs from house and home because we had
Covered his shape with dirt and planted trees;

And then kneel down and rip with fingernails   13
A trench to pour the enemy Atlantic
Into our basin, and the water rush,
With the streets full and all the voices frantic.

That was the summer I expected him.   17
Later the high and watchful sun instead
Walked low behind the house, and school began,
And winter pulled a sheet over his head.

The Darkling Thrush

I leant upon a coppice gate
    When Frost was spectre-gray,
And Winter's dregs made desolate
    The weakening eye of day.
The tangled bine-stems scored the sky   5
    Like strings from broken lyres,
And all mankind that haunted nigh
    Had sought their household fires.

Darkling: in the dark. 1 *coppice:* thicket. 5 *bine:* climbing plant. 5 *scored:*
marked lines on. 7 *haunted:* dwelled.

The land's sharp features seemed to be   9
  The Century's corpse outleant,
His crypt the cloudy canopy,
  The wind his death-lament.
The ancient pulse of germ and birth   13
  Was shrunken hard and dry,
And every spirit upon earth
  Seemed fervourless as I.

At once a voice arose among   17
  The bleak twigs overhead
In a full-hearted evensong
  Of joy illimited;
An aged thrush, frail, gaunt and small,   21
  In blast-beruffled plume,
Had chosen thus to fling his soul
  Upon the growing gloom.

So little cause for carolings   25
  Of such ecstatic sound
Was written on terrestrial things
  Afar or nigh around,
That I could think there trembled through   29
  His happy good-night air
Some blessed Hope, whereof he knew
  And I was unaware.

December 1900

Case

A

1. The primary theme is the despair of the speaker at the end of the century.

2. Even the "joy illimited" of the thrush's song is nullified by the speaker's realization in the last stanza that such optimism is a delusion.

B

1. The primary theme is the transition from despair (Stanzas 1-2) to "blessed hope" (Stanzas 3-4).

10 *outleant:* stretched out.   20 *illimited:* unlimited.   22 *plume:* feathers.

2. The "ecstatic sound" of the thrush's song in the face of "growing gloom" is evidence to the speaker that there *is* beauty in the universe, even though he himself is ordinarily "unaware" of it.

C

1. The primary theme is a hesitant awareness of the possibility of hope in the midst of despair.

2. The poem ends not with a "moral" but with a delicately poised expression of optimism and pessimism, skepticism and belief.

The Phantom Horsewoman

I

Queer are the ways of a man I know:
    He comes and stands
    In a careworn craze,
    And looks at the sands
    And the seaward haze   5
    With moveless hands
    And face and gaze,
    Then turns to go . . .
And what does he see when he gazes so?

II

They say he sees as an instant thing   10
    More clear than to-day,
    A sweet soft scene
    That once was in play
    By that briny green;
    Yes, notes alway   15
    Warm, real, and keen,
    What his back years bring—
A phantom of his own figuring.

III

Of this vision of his they might say more: 19
    Not only there
    Does he see this sight,

But everywhere
In his brain—day, night,
As if on the air   24
It were drawn rose bright—
Yea, far from that shore
Does he carry this vision of heretofore:

IV

A ghost-girl-rider. And though, toil-tried,   28
  He withers daily,
  Time touches her not,
  But she still rides gaily
  In his rapt thought
  On that shagged and shaly   33
  Atlantic spot,
  And as when first eyed
Draws rein and sings to the swing of the tide.

In Time of "The Breaking of Nations"

I

Only a man harrowing clods
  In a slow silent walk
With an old horse that stumbles and nods
  Half asleep as they stalk.

II

Only thin smoke without flame   5
  From the heaps of couch-grass;
Yet this will go onward the same
  Though Dynasties pass.

III

Yonder a maid and her wight   9
  Come whispering by:
War's annals will fade into night
  Ere their story die.

---

33 *shaly:* rocky.

"*The Breaking of Nations*": see Jeremiah 51:20 (Robinson and Rideout).
9 *wight:* man.

The Oxen

Christmas Eve, and twelve of the clock.
   "Now they are all on their knees,"
An elder said as we sat in a flock
   By the embers in hearthside ease.

We pictured the meek mild creatures where   5
   They dwelt in their strawy pen,
Nor did it occur to one of us there
   To doubt they were kneeling then.

So fair a fancy few would weave   9
   In these years! Yet, I feel,
If someone said on Christmas Eve,
   "Come; see the oxen kneel

"In the lonely barton by yonder coomb   13
   Our childhood used to know,"
I should go with him in the gloom,
   Hoping it might be so.

Virtue

Sweet day, so cool, so calm, so bright
The bridal of the earth and sky:
The dew shall weep thy fall tonight,
      For thou must die.

Sweet rose, whose hue, angry and brave,   5
Bids the rash gazer wipe his eye:
Thy root is ever in its grave,
      And thou must die.

Sweet spring, full of sweet days and roses,   9
A box where sweets compacted lie:
My music shows ye have your closes,
      And all must die.

Only a sweet and virtuous soul,   13
Like seasoned timber, never gives;
But though the whole world turn to coal,
      Then chiefly lives.

13 *barton:* farmyard.   13 *coomb:* valley.

---

5 *brave:* splendid.   15 *coal:* cinder.

The Collar

I struck the board and cry'd, No more.
        I will abroad.
What? shall I ever sigh and pine?
My lines and life are free; free as the road,
    Loose as the wind, as large as store.   5
        Shall I be still in suit?
Have I no harvest but a thorn
To let me blood, and not restore
What I have lost with cordial fruit?
            Sure there was wine   10
Before my sighs did dry it: there was corn
        Before my tears did drown it.
    Is the year only lost to me?
        Have I no bays to crown it?
No flowers, no garlands gay? all blasted?   15
            All wasted?
    Not so, my heart: but there is fruit,
        And thou hast hands.
    Recover all thy sigh-blown age
On double pleasures: leave thy cold dispute   20
Of what is fit, and not. Forsake thy cage,
        Thy rope of sands,
Which petty thoughts have made, and made to thee
    Good cable, to enforce and draw,
            And be thy law,   25
While thou didst wink and wouldst not see.
        Away; take heed:
        I will abroad.
Call in thy death's head there: tie up thy fears.
        He that forbears   30
    To suit and serve his need
        Deserves his load.
But as I rav'd and grew more fierce and wild
        At every word,
    Me thoughts I heard one calling, *Child!*
        And I reply'd, *My Lord.*   36

5 *store:* abundance.   6 *suit:* bondage.   11 *corn:* grain.

Another Grace for a Child

Here a little child I stand,
Heaving up my either hand.
Cold as paddocks though they be,   3
Here I lift them up to Thee,
For a benison to fall
On our meat, and on us all. *Amen.*

Upon Julia's Clothes

Whenas in silks my Julia goes,
Then, then (methinks) how sweetly flows
That liquefaction of her clothes.

Next, when I cast mine eyes, and see   4
That brave vibration each way free—
O, how that glittering taketh me!

Critique

1. . . . A fresh and unaffected sensuality pervades the poem. Not only is the speaker's excitement expressed by 'then, then,' but from the flow of the clothes and their vibration the hint of the body beneath is not absent. The full emphasis and the fall of the third line express how well the spectator's excitement is satisfied by the downward flow of the silk. We may even derive from 'liquefaction' a hint of the word 'satisfaction.' 'Liquefaction' is a sophisticated word, and as such is more important than as describing a quality of silk which (incidentally) had been already indicated in the word 'flows.' More important, probably, than any of the factors noted above is the contrast on which the poem is constructed. The spectator first sees the downward flow of Julia's silks and he experiences

3 *paddocks:* frogs.

5 *brave:* splendid.

satisfaction. He then sees the silks vibrating, perhaps moving in little horizontal eddies, and he is captivated. . . .

(E. M. W. Tillyard)

2. His subject, surely, is nothing more, or less, than in stanza 1, Julia dressed; in stanza 2, Julia undressed. The word *next* must introduce a distinct change if the whole line "Next, when I cast mine eyes, and see" is not to become a waste of words intolerable in so short a poem and if all the last three lines are not to fall into flat anticlimax. The change is from Julia's motion as she walks ("goes," in seventeenth-century English) in the liquid flowing movement of silk, to the rhythmical motion back and forth, "each way free," of her unencumbered naked limbs, the contrast being marked by the symmetrical "when" formula and the triplet rhymes. . . .

I may add the unpublished suggestion of Professor Irwin Griggs that Herrick's title seems to weigh in favor of this interpretation, "because it makes the subject Julia's *clothes,* not just *silk* or how pretty she is in silk." (Elisabeth Schneider)

3. Along with her contention that Julia must discard her silks between stanzas 1 and 2 if the poet is to say "anything distinctly new" in the last tercet, Miss Schneider . . . rules out other possibilities. This is not justifiable.

Julia could well keep her silks, and yet gain variety of impression by presenting first a front view (stanza), and then a rear view (stanza 2) as she strolls by the author's vantage. In fact, the title and his emphasis on the silks in the first tercet ("then, then") indicate that Herrick's bit is a brief and simple dissertation on Julia *in* clothes (Daniels, Exp., March, 1942, i, 35), making the point that her charms are most effective when adorned in silk.

Also, we need not concede the necessity of Julia's naked flaunting of her wares in stanza 2, since we can gain both continuity and progress from stanza to stanza if we consider that Julia is engaged in a short but skilled demonstration of effective packaging, with Herrick as both observer and target of a technique that "taketh" Man (male) through the subtler magnetism of the veiled.

Silk-clad, she walks past only once. As she approaches, her façade charms "sweetly" (stanza 1) with its "liquefaction" of draped silks, mildly alerting her object (Herrick). Then, as she passes, perhaps drawing her silks a trifle snugly about her, *her* Herrick responds with a *double-take* to receive the full magic of "that brave vibration, each way free.". . . (Nat Henry)

4. Herrick's simple lyric "Upon Julia's Clothes" has evoked a variety of responses from modern readers, very few alike. Yet, for all the critical disagreement, there is unanimity in starting with an assumption that, from the poem's outset, the speaker reacts to the *sight* of Julia's bewitching clothes. . . . This assumption of a visual experience, while understandable in view of our overreliance upon this sense, is nevertheless a major cause of our difficulty with so apparently simple a poem. For, in actual fact, the speaker's first allusion to his glimpse of Julia occurs not at all in the opening stanza but in the initial line of the second. And there, by reiteration, he emphasizes it ("I cast mine eyes and see"). That he intends to suggest his first view of her at this point is evident from the syntax. For he does not begin "When next I cast mine eyes," which certainly would imply a second look and, further, would achieve an easy metrical regularity. Instead, it is "Next, when I cast mine eyes." The initial and structurally significant word, occurring outside the clause, does not modify "cast" but serves as the conjunctive pivot which turns us away from some previous experience to a succeeding visual one. Further emphasizing this turn is the slight metrical irregularity which produces a strong anticipatory stress at just this fulcrum point.

What, then, is the nature of the experience at the poem's opening? If we can escape the tyranny of sight and listen to the poem as the speaker in it listens to the sound made by his Julia's clothes, we may be able to share that experience, for it is one of imaginative hearing. As Daniels has shown . . . except for part of the second line when the speaker's quickened emotions jar the rhythm, the stanza is liltingly smooth as it records Julia's silken walk. And in these two and a half lines, the sibilants and liquid *l*'s converge in nearly every important word ("silks," "Julia," sweetly flowes," "liquefaction," "clothes") to evoke the very sound of flowing liquid the speaker imagined he was hearing. . . . (WILLIAM O. HARRIS)

BIBLIOGRAPHY

Harris, W. O., *Explicator*, **21** (Dec. 1962), 29; Henry, N., *Explicator*, **14** (Dec. 1955), 15; Schneider, E., *Explicator*, **13** (Mar. 1955), 30; Tillyard, E. M. W., *Essays and Studies by Members of the English Association*, **20** (1935), 19.

The Last Leaf

I saw him once before,
As he passed by the door,
    And again
The pavement stones resound,   4
As he totters o'er the ground
    With his cane.

They say that in his prime,   7
Ere the pruning-knife of Time
    Cut him down,
Not a better man was found   10
By the Crier on his round
    Through the town.

But now he walks the streets,   13
And he looks at all he meets
    Sad and wan,
And he shakes his feeble head,   16
That it seems as if he said,
    "They are gone."

The mossy marbles rest   19
On the lips that he has pressed
    In their bloom,
And the names he loved to hear   22
Have been carved for many a year
    On the tomb.

My grandmamma has said—   25
Poor old lady, she is dead
    Long ago—
That he had a Roman nose,   28
And his cheek was like a rose
    In the snow.

But now his nose is thin,   31
And it rests upon his chin
    Like a staff,
And a crook is in his back,   34
And a melancholy crack
    In his laugh.

I know it is a sin   37
For me to sit and grin
    At him here;
But the old three-cornered hat,   40
And the breeches, and all that,
    Are so queer!

And if I should live to be   43
The last leaf upon the tree
    In the spring,
Let them smile, as I do now,   46
At the old forsaken bough
    Where I cling.

Spring

Nothing is so beautiful as spring—
    When weeds, in wheels, shoot long and lovely and lush;
    Thrush's eggs look little low heavens, and thrush
Through the echoing timber does so rinse and wring
The ear, it strikes like lightnings to hear him sing;   5
    The glassy peartree leaves and blooms, they brush
    The descending blue; that blue is all in a rush
With richness; the racing lambs too have fair their fling.

What is all this juice and all this joy?   9
    A strain of the earth's sweet being in the beginning
In Eden garden.—Have, get, before it cloy,
    Before it cloud, Christ, lord, and sour with sinning,
Innocent mind and Mayday in girl and boy,
    Most, O maid's child, thy choice and worthy the winning. 14

Spring and Fall:

To a Young Child

Márgarét, are you grieving
Over Goldengrove unleaving?
Leáves, like the things of man, you

With your fresh thoughts care for, can you?
Áh! ás the heart grows older   5
It will come to such sights colder
By and by, nor spare a sigh
Though worlds of wanwood leafmeal lie;
And yet you wíll weep and know why.
Now no matter, child, the name: 10
Sórrow's spríngs áre the same.
Nor mouth had, no nor mind, expressed
What heart heard of, ghost guessed:
It ís the blight man was born for,
It is Margaret you mourn for.   15

Case

A

1. The primary theme is man's mortality—"the blight man was born for."

2. The speaker's questions and reflections imply that the cause of Margaret's grief is the fate that hangs over leaves, mankind, and Margaret.

3. Although the child will some day understand rationally the cause of her grief, lines 12-13 imply that the awareness of mortality can arise intuitively—as it has with her.

B

1. The primary theme is the contrast between a child's sensitivity and an adult's rationality.

2. Where Margaret is characterized by the phrases "grieving," "fresh thoughts," "care for," "sigh," "weep," "heart heard," "ghost guessed," and "mourn," the speaker characterizes himself in his use of "like the things of man," "older," "colder," "worlds of wanwood,"

8 *wanwood leafmeal:* Since the obsolete prefix "wan-" has the effect of "not" and the almost obsolete suffix "-meal" has the effect of "measured by" (cf. "piecemeal"), the phrase probably intensifies a literal meaning of "many leaves fallen from trees," leaving the wood "wan." 12-13: Neither mouth nor mind had expressed that which the heart heard and the soul guessed.

"no matter, child, the name," "Sorrow's springs," "mind," and "blight."

3. The poem skillfully manages a tone not only of melancholy but also of irony, as in the symbolic contrast of the title, the rhetorical questions of 1-4, the hyperbole of 7-8, and the paradox of the closing lines.

BIBLIOGRAPHY

Drew, E., *Poetry: A Modern Guide*, 1959, pp. 107-9; Empson, W., *Seven Types of Ambiguity*, 1930, pp. 187-88; 1947 ed., pp. 148-49; Gardner, W. H., *Gerard Manley Hopkins*, II, 1949, 309-10.

Thou Art Indeed Just, Lord, If I Contend

Justus quidem tu es, Domine, si disputem tecum: verumtamen justa loquar ad te: Quare via impiorum prosperatur? &c.

Thou art indeed just, Lord, if I contend
With thee; but, sir, so what I plead is just.
Why do sinners' ways prosper? and why must
Disappointment all I endeavour end?
    Wert thou my enemy, O thou my friend,   5
How wouldst thou worse, I wonder, than thou dost
Defeat, thwart me? Oh, the sots and thralls of lust
Do in spare hours more thrive than I that spend,
Sir, life, upon thy cause. See, banks and brakes   9
Now, leavèd how thick! lacèd they are again
With fretty chervil, look, and fresh wind shakes
Them; birds build—but not I build; no, but strain,
Time's eunuch, and not breed one work that wakes.
Mine, O thou lord of life, send my roots rain.   14

Justus . . . &c.: Vulgate version of Jeremiah 12:1, which lines 1-3 paraphrase. 7 *sots and thralls:* fools and slaves.   9 *brakes:* bushes.   11 *fretty chervil:* intertwining plant.

God's Grandeur

The world is charged with the grandeur of God.
  It will flame out, like shining from shook foil;
  It gathers to a greatness, like the ooze of oil
Crushed. Why do men then now not reck his rod?
Generations have trod, have trod, have trod;   5
  And all is seared with trade, bleared, smeared with toil;
  And wears man's smudge and shares man's smell: the soil
Is bare now, nor can foot feel, being shod.

And for all this, nature is never spent;   9
  There lives the dearest freshness deep down things;
And though the last lights off the black West went
  Oh, morning, at the brown brink eastward, springs—
Because the Holy Ghost over the bent
  World broods with warm breast and with ah! bright wings.   14

Heaven-Haven

A Nun Takes the Veil

  I have desired to go
    Where springs not fail,
To fields where flies no sharp and sided hail
  And a few lilies blow.

  And I have asked to be   5
    Where no storms come,
Where the green swell is in the havens dumb,
  And out of the swing of the sea.

Felix Randal

Felix Randal the farrier, O he is dead then? my duty all ended,
Who have watched his mould of man, big-boned and hardy-handsome

---

4 *reck:* heed.

---

4 *blow:* blossom.

---

1 *farrier:* blacksmith.

Pining, pining, till time when reason rambled in it and some
Fatal four disorders, fleshed there, all contended?

Sickness broke him. Impatient he cursed at first, but mended   5
Being anointed and all; though a heavenlier heart began some
Months earlier, since I had our sweet reprieve and ransom
Tendered to him. Ah well, God rest him all road ever he offended!

This seeing the sick endears them to us, us too it endears.   9
My tongue had taught thee comfort, touch had quenched thy tears,
Thy tears that touched my heart, child, Felix, poor Felix Randal;

How far from then forethought of, all thy more boisterous years,   12
When thou at the random grim forge, powerful amidst peers,
Didst fettle for the great grey drayhorse his bright and battering sandal!

Pied Beauty

Glory be to God for dappled things—
    For skies of couple-color as a brinded cow;
      For rose-moles all in stipple upon trout that swim;
Fresh-firecoal chestnut-falls; finches' wings;   4
    Landscape plotted and pieced—fold, fallow, and plough,
      And áll trádes, their gear and tackle and trim.

All things counter, original, spare, strange;   7
    Whatever is fickle, freckled (who knows how?)
      With swift, slow; sweet, sour; adazzle, dim;
He fathers-forth whose beauty is past change: 10
      Praise him.

6-8 *Being anointed . . . Tendered to him:* reference to last rites.   8 *rest him:*
give him rest from.   13 *random:* possibly "built with stones of irregular shapes
and sizes" (Gardner), or an obsolete usage referring to powerful force.   13
powerful amidst peers: conventional phrase in Old English poetry.   14 *fettle:*
fix.   14 *drayhorse:* cart-horse.

2 *couple:* two.   2 *brinded:* spotted.   3 *rose-moles:* red spots.   5 *fold, fallow,
and plough:* sheepfolds, unploughed fields, and ploughed fields.   6 *trim:* equip-
ment.   8 *Whatever:* object of verb "fathers-forth" (10).

The Windhover

To Christ Our Lord

I caught this morning morning's minion, king~~dom of daylight~~'s

down of daylight's dauphin, dapple-dawn-drawn Falcon, in his riding

    Of the rolling level underneath him steady air, and striding

High there, how he rung upon the rein of a wimpling wing

In his ecstasy! then off, off forth on swing,   5

    As a skate's heel sweeps smooth on a bow-bend: the hurl and gliding

    Rebuffed the big wind. My heart in hiding

Stirred for a bird,—the achieve of, the mastery of the thing!

Brute beauty and valor and act, oh, air, pride, plume, here   9

    Buckle! AND the fire that breaks from thee then, a billion

Times told lovelier, more dangerous, O my chevalier!

No wonder of it: shéer plód makes plough down sillion   12

Shine, and blue-bleak embers, ah my dear,

    Fall, gall themselves, and gash gold-vermillion.

Case

A

1. The primary theme is the powerful beauty of Christ and its effect on the poet-priest.

2. The poem equates the bird with a royal, heavenly Christ by the subtitle, by calling it "minion," "dauphin," and "chevalier" possessing "valor," "pride," and "plume," and by stressing its "mastery" of the heavens.

3. Comparing the hawk's "buckling" to Christ's existing in this world, the poet-priest concludes that even his own ephemeral work brings some beauty to the world.

4. Although the extravagance of metaphor and symbol is matched by the expansive sprung rhythm, the careful use of alliteration and assonance in every line maintains a compact whole.

Windhover: small hawk that hovers in the wind. 1 *minion:* court favorite. 2 *dauphin:* French king's eldest son. 2 *dapple:* spotted. 4 *rung:* rose in a spiral. 4 *wimpling:* rippling. 9 *plume:* plumage. 10 *Buckle:* possibly both "fasten" and "crumple" (Gardner). 11 *told:* counted. 11 *chevalier:* horseman, knight. 12 *sillion:* strip of land. 14 *gall:* crack open.

B

1. Despite the dedication, the primary theme is the beauty of a hawk as it hovers in the sky and then plunges toward the earth.

2. The octave of this Petrarchan sonnet embodies the hovering flight of the bird in the wind and the speaker's admiration for the achievement, with the sprung rhythm of 3-6 reinforcing the description.

3. The opening lines of the sestet call to mind the dive of the hawk, the fall being even lovelier than the hovering flight.

4. The last three lines of the poem provide analogies to the windhover's dive in the progress of a shining ploughshare and the fire of falling embers.

BIBLIOGRAPHY

Drew, E., *Poetry: A Modern Guide*, 1959, pp. 248-52; Empson, W., *Seven Types of Ambiguity*, 1930, pp. 284-86; 1955 ed., pp. 254-56; Friar K., and J. M. Brinnin, *Modern Poetry*, 1951, p. 504; Gardner, W. H., *Gerard Manley Hopkins*, I (1944), 180-84; Gwynn, F. L., *Modern Language Notes*, **66** (June 1951), 366-70; Lees, F. N., *Scrutiny*, 17 (Spring 1950), 32-38; Peters, W. A. M., *Gerard Manley Hopkins*, 1948, pp. 85-86; Stauffer, D. A., *The Nature of Poetry*, 1946, pp. 41-42; Woodring, C., *Western Review*, 15 (Autumn 1950), 61-64.

Loveliest of Trees

Loveliest of trees, the cherry now
Is hung with bloom along the bough,
And stands about the woodland ride
Wearing white for Eastertide.

Now, of my threescore years and ten,   5
Twenty will not come again,
And take from seventy springs a score,
It only leaves me fifty more.

And since to look at things in bloom   9
Fifty springs are little room,
About the woodlands I will go
To see the cherry hung with snow.

3 *ride:* road for riding.   5 *threescore years and ten:* allotted span of life (Psalms 90:10).

To an Athlete Dying Young

The time you won your town the race
We chaired you through the market-place;
Man and boy stood cheering by,
And home we brought you shoulder-high.

To-day, the road all runners come,   5
Shoulder-high we bring you home,
And set you at your threshold down,
Townsman of a stiller town.

Smart lad, to slip betimes away   9
From fields where glory does not stay,
And early though the laurel grows
It withers quicker than the rose.

Eyes the shady night has shut   13
Cannot see the record cut,
And silence sounds no worse than cheers
After earth has stopped the ears:

Now you will not swell the rout   17
Of lads that wore their honors out,
Runners whom renown outran
And the name died before the man.

So set, before its echoes fade,   21
The fleet foot on the sill of shade,
And hold to the low lintel up
The still-defended challenge-cup.

And round that early-laurelled head   25
Will flock to gaze the strengthless dead,
And find unwithered on its curls
The garland briefer than a girl's.

Case

A

1. The poem is primarily a personal elegy, a lament expressing
the poet's grief for the death of a young friend.

9 *betimes:* early.   22-23 *sill of shade, lintel:* doorway of death.

2. It explores the pathos inherent in the departure of the intelligent ("Smart lad," 9), young athlete, who will now never have the opportunity of repeating his victories.

3. In his grieving affection, the poet softens the unpleasantness of death by employing at least a half-dozen euphemisms for it.

B

1. The poem is primarily an impersonal elegy, an ironical comment on the benefits conferred by premature death.

2. The speaker, who may or may not have been close to the young man, embodies an ambiguous feeling of sorrow and consolation by conceiving the paradox of fortunate death.

3. This paradox is kept constantly before the reader by a number of nicely balanced contrasts: the two trips in which the athlete is brought home (described in repeated terms), the foot-race and the race of life, and the double references to "laurel," "rose," and "wither."

BIBLIOGRAPHY

Brooks, C., and R. P. Warren, *Understanding Poetry*, 1934 ed., pp. 267-69; 1950 ed., pp. 385-87, 625-27; 1960 ed., pp. 546-48; Myers, W. L., *Explicator*, **11** (Feb. 1953), 23; Nitchie, E., *Explicator*, **10** (June 1952), 57.

Terence, This Is Stupid Stuff

'Terence, this is stupid stuff:
You eat your victuals fast enough;
There can't be much amiss, 'tis clear,
To see the rate you drink your beer.
But oh, good lord, the verse you make,   5
It gives a chap the belly-ache.
The cow, the old cow, she is dead;
It sleeps well, the horned head:
We poor lads, 'tis our turn now
To hear such tunes as killed the cow.   10
Pretty friendship 'tis to rhyme

1 *this:* this poetry.   7-8: pedestrian parody of "Terence's" verse.

Your friends to death before their time
Moping melancholy mad:
Come, pipe a tune to dance to, lad.'

Why, if 'tis dancing you would be,   15
There's brisker pipes than poetry.
Say, for what were hop-yards meant,
Or why was Burton built on Trent?
Oh many a peer of England brews
Livelier liquor than the Muse,   20
And malt does more than Milton can
To justify God's ways to man.
Ale, man, ale's the stuff to drink
For fellows whom it hurts to think:
Look into the pewter pot   25
To see the world as the world's not.
And faith, 'tis pleasant till 'tis past:
The mischief is that 'twill not last.
Oh, I have been to Ludlow fair
And left my necktie God knows where,   30
And carried half-way home, or near,
Pints and quarts of Ludlow beer:
Then the world seemed none so bad,
And I myself a sterling lad;
And down in lovely muck I've lain,   35
Happy till I woke again.
Then I saw the morning sky:
Heigho, the tale was all a lie;
The world, it was the old world yet,
I was I, my things were wet,   40
And nothing now remained to do
But begin the game anew.

Therefore, since the world has still   43
Much good, but much less good than ill,
And while the sun and moon endure
Luck's a chance, but trouble's sure,
I'd face it as a wise man would,
And train for ill and not for good.   48
'Tis true, the stuff I bring for sale

17 *hop:* plant used in making beer.   18 *Burton . . . on Trent* [River]: location
of famous breweries.   22: stated aim of *Paradise Lost.*

Is not so brisk a brew as ale:
Out of a stem that scored the hand
I wrung it in a weary land.
But take it: if the smack is sour,   53
The better for the embittered hour;
It should do good to heart and head
When your soul is in my soul's stead;
And I will friend you, if I may,
In the dark and cloudy day.

There was a king reigned in the East: 59
There, when kings will sit to feast,
They get their fill before they think
With poisoned meat and poisoned drink.
He gathered all that springs to birth
From the many-venomed earth;   64
First a little, thence to more,
He sampled all her killing store;
And easy, smiling, seasoned sound,
Sate the king when healths went round.
They put arsenic in his meat   69
And stared aghast to watch him eat;
They poured strychnine in his cup
And shook to see him drink it up:
They shook, they stared as white's their shirt:
Them it was their poison hurt.   74
—I tell the tale that I heard told.
Mithridates, he died old.

Easter Hymn

If in that Syrian garden, ages slain,
You sleep, and know not you are dead in vain,
Nor even in dreams behold how dark and bright
Ascends in smoke and fire by day and night   4
The hate you died to quench and could but fan.
Sleep well and see no morning, son of man.

51 *scored:* scratched.   56 *stead:* place.

But if, the grave rent and the stone rolled by,   7
At the right hand of majesty on high
You sit, and sitting so remember yet
Your tears, your agony and bloody sweat,   10
Your cross and passion and the life you gave,
Bow hither out of heaven and see and save.

I to My Perils

I to my perils
  Of cheat and charmer
  Came clad in armour
    By stars benign.
Hope lies to mortals   5
  And most believe her,
  But man's deceiver
    Was never mine.

The thoughts of others   9
  Were light and fleeting,
  Of lovers' meeting
    Or luck or fame.
Mine were of trouble,   13
  And mine were steady,
  So I was ready
    When trouble came.

The Death of the Ball Turret Gunner

From my mother's sleep I fell into the State,
And I hunched in its belly till my wet fur froze.
Six miles from earth, loosed from its dream of life,
I woke to black flak and the nightmare fighters.
When I died they washed me out of the turret with a hose.   5

4 *flak:* anti-aircraft shell bursts.

On My First Son

Farewell, thou child of my right hand, and joy;
  My sin was too much hope of thee, lov'd boy.
Seven years tho' wert lent to me, and I thee pay,
  Exacted by thy fate, on the just day.
O, could I lose all father now. For why   5
  Will man lament the state he should envy?
To have so soon scap'd world's and flesh's rage,
  And, if no other misery, yet age?
Rest in soft peace and, ask'd, say here doth lie
  BEN JONSON his best piece of *poetry*.   10
For whose sake, hence-forth, all his vows be such,
  As what he loves may never like too much.

Her Triumph

See the chariot at hand here of love,
  Wherein my lady rideth!
Each that draws is a swan, or a dove,
  And well the car love guideth.
As she goes, all hearts do duty
      Unto her beauty;   6
And enamour'd, do wish, so they might
      But enjoy such a sight,
  That they still were to run by her side,
Through swords, through seas, whither she would ride.

Do but look on her eyes, they do light   11
  All that love's world compriseth!
Do but look on her hair, it is bright
  As love's star when it riseth!
Do but mark, her forehead's smoother
      Than words that soothe her!   16
And from her arched brows, such a grace
      Sheds itself through the face,
  As alone there triumphs to the life
All the gain, all the good, of the elements' strife.

5 *father:* fatherhood.   12 *may never:* may he never.

10 *whither:* emended from *whether* by Hebel and Hudson.

Have you seen but a bright lily grow,   21
   Before rude hands have touch'd it?
Have you mark'd but the fall of the snow
   Before the soil hath smutch'd it?
Have you felt the wool o' the beaver?
      Or swan's down ever?   26
Or have smelt o' the bud o' the brier?
      Or the nard i' the fire?
Or have tasted the bag o' the bee?
O so white! O so soft! O so sweet is she!

On First Looking into Chapman's Homer

Much have I travell'd in the realms of gold,
   And many goodly states and kingdoms seen;
   Round many western islands have I been
Which bards in fealty to Apollo hold.
Oft of one wide expanse had I been told   5
   That deep-brow'd Homer ruled as his demesne;
   Yet did I never breathe its pure serene
Till I heard Chapman speak out loud and bold:
Then felt I like some watcher of the skies   9
   When a new planet swims into his ken;
   Or like stout Cortez when with eagle eyes
He star'd at the Pacific—and all his men
Look'd at each other with a wild surmise—
   Silent, upon a peak in Darien.   14

---

28 *nard:* fragrant plant.

Chapman's Homer: George Chapman (c. 1600) translated the *Iliad* and *Odyssey*.
4 *fealty:* feudal fidelity to lord. 4 *Apollo:* as god of poetry. 6 *demesne:*
domain. 10 *ken:* sight. 14 *Darien:* Panama.

The Eve of St. Agnes

I

St. Agnes' Eve—Ah, bitter chill it was!
The owl, for all his feathers, was a-cold;
The hare limp'd trembling through the frozen grass,
And silent was the flock in woolly fold:
Numb were the Beadsman's fingers, while he told   5
His rosary, and while his frosted breath,
Like pious incense from a censer old,
Seem'd taking flight for heaven, without a death,
Past the sweet Virgin's picture, while his prayer he saith.

II

His prayer he saith, this patient, holy man;   10
Then takes his lamp, and riseth from his knees,
And back returneth, meagre, barefoot, wan,
Along the chapel aisle by slow degrees:
The sculptured dead, on each side, seem to freeze,
Emprison'd in black, purgatorial rails: 15
Knights, ladies, praying in dumb orat'ries,
He passeth by; and his weak spirit fails
To think how they may ache in icy hoods and mails.

III

Northward he turneth through a little door,   19
And scarce three steps, ere Music's golden tongue
Flatter'd to tears this aged man and poor;
But no—already had his deathbell rung;
The joys of all his life were said and sung:
His was harsh penance on St. Agnes' Eve: 24
Another way he went, and soon among
Rough ashes sat he for his soul's reprieve,
And all night kept awake, for sinners' sake to grieve.

IV

That ancient Beadsman heard the prelude soft;   28
And so it chanc'd, for many a door was wide,
From hurry to and fro. Soon, up aloft,

The Eve of St. Agnes: January 21, anniversary of the martyrdom of the Roman virgin Agnes.   5 *Beadsman:* prays for patrons.   16 *orat'ries:* chapels.

The silver, snarling trumpets 'gan to chide:
The level chambers, ready with their pride,
Were glowing to receive a thousand guests: 33
The carved angels, ever eager-ey'd,
Star'd, where upon their heads the cornice rests,
With hair blown back, and wings put cross-wise on their breasts.

V

At length burst in the argent revelry,   37
With plume, tiara, and all rich array,
Numerous as shadows haunting faerily
The brain, new stuff'd, in youth, with triumphs gay
Of old romance. These let us wish away,
And turn, sole-thoughted, to one Lady there,   42
Whose heart had brooded, all that wintry day,
On love, and wing'd St. Agnes' saintly care,
As she had heard old dames full many times declare.

VI

They told her how, upon St. Agnes' Eve,   46
Young virgins might have visions of delight,
And soft adorings from their loves receive
Upon the honey'd middle of the night,
If ceremonies due they did aright:
As, supperless to bed they must retire,   51
And couch supine their beauties, lilly white;
Nor look behind, nor sideways, but require
Of Heaven with upward eyes for all that they desire.

['Twas said her future lord would there appear,   55
Offering as sacrifice—all in the dream—
Delicious food even to her lips brought near:
Viands and wine and fruit and sugared cream,
To touch her palate with the fine extreme
Of relish; then soft music heard; and then   60
More pleasures followed in a dizzy stream
Palpable almost; then to wake again
Warm in the virgin morn, no weeping Magdalen.]

VII

Full of this whim was thoughtful Madeline: 64
The music, yearning like a god in pain,

37 *argent:* silver.   41 *romance:* tales of chivalry.   55-63: This manuscript
stanza (de Sélincourt edition, 1905) explains some of the later action.   62
Palpable: tangible.   63 *Magdalen:* penitent prostitute.

She scarcely heard; her maiden eyes divine,
Fix'd on the floor, saw many a sweeping train
Pass by—she heeded not at all: in vain
Came many a tiptoe, amorous cavalier,   69
And back retir'd; not cool'd by high disdain,
But she saw not: her heart was otherwhere:
She sighed for Agnes' dreams, the sweetest of the year.

VIII

She danc'd along with vague, regardless eyes,   73
Anxious her lips, her breathing quick and short:
The hallow'd hour was near at hand; she sighs
Amid the timbrels, and the throng'd resort
Of whisperers in anger, or in sport;
'Mid looks of love, defiance, hate, and scorn,   78
Hoodwink'd with faery fancy; all amort,
Save to St. Agnes and her lambs unshorn,
And all the bliss to be before tomorrow morn.

IX

So, purposing each moment to retire,   82
She linger'd still. Meantime, across the moors,
Had come young Porphyro, with heart on fire
For Madeline. Beside the portal doors,
Buttress'd from moonlight, stands he, and implores
All saints to give him sight of Madeline,   87
But for one moment in the tedious hours,
That he might gaze and worship all unseen;
Perchance speak, kneel, touch, kiss—in sooth such things have been.

X

He ventures in: let no buzz'd whisper tell;   91
All eyes be muffled, or a hundred swords
Will storm his heart, Love's fev'rous citadel:
For him, those chambers held barbarian hordes,
Hyena foemen, and hot-blooded lords,
Whose very dogs would execrations howl   96
Against his lineage: not one breast affords
Him any mercy, in that mansion foul,
Save one old beldame, weak in body and in soul.

76 *timbrels:* tambourines. 76 *resort:* crowd. 79 *amort:* death-like. 86 *Buttress'd:* hidden by a buttress. 99 *beldame:* old woman.

XI

Ah, happy chance! the aged creature came,   100
Shuffling along with ivory-headed wand,
To where he stood, hid from the torch's flame,
Behind a broad hall-pillar, far beyond
The sound of merriment and chorus bland:
He startled her; but soon she knew his face,   105
And grasp'd his fingers in her palsied hand,
Saying, "Mercy, Porphyro! hie thee from this place;
"They are all here tonight, the whole blood-thirsty race!

XII

_"Get hence! get hence! there's dwarfish Hildebrand;   109
"He had a fever late, and in the fit
"He cursed thee and thine, both house and land;
"Then there's that old Lord Maurice, not a whit
"More tame for his gray hairs—Alas me! flit!
"Flit like a ghost away."—"Ah, Gossip dear,   114
"We're safe enough; here in this armchair sit,
"And tell me how"—"Good Saints! not here, not here;
"Follow me, child, or else these stones will be thy bier."

XIII

He follow'd through a lowly arched way,   118
Brushing the cobwebs with his lofty plume,
And as she mutter'd "Well-a—well-a-day!"
He found him in a little moonlight room,
Pale, lattic'd, chill, and silent as a tomb.
"Now tell me where is Madeline," said he,   123
"O tell me, Angela, by the holy loom
"Which none but secret sisterhood may see,
"When they St. Agnes' wool are weaving piously."

XIV

"St. Agnes! Ah! it is St. Agnes' Eve—   127
"Yet men will murder upon holy days:
"Thou must hold water in a witch's sieve,
"And be liege-lord of all the Elves and Fays,
"To venture so: it fills me with amaze
"To see thee, Porphyro!—St. Agnes' Eve!   132

114 _Gossip:_ godmother, friend.   130 _Fays:_ fairies.

"God's help! my lady fair the conjurer plays
"This very night: good angels her deceive!
"But let me laugh awhile, I've mickle time to grieve."

XV

Feebly she laugheth in the languid moon,   136
While Porphyro upon her face doth look,
Like puzzled urchin on an aged crone
Who keepeth closed a wond'rous riddle-book,
As spectacled she sits in chimney nook.
But soon his eyes grew brilliant, when she told   141
His lady's purpose; and he scarce could brook
Tears, at the thought of those enchantments cold,
And Madeline asleep in lap of legends old.

XVI

Sudden a thought came like a full-blown rose,   145
Flushing his brow, and in his pained heart
Made purple riot; then doth he propose
A stratagem, that makes the beldame start:
"A cruel man and impious thou art:
"Sweet lady, let her pray, and sleep, and dream   150
"Alone with her good angels, far apart
"From wicked men like thee. Go, go!—I deem
"Thou canst not surely be the same that thou didst seem."

XVII

"I will not harm her, by all saints I swear,"   154
Quoth Porphyro: "O may I ne'er find grace
"When my weak voice shall whisper its last prayer,
"If one of her soft ringlets I displace,
"Or look with ruffian passion in her face;
"Good Angela, believe me by these tears,   159
"Or I will, even in a moment's space,
"Awake, with horrid shout, my foemen's ears,
"And beard them, though they be more fang'd than wolves and bears."

XVIII

"Ah! why wilt thou affright a feeble soul?   163
"A poor, weak, palsy-stricken, churchyard thing,
"Whose passing-bell may ere the midnight toll;

135 *mickle:* a great deal of.   142 *brook:* hold back.   145 *blown:* blossomed.

"Whose prayers for thee, each morn and evening,
"Were never miss'd."—Thus plaining, doth she bring
A gentler speech from burning Porphyro;   168
So woeful, and of such deep sorrowing,
That Angela gives promise she will do
Whatever he shall wish, betide her weal or woe.

XIX

Which was, to lead him, in close secrecy,   172
Even to Madeline's chamber, and there hide
Him in a closet, of such privacy
That he might see her beauty unespy'd,
And win perhaps that night a peerless bride,
While legion'd faeries pac'd the coverlet,   177
And pale enchantment held her sleepy-ey'd.
Never on such a night have lovers met,
Since Merlin paid his Demon all the monstrous debt.

XX

"It shall be as thou wishest," said the Dame: 181
"All cates and dainties shall be stored there
"Quickly on this feast-night: by the tambour frame
"Her own lute thou wilt see; no time to spare,
"For I am slow and feeble, and scarce dare
"On such a catering trust my dizzy head.   186
"Wait here, my child, with patience; kneel in prayer
"The while. Ah! thou must needs the lady wed,
"Or may I never leave my grave among the dead."

XXI

So saying, she hobbled off with busy fear.   190
The lover's endless minutes slowly pass'd;
The dame returned, and whisper'd in his ear
To follow her; with aged eyes aghast
From fright of dim espial. Safe at last,
Through many a dusky gallery, they gain   195
The maiden's chamber, silken, hush'd, and chaste;
Where Porphyro took covert, pleas'd amain.
His poor guide hurried back with agues in her brain.

171 *weal:* prosperity.   180: The magician Merlin was bewitched by his mistress Vivien, the Lady of the Lake.   182 *cates:* delicacies.   183 *tambour frame:* for embroidering.   184 *lute:* stringed instrument.   197 *amain:* exceedingly.   198 *agues:* chills and fevers.

XXII

Her falt'ring hand upon the balustrade,   199
Old Angela was feeling for the stair,
When Madeline, St. Agnes' charmed maid,
Rose, like a mission'd spirit, unaware:
With silver taper's light, and pious care,
She turn'd, and down the aged gossip led   204
To a safe level matting. Now prepare,
Young Porphyro, for gazing on that bed;
She comes, she comes again, like ring-dove fray'd and fled.

XXIII

Out went the taper as she hurried in;   208
Its little smoke, in pallid moonshine, died;
She clos'd the door, she panted, all akin
To spirits of the air, and visions wide:
No uttered syllable, or, woe betide!
But to her heart, her heart was voluble,   213
Paining with eloquence her balmy side;
As though a tongueless nightingale should swell
Her throat in vain, and die, heart-stifled, in her dell.

XXIV

A casement high and triple-arch'd there was,   217
All garlanded with carven imag'ries
Of fruits, and flowers, and bunches of knot-grass,
And diamonded with panes of quaint device,
Innumerable of stains and splendid dyes,
As are the tiger-moth's deep-damask'd wings;   222
And in the midst, 'mong thousand heraldries,
And twilight saints, and dim emblazonings,
A shielded scutcheon blush'd with blood of queens and kings.

XXV

Full on this casement shone the wintry moon,   226
And threw warm gules on Madeline's fair breast,
As down she knelt for heaven's grace and boon;
Rose-bloom fell on her hands, together prest,
And on her silver cross soft amethyst,
And on her hair a glory, like a saint: 231

207 *fray'd:* frightened.   223-25 *heraldries, emblazonings, scutcheon:* coats of
arms.   227 *gules:* red marks.   231 *glory:* halo.

She seem'd a splendid angel, newly drest,
Save wings, for heaven:—Porphyro grew faint:
She knelt, so pure a thing, so free from mortal taint.

XXVI

Anon his heart revives: her vespers done,   235
Of all its wreathed pearls her hair she frees;
Unclasps her warmed jewels one by one;
Loosens her fragrant bodice; by degrees
Her rich attire creeps rustling to her knees.
Half-hidden, like a mermaid in seaweed,   240
Pensive awhile she dreams awake, and sees,
In fancy, fair St. Agnes in her bed,
But dares not look behind, or all the charm is fled.

XXVII

Soon, trembling in her soft and chilly nest,   .   244
In sort of wakeful swoon, perplex'd she lay,
Until the poppied warmth of sleep oppress'd
Her soothed limbs, and soul fatigued away;
Flown, like a thought, until the morrow-day;
Blissfully haven'd both from joy and pain;   249
Clasp'd like a missal where swart Paynims pray;
Blinded alike from sunshine and from rain,
As though a rose should shut, and be a bud again.

XXVIII

Stol'n to this paradise, and so entranced,   253
Porphyro gaz'd upon her empty dress,
And listen'd to her breathing, if it chanced
To wake into a slumberous tenderness;
Which when he heard, that minute did he bless,
And breath'd himself: then from the closet crept,   258
Noiseless as fear in a wide wilderness,
And over the hush'd carpet, silent, stepped,
And 'tween the curtains peep'd, where, lo!—how fast she slept.

XXIX

Then by the bedside, where the faded moon   262
Made a dim, silver twilight, soft he set
A table, and, half anguish'd, threw thereon

250 *missal:* prayer-book.   250 *swart Paynims:* dark pagans.

A cloth of woven crimson, gold, and jet:—
O for some drowsy Morphean amulet!
The boisterous, midnight, festive clarion,   267
The kettle-drum, and far-heard clarionet,
Affray his ears, though but in dying tone:—
The hall door shuts again, and all the noise is gone.

XXX

And still she slept an azure-lidded sleep,   271
In blanched linen, smooth, and lavender'd,
While he from forth the closet brought a heap
Of candied apple, quince, and plum, and gourd;
With jellies soother than the creamy curd,
And lucent syrups, tinct with cinnamon;   276
Manna and dates, in argosy transferr'd
From Fez; and spiced dainties, every one,
From silken Samarcand to cedar'd Lebanon.

XXXI

These delicates he heaped with glowing hand   280
On golden dishes and in baskets bright
Of wreathed silver: sumptuous they stand
In the retired quiet of the night,
Filling the chilly room with perfume light.—
"And now, my love, my seraph fair, awake!   285
"Thou art my heaven, and I thine eremite:
"Open thine eyes, for meek St. Agnes' sake,
"Or I shall drowse beside thee, so my soul doth ache."

XXXII

Thus whispering, his warm, unnerved arm   289
Sank in her pillow. Shaded was her dream
By the dusk curtains:—'twas a midnight charm
Impossible to melt as iced stream:
The lustrous salvers in the moonlight gleam;
Broad golden fringe upon the carpet lies: 294
It seem'd he never, never could redeem
From such a steadfast spell his lady's eyes;
So mus'd awhile, entoiled in woofed phantasies.

266 *Morphean amulet:* opiate. Morpheus was god of dreams.   272 *blanched:*
whitened.   272 *lavender'd:* perfumed with lavender flowers.   276 *lucent:*
bright.   277 *Manna:* food from heaven.   286 *eremite:* religious hermit.   293
salvers: trays.   297 *woofed:* woven.

XXXIII

Awakening up, he took her hollow lute,—   298
Tumultuous,—and, in chords that tenderest be,
He play'd an ancient ditty, long since mute,
In Provence call'd, "La belle dame sans mercy,"
Close to her ear touching the melody;—
Wherewith disturb'd she utter'd a soft moan: 303
He ceas'd—she panted quick—and suddenly
Her blue affrayed eyes wide open shone:
Upon his knees he sank, pale as smooth-sculptured stone.

XXXIV

Her eyes were open, but she still beheld,   307
Now wide awake, the vision of her sleep:
There was a painful change, that nigh expell'd
The blisses of her dream so pure and deep
At which fair Madeline began to weep,
And moan forth witless words with many a sigh;   312
While still her gaze on Porphyro would keep;
Who knelt, with joined hands and piteous eye,
Fearing to move or speak, she look'd so dreamingly.

XXXV

"Ah, Porphyro!" said she, "but even now   316
"Thy voice was at sweet tremble in mine ear,
"Made tunable with every sweetest vow;
"And those sad eyes were spiritual and clear.
"How chang'd thou art; how pallid, chill, and drear!
"Give me that voice again, my Porphyro,   321
"Those looks immortal, those complainings dear!
"Oh, leave me not in this eternal woe,
"For if thou diest, my Love, I know not where to go."

XXXVI

Beyond a mortal man impassion'd far   325
At these voluptuous accents, he arose,
Ethereal, flush'd, and like a throbbing star
Seen mid the sapphire heaven's deep repose;
Into her dream he melted, as the rose
Blendeth its odor with the violet,—   330

301 *Provence:* medieval French kingdom.   301 *"La belle dame sans merci":*
"The Beautiful Merciless Lady."

Solution sweet: meantime the frost-wind blows
Like Love's alarum, pattering the sharp sleet
Against the window-panes; St. Agnes' moon hath set.

XXXVII

'Tis dark: quick pattereth the flaw-blown sleet.   334
"This is no dream, my bride, my Madeline!"
'Tis dark: the iced gusts still rave and beat.
"No dream, alas! alas! and woe is mine!
"Porphyro will leave me here to fade and pine.
"Cruel! what traitor could thee hither bring?   339
"I curse not, for my heart is lost in thine,
"Though thou forsakest a deceived thing;—
"A dove forlorn and lost with sick unpruned wing."

XXXVIII

"My Madeline! sweet dreamer! lovely bride!   343
"Say, may I be for aye thy vassal blest?
"Thy beauty's shield, heart-shap'd and vermeil dy'd?
"Ah, silver shrine, here will I take my rest
"After so many hours of toil and quest,
"A famish'd pilgrim,—sav'd by miracle.   348
"Though I have found, I will not rob thy nest
"Saving of thy sweet self; if thou think'st well
"To trust, fair Madeline, to no rude infidel.

XXXIX

"Hark! 'tis an elfin-storm from faery land.   352
"Of haggard seeming, but a boon indeed:
"Arise—arise! the morning is at hand;—
"The bloated wassaillers will never heed:
"Let us away, my love, with happy speed;
"There are no ears to hear, or eyes to see,—   357
"Drown'd all in Rhenish and the sleepy mead:
"Awake! arise! my love, and fearless be,
"For o'er the southern moors I have a home for thee."

XL

She hurried at his words, beset with fears,   361
For there were sleeping dragons all around,

334 *flaw:* gust.   345 *vermeil:* bright red.   353 *haggard:* witch-like.   353 *boon:* blessing.   358 *Rhenish, mead:* wine, liquor.

At glaring watch, perhaps, with ready spears—
Down the wide stairs a darkling way they found.
In all the house was heard no human sound.
A chain-drooped lamp was flickering by each door;   366
The arras, rich with horseman, hawk, and hound,
Flutter'd in the besieging wind's uproar;
And the long carpets rose along the gusty floor.

XLI

They glide, like phantoms, into the wide hall;   370
Like phantoms, to the iron porch they glide;
Where lay the Porter, in uneasy sprawl,
With a huge empty flaggon by his side:
The wakeful bloodhound rose, and shook his hide,
But his sagacious eye an inmate owns: 375
By one, and one, the bolts full easy slide:—
The chains lie silent on the footworn stones;—
The key turns, and the door upon its hinges groans.

XLII

And they are gone: aye, ages long ago   379
These lovers fled away into the storm.
That night the Baron dreamt of many a woe,
And all his warrior-guests, with shade and form
Of witch, and demon, and large coffin-worm,
Were long be-nightmar'd. Angela the old   384
Died palsy-twitch'd, with meagre face deform;
The Beadsman, after thousand aves told,
For aye unsought for slept among his ashes cold.

Ode to a Nightingale

My heart aches, and a drowsy numbness pains
    My sense, as though of hemlock I had drunk,
Or emptied some dull opiate to the drains
    One minute past, and Lethe-wards had sunk:

367 *arras:* tapestry.   375 *owns:* recognizes.   386 *aves:* Hail Marys.

2 *hemlock:* sedative herb.   4 *Lethe:* river of forgetfulness in Hades.

'Tis not through envy of thy happy lot,
 But being too happy in thine happiness,—   6
  That thou, light winged Dryad of the trees,
   In some melodious plot
  Of beechen green, and shadows numberless,
  Singest of summer in full-throated ease.

O, for a draught of vintage! that had been   11
 Cooled a long age in the deep-delved earth,
Tasting of Flora and the country green,
 Dance, and Provençal song, and sunburnt mirth!
O for a beaker full of the warm South,
 Full of the true, the blushful Hippocrene,   16
  With beaded bubbles winking at the brim,
   And purple-stained mouth;
  That I might drink, and leave the world unseen,
  And with thee fade away into the forest dim:

Fade far away, dissolve, and quite forget   21
 What thou among the leaves hast never known,
The weariness, the fever, and the fret
 Here, where men sit and hear each other groan;
Where palsy shakes a few, sad, last gray hairs,
 Where youth grows pale, and spectre-thin, and dies; 26
  Where but to think is to be full of sorrow
   And leaden-eyed despairs,
  Where Beauty cannot keep her lustrous eyes,
  Or new Love pine at them beyond to-morrow.

Away! away! for I will fly to thee,   31
 Not charioted by Bacchus and his pards,
But on the viewless wings of Poesy,
 Though the dull brain perplexes and retards:
Already with thee! tender is the night,
 And haply the Queen-Moon is on her throne,   36
  Clustered around by all her starry Fays;
   But here there is no light,
Save what from heaven is with the breezes blown
 Through verdurous glooms and winding mossy ways.

I cannot see what flowers are at my feet,   41
 Nor what soft incense hangs upon the boughs,

7 *Dryad:* tree-nymph. 13 *Flora:* goddess of flowers. 14 *Provençal song:*
Provence, in southern France, home of medieval troubadours. 16 *Hippocrene:*
fountain of the Muses. 32 *Bacchus and his pards:* The god of wine had a
chariot drawn by leopards. 36 *haply:* perhaps.

But, in embalmed darkness, guess each sweet
   Wherewith the seasonable month endows
The grass, the thicket, and the fruit-tree wild;
   White hawthorn, and the pastoral eglantine;   46
      Fast fading violets covered up in leaves;
         And mid-May's eldest child,
   The coming musk-rose, full of dewy wine,
      The murmurous haunt of flies on summer eves.

Darkling I listen; and, for many a time   51
   I have been half in love with easeful Death,
Called him soft names in many a mused rhyme,
   To take into the air my quiet breath;
Now more than ever seems it rich to die,
   To cease upon the midnight with no pain,   56
      While thou art pouring forth thy soul abroad
         In such an ecstasy!
   Still wouldst thou sing, and I have ears in vain—
      To thy high requiem become a sod.

Thou wast not born for death, immortal Bird!   61
   No hungry generations tread thee down;
The voice I hear this passing night was heard
   In ancient days by emperor and clown:
Perhaps the self-same song that found a path
   Through the sad heart of Ruth, when, sick for home,   66
      She stood in tears amid the alien corn;
         The same that oft-times hath
   Charm'd magic casements, opening on the foam
      Of perilous seas, in faery lands forlorn.

Forlorn! the very word is like a bell   71
   To toll me back from thee to my sole self!
Adieu! the fancy cannot cheat so well
   As she is fam'd to do, deceiving elf.
Adieu! adieu! thy plaintive anthem fades
   Past the near meadows, over the still stream,   76
      Up the hill-side; and now 'tis buried deep
         In the next valley-glades:
   Was it a vision, or a waking dream?
      Fled is that music:—Do I wake or sleep?

43 *embalmed:* fragrant. 46 *pastoral eglantine:* country honeysuckle. 64
clown: rustic. 66 *Ruth:* heroine of the Old Testament Book of Ruth. After her
husband's death, she went to his mother's land and worked in the fields. 67
corn: grain. 73 *fancy:* inventive faculty.

Case

A

1. The primary theme is the immortality of beauty created by the nightingale's song.

2. Hearing but not seeing the bird gives it a disembodied, spiritual quality, and the variety of occasions when others have heard it (Stanza 7) emphasizes its agelessness.

3. Although neither wine, poetry, nor death can join the mortal man to the "immortal Bird," the poem's speaker has still been in contact with eternal beauty.

B

1. The primary theme is the fleeting and deceptive quality of the esthetic experience.

2. The poet's response to the nightingale's song involves successive consideration of "drowsy numbness" (Stanza 1), intoxication (Stanza 2), olfactory stimulation (Stanza 5), the death-wish (Stanza 6), and fantasy (Stanza 7).

3. As a member of the real world, "Where Beauty cannot keep her lustrous eyes," the poet ends by berating his "fancy" as a "deceiving elf" and doubting the transitory "vision" of the nightingale as merely a "waking dream."

C

1. The primary theme is the unity of opposing forces and feelings in the experience of beauty.

2. The poet's response involves such dual reactions as feeling both heartache and happiness, appealing to both real wine and the "viewless wings of poesy," and finding the song both ecstatic and "plaintive."

3. Although the poem sets the bird transcendently above man—in the trees, in the bright night above the darkness, and in immortality—the imagery throughout actually emphasizes humanity in all its sensuousness and mortality.

BIBLIOGRAPHY

Adams, R. M., *Strains of Discord,* 1958, pp. 65-68; Blair, W., and W. K. Chandler, *Approaches to Poetry,* 1936, pp. 552-56; Brooks, C., *Modern Poetry and the Tradition,* 1939, p. 31; ———, and R. P. Warren, *Under-*

standing Poetry, 1950 ed., pp. 338-45; 1960 ed., pp. 426-31; Bush, D., *Mythology and the Romantic Tradition,* 1937, pp. 107-8; Daniels, E., *The Art of Reading Poetry,* 1941, pp. 368-72; Fogle, R. H., *The Imagery of Shelley and Keats,* 1949, pp. 119-22; ———, *Modern Language Quarterly,* **8** (Mar. 1947), 81-84; ———, *PMLA,* **68** (Mar. 1953), 211-22; Ford, N. F., *Studies in Philology,* **45** (July 1948), 489-90; Knight, G. W., *The Starlit Dome,* 1941, pp. 298-300; Leavis, F. L., *Revaluation,* 1936, 1947, pp. 244-52; McLuhan, H. M., *University of Toronto Quarterly,* **12** (Jan. 1943), 167-79; Pettet, E. C., *On the Poetry of Keats,* 1957, pp. 251-81; Pitcher, S. M., *Explicator,* **3** (Mar. 1945), 39; Rosenthal, M. L., and A. J. M. Smith, *Exploring Poetry,* 1955, pp. 505-7; Sypher, W., *Virginia Quarterly Review,* **25** (Summer 1949), 425; Wasserman, E. R., *The Finer Tone,* 1953, pp. 178-223.

Ode on a Grecian Urn

Thou still unravish'd bride of quietness,
    Thou foster-child of silence and slow time,
Sylvan historian, who canst thus express
    A flowery tale more sweetly than our rhyme:
What leaf-fring'd legend haunts about thy shape
    Of deities or mortals, or of both,   6
        In Tempe or the dales of Arcady?
What men or gods are these? What maidens loth?
    What mad pursuit? What struggle to escape?
        What pipes and timbrels? What wild ecstasy?

Heard melodies are sweet, but those unheard   11
    Are sweeter; therefore, ye soft pipes, play on;
Not to the sensual ear, but, more endear'd,
    Pipe to the spirit ditties of no tone:
Fair youth, beneath the trees, thou canst not leave
    Thy song, nor ever can those trees be bare;   16
        Bold Lover, never, never canst thou kiss,
Though winning near the goal—yet, do not grieve;
    She cannot fade, though thou hast not thy bliss,
        For ever wilt thou love, and she be fair!

Ah, happy, happy boughs! that cannot shed   21
    Your leaves, nor ever bid the Spring adieu:

3 *Sylvan:* of the forest.   7 *Tempe, Arcady:* pleasant places in Greece.   10 *timbrels:* tambourines.

And, happy melodist, unwearied,
  For ever piping songs for ever new;
More happy love! more happy, happy love!
    For ever warm and still to be enjoyed,   26
      For ever panting, and for ever young;
All breathing human passion far above,
  That leaves a heart high-sorrowful and cloy'd,
    A burning forehead, and a parching tongue.

Who are these coming to the sacrifice?   31
  To what green altar, O mysterious priest,
Lead'st thou that heifer lowing at the skies,
  And all her silken flanks with garlands dressed?
What little town by river or sea shore,
    Or mountain-built with peaceful citadel,   36
      Is emptied of this folk, this pious morn?
And, little town, thy streets for evermore
  Will silent be; and not a soul to tell
    Why thou art desolate, can e'er return.

O Attic shape! Fair attitude! with brede   41
  Of marble men and maidens overwrought,
With forest branches and the trodden weed;
  Thou, silent form, dost tease us out of thought
As doth eternity: Cold Pastoral!
    When old age shall this generation waste,   46
      Thou shalt remain, in midst of other woe
Than ours, a friend to man, to whom thou sayst,
  "Beauty is truth, truth beauty,"—that is all
    Ye know on earth, and all ye need to know.

---

41 *brede:* embroidery.   42 *overwrought:* decorated.   49-50: The identity of speaker and audience in these lines is a crucial critical question bearing on the whole poem. According to R. M. Adams, "A textual confusion may throw a bit of light here. The four extant transcripts of Keats's lost manuscript agree in placing only a comma and dash in the penultimate line,

    Beauty is truth, truth beauty,—that is all. . . .

But the magazine text of January 1820 alters the comma to a period, and the text published in volume form (June 1820) adds inverted commas around 'Beauty is truth, truth beauty.' Keats's tendency is thus to separate by increasingly high barriers the urn's motto from the last line and a half of the poem" (*Strains of Discord,* 1958, p. 70: second sentence revised by Adams for this note).

Case

A

1. The primary theme of the ode is that "Beauty is truth, truth beauty"—that is, the beauty of enduring works of art like the urn constitutes truth.

2. The lasting beauty of the idealized human figures carved on the urn is contrasted with the effects of ephemeral "human passion" (28).

3. Addressing mankind in general, the urn speaks the last two lines of the poem.

B

1. The primary theme of the poem is that "Beauty is truth, truth beauty"—that is, the creative imagination is the best means for apprehending essential truth.

2. Although a concrete artifact is the overt subject of the ode, the abstract imagination is the actual requisite for hearing the "unheard melodies," for fulfilling the lover's attempt to kiss, for re-creating the ceremony and the town, and for appreciating the transcendent meaning that "dost tease us out of [rational] thought."

3. After quoting the urn's message (49), the poet emphasizes the importance of the message to the reader (49-50).

C

1. The primary theme of the poem is that "Beauty is truth, truth beauty" is a limited view of the nature of human existence.

2. Throughout the ode "on" (not "to") the ancient work of art, there is an undercurrent of awareness that a great gulf exists between such suspended animation and the moving realities of human life, full of "woe" (47) though these realities may be.

3. For this reason, the poem's speaker finally rebukes the figures on the urn (49-50), after quoting their composite message to "man" (48-49).

BIBLIOGRAPHY

Abrams, M. H., *University of Toronto Quarterly,* **27** (Jan. 1958), 124-27; Adams, R. M., *Strains of Discord,* 1958, pp. 68-71; Basler, R. P., *Explicator,* **4** (Oct. 1945), 6; Bateson, F. W., *English Poetry,* 1950, pp. 217-22; Berkelman, R., *South Atlantic Quarterly,* **57** (Summer 1958), 354-58;

Bloom, H., *The Visionary Company*, 1961, pp. 406-10; Bowra, C. M., *The Romantic Imagination*, 1949, pp. 126-48; Brooks, C., *The Well Wrought Urn*, 1947, pp. 139-52; Hamm, V. W., *Explicator*, 3 (May 1945), 56; Havens, R. D., *Modern Philology*, 24 (Nov. 1926), 209-14; Murry, J. M., *Keats*, 1930, 1962, pp. 210-26; Patterson, C. I., *ELH*, 21 (Sept. 1954), 208-20; Perkins, D., *The Quest for Permanence*, 1959, pp. 233-42; Pettet, E. C., *On the Poetry of Keats*, 1957, pp. 316-47; Pettigrew, R. C., *Explicator*, 5 (Nov. 1946), 13; Shipman, M. E., *PMLA*, 44 (Sept. 1929), 929-34; Snow, R., *PMLA*, 43 (Dec. 1928), 1142-49; Stallman, R. W., *University of Toronto Quarterly*, 16 (Jan. 1947), 155-56; Whitley, A., *Keats-Shelley Memorial Bulletin*, 5 (1953), 1-3; Wigod, J. D., *PMLA*, 72 (Mar. 1957), 113-21; Wilcox, S. C., *Explicator*, 7 (Apr. 1949), 47; ———, *Personalist*, 31 (Spring 1950), 149-56.

Ode to Psyche

O Goddess! hear these tuneless numbers, wrung
    By sweet enforcement and remembrance dear,
And pardon that thy secrets should be sung
    Even into thine own soft-conched ear:
Surely I dreamt today, or did I see   5
    The winged Psyche with awaken'd eyes?
I wander'd in a forest thoughtlessly,
    And, on the sudden, fainting with surprise,
Saw two fair creatures, couched side by side
    In deepest grass, beneath the whisp'ring roof   10
Of leaves and trembled blossoms, where there ran
    A brooklet, scarce espied:

Mid hush'd, cool-rooted flowers, fragrant-eyed,
    Blue, silver-white, and budded Tyrian,
They lay calm-breathing on the bedded grass;   15
    Their arms embraced, and their pinions too;
    Their lips touch'd not, but had not bade adieu,
As if disjoined by soft-handed slumber,
And ready still past kisses to outnumber
    At tender eye-dawn of aurorean love: 20
        The winged boy I knew;

Psyche: a princess, whose name means "soul." Cupid fell in love with her, and after much tribulation, she became immortal like him.   1 *numbers:* metrical lines.   14 *Tyrian:* purple.

But who wast thou, O happy, happy dove?
     His Psyche true!

O latest born and loveliest vision far   24
     Of all Olympus' faded hierarchy!
Fairer than Phœbe's sapphire-region'd star,
     Or Vesper, amorous glow-worm of the sky;
Fairer than these, though temple thou hast none,
     Nor altar heap'd with flowers;   29
Nor virgin-choir to make delicious moan
     Upon the midnight hours;
No voice, no lute, no pipe, no incense sweet
     From chain-swung censer teeming;
No shrine, no grove, no oracle, no heat   34
     Of pale-mouth'd prophet dreaming.

O brightest! though too late for antique vows,   36
     Too, too late for the fond believing lyre,
When holy were the haunted forest boughs,
     Holy the air, the water, and the fire;
Yet even in these days so far retir'd
     From happy pieties, thy lucent fans,   41
     Fluttering among the faint Olympians,
I see, and sing, by my own eyes inspired.
So let me be thy choir, and make a moan
     Upon the midnight hours;
Thy voice, thy lute, thy pipe, thy incense sweet   46
     From swinged censer teeming;
Thy shrine, thy grove, thy oracle, thy heat
     Of pale-mouth'd prophet dreaming.

Yes, I will be thy priest, and build a fane   50
     In some untrodden region of my mind,
Where branched thoughts, new grown with pleasant pain
     Instead of pines shall murmur in the wind:
Far, far around shall those dark-cluster'd trees
     Fledge the wild-ridged mountains steep by steep;   55
And there by zephyrs, streams, and birds, and bees,
     The moss-lain Dryads shall be lull'd to sleep;
And in the midst of this wide quietness
A rosy sanctuary will I dress

---

24 *latest born:* The myth of Cupid and Psyche appears in *The Golden Ass* of
Apuleius (A.D. second century). 26 *Phœbe's . . . star:* Diana's, i.e., the moon.
27 *Vesper:* the evening-star, Venus. 32 *lute:* mandolin-like instrument. 41
lucent fans: bright wings. 50 *fane:* temple. 55 *Fledge:* cover with feathers.
57 *Dryads:* Greek tree-nymphs.

With the wreath'd trellis of a working brain,   60
    With buds, and bells, and stars without a name,
With all the gardener Fancy e'er could feign,
    Who breeding flowers, will never breed the same:
And there shall be for thee all soft delight
    That shadowy thought can win,   65
A bright torch, and a casement ope at night,
    To let the warm Love in!

To Autumn

Season of mists and mellow fruitfulness,
    Close bosom-friend of the maturing sun:
Conspiring with him how to load and bless
    With fruit the vines that round the thatch-eves run;
To bend with apples the moss'd cottage-trees,
    And fill all fruit with ripeness to the core;   6
        To swell the gourd, and plump the hazel shells
With a sweet kernel; to set budding more,
    And still more, later flowers for the bees,
    Until they think warm days will never cease,
        For Summer has o'er-brimm'd their clammy cells.

Who hath not seen thee oft amid thy store?   12
    Sometimes whoever seeks abroad may find
Thee sitting careless on a granary floor,
    Thy hair soft-lifted by the winnowing wind;
Or on a half-reap'd furrow sound asleep,
    Drows'd with the fume of poppies, while thy hook   17
        Spares the next swath and all its twined flowers:
And sometimes like a gleaner thou dost keep
    Steady thy laden head across a brook;
    Or by a cyder-press, with patient look,
        Thou watchest the last oozings hours by hours.

Where are the songs of Spring? Ay, where are they?   23
    Think not of them, thou hast thy music too,—

62 *Fancy:* inventive faculty.   62 *feign:* produce.   66-67: In Apuleius'
story, Cupid ("Love") at first visited Psyche incognito at night.

17 *hook:* sickle.

While barred clouds bloom the soft-dying day,
  And touch the stubble-plains with rosy hue;
Then in a wailful choir the small gnats mourn
  Among the river sallows, borne aloft   28
    Or sinking as the light wind lives or dies;
And full-grown lambs loud bleat from hilly bourn;
  Hedge-crickets sing; and now with treble soft
  The red-breast whistles from a garden-croft;
    And gathering swallows twitter in the skies.

Case

A

1. The poem is a carefully constructed evocation of autumnal feeling.

2. The structure rests partially on the self-containment of the stanzas, each of which embodies a different aspect of Autumn: The first stanza is concerned with autumnal ripeness, the second with autumnal drowsiness, and the third with autumnal music.

3. The structure rests partially on the personification of Autumn as a woman, a fruitful female who in Stanza 1 "conspires" with the male sun to produce abundant offspring, and who is described as a woman in Stanza 2.

4. The structure is completed in the last stanza by the imagery of the "dying day," the fields of "stubble," the lambs that are now "full-grown," and the swallows possibly "gathering" to migrate south.

B

1. Careful analysis discloses weaknesses that spoil the effect of the whole.

2. The imagery directed primarily to the eye in Stanzas 1 and 2 is suddenly shifted in Stanza 3 to imagery that somewhat noisily commands the ear.

3. The gap between Stanzas 1-2 and 3 is widened by the inexplicable abandonment of the female personification—who has never actually been identified as feminine.

28 *sallows:* willow-trees.   30 *bourn:* region.   32 *croft:* area.

4. Finally, the poem has the major flaw of inconclusiveness: Instead of coming to a satisfactory resolution of Autumn's difference from Spring and Summer, it just stops, leaving one with the feeling that the poet could have added or subtracted a stanza without making much difference.

BIBLIOGRAPHY

Brower, R. R., *The Fields of Light*, 1951, pp. 38-41; Frost, R., quoted by R. L. Cook in *College English*, **17** (May 1956), 437-38; Knight, G. W., *The Starlit Dome*, 1941, pp. 300-1; Unger, L., *Western Review*, **14** (Summer 1950), ———, and W. V. O'Connor, *Poems for Study*, 1953, pp. 454-56.

Ode on Melancholy

No, no, go not to Lethe, neither twist
    Wolf's-bane, tight-rooted, for its poisonous wine;
Nor suffer thy pale forehead to be kiss'd
    By nightshade, ruby grape of Proserpine;
Make not your rosary of yew-berries,
    Nor let the beetle, nor the death-moth be   6
      Your mournful Psyche, nor the downy owl
A partner in your sorrow's mysteries;
    For shade to shade will come too drowsily,
      And drown the wakeful anguish of the soul.

But when the melancholy fit shall fall   11
    Sudden from heaven like a weeping cloud,
That fosters the droop-headed flowers all,
    And hides the green hill in an April shroud;
Then glut thy sorrow on a morning rose,
    Or on the rainbow of the salt sand-wave,   16
      Or on the wealth of globed peonies;
Or if thy mistress some rich anger shows,
    Emprison her soft hand, and let her rave,
      And feed deep, deep upon her peerless eyes.

1 *Lethe:* river of forgetfulness in Hades. 4 *Proserpine:* queen of Hades. 5 *yew:* tree associated with mourning. 7 *Psyche:* goddess, beloved by Cupid; the soul, often symbolized by a butterfly. 8 *mysteries:* religious rites. 9 *shade:* inhabitant of Hades. 11 *fit:* mood.

She dwells with Beauty—Beauty that must die;   21
And Joy, whose hand is ever at his lips
Bidding adieu; and aching Pleasure nigh,
    Turning to Poison while the bee-mouth sips:
Ay, in the very temple of Delight
    Veil'd Melancholy has her sovran shrine,   26
        Though seen of none save him whose strenuous tongue
    Can burst Joy's grape against his palate fine;
His soul shall taste the sadness of her might,
    And be among her cloudy trophies hung.

Little Elegy

for a child who skipped rope

Here lies resting, out of breath,
Out of turns, Elizabeth
Whose quicksilver toes not quite
Cleared the whirring edge of night.

Earth whose circles round us skim   5
Till they catch the lightest limb,
Shelter now Elizabeth
And for her sake trip up Death.

The Exequy

Accept, thou shrine of my dead saint,
Instead of dirges, this complaint;
And for sweet flowers to crown thy hearse,
Receive a strew of weeping verse   4
From thy griev'd friend, whom thou might'st see
Quite melted into tears for thee.

    Dear loss! since thy untimely fate   7
My task hath been to meditate

Exequy: funeral.

On thee, on thee; thou art the book,
The library whereon I look,
Though almost blind. For thee, lov'd clay,
I languish out, not live, the day,   12
Using no other exercise
But what I practise with mine eyes;
By which wet glasses I find out
How lazily time creeps about
To one that mourns: this, only this,   17
My exercise and bus'ness is.
So I compute the weary hours
With sighs dissolved into showers.

   Nor wonder if my time go thus   21
Backward and most preposterous;
Thou hast benighted me; thy set
This eve of blackness did beget,
Who was't my day (though overcast
Before thou had'st thy noon-tide passed);   26
And I remember must in tears,
Thou scarce had'st seen so many years
As day tells hours. By the clear sun
My love and fortune first did run;
But thou wilt never more appear   31
Folded within my hemisphere,
Since both thy light and motion
Like a fled star is fall'n and gone,
And twixt me and my soul's dear wish
An earth now interposed is,   36
Which such a strange eclipse doth make
As ne'er was read in almanac.

   I could allow thee for a time   39
To darken me and my sad clime;
Were it a month, a year, or ten,
I would thy exile live till then,
And all that space my mirth adjourn,
So thou wouldst promise to return,   44
And putting off thy ashy shroud,
At length disperse this sorrow's cloud.

   But woe is me! the longest date   47
Too narrow is to calculate

29 *tells:* counts.

These empty hopes; never shall I
Be so much blest as to descry
A glimpse of thee, till that day come   51
Which shall the earth to cinders doom,
And a fierce fever must calcine
The body of this world like thine,
My little world! That fit of fire
Once off, our bodies shall aspire   56
To our souls' bliss: then we shall rise
And view ourselves with clearer eyes
In that calm region, where no night
Can hide us from each other's sight.

Meantime, thou hast her, earth; much good   61
May my harm do thee. Since it stood
With heaven's will I might not call
Her longer mine, I give thee all
My short-liv'd right and interest
In her whom living I loved best;   66
With a most free and bounteous grief,
I give thee what I could not keep.
Be kind to her, and prithee look
Thou write into thy Dooms-day book
Each parcel of this rarity   71
Which in thy casket shrin'd doth lie.
See that thou make thy reck'ning straight,
And yield her back again by weight;
For thou must audit on thy trust
Each grain and atom of this dust,   76
As thou wilt answer Him that lent,
Not gave thee, my dear monument.

So close the ground, and 'bout her shade   79
Black curtains draw, my bride is laid.

Sleep on, my love, in thy cold bed,   81
Never to be disquieted!
My last good-night! Thou wilt not wake
Till I thy fate shall overtake;
Till age, or grief, or sickness must

---

51 *that day:* Judgment Day, the Day of Doom.   53 *calcine:* burn up.   69
prithee: I pray thee.   70 *Dooms-day book:* records for Judgment Day.

Marry my body to that dust   86
It so much loves, and fill the room
My heart keeps empty in thy tomb.
Stay for me there; I will not fail
To meet thee in that hollow vale.
And think not much of my delay;   91
I am already on the way,
And follow thee with all the speed
Desire can make, or sorrows breed.
Each minute is a short degree,
And ev'ry hour a step towards thee.   96
At night when I betake to rest,
Next morn I rise nearer my west
Of life, almost by eight hours' sail,
Than when sleep breath'd his drowsy gale.

   Thus from the sun my bottom steers,   101
And my day's compass downward bears:
Nor labor I to stem the tide
Through which to thee I swiftly glide.

   'Tis true, with shame and grief I yield, 105
Thou like the van first took'st the field,
And gotten hath the victory
In thus adventuring to die
Before me, whose more years might crave
A just precedence in the grave.   110
But hark! my pulse like a soft drum
Beats my approach, tells thee I come;
And slow howe'er my marches be,
I shall at last sit down by thee.

   The thought of this bids me go on,   115
And wait my dissolution
With hope and comfort. Dear (forgive
The crime), I am content to live
Divided, with but half a heart,
Till we shall meet and never part.   120

101 *bottom:* ship.   106 *van:* vanguard, front lines.

Psalm 137

By the rivers of Babylon, there we sat down, yea, we wept, when we
remembered Zion.
We hanged our harps upon the willows in the midst thereof.
For they that carried us away captive required of us a song; and they
that wasted us required of us mirth, saying, Sing us one of the
songs of Zion.
How shall we sing the Lord's song in a strange land?
If I forget thee, O Jerusalem, let my right hand forget her cunning.   5
If I do not remember thee, let my tongue cleave to the roof of my
mouth, if I prefer not Jerusalm above my chief joy.
Remember, O Lord, the children of Edom in the day of Jerusalem,
who said, Raze it, raze it, even to the foundation thereof.
O daughter of Babylon, who art to be destroyed, happy shall he be
that rewardeth thee as thou hast served us.
Happy shall he be that taketh and dasheth thy little ones against the
stones.   9

Danny Deever

"What are the bugles blowin' for?" said Files-on-Parade.
"To turn you out, to turn you out," the Colour-Sergeant said.
"What makes you look so white, so white?" said Files-on-Parade.
"I'm dreadin' what I've got to watch," the Colour-Sergeant said.
  For they're hangin' Danny Deever, you can hear the Dead March
      play,   5
  The Regiment's in 'ollow square—they're hangin' him to-day;
  They've taken of his buttons off an' cut his stripes away,
  An' they're hangin' Danny Deever in the mornin'.

"What makes the rear-rank breathe so 'ard?" said Files-on-Parade.   9
"It's bitter cold, it's bitter cold," the Colour-Sergeant said.
"What makes that front-rank man fall down?" says Files-on-Parade.
"A touch o' sun, a touch o' sun," the Colour-Sergeant said.
  They are hangin' Danny Deever, they are marchin' of 'im round.   13

1 *Babylon:* where the Jews were in captivity; *Zion:* hill of the Temple in
Jerusalem.   8 *daughter of Babylon:* i.e., the city.

1 *Files-on-Parade:* noncommissioned officer charged with closing up files in
military formation.

They 'ave 'alted Danny Deever by 'is coffin on the ground;
An' 'e'll swing in 'arf a minute for a sneakin' shootin' hound—
O they're hangin' Danny Deever in the mornin'!

"'Is cot was right-'and cot to mine," said Files-on-Parade.   17
"'E's sleepin' out an' far to-night,' the Colour-Sergeant said.
"I've drunk 'is beer a score o' times," said Files-on-Parade.
"'E's drinkin' bitter beer alone," the Colour-Sergeant said.
   They are hangin' Danny Deever, you must mark 'im to 'is place,   21
   For 'e shot a comrade sleepin'—you must look 'im in the face;
   Nine 'undred of 'is county an' the Regiment's disgrace,
   While they're hangin' Danny Deever in the mornin'.

"What's that so black agin the sun?" said Files-on-Parade.   25
"It's Danny fightin' 'ard for life," the Colour-Sergeant said.
"What's that that whimpers over'ead?" said Files-on-Parade.
"It's Danny's soul that's passin' now," the Colour-Sergeant said.
   For they're done with Danny Deever, you can 'ear the quickstep
      play,   29
   The Regiment's in column, an' they're marchin' us away;
   Ho! the young recruits are shakin', an' they'll want their beer today,
   After hangin' Denny Deever in the mornin'!

The Jacob's Ladder

The stairway is not
a thing of gleaming strands
a radiant evanescence
for angels' feet that only glance in their tread, and need not
touch the stone.

It is of stone.   6
A rosy stone that takes
a glowing tone of softness
only because behind it the sky is a doubtful, a doubting
night gray.

A stairway of sharp   11
angles, solidly built.
One sees that the angels must spring

Jacob's Ladder: see Genesis 28:12.

down from one step to the next, giving a little
lift of the wings:

and a man climbing   16
must scrape his knees, and bring
the grip of his hands into play. The cut stone
consoles his groping feet. Wings brush past him.
The poem ascends.

Paul Revere's Ride

Listen, my children, and you shall hear
Of the midnight ride of Paul Revere,
On the eighteenth of April, in Seventy-five;
Hardly a man is now alive
Who remembers that famous day and year.

He said to his friend, "If the British march   6
By land or sea from the town tonight,
Hang a lantern aloft in the belfry arch
Of the North Church tower as a signal light,—
One, if by land, and two, if by sea;
And I on the opposite shore will be,   11
Ready to ride and spread the alarm
Through every Middlesex village and farm,
For the country folk to be up and to arm."
Then he said, "Good night!" and with muffled oar   15
Silently rowed to the Charlestown shore,
Just as the moon rose over the bay,
Where swinging wide at her moorings lay
The Somerset, British man-of-war;
A phantom ship, with each mast and spar   20
Across the moon like a prison bar,
And a huge black hulk, that was magnified
By its own reflection in the tide.

Meanwhile, his friend, through alley and street,   24
Wanders and watches with eager ears,
Till in the silence around him he hears
The muster of men at the barrack door,
The sound of arms, and the tramp of feet,

And the measured tread of the grenadiers,   29
Marching down to their boats on the shore.

Then he climbed the tower of the Old North Church,   31
By the wooden stairs, with stealthy tread,
To the belfry-chamber overhead,
And startled the pigeons from their perch
On the sombre rafters, that round him made
Masses and moving shapes of shade,—   36
By the trembling ladder, steep and tall,
To the highest window in the wall,
Where he paused to listen and look down
A moment on the roofs of the town,
And the moonlight flowing over all.   41
Beneath, in the churchyard, lay the dead,
In their night-encampment on the hill,
Wrapped in silence so deep and still
That he could hear, like a sentinel's tread,
The watchful night-wind, as it went   46
Creeping along from tent to tent,
And seeming to whisper, "All is well!"
A moment only he feels the spell
Of the place and the hour, and the secret dread
Of the lonely belfry and the dead;   51
For suddenly all his thoughts are bent
On a shadowy something far away,
Where the river widens to meet the bay,—
A line of black that bends and floats
On the rising tide, like a bridge of boats.

Meanwhile, impatient to mount and ride,   57
Booted and spurred, with a heavy stride
On the opposite shore walked Paul Revere.
Now he patted his horse's side,
Now gazed at the landscape far and near,
Then, impetuous, stamped the earth,   62
And turned and tightened his saddle-girth;
But mostly he watched with eager search
The belfry-tower of the Old North Church,
As it rose above the graves on the hill,
Lonely and spectral and sombre and still.   67
And lo! as he looks, on the belfry's height
A glimmer, and then a gleam of light!
He springs to the saddle, the bridle he turns,

But lingers and gazes, till full on his sight
A second lamp in the belfry burns!

A hurry of hoofs in a village street,   73
A shape in the moonlight, a bulk in the dark,
And beneath, from the pebbles, in passing, a spark
Struck out by a steed flying fearless and fleet:
That was all! And yet, through the gloom and the light,
The fate of a nation was riding that night;   78
And the spark struck out by that steed, in his flight,
Kindled the land into flame with its heat.
He has left the village and mounted the steep,
And beneath him, tranquil and broad and deep,
Is the Mystic, meeting the ocean tides;   83
And under the alders, that skirt its edge,
Now soft on the sand, now loud on the ledge,
Is heard the tramp of his steed as he rides.

It was twelve by the village clock   87
When he crossed the bridge into Medford town.
He heard the crowing of the cock,
And the barking of the farmer's dog,
And felt the damp of the river fog,
That rises after the sun goes down.

It was one by the village clock,   93
When he galloped into Lexington.
He saw the gilded weathercock
Swim in the moonlight as he passed,
And the meeting-house windows, blank and bare,
Gaze at him with a spectral glare,   98
As if they already stood aghast
At the bloody work they would look upon.

It was two by the village clock,   101
When he came to the bridge in Concord town.
He heard the bleating of the flock,
And the twitter of birds among the trees,
And felt the breath of the morning breeze
Blowing over the meadows brown.   106
And one was safe and asleep in his bed
Who at the bridge would be first to fall,
Who that day would be lying dead,
Pierced by a British musket-ball.

You know the rest. In the books you have read,   111
How the British Regulars fired and fled,—
How the farmers gave them ball for ball,
From behind each fence and farm-yard wall,
Chasing the red-coats down the lane,
Then crossing the fields to emerge again   116
Under the trees at the turn of the road,
And only pausing to fire and load.

So through the night rode Paul Revere;   119
And so through the night went his cry of alarm
To every Middlesex village and farm,—
A cry of defiance and not of fear,
A voice in the darkness, a knock at the door,
And a word that shall echo forevermore!   124
For, borne on the night-wind of the Past,
Through all our history, to the last,
In the hour of darkness and peril and need,
The people will waken and listen to hear
The hurrying hoof-beats of that steed,
And the midnight message of Paul Revere.   130

The End of the World

Quite unexpectedly as Vasserot
The armless ambidextrian was lighting
A match between his great and second toe
And Ralph the lion was engaged in biting
The neck of Madame Sossman while the drum   5
Pointed, and Teeny was about to cough
In waltz-time swinging Jocko by the thumb—
Quite unexpectedly the top blew off:

And there, there overhead, there, there, hung over   9
Those thousands of white faces, those dazed eyes,
There in the starless dark the poise, the hover,
There with vast wings across the canceled skies,
There in the sudden blackness the black pall
Of nothing, nothing, nothing—nothing at all.   14

6 *Pointed:* called attention to the act.

Ars Poetica

A poem should be palpable and mute
As a globed fruit,

Dumb
As old medallions to the thumb,

Silent as the sleeve-worn stone   5
Of casement ledges where the moss has grown—

A poem should be wordless
As the flight of birds.

❋

A poem should be motionless in time   9
As the moon climbs,

Leaving, as the moon releases
Twig by twig the night-entangled trees,

Leaving, as the moon behind the winter leaves,   13
Memory by memory the mind—

A poem should be motionless in time
As the moon climbs.

❋

A poem should be equal to: 17
Not true.

For all the history of grief
An empty doorway and a maple leaf.

For love   21
The leaning grasses and two lights above the sea—

A poem should not mean
But be.

You, Andrew Marvell

And here face down beneath the sun
And here upon earth's noonward height

Andrew Marvell: see "To His Coy Mistress" (p. 206), especially lines 5-7, 21-24.   1 *here:* the Illinois lake shore, according to MacLeish.

To feel the always coming on
The always rising of the night:

To feel creep up the curving east   5
The earthy chill of dusk and slow
Upon those under lands the vast
And ever climbing shadow grow

And strange at Ecbatan the trees   9
Take leaf by leaf the evening strange
The flooding dark about their knees
The mountains over Persia change

And now at Kermanshah the gate   13
Dark empty and the withered grass
And through the twilight now the late
Few travelers in the westward pass

And Baghdad darken and the bridge   17
Across the silent river gone
And through Arabia the edge
Of evening widen and steal on

And deepen on Palmyra's street   21
The wheel rut in the ruined stone
And Lebanon fade out and Crete
High through the clouds and overblown

And over Sicily the air   25
Still flashing with the landward gulls
And loom and slowly disappear
The sails above the shadowy hulls

And Spain go under and the shore   29
Of Africa the gilded sand
And evening vanish and no more
The low pale light across that land

Nor now the long light on the sea: 33

And here face downward in the sun
To feel how swift how secretly
The shadow of the night comes on . . .

9 *Ecbatan* (now Hamadan), 13 *Kermanshah,* 17 *Baghdad,* 21 *Palmyra:* ancient
cities in the Near East, lying roughly in a line from east to west.

The Passionate Shepherd to His Love

Come live with me and be my love,
And we will all the pleasures prove
That valleys, groves, hills, and fields,
Woods, or steepy mountain yields.

And we will sit upon the rocks,   5
Seeing the shepherds feed their flocks,
By shallow rivers, to whose falls
Melodious birds sing madrigals.

And I will make thee beds of roses   9
And a thousand fragrant posies,
A cap of flowers, and a kirtle
Embroidered all with leaves of myrtle;

A gown made of the finest wool,   13
Which from our pretty lambs we pull;
Fair lined slippers for the cold,
With buckles of the purest gold;

A belt of straw and ivy-buds   17
With coral clasps and amber studs:
And if these pleasures may thee move,
Come live with me and be my love.

The shepherd's swains shall dance and sing   21
For thy delight each May morning:
If these delights thy mind may move,
Then live with me and be my love.

The Garden

How vainly men themselves amaze
To win the palm, the oak, or bays;
And their uncessant labours see
Crown'd from some single herb or tree,
Whose short and narrow verged shade   5

Note: cf. Ralegh's "The Nymph's Reply to the Shepherd" (p. 233).   11 *kirtle:*
gown.   21 *swains:* young men.

2 *palm, oak, bays:* for victories.

Does prudently their toils upbraid;
While all flow'rs and all trees do close
To weave the garlands of repose.

Fair Quiet, have I found thee here,   9
And Innocence thy sister dear!
Mistaken long, I sought you then
In busy companies of men.
Your sacred plants, if here below,   13
Only among the plants will grow;
Society is all but rude,
To this delicious solitude.

No white nor red was ever seen   17
So am'rous as this lovely green.
Fond lovers, cruel as their flame,
Cut in these trees their mistress' name.
Little, alas, they know or heed,   21
How far these beauties hers exceed!
Fair trees! where s'e'er your barks I wound,
No name shall but your own be found.

When we have run our passion's heat,   25
Love hither makes his best retreat.
The gods, that mortal beauty chase,
Still in a tree did end their race;
Apollo hunted Daphne so,   29
Only that she might laurel grow.
And Pan did after Syrinx speed,
Not as a nymph, but for a reed.

What wond'rous life is this I lead!   33
Ripe apples drop about my head;
The luscious clusters of the vine
Upon my mouth do crush their wine:
The nectaren and curious peach   37
Into my hands themselves do reach;
Stumbling on melons, as I pass,
Insnar'd with flow'rs, I fall on grass.

Mean while the mind, from pleasure less,   41
Withdraws into its happiness:

16 *To:* compared to.   17 *white nor red:* "of a lady's face" (Dean).   27-32:
According to Ovid, Daphne was turned into a laurel to escape Apollo; Syrinx,
to escape Pan, into a reed—which Pan used to make his pipes.   37 *curious:*
excellent.

The mind, that ocean where each kind
Does straight its own resemblance find;
Yet it creates, transcending these,   45
Far other worlds, and other seas,
Annihilating all that's made
To a green thought in a green shade.

Here at the fountain's sliding foot,   49
Or at some fruit-tree's mossy root,
Casting the body's vest aside,
My soul into the boughs does glide;
There like a bird it sits and sings,   53
Then whets and combs its silver wings,
And, till prepar'd for longer flight,
Waves in its plumes the various light.

Such was that happy Garden-state,   57
While man there walked without a mate:
After a place so pure, and sweet,
What other help could yet be meet!
But 'twas beyond a mortal's share   61
To wander solitary there:
Two Paradises 'twere in one,
To live in Paradise alone.

How well the skilful gardener drew   65
Of flow'rs and herbs this dial new!
Where from above, the milder sun
Does through a fragrant zodiac run;
And, as it works, th' industrious bee   69
Computes its time as well as we!
How could such sweet and wholesome hours
Be reckon'd but with herbs and flow'rs!

To His Coy Mistress

  Had we but world enough, and time,
This coyness, lady, were no crime.
We would sit down, and think which way
To walk, and pass our long love's day.
Thou by the Indian Ganges' side   5
Should'st rubies find: I by the tide

43 *kind:* species.   57 *Garden-state:* Eden.   60 *meet:* suitable.

Of Humber would complain. I would
Love you ten years before the Flood,
And you should, if you please, refuse
Till the conversion of the Jews.   10
My vegetable love should grow
Vaster than empires and more slow:
An hundred years should go to praise
Thine eyes, and on thy forehead gaze.
Two hundred to adore each breast: 15
But thirty thousand to the rest.
An age at least to every part,
And the last age should show your heart.
For, lady, you deserve this state,
Nor would I love at lower rate.

But at my back I always hear   21
Time's winged chariot hurrying near:
And yonder all before us lie
Deserts of vast eternity.
Thy beauty shall no more be found,
Nor, in thy marble vault, shall sound   26
My echoing song: then worms shall try
That long-preserv'd virginity:
And your quaint honour turn to dust;
And into ashes all my lust.
The grave's a fine and private place,   31
But none I think do there embrace.

Now, therefore, while the youthful hue   33
Sits on thy skin like morning dew,
And while thy willing soul transpires
At every pore with instant fires,
Now let us sport us while we may;
And now, like am'rous birds of prey,   38
Rather at once our time devour,
Than languish in his slow-chappt pow'r.
Let us roll all our strength, and all
Our sweetness, up into one ball:
And tear our pleasures with rough strife,   43
Thorough the iron gates of life;
Thus, though we cannot make our sun
Stand still, yet we will make him run.

7 *Humber:* river in England.   34 *dew:* originally *glew* (meaning uncertain).
40 *chappt:* devouring (*chap:* jaw).

Case

A

1. Here, under the guise of subtle and witty intellectual disputation, lies a bold sexual appeal.
2. The speaker's light tone in Section 1 and his solemnity in the other two sections screen the indelicate nature of his entreaty, but close analysis reveals the insidiousness of such items as the slanted words "coyness" and "crime," the sensual catalogue of 14-18, the pictorial immediacy of 27-28, and the choice of "sport" and "pleasures" to characterize love.
3. The primary theme is masculine "lust" (30) versus feminine "honour" (29).

B

1. The poem is a novel philosophical commentary constructed on the conventional frame of a lover's complaint against his hardhearted mistress.
2. The speaker's awareness of omnipresent death emerges most dramatically in the middle section—in contrast to the ironically exaggerated protestation of Section 1 and the direct exhortation of Section 3.
3. The primary theme is the affirmation of man's limited vitality versus the ultimate power of mortality.

BIBLIOGRAPHY

Brooks, C., J. T. Purser, and R. P. Warren, *An Approach to Literature,* 1952, pp. 393-95; Cunningham, J. V., *Modern Philology,* **51** (Aug. 1953), 34-38; Henn, T. R., *The Apple and the Spectroscope,* 1951, pp. 25-33; Roberts, J. H., *Explicator,* 1 (Dec. 1942), 17.

The Portent

Hanging from the beam,
　Slowly swaying (such the law),
Gaunt the shadow on your green,
　Shenandoah!　　　　　　　4

4 *Shenandoah:* Virginia valley where in 1859 John Brown was hanged after leading an unsuccessful Abolitionist rebellion.

The cut is on the crown
  (Lo, John Brown),
And the stabs shall heal no more.

Hidden in the cap   8
  Is the anguish none can draw;
So your future veils its face,
  Shenandoah!
But the streaming beard is shown   12
  (Weird John Brown),
The meteor of the war.

Thus Piteously Love Closed What He Begat
(No. 50 from Modern Love)

Thus piteously Love closed what he begat:
The union of this ever-diverse pair!
These two were rapid falcons in a snare,
Condemned to do the flitting of the bat.
Lovers beneath the singing sky of May,   5
They wandered once; clear as the dew on flowers:
But they fed not on the advancing hours:
Their hearts held cravings for the buried day.
Then each applied to each that fatal knife,
Deep questioning, which probes to endless dole. 10
Ah, what a dusty answer gets the soul
When hot for certainties in this our life!—
In tragic hints here see what evermore
Moves dark as yonder midnight ocean's force,
Thundering like ramping hosts of warrior horse,
To throw that faint thin line upon the shore!   16

Lucifer in Starlight

On a starred night Prince Lucifer uprose.
Tired of his dark dominion swung the fiend

5, 7: The wound is on the head for a long time to come.   8 *cap:* hanged man's
hood.   13 *Weird:* fatefully prophetic.

Lucifer: Satan's name before he rebelled against God and was expelled from
Heaven.

Above the rolling ball in cloud part screened,
Where sinners hugged their spectre of repose.
Poor prey to his hot fit of pride were those.   5
And now upon his western wing he leaned,
Now his huge bulk o'er Afric's sands careened,
Now the black planet shadowed Arctic snows.
Soaring through wider zones that pricked his scars   9
With memory of the old revolt from Awe,
He reached a middle height, and at the stars,
Which are the brain of heaven, he looked, and sank.
Around the ancient track marched, rank on rank,
The army of unalterable law.   14

Wind on the Lyre

That was the chirp of Ariel
You heard, as overhead it flew,
The farther going more to dwell,
And wing our green to wed our blue;
But whether note of joy or knell,   5
Not his own Father-singer knew;
Nor yet can any mortal tell,
Save only how it shivers through;
The breast of us a sounded shell,
The blood of us a lighted dew.   10

3 *rolling ball:* Earth.   4 *spectre:* illusion.   10 *Awe:* i.e., God.

6 *Father-singer:* Shakespeare, who created Ariel in *The Tempest* (Trevelyan).

Lycidas

In this Monody the Author bewails a learned Friend, unfortunately drown'd in his Passage from Chester on the Irish Seas, 1637. And by occasion foretells the ruin of our corrupted Clergy then in their height.

Yet once more, O ye laurels, and once more
Ye myrtles brown, with ivy never sere,
I come to pluck your berries harsh and crude,
And with forc'd fingers rude,
Shatter your leaves before the mellowing year.   5
Bitter constraint, and sad occasion dear,
Compels me to disturb your season due:
For Lycidas is dead, dead ere his prime,
Young Lycidas, and hath not left his peer:
Who would not sing for Lycidas? he well knew   10
Himself to sing, and build the lofty rhyme.
He must not float upon his watery bier
Unwept, and welter to the parching wind,
Without the meed of some melodious tear.
    Begin then, Sisters of the sacred well,   15
That from beneath the seat of Jove doth spring,
Begin, and somewhat loudly sweep the string.
Hence with denial vain, and coy excuse,
So may some gentle muse
With lucky words favour my destin'd urn,   20
And as he passes turn,
And bid fair peace be to my sable shroud.
For we were nursed upon the self-same hill,
Fed the same flock, by fountain, shade, and rill.
    Together both, ere the high lawns appear'd   25
Under the opening eye-lids of the morn,
We drove a-field, and both together heard
What time the gray-fly winds her sultry horn,
Batt'ning our flocks with the fresh dews of night,
Oft till the star that rose, at ev'ning bright   30
Toward heav'n's descent had slop'd his westering wheel.

Friend: Edward King, a 25-year-old scholar in Milton's college at Cambridge, expected to have a brilliant career in poetry and the church. 1-2 *laurels, myrtles, ivy:* evergreens used for wreaths to crown prize-winning poets; sacred to Apollo (poetry), Venus (love), and Bacchus (wine and vitality), respectively. 3 *crude:* unripe. 13 *welter to the parching:* be tossed by the withering. 14 *meed:* reward. 15-16 *Sisters . . . spring:* the Nine Muses. 17 *string:* strings of pastoral lyre. 19 *muse:* poet. 20 *urn:* burial urn. 28 *winds:* blows.

Meanwhile the rural ditties were not mute,
Temper'd to th' oaten flute,
Rough Satyrs danc'd, and Fauns with clov'n heel
From the glad sound would not be absent long,   35
And old Damætas lov'd to hear our song.
    But O the heavy change, now thou art gone,
Now thou art gone, and never must return!
Thee Shepherd, thee the woods, and desert caves,
With wild thyme and the gadding vine o'ergrown,   40
And all their echoes, mourn.
The willows, and the hazel copses green,
Shall now no more be seen,
Fanning their joyous leaves to thy soft lays.
As killing as the canker to the rose,   45
Or taint-worm to the weanling herds that graze,
Or frost to flowers, that their gay wardrobe wear,
When first the white-thorn blows;
Such, Lycidas, thy loss to shepherd's ear.
    Where were ye Nymphs when the remorseless deep   50
Clos'd o'er the head of your lov'd Lycidas?
For neither were ye playing on the steep,
Where your old Bards, the famous Druids lie,
Nor on the shaggy top of Mona high,
Nor yet where Deva spreads her wizard stream: 55
Ay me, I fondly dream!
Had ye been there . . . for what could that have done?
What could the Muse her self that Orpheus bore,
The Muse her self, for her enchanting son
Whom universal nature did lament,   60
When by the rout that made the hideous roar,
His gory visage down the stream was sent,
Down the swift Hebrus to the Lesbian shore.
    Alas! What boots it with uncessant care
To tend the homely slighted shepherd's trade,   65
And strictly meditate the thankless Muse,
Were it not better done as others use,

36 *Damætas:* pastoral name, usually considered to refer to a tutor at Cambridge.
42 *copses:* groves.   44 *lays:* songs.   48 *blows:* blooms.   52-55: Welsh places
on Irish Sea.   56 *fondly:* foolishly.   58-63 *the Muse . . . shore:* Calliope, muse
of epic poetry, was the mother of the supreme poet Orpheus, who was torn to
pieces by Thracian women, who threw his head into the river.   64 *boots:* benefits.   66: conscientiously study the difficult art of poetry.   67 *use:* do.

To sport with Amaryllis in the shade,
Or with the tangles of Neæra's hair?
Fame is the spur that the clear spirit doth raise   70
(That last infirmity of noble mind)
To scorn delights, and live laborious days;
But the fair guerdon when we hope to find,
And think to burst out into sudden blaze,
Comes the blind Fury with th' abhorred shears,   75
And slits the thin-spun life. But not the praise,
Phoebus replied, and touch'd my trembling ears;
Fame is no plant that grows on mortal soil,
Nor in the glistering foil
Set off to th' world, nor in broad rumour lies,   80
But lives and spreads aloft by those pure eyes,
And perfect witness of all-judging Jove;
As he pronounces lastly on each deed,
Of so much fame in Heav'n expect thy meed.
    O Fountain Arethuse, and thou honour'd flood,   85
Smooth-sliding Mincius, crown'd with vocal reeds,
That strain I heard was of a higher mood:
But now my Oat proceeds,
And listens to the Herald of the Sea
That came in Neptune's plea.   90
He ask'd the waves, and ask'd the felon winds,
What hard mishap hath doom'd this gentle swain?
And question'd every gust of rugged wings
That blows from off each beaked promontory;
They knew not of his story,   95
And sage Hippotades their answer brings,
That not a blast was from his dungeon stray'd,
The air was calm, and on the level brine,
Sleek Panope with all her sisters play'd.
It was that fatal and perfidious bark   100
Built in th' eclipse, and rigg'd with curses dark,
That sunk so low that sacred head of thine.
    Next Camus, reverend sire, went footing slow,
His mantle hairy, and his bonnet sedge,

68-69 *Amaryllis . . . Neæra:* pastoral shepherdesses.   73 *guerdon:* reward.   77
Phoebus: Apollo, god of poetry.   80 *rumour:* reputation.   85, 86 *Arethuse,*
Mincius: waters associated with pastoral poets Theocritus and Virgil.   88 *Oat:*
pastoral pipe.   89 *Herald of the Sea:* Triton.   96 *Hippotades:* Aeolus, god of
the winds.   99 *Panope . . . sisters:* sea nymphs.   103 *Camus:* personification
of river Cam in Cambridge University.   104 *sedge:* grass-like plant.

Inwrought with figures dim, and on the edge   105
Like to that sanguine flower inscrib'd with woe.
Ah! Who hath reft (quoth he) my dearest pledge?
Last came, and last did go,
The Pilot of the Galilean lake,
Two massy keys he bore of metals twain,   110
(The golden opes, the iron shuts amain).
He shook his miter'd locks, and stern bespake,
How well could I have spar'd for thee young swain,
Enow of such as for their bellies' sake,
Creep and intrude, and climb into the fold!   115
Of other care they little reck'ning make,
Than how to scramble at the shearers' feast,
And shove away the worthy bidden guest;
Blind mouths! that scarce themselves know how to hold
A sheep-hook, or have learn'd aught else the least   120
That to the faithful herdsman's art belongs!
What recks it them? What need they? They are sped;
And when they list, their lean and flashy songs
Grate on their scrannel pipes of wretched straw,
The hungry sheep look up, and are not fed,   125
But swoln with wind, and the rank mist they draw,
Rot inwardly, and foul contagion spread:
Besides what the grim Wolf with privy paw
Daily devours apace, and nothing said,
But that two-handed engine at the door,   130
Stands ready to smite once, and smite no more.
     Return Alpheus, the dread voice is past,
That shrunk thy streams; return Sicilian Muse,
And call the vales, and bid them hither cast
Their bells, and flowerets of a thousand hues.   135
Ye valleys low where the mild whispers use,
Of shades and wanton winds, and gushing brooks,

106 *sanguine flower . . . woe:* usually considered to refer to the hyacinth,
sprung from the blood (*sanguine*) of Hyacinthus after his death, with markings that look like the Greek letters AI (alas).   107 *reft:* robbed.   109-112
Pilot . . . keys: St. Peter, former fisherman, bears the keys to Heaven.   111
amain: powerfully.   112 *mitred:* with ecclesiastical hat.   119 *Blind mouths:*
selfish feeders.   122 *What recks it them:* What do they care?   122 *sped:* satisfied.   123 *list:* like, wish.   124 *scrannel:* thin.   128 *privy:* stealthy.   129 *apace:*
swiftly.   130 *two-handed engine:* weapon that requires two hands to wield;
meaning obscure.   132 *Alpheus:* pastoral river.   133 *Sicilian:* Theocritus was
Sicilian.   136 *use:* dwell.   138 *swart star:* Sirius, "black" because associated
with heat (Mack).

On whose fresh lap the swart star sparely looks,
Throw hither all your quaint enameled eyes,
That on the green turf suck the honied showers,   140
And purple all the ground with vernal flowers.
Bring the rathe primrose that forsaken dies,
The tufted crow-toe, and pale jessamine,
The white pink, and the pansy freaked with jet,
The glowing violet,   145
The musk-rose, and the well-attir'd woodbine,
With cowslips wan that hang the pensive head,
And every flower that sad embroidery wears:
Bid Amaranthus all his beauty shed,
And daffadillies fill their cups with tears,   150
To strew the laureate hearse where Lycid lies.
For so to interpose a little ease,
Let our frail thoughts dally with false surmise.
Ay me! Whilst thee the shores, and sounding seas
Wash far away, where'er they bones are hurled,   155
Whether beyond the stormy Hebrides,
Where thou perhaps under the whelming tide
Visit'st the bottom of the monstrous world;
Or whether thou to our moist vows deny'd,
Sleep'st by the fable of Bellerus old,   160
Where the great vision of the guarded mount
Looks toward Namancos and Bayona's hold;
Look homeward Angel now, and melt with ruth,
And, O ye dolphins, waft the hapless youth.
    Weep no more, woful Shepherds weep no more,   165
For Lycidas your sorrow is not dead,
Sunk though he be beneath the watery floor,
So sinks the day-star in the ocean bed,
And yet anon repairs his drooping head,
And tricks his beams, and with new spangled ore,   170
Flames in the forehead of the morning sky:
So Lycidas sunk low, but mounted high,
Through the dear might of Him that walk'd the waves;
Where other groves, and other streams along,
With nectar pure his oozy locks he laves,   175

139 *enameled:* decorated.   142 *rathe:* early.   151 *laureate:* crowned with
laurel.   158 *monstrous world:* world of monsters, the sea.   159 *moist:* tearful.
160-62: Archangel Michael was said to sit at the southwest tip (Bellerium) of
England, looking toward Spain (Namancos and Bellona) (Mack).   163 *ruth:*
pity.   168 *day-star:* sun.   170 *tricks:* adorns.

And hears the unexpressive nuptial Song,
In the blest kingdoms meek of joy and love.
There entertain him all the Saints above,
In solemn troops, and sweet societies
That sing, and singing in their glory move,   180
And wipe the tears for ever from his eyes.
Now Lycidas the Shepherds weep no more;
Henceforth thou art the Genius of the shore,
In thy large recompense, and shalt be good
To all that wander in that perilous flood.   185
   Thus sang the uncouth Swain to th' oaks and rills,
While the still morn went out with sandals gray,
He touch'd the tender stops of various quills,
With eager thought warbling his Doric lay:
And now the sun had stretch'd out all the hills,   190
And now was dropt into the western bay;
At last he rose, and twitch'd his mantle blue:
To-morrow to fresh woods, and pastures new.

Case

Note: For purposes of analysis, the poem has been divided into the following main sections: I (Stanzas 1-6), II (7-8), III (9-11).

A

1. The primary theme of the poem is death and its eventual con-
quest by Christian immortality.

2. In Section I the poet mourns the premature death of a friend
and fellow-poet.

3. Stanzas (they are actually irregular verse-paragraphs) 1-3 present three reasons for the elegy: the fact that Lycidas was a poet
himself, the speaker's desire to be similarly mourned, and the happy
friendship—set forth in pastoral terms—of the two young men.

4. Stanza 4 points to the change in Nature, which now reflects
the sadness of Lycidas's death.

5. But (the poet recognizes in Stanzas 5-6) neither pagan spirits
nor hard work could, or can, prevail against inexorable death.

176 *unexpressive:* indescribable. 176 *nuptial:* "Blessed are they that are called
to the marriage supper of the Lamb" (Revelation 19:9) (Mack). 183 *Genius:*
guardian spirit. 186 *uncouth:* unlearned, unknown. 189 *Doric:* Greek pastoral dialect. 192 *twitch'd:* grabbed.

6. In Phoebus's assurance (76-84) that the reward of fame is a matter for "all-judging Jove" to bestow in "heaven," the poet resolves the frustration of Lycidas's *poetic* career, at the same time foreshadowing the final consolation described in Section III.

7. Section II of the poem considers Lycidas's premature death from the point of view of his promise as a Christian scholar and churchman.

8. It begins (in Stanza 7) with an accusation of guilt against the "perfidious" ship (100) that sank Lycidas's "sacred" person (102); that is, against a treacherous agent that frustrated Lycidas's *religious* future.

9. It continues (in Stanza 8) with a brief, gentle lament by a spirit representing the University (103-7), and a harsh blast by St. Peter, representing the Christian Church, against the corrupt clergy who counteract such a worthy priest as Lycidas would have become.

10. It ends (130-31) with a prediction of some kind of divine punishment for the evil clergy.

11. In Section III the poet sees the negativeness and frustration of Lycidas's early death conquered by the young man's ascent into Heaven through Christ (172-81).

12. Stanza 9 provides a transition from harshness to relief, by means of (a) the flowers that, called to an imagined funeral, are still brilliantly colorful, and (b) the watery grave that, despite all its negating reality, still provides the setting for resurrection (161-64, 167-75).

13. The last stanza of the poem reveals the fact that after a day's meditation and song the poet has resolved his own sorrow for Lycidas.

14. The poet's tone has ranged from reluctance (Stanzas 1-2) to active lamentation (Stanzas 3-4), from mild to bitter indignation (Stanzas 5-8), back to personal mourning (Stanza 9), thence reversing to triumph (Stanza 10), and ending with calm confidence (Stanza 11).

B

1. The primary theme of the poem is the proper destiny of a poet.

2. As well as expressing grief, the opening lines point to a conflict between the poet's artistic conscience and the demands made upon it.

3. Although the poet notes (Stanzas 3-4) the change in nature since the death of the poet Lycidas, he finds the nature spirits ("Nymphs," 50) inadequate to the job of protecting him—though no less so than "the Muse her self" (58), who could not save her own son, the famed poet Orpheus.

4. The poet begins Stanza 6 despairingly, noting that artistic labor is often cut off prematurely (72-76), but he ends the stanza —and the first major section of the poem—with the partial consolation, supplied by Apollo, that fame comes only after death.

5. The second major section of the poem expresses more frustration: nature's lack of responsibility in the death of the young poet Lycidas (91-99), the mysterious cause of the drowning (100-2), and the fact that whereas Lycidas, likely scholar and clergyman, has been destroyed, evil ecclesiastics continue to flourish.

6. At the beginning of Section III, in Stanzas 9-10, the poet calls up the beauty of nature in the form of flowers, and attempts to find sympathy there (149-51), only to face the reality that such a notion is a "false surmise" (153), and that Lycidas is actually a corpse tossed by the sea.

7. At this point of hopelessness, the chance association of a possible resting place for Lycidas's body with St. Michael the Archangel brings the poet to a prayer to the Angel for mercy (160-63).

8. With the almost fortuitous transition to Christian faith ending Stanza 9, the poem reverses itself: Death is not final, because through Christ there is resurrection (172-73).

9. The conclusion of the poem's submerged argument is that the true harmony of the poet with the universe lies in the "blest kingdoms" of Heaven (177) rather than in nature or poetic fame.

10. The firmness of the poet's final conviction is emphasized by the regularity of Stanzas 10-11: There are none of the short or unrhymed lines that give fitful variations to every other stanza; and Stanza 11 is actually in a traditional stanza form—the ottava rima —which helps to embody a feeling of unity, resolution of conflict, and assurance.

BIBLIOGRAPHY

Abrams, M. H., in *Varieties of Literary Experience*, S. Burnshaw, ed., 1962, pp. 1-23; Adams, R. P., *PMLA*, 64 (Mar. 1949), 183-88; Brooks, C., and J. E. Hardy, *Poems of Mr. John Milton*, 1951, pp. 169-86; Daiches, D., *A Study of Literature*, 1948, pp. 170-95; French, J. M.,

Studies in Philology, **50** (July 1953), 485-90; Mack, M., ed., *Milton,* 1950, pp. 9-11, 67-74; Mayerson, C. W., *PMLA,* **64** (Mar. 1949), 189-207; Ross, M. M., *University of Toronto Quarterly,* **17** (July 1948), 358-60; Shumaker, W., *PMLA,* **66** (June 1951), 485-94; Thomas, W., and S. G. Brown, *Reading Poems,* 1941, pp. 692-94; Tillyard, E. M. W., *Milton,* 1930, pp. 80-85; ———, *Poetry Direct and Oblique,* 1934, pp. 208-13; 1945 ed., pp. 9-10, 81-84; Wagenknecht, E., *College English,* **7** (Apr. 1946), 393-97.

When I Consider How My Light Is Spent

When I consider how my light is spent
   Ere half my days in this dark world and wide,
   And that one talent which is death to hide
   Lodg'd with me useless, though my soul more bent
To serve therewith my Maker, and present   5
   My true account, lest he returning chide,
   "Doth God exact day-labour, light deny'd?"
   I fondly ask. But Patience, to prevent
That murmur, soon replies, "God doth not need   9
   Either man's work or his own gifts. Who best
   Bear his mild yoke, they serve him best. His state
Is kingly: thousands at his bidding speed,
   And post o'er land and ocean without rest;
   They also serve who only stand and wait."   14

Critique

1. ... Considered in relation to the rest of Milton's works this is an extremely difficult and strange poem. There is a tone of self-abasement found but once again in Milton. In a way the theme is that of *Lycidas:* the ranking of the state of mind above the deed. But the conception of the deed is quite different. In *Lycidas* the deed is personal, the exercise of Milton's creative faculty: in the sonnet it is the passive yielding to God's command; Milton crouches

Title: often entitled "On His Blindness."   8 *fondly:* foolishly.

in humble expectation, like a beaten dog ready to wag its tail at the smallest token of its master's attention. In view of Milton's normal self-confidence, of his belief in the value of his own undertakings, I cannot but see in the sonnet the signs of his having suffered an extraordinary exhaustion of vitality. Yet for all this weakness the sonnet shows the nature of Milton's greatness and the promise of recovery. . . .   (E. M. W. TILLYARD)

2. . . . There is, I believe, in English literature no human tragedy so simply depicted as that of the foregoing sonnet. It is a tragedy because, though the end is peaceful, it is the renunciation of poetic achievement seemingly impossible in blindness. It is a tragedy because it contains a conflict, controlled and well-ordered, but obviously a struggle. It is likewise a tragedy because it is the expression of one who has suffered almost beyond human endurance and has emerged without bitterness of spirit or reproach against his grievous fate.

The "beaten dog" attitude portrayed by Tillyard is to me not apparent and is in no sense compatible with the lofty resignation which a majority of readers usually find in this sonnet. . . .

(ELEANOR G. BROWN) [Miss Brown is herself blind.]

3. For many readers this poem is principally interesting biographically. Milton was blind; and here he tells us how he felt about it. Really the biographical note is of the smallest significance. To know that the sonnet was written by a blind man may, perhaps, give it added poignancy, but a poem quite as effective, on the same subject, might conceivably have been written by a good poet with two good eyes. . . . The reader who finds in it an eloquent statement of courage in adversity has gone farther than the one who rests in biography, though even he has not advanced very far with the poem. Analysis can teach us more. The first two lines suggest the image of a man trying to walk in the dark when the light he was carrying has gone out. The idea of the darkness of being blind is sharpened and emphasized by making the world also *dark*, and *wide*, and with that last phrase the common Biblical figure of life as a pilgrimage through the darkness of a hostile world is hinted at. In this allusion the whole poem, when we come to look back at it, will be found tied together. For the rest is centered in the Biblical metaphor of a master and a servant. The words *talent* and *hide* (3), *account* (6), and *day-labour* (7) are clues which ought to put an observant reader on the right track. The servant in the parable

who hid his lord's money is the key. Having discovered this, a reader should, if the parable of the talents is not familiar to him, reread it to get the details in his mind; for the crux of the poem is the effectiveness of the poet's adaptation of the parable to the purposes of his sonnet, the play between parable and poem. In the parable the one-talent man was afraid and hid the money; in the sonnet the poet is afraid he will be obliged, because he cannot see, to hide his talent for writing, and he knows such procedure is death; it is death for the mind and spirit of an artist if he cannot find expression through his art. . . . The talent is taken from the one who acted but acted wrong, while the poet, afraid he cannot act and so will be wrong—really failing to act at all—is reassured, "They also serve who only stand and wait." (EARL DANIELS)

4. . . . I suggest that "days" in the second line of Milton's sonnet on his blindness should be interpreted to mean *working* days. If Milton's blindness became complete when he was about forty-four, considerably more than half his total life expectancy had passed, but somewhat less than half of a normal *working* life. This reading is in accordance with the reference to "day-labor" in the seventh line. . . . (DONALD C. DORIAN)

5. . . . The poem is *not* on his blindness. . . .

. . . The poem is usually dated 1652 (the year Milton went blind) or 1655 . . . . [But] If we assume that he was thinking [in line 2] of the Biblical threescore and ten years as the span of life, it means that he was just shy of 35 when he wrote the poem; but he was . . . 44 or 47 if we accept either of the two dates usually assigned. . . . I will set 1642—his 34th year—as the probable date of composition.

What happens if we accept this date? . . . It means that the subject cannot be his blindness, for he will not be blind till another ten years have passed. . . .

. . . If, then, . . . the poem was . . . not written on the loss of his sight, what *was* the subject? The first line has been taken to mean he is blind, "light" meaning "eyesight"—but surely "light" is commonly used in other meanings, as "inspiration" for example. I believe it means "inspiration" in the poem, and I read the poem thus: In a time of stress and doubt he considers that possibly his God-given inspiration is already spent, before half his life is lived, even though he sees the world to be dark and wide and desperately in need of the light of the poet's words. The first line may mean not only that his inspiration is exhausted, but also that it is being spent or employed in other ways . . . than those called for by the poet's noble duty, *i.e.* *mis*spent. He further considers the fact that his "one talent"—his supreme gift or ability, the ability to fulfill the poet's function—is useless (and/or "unused"?). And yet his soul is more bent to serve God therewith (with this talent) than it is to serve mankind with . . . any other business than the producing of great poetry, lest God punish him for not fulfilling his true function. Therefore he is foolishly tempted to ask if God expects him to struggle to use that talent even though the necessary inspiration is denied him. Patience then replies that God does not need his efforts, and he will be serving God if he merely stands waiting . . . , ready to begin his true work when inspiration is again given him.

If the poem is taken to be on his blindness, line 2 is, as noted, a problem. So also is "wide" in the same line—the world is "dark" to the blind man, but hardly "wide." And in the last line, the word "wait[e]"—"wait[e]" for *what?* For the highly improbable return of his eyesight? For death, even though he has not lived half his days? I believe that these questions are answered satisfactorily by the reading I have proposed. . . . (LYSANDER KEMP)

BIBLIOGRAPHY

Brown, E. G., *Milton's Blindness*, 1934, p. 52; Daniels, E., *The Art of Reading Poetry*, 1941, pp. 35-36; Dorian, D. C., *Explicator*, 10 (Dec. 1951), 16; Kemp, L., *Hopkins Review*, 6 (Fall 1952), 80-83; Tillyard, E. M. W., *Milton*, 1930, p. 190.

The Private Dining Room

Miss Rafferty wore taffeta,
Miss Cavendish wore lavender.
We ate pickerel and mackerel
And other lavish provender.
Miss Cavendish was Lalage,
Miss Rafferty was Barbara.
We gobbled pickled mackerel
And broke the candelabara,
Miss Cavendish in lavender,

7

In taffeta, Miss Rafferty,
The girls in taffeta lavender,
And we, of course, in mufti.

Miss Rafferty wore taffeta, 13
The taffeta was lavender,
Was lavend, lavender, lavenderest,
As the wine improved the provender.
Miss Cavendish wore lavender,
The lavender was taffeta.
We boggled mackled pickerel, 19
And bumpers did we quaffeta.
And Lalage wore lavender,
And lavender wore Barbara,
Rafferta taffeta Cavender lavender
Barbara abracadabra.

Miss Rafferty in taffeta 25
Grew definitely raffisher.
Miss Cavendish in lavender
Grew less and less stand-offisher.
With Lalage and Barbara
We grew a little pickereled,
We ordered Mumm and Roederer 31
Because the bubbles tickereled.
But lavender and taffeta
Were gone when we were soberer.
I haven't thought for thirty years
Of Lalage and Barbara.

Adieu, Farewell, Earth's Bliss

Adieu, farewell, earth's bliss.
This world uncertain is,
Fond are life's lustful joys,
Death proves them all but toys; 4
None from his darts can fly;
I am sick, I must die:
    Lord, have mercy on us.

3 *Fond:* foolish.

Rich men, trust not in wealth,   8
Gold cannot buy you health;
Physic himself must fade.
All things to end are made,   11
The plague full swift goes by;
I am sick, I must die.
      Lord, have mercy on us.

Beauty is but a flower,   15
Which wrinkles will devour,
Brightness falls from the air,
Queens have died young and fair,   18
Dust hath closed Helen's eye.
I am sick, I must die:
      Lord, have mercy on us.

Strength stoops unto the grave,   22
Worms feed on Hector brave,
Swords may not fight with fate,
Earth still holds ope her gate.   25
Come, come, the bells do cry.
I am sick, I must die:
      Lord, have mercy on us.

Wit with his wantonness   29
Tasteth death's bitterness:
Hell's executioner
Hath no ears for to hear   31
What vain art can reply.
I am sick, I must die:
      Lord, have mercy on us.

Haste therefore each degree,   36
To welcome destiny:
Heaven is our heritage,
Earth but a player's stage,   39
Mount we unto the sky.
I am sick, I must die.
      Lord, have mercy on us!

10 *Physic:* the physician.   29 *Wit with his wantonness:* intellectuality in its extravagance.   36 *degree:* rank of society.

The Goose Fish

On the long shore, lit by the moon
To show them properly alone,
Two lovers suddenly embraced
So that their shadows were as one.
The ordinary night was graced　　　　　5
For them by the swift tide of blood
That silently they took at flood,
And for a little time they prized
　　Themselves emparadised.

Then, as if shaken by stage-fright　　　　10
Beneath the hard moon's bony light,
They stood together on the sand
Embarrassed in each other's sight
But still conspiring hand in hand,
Until they saw, there underfoot,　　　　15
As though the world had found them out,
The goose fish turning up, though dead,
　　His hugely grinning head.

There in the china light he lay,　　　　19
Most ancient and corrupt and grey.
They hesitated at his smile,
Wondering what it seemed to say
To lovers who a little while
Before had thought to understand,　　　　24
By violence upon the sand,
The only way that could be known
　　To make a world their own.

It was a wide and moony grin　　　　28
Together peaceful and obscene;
They knew not what he would express,
So finished a comedian
He might mean failure or success,
But took it for an emblem of　　　　33
Their sudden, new and guilty love
To be observed by, when they kissed,
　　That rigid optimist.

So he became their patriarch,　　　　37
Dreadfully mild in the half dark.

His throat that the sand seemed to choke,
His picket teeth, these left their mark
But never did explain the joke
That so amused him, lying there   42
While the moon went down to disappear
Along the still and tilted track
That bears the zodiac.

To Helen

Helen, thy beauty is to me
    Like those Nicéan barks of yore
That gently, o'er a perfumed sea,
    The weary, way-worn wanderer bore
    To his own native shore.

On desperate seas long wont to roam,   6
    Thy hyacinth hair, thy classic face,
Thy Naiad airs have brought me home
    To the glory that was Greece,
    And the grandeur that was Rome.

Lo! in yon brilliant window-niche   11
    How statue-like I see thee stand,
The agate lamp within thy hand,
    Ah, Psyche, from the regions which
    Are Holy-Land!

Epistle

To Miss Blount, on her leaving
the Town, after the Coronation.

As some fond virgin, whom her mother's care
Drags from the town to wholsom country air,
Just when she learns to roll a melting eye,

2, 4 *Nicéan, wanderer:* reference in doubt; see E. D. Snyder, *CJ*, **48** (Feb. 1953), 161-69.   8 *Naiad:* nymph-like.   14 *Psyche:* beloved of Cupid.

1 *fond:* infatuated.

And hear a spark, yet think no danger nigh;
From the dear man unwilling she must sever,   5
Yet takes one kiss before she parts for ever:
Thus from the world fair *Zephaltndu* flew,
Saw others happy, and with sighs withdrew;
Not that their pleasures caus'd her discontent,
She sigh'd not that They stay'd, but that She went.   10
   She went, to plain-work, and to purling brooks,
Old-fashion'd halls, dull aunts, and croaking rooks,
She went from Op'ra, park, assembly, play,
To morning walks, and pray'rs three hours a day;
To pass her time 'twixt reading and Bohea,   15
To muse, and spill her solitary Tea,
Or o'er cold coffee trifle with the spoon,
Count the slow clock, and dine exact at noon;
Divert her eyes with pictures in the fire,
Hum half a tune, tell stories to the squire;   20
Up to her godly garret after sev'n,
There starve and pray, for that's the way to heav'n.
   Some Squire, perhaps, you take delight to rack;
Whose game is Whisk, whose treat a toast in sack,
Who visits with a gun, presents you birds,   25
Then gives a smacking buss, and cries—No words!
Or with his hound comes hollowing from the stable,
Makes love with nods, and knees beneath a table;
Whose laughs are hearty, tho' his jests are coarse,
And loves you best of all things—but his horse.   30
   In some fair evening, on your elbow laid,
You dream of triumphs in the rural shade;
In pensive thought recall the fancy'd scene,
See Coronations rise on ev'ry green;
Before you pass th' imaginary sights   35
Of Lords, and Earls, and Dukes, and garter'd Knights;
While the spread Fan o'ershades your closing eyes;
Then give one flirt, and all the vision flies.
Thus vanish sceptres, coronets, and balls,
And leave you in lone woods, or empty walls.   40
   So when your slave, at some dear, idle time,
(Not plagu'd with headachs, or the want of rhime)
Stands in the streets, abstracted from the crew,

4 *spark:* suitor. 7 *Zephalinda:* fanciful name for Miss Blount. 11 *plain-work:* simple needle-work. 15 *Bohea:* tea. 24 *Whisk:* whist. 24 *toast in sack:* toast soaked in wine. 36 *garter'd Knights:* Knights of the Garter, the highest British order. 42 *want:* lack.

And while he seems to study, thinks of you:
Just when his fancy points your sprightly eyes,   45
Or sees the blush of soft *Parthenia* rise,
Gay pats my shoulder, and you vanish quite;
Streets, chairs, and coxcombs rush upon my sight;
Vext to be still in town, I knit my brow,
Look sow'r, and hum a tune—as you may now.   50

Case

A

1. The poem is a poet's pleasant, light-hearted expression of sympathy to a lady friend.

2. The poet establishes a mock-serious tone in the first section by using exaggerated diction.

3. Sections 2, 3, and 4 carry out this playfulness by showing Zephalinda subjected to horrors that are more comic and boring than terrible, and by describing the world for which she longs in terms of childlike daydreams rather than serious desires.

4. After almost becoming serious about his separation from Zephalinda (41-44), the poet returns to the light tone, ending the epistle by sharing the lady's boredom himself.

B

1. Under the guise of cheering up a lady, the poet unconsciously seeks to impress her with his own superiority.

2. By his catalogue (Sections 2 and 3) of stupid country life, the poet implies that if Zephalinda were in the city with him, she would be in far superior company.

3. In Section 4, the poet sympathetically depicts the forlorn Zephalinda dreaming of colorful pomp—only to puncture the pleasant dream and return her to ugly reality.

4. The final thrust is the speaker's acknowledgment (Section 5) that even when—at "idle" times, when not sick or busy, to be sure—he is thinking of the lady (and, incidentally, of her sister, too), the arrival of one of his city friends can cause the vision to vanish completely.

44 *study:* meditate.   46 *Parthenia:* possibly a fanciful name for Miss Blount's sister (Ault and Butt).   47 *Gay:* John Gay, poet and playwright, friend of Pope.   48 *chairs:* sedan-chairs.   48 *coxcombs:* fools.

From *An Essay on Man, Epistle II*

I. Know then thyself, presume not God to scan;
The proper study of Mankind is Man.
Plac'd on this isthmus of a middle state,
A being darkly wise, and rudely great:
With too much knowledge for the Sceptic side,   5
With too much weakness for the Stoic's pride,
He hangs between; in doubt to act, or rest,
In doubt to deem himself a God, or Beast;
In doubt his Mind or Body to prefer,
Born but to die, and reas'ning but to err;   10
Alike in ignorance, his reason such,
Whether he thinks too little, or too much:
Chaos of Thought and Passion, all confus'd;
Still by himself abus'd, or disabus'd;
Created half to rise, and half to fall;   15
Great lord of all things, yet a prey to all;
Sole judge of Truth, in endless Error hurl'd:
The glory, jest, and riddle of the world!

Sestina: Altaforte

LOQUITUR: *En* Bertrans de Born.
   Dante Alighieri put this man in hell for that he was a
   stirrer up of strife.
   Eccovi!
   Judge ye!
   Have I dug him up again?
The scene is at his castle, Altaforte. "Papiols" is his jongleur.
"The Leopard," the *device* of Richard (Coeur de Lion).

I

Damn it all! all this our South stinks peace.
You whoreson dog, Papiols, come! Let's to music!
I have no life save when the swords clash.

Sestina: French form of six 6-line stanzas with the end-words repeated in each stanza in a different order. *Loquitur: En Bertrans de Born:* spoken by Bertrans de Born, famous poet of medieval Provence. *hell:* in the *Divine Comedy. Eccovi!:* Here you are! *jongleur:* minstrel. *device:* sign. 1 *South:* of France.

But ah! when I see the standards gold, vair, purple, opposing   4
And the broad fields beneath them turn crimson,
Then howl I my heart nigh mad with rejoicing.

II

In hot summer have I great rejoicing   7
When the tempests kill the earth's foul peace,
And the lightnings from black heav'n flash crimson,
And the fierce thunders roar me their music   10
And the winds shriek through the clouds mad, opposing,
And through all the riven skies God's swords clash.

III

Hell grant soon we hear again the swords clash!   13
And the shrill neighs of destriers in battle rejoicing,
Spiked breast to spiked breast opposing!
Better one hour's stour than a year's peace   16
With fat boards, bawds, wine and frail music!
Bah! there's no wine like the blood's crimson!

IV

And I love to see the sun rise blood-crimson.   19
And I watch his spears through the dark clash
And it fills all my heart with rejoicing
And pries wide my mouth with fast music   22
When I see him so scorn and defy peace,
His lone might 'gainst all darkness opposing.

V

The man who fears war and squats opposing   25
My words for stour, hath no blood of crimson
But is fit only to rot in womanish peace
Far from where worth's won and the swords clash   28
For the death f such sluts I go rejoicing;
Yea, I fill all the air with my music.

VI

Papiols, Papiols, to the music!   31
There's no sound like to swords swords opposing,
No cry like the battle's rejoicing

4 *vair:* alternately blue and silver.   14 *destriers:* warhorses.   16, 26 *stour:* fight.

When our elbows and swords drip the crimson   34
And our charges 'gainst "The Leopard's" rush clash.
May God damn for ever all who cry "Peace!"

VII

And let the music of the swords make them crimson!   37
Hell grant soon we hear again the swords clash!
Hell blot black for alway the thought "Peace"!

In a Station of the Metro

The apparition of these faces in the crowd;
Petals on a wet, black bough.

Critique

1. In the first line the word "apparition" suggests the supernatural
or the immaterial and a sudden and unexpected appearance. The
faces are not those of a crowd, but "these faces in the crowd," a
selection which emphasizes the special, even unique, quality of
an apparition and, since only faces are mentioned, reinforces the
idea of a bodiless substance. The faces . . . are the faces in the
windows of a train which has drawn up at the station, for the
likeness can only be between the faces framed in the windows of
the long, dark train and petals which have fallen on a bough
after a rain. The important point of similarity is that the train has
made one of its momentary stops, just as the bough is only momentarily black because it is wet from the rain which has just broken
the petals from their stem. Both situations, the train's stop and a
moment during the rain, are quickly over . . . . The vision of beauty
has occurred in the one instant before it vanishes. . . .

(THOMAS A. HANZO)

2. . . . Pound writes:

Three years ago in Paris I got out of a "metro" train at La Concorde,
and saw suddenly a beautiful face, and then another and another, and

Metro: Paris subway.

then a beautiful child's face, and then another beautiful woman, and I
tried all that day to find words for what this had meant to me, and
I could not find any words that seemed to me worthy, or as lovely as
that sudden emotion. . . .
    . . . I wrote a thirty-line poem, and destroyed it because it was what
we call work "of second intensity." Six months later I made a poem
half that length; a year later I made the following hokku-like sentence:—

> "The apparition of these faces in the crowd:
> Petals, on a wet, black bough."

I dare say it is meaningless unless one has drifted into a certain vein of
thought. In a poem of this sort one is trying to record the precise
instant when a thing outward and objective transforms itself,' or darts
into a thing inward and subjective.

Happily, Pound's explanation keeps "these faces" precisely where
the poem places them, "in the crowd," and makes unnecessary the
visual embarrassment of Mr. Hanzo's reading . . . , which fails to
recognize that the subway platform and the interior of the train
would both be lighted and that the exterior of Metro carriages has
always been more colorful than dark. . . .   (JOHN J. ESPEY)

BIBLIOGRAPHY

Espey, J. J., *Explicator,* 11 (June 1953), 59; Hanzo, T. A., *Explicator,* 11
(Feb. 1953), 26.

Envoi (1919)

Go, dumb-born book,
Tell her that sang me once that song of Lawes:
Hadst thou but song
As thou hast subjects known,   4
Then were there cause in thee that should condone
Even my faults that heavy upon me lie,
And build her glories their longevity.

Tell her that sheds   8
Such treasure in the air,

Envoi: concluding dedication.   2 *Lawes:* composer who wrote music for poems
of Waller (23).

Recking naught else but that her graces give
Life to the moment,
I would bid them live
As roses might, in magic amber laid,   13
Red overwrought with orange and all made
One substance and one colour
Braving time.

Tell her that goes   17
With song upon her lips
But sings not out the song, nor knows
The maker of it, some other mouth
May be as fair as hers,
Might, in new ages, gain her worshippers,   22
When our two dusts with Waller's shall be laid,
Siftings on siftings in oblivion,
Till change hath broken down
All things save Beauty alone.

The Nymph's Reply to the Shepherd

If all the world and love were young,
And truth in every shepherd's tongue,
These pretty pleasures might me move
To live with thee, and be thy love.

Time drives the flocks from field to fold,   5
When rivers rage, and rocks grow cold,
And Philomel becometh dumb;
The rest complain of cares to come.

The flowers do fade, and wanton fields   9
To wayward winter reckoning yields;
A honey tongue, a heart of gall,
Is fancy's spring, but sorrow's fall.

Thy gowns, thy shoes, thy beds of roses,   13
Thy cap, thy kirtle, and thy posies

10 *Recking:* heeding.   23 *Waller:* Edmund Waller, seventeenth-century British
poet, whose "Go, Lovely Rose" (p. 295) Pound is imitating.

Note: Cf. Marlowe's "The Passionate Shepherd to His Love" (p. 204).
7 *Philomel:* the nightingale.   9 *wanton:* fertile.   14 *kirtle:* gown.

Soon break, soon wither, soon forgotten:
In folly ripe, in reason rotten.

Thy belt of straw and ivy buds,   17
Thy coral clasps and amber studs,
All these in me no means can move
To come to thee, and be thy love.

But could youth last, and love still breed,   21
Had joys no date, nor age no need,
Then these delights my mind might move
To live with thee, and be thy love.

Winter Remembered

Two evils, monstrous either one apart,
Possessed me, and were long and loath at going:
A cry of Absence, Absence, in the heart,
And in the wood the furious winter blowing.

Think not, when fire was bright upon my bricks,   5
And past the tight boards hardly a wind could enter,
I glowed like them, the simple burning sticks,
Far from my cause, my proper heat and centre.

Better to walk forth in the murderous air   9
And wash my wound in the snows; that would be healing;
Because my heart would throb less painful there,
Being caked with cold, and past the smart of feeling.

And where I went, the hugest winter blast   13
Would have this body bowed, these eyeballs streaming,
And though I think this heart's blood froze not fast
It ran too small to spare one drop for dreaming.

Dear love, these fingers that had known your touch,   17
And tied our separate forces first together,
Were ten poor idiot fingers not worth much,
Ten frozen parsnips hanging in the weather.

Bells for John Whitesides' Daughter

There was such speed in her little body,
And such lightness in her footfall,
It is no wonder her brown study
Astonishes us all.

Her wars were bruited in our high window.   5
We looked among orchard trees and beyond,
Where she took arms against her shadow,
Or harried unto the pond

The lazy geese, like a snow cloud   9
Dripping their snow on the green grass,
Tricking and stopping, sleepy and proud,
Who cried in goose, Alas,

For the tireless heart within the little   13
Lady with rod that made them rise
From their noon apple dreams, and scuttle
Goose-fashion under the skies!

But now go the bells, and we are ready;   17
In one house we are sternly stopped
To say we are vexed at her brown study,
Lying so primly propped.

Critique

1. ... Now the peculiar effect of this admirable little poem is
largely implied in the words *astonishes* and *vexed*. First, simple
grief is not the content of the primary statement. We are astonished
at this event, which, though common to nature, has upset our human calculation. Second, it is not a poem whose aim is unvarnished
pathos of recollection. Third, the resolution of the grief is not on a
compensatory basis, as is common in the elegy formula. It is something more modest. The word *vexed* indicates its nature: the aston-
ishment, the pathos, are absorbed into the total body of the mourner's
experiences and given perspective so that the manly understate-

3, 19 *brown study:* attitude of musing.   5 *bruited:* reported.

ment is all that is to be allowed. We are shaken, but not as a leaf.

(ROBERT PENN WARREN)

2. ... Stanzas two, three, and four, which show the child in life, do not keep saying that she was lively; they do not say it at all. Instead they use a special image of liveliness: the image of war. This not only gives a picture of the ultimate in physical energy, but by its irony—the irony of a little girl as a warrior—it further counteracts the danger of the obvious. A similar ironic counter-action lies in the humorous lament of the victims, who "cried in goose, Alas." Only the word *tireless* (l. 13) literally names the thing being communicated to us . . . .   (ROBERT B. HEILMAN)

BIBLIOGRAPHY

Heilman, R. B., *Pacific Spectator*, 5 (Autumn 1951), 459; Warren, R. P., *Virginia Quarterly Review*, 11 (Jan. 1935), 106.

The Equilibrists

Full of her long white arms and milky skin
He had a thousand times remembered sin.
Alone in the press of people travelled he,
Minding her jacinth and myrrh and ivory.

Mouth he remembered: the quaint orifice   5
From which came heat that flamed upon the kiss,
Till cold words came down spiral from the head,
Grey doves from the officious tower illsped.

Body: it was a white field ready for love.   9
On her body's field, with the gaunt tower above,
The lilies grew, beseeching him to take,
If he would pluck and wear them, bruise and break.

Eyes talking: Never mind the cruel words,   13
Embrace my flowers but not embrace the swords.
But what they said, the doves came straightway flying
And unsaid: Honor, Honor, they came crying.

Importunate her doves. Too pure, too wise,   17
Clambering on his shoulder, saying, Arise,
Leave me now, and never let us meet,
Eternal distance now command thy feet.

Predicament indeed, which thus discovers   21
Honor among thieves, Honor between lovers.
O such a little word is Honor, they feel!
But the grey word is between them cold as steel.

At length I saw these lovers fully were come   25
Into their torture of equilibrium:
Dreadfully had forsworn each other, and yet
They were bound each to each, and they did not forget.

And rigid as two painful stars, and twirled   29
About the clustered night their prison world,
They burned with fierce love always to come near,
But Honor beat them back and kept them clear.

Ah, the strict lovers, they are ruined now!   33
I cried in anger. But with puddled brow
Devising for those gibbeted and brave
Came I descanting: Man, what would you have?

For spin your period out, and draw your breath,   37
A kinder saeculum begins with Death.
Would you ascend to Heaven and bodiless dwell?
Or take your bodies honorless to Hell?

In Heaven you have heard no marriage is,   41
No white flesh tinder to your lecheries,
Your male and female tissue sweetly shaped
Sublimed away, and furious blood escaped.

Great lovers lie in Hell, the stubborn ones   45
Infatuate of the flesh upon the bones;
Stuprate, they rend each other when they kiss;
The pieces kiss again—no end to this.

But still I watched them spinning, orbited nice,   49
Their flames were not more radiant than their ice.
I dug in the quiet earth and wrought the tomb
And made these lines to memorize their doom:—

Equilibrists lie here; stranger, tread light;   53
Close, but untouching in each other's sight;
Mouldered the lips and ashy the tall skull,
Let them lie perilous and beautiful.

35 *gibbeted:* hanged, or defamed.   38 *saeculum:* age.   47 *Stuprate:* ravished.

Naming of Parts

To-day we have naming of parts. Yesterday,
We had daily cleaning. And to-morrow morning,
We shall have what to do after firing. But to-day,
To-day we have naming of parts. Japonica   4
Glistens like coral in all of the neighbouring gardens,
    And to-day we have naming of parts.

This is the lower sling swivel. And this   7
Is the upper sling swivel, whose use you will see,
When you are given your slings. And this is the piling swivel,
Which in your case you have not got. The branches   10
Hold in the gardens, their silent, eloquent gestures,
    Which in our case we have not got.

This is the safety-catch, which is always released   13
With an easy flick of the thumb. And please do not let me
See anyone using his finger. You can do it quite easy
If you have any strength in your thumb. The blossoms   16
Are fragile and motionless, never letting anyone see
    Any of them using their finger.

And this you can see is the bolt. The purpose of this   19
Is to open the breech, as you see. We can slide it
Rapidly backwards and forwards: we call this
Easing the spring. And rapidly backwards and forwards   22
The early bees are assaulting and fumbling the flowers:
    They call it easing the Spring.

They call it easing the Spring: it is perfectly easy   25
If you have any strength in your thumb: like the bolt,
And the breech, and the cocking-piece, and the point of balance,
Which in our case we have not got; and the almond-blossom   28
Silent in all of the gardens and the bees going backwards and forwards,
    For to-day we have naming of parts.

Luke Havergal

    Go to the western gate, Luke Havergal,
    There where the vines cling crimson on the wall,
    And in the twilight wait for what will come.
    The leaves will whisper there of her, and some,

Like flying words, will strike you as they fall;   5
But go, and if you listen she will call.
Go to the western gate, Luke Havergal—
Luke Havergal.

No, there is not a dawn in eastern skies   9
To rift the fiery night that's in your eyes;
But there, where western glooms are gathering,
The dark will end the dark, if anything:
God slays Himself with every leaf that flies,   13
And hell is more than half of paradise.
No, there is not a dawn in eastern skies—
In eastern skies.

Out of a grave I come to tell you this,   17
Out of a grave I come to quench the kiss
That flames upon your forehead with a glow
That blinds you to the way that you must go.
Yes, there is yet one way to where she is,   21
Bitter, but one that faith may never miss.
Out of a grave I come to tell you this—
To tell you this.

There is the western gate, Luke Havergal,   25
There are the crimson leaves upon the wall.
Go, for the winds are tearing them away—
Nor think to riddle the dead words they say,
Nor any more to feel them as they fall;   29
But go, and if you trust her she will call.
There is the western gate, Luke Havergal—
Luke Havergal.

Critique

1. ... Theodore Roosevelt ... wrote: "I am not sure that I understand 'Luke Havergal', but I am entirely sure that I like it." Readers
less extroverted and less occupied than Roosevelt may agree with
the latter part of this presidential proclamation and yet feel less
satisfied until they *do* understand the poem . . . . And even if, after
long reflection, we decide tentatively that "she" is the woman,
now dead, whom Luke has loved; that the voice is that of his own

grief and longing; and that "the western gate" is self-inflicted death, we still do not *quite* know. Robinson's own references to the poem—once as "my uncomfortable abstraction" and again as "a piece of deliberate degeneration"—still leave the picture far from clear.

(ELLSWORTH BARNARD)

2. Three persons are involved in the situation: (a) the mysterious speaker "out of a grave" who counsels (b) Luke how to hear (c) his loved one call. Luke is advised to go to the western gate, to wait in the twilight, to seek the dark (completion, certainty) that will end the dark (incompleteness, doubt) of Luke's blindness (line 20). He is specifically warned not to look for a dawn in eastern skies (renewal, the return of his lost loved one in a new day). The "western gate," then, seems the goal of faith (line 22) and trust (line 30) in the woman Luke seeks. On the one hand, the speaker offers ambiguous advice about the power of the dark to end the dark: "if anything" the speaker qualifies, the dark will end Luke's uncertainty and doubt. Later, on the other hand, the speaker's advice becomes more positive and clear: "If you trust her, she will call" (line 30). . . .

One more tentative suggestion. Luke has to learn from God's slaying himself, i.e., a part of himself in nature's seasonal death, that there is no perfection by itself alone, that all is relative, with pleasure amounting to less than half of life (line 14). Luke is blinded (line 20) because he expects absolute, rather than relative, love. . . . To win her voice he must learn to abandon the hope for more . . . . (WALTER GIERASCH)

BIBLIOGRAPHY

Barnard, E., *Edwin Arlington Robinson*, 1952, p. 44; Gierasch, W., *Explicator*, 3 (Oct. 1944), 8.

Cliff Klingenhagen

Cliff Klingenhagen had me in to dine
With him one day; and after soup and meat,
And all the other things there were to eat,
Cliff took two glasses and filled one with wine

And one with wormwood. Then, without a sign   5
For me to choose at all, he took the draught
Of bitterness himself, and lightly quaffed
It off, and said the other one was mine.

And when I asked him what the deuce he meant   9
By doing that, he only looked at me
And smiled, and said it was a way of his.
And though I know the fellow, I have spent
Long time a-wondering when I shall be
As happy as Cliff Klingenhagen is.   14

Richard Cory

Whenever Richard Cory went down town,
We people on the pavement looked at him:
He was a gentleman from sole to crown,
Clean favored, and imperially slim.

And he was always quietly arrayed,   5
And he was always human when he talked;
But still he fluttered pulses when he said,
"Good-morning," and he glittered when he walked.

And he was rich—yes, richer than a king—   9
And admirably schooled in every grace:
In fine, we thought that he was everything
To make us wish that we were in his place.

So on we worked, and waited for the light,   13
And went without the meat, and cursed the bread;
And Richard Cory, one calm summer night,
Went home and put a bullet through his head.

Miniver Cheevy

Miniver Cheevy, child of scorn,
    Grew lean while he assailed the seasons;
He wept that he was ever born,
    And he had reasons.

Miniver loved the days of old   5
　　When swords were bright and steeds were prancing;
The vision of a warrior bold
　　Would set him dancing.

Miniver sighed for what was not,   9
　　And dreamed, and rested from his labors;
He dreamed of Thebes and Camelot,
　　And Priam's neighbors.

Miniver mourned the ripe renown   13
　　That made so many a name so fragrant;
He mourned Romance, now on the town,
　　And Art, a vagrant.

Miniver loved the Medici,   17
　　Albeit he had never seen one;
He would have sinned incessantly
　　Could he have been one.

Miniver cursed the commonplace   21
　　And eyed a khaki suit with loathing;
He missed the medieval grace
　　Of iron clothing.

Miniver scorned the gold he sought,   25
　　But sore annoyed was he without it;
Miniver thought, and thought, and thought,
　　And thought about it.

Miniver Cheevy, born too late,   29
　　Scratched his head and kept on thinking;
Miniver coughed, and called it fate,
　　And kept on drinking.

Mr. Flood's Party

Old Eben Flood, climbing alone one night
Over the hill between the town below
And the forsaken upland hermitage
That held as much as he should ever know
On earth again of home, paused warily.   5

The road was his with not a native near;
And Eben, having leisure, said aloud,
For no man else in Tilbury Town to hear:

"Well, Mr. Flood, we have the harvest moon   9
Again, and we may not have many more;
The bird is on the wing, the poet says,
And you and I have said it here before.
Drink to the bird." He raised up to the light   13
The jug that he had gone so far to fill,
And answered huskily: "Well, Mr. Flood,
Since you propose it, I believe I will."

Alone, as if enduring to the end   17
A valiant armor of scarred hopes outworn,
He stood there in the middle of the road
Like Roland's ghost winding a silent horn.
Below him, in the town among the trees,   21
Where friends of other days had honored him,
A phantom salutation of the dead
Rang thinly till old Eben's eyes were dim.

Then, as a mother lays her sleeping child   25
Down tenderly, fearing it may awake,
He set the jug down slowly at his feet
With trembling care, knowing that most things break;
And only when assured that on firm earth   29
It stood, as the uncertain lives of men
Assuredly did not, he paced away,
And with his hand extended paused again:

"Well, Mr. Flood, we have not met like this   33
In a long time; and many a change has come
To both of us, I fear, since last it was
We had a drop together. Welcome home!"
Convivially returning with himself,   37
Again he raised the jug up to the light;
And with an acquiescent quaver said:
"Well, Mr. Flood, if you insist, I might.

11 *the poet*: Edward Fitzgerald, in the *Rubáiyát of Omar Khayyám*, line 28.
17-24: The hero of the medieval French romance, *The Song of Roland*, dies
fighting for Charlemagne against the pagans. Before he dies, he blows his miraculous horn to summon aid, and receives an answer from the king's horns, but
the army arrives too late.

"Only a very little, Mr. Flood—   41
For auld lang syne. No more, sir; that will do."
So, for the time, apparently it did,
And Eben evidently thought so too;
For soon amid the silver loneliness   45
Of night he lifted up his voice and sang,
Secure, with only two moons listening,
Until the whole harmonious landscape rang—

"For auld lang syne." The weary throat gave out.   49
The last word wavered; and the song being done,
He raised again the jug regretfully
And shook his head, and was again alone.
There was not much that was ahead of him,   53
And there was nothing in the town below—
Where strangers would have shut the many doors
That many friends had opened long ago.

Case

A

1. The poem humorously characterizes an alcoholic old codger ostracized by the community.

2. Mr. Flood's chronic alcoholism is revealed by the typical activity of drinking alone, getting drunk, talking to himself, going through the physical motions of an illusory situation, weeping, and pitying himself.

3. Despite the poignancy of the situation, the tone of the poet is for the most part light and witty, as in the contrast between Mr. Flood and Roland.

B

1. The poem sympathetically characterizes a respectable old man who has outlived his time.

2. Eben Flood, once known and liked by men who have since died, attempts to cheer himself up by a mild, circumspect, and rather unaccustomed intoxication.

3. Despite Eben's shortcomings, the poet's tone is sympathetic, as in the comparison between Mr. Flood and Roland.

BIBLIOGRAPHY

Brooks, C., and R. P. Warren, *Understanding Poetry*, 1950 ed., pp. 172-73; 1960 ed., pp. 214-18; Jacobs, W. D., *College English*, **12** (Nov. 1950), 110; Owney, E. S., *Explicator*, **8** (Apr. 1950), 47.

My Papa's Waltz

The whiskey on your breath
Could make a small boy dizzy;
But I hung on like death:
Such waltzing was not easy.

We romped until the pans   5
Slid from the kitchen shelf;
My mother's countenance
Could not unfrown itself.

The hand that held my wrist   9
Was battered on one knuckle;
At every step you missed
My right ear scraped a buckle.

You beat time on my head   13
With a palm caked hard by dirt,
Then waltzed me off to bed
Still clinging to your shirt.

Elegy for Jane

My Student, Thrown by a Horse

I remember the neckcurls, limp and damp as tendrils;
And her quick look, a sidelong pickerel smile;
And how, once startled into talk, the light syllables leaped for her,
And she balanced in the delight of her thought,
A wren, happy, tail into the wind,   5
Her song trembling the twigs and small branches.

The shade sang with her;
The leaves, their whispers turned to kissing;
And the mold sang in the bleached valleys under the rose.

Oh, when she was sad, she cast herself down into such a pure depth, 10
Even a father could not find her:
Scraping her cheek against straw;
Stirring the clearest water.

My sparrow, you are not here,   14
Waiting like a fern, making a spiny shadow.
The sides of wet stones cannot console me,
Nor the moss, wound with the last light.

If only I could nudge you from this sleep,   18
My maimed darling, my skittery pigeon.
Over this damp grave I speak the words of my love:
I, with no rights in this matter,
Neither father nor lover.   22

The Woodspurge

The wind flapped loose, the wind was still,
Shaken out dead from tree and hill:
I had walked on at the wind's will,—
I sat now, for the wind was still.

Between my knees my forehead was,—   5
My lips, drawn in, said not Alas!
My hair was over in the grass,
My naked ears heard the day pass.

My eyes, wide open, had the run   9
Of some ten weeds to fix upon;
Among those few, out of the sun,
The woodspurge flowered, three cups in one.

From perfect grief there need not be   13
Wisdom or even memory:
One thing then learnt remains to me,—
The woodspurge has a cup of three.

When Icicles Hang by the Wall

When icicles hang by the wall,
And Dick the shepherd blows his nail,
And Tom bears logs into the hall,
And milk comes frozen home in pail:
When blood is nipped, and ways be foul,   5
Then nightly sings the staring owl,
Tu-whit tu-who:
    A merry note,
    While greasy Joan doth keel the pot.

When all aloud the wind doth blow,   10
And coughing drowns the parson's saw,
And birds sit brooding in the snow,
And Marian's nose looks red and raw:
When roasted crabs hiss in the bowl,   14
Then nightly sings the staring owl,
Tu-whit tu-who:
    A merry note,
    While greasy Joan doth keel the pot.

When to the Sessions of Sweet Silent Thought

(Sonnet 30)

When to the sessions of sweet silent thought
I summon up remembrance of things past,
I sigh the lack of many a thing I sought,
And with old woes new wail my dear time's waste.
Then can I drown an eye, unused to flow,   5
For precious friends hid in death's dateless night,
And weep afresh love's long since cancelled woe,
And moan th'expense of many a vanished sight.
Then can I grieve at grievances foregone,   9
And heavily from woe to woe tell o'er
The sad account of fore-bemoaned moan,
Which I new pay as if not paid before.
    But if the while I think on thee, dear friend,
    All losses are restored, and sorrows end.   14

2 *his nail:* on his finger-nails. 5 *ways:* roads. 8 *keel:* cool against boiling
over. 11 *saw:* saying. 14 *crabs:* crab-apples.

8 *expense:* loss. 10 *tell:* count.

Critique

A

[The following analysis by Stephen C. Pepper considers the sonnet from four points of view: (1) the poem as a source of pleasure, (2) the poem as an experience of a unique quality, (3) the poem as an organic whole, and (4) the poem as an expression of universal or archetypal norms.]

1. . . . What immediate pleasures are to be found in this poem?
. . .

Consider its sensuous character. It flows with ease in the reading. Over an underlying five stress pulsing of iambic meter broad explicit rhythms of speech follow the movement of thought and emotion. There is constant rhythmic variety from line to line. . . .

Turn to the sounds themselves, the pleasant sequences of the consonants and vowels. . . . The poem is rich in alliteration and assonances, the *s*'s in the first three lines, the *w*'s in the fourth, and so on. . . .

And now consider the imagery and thought which are the special medium of poetry. . . . Pick a few of the most striking images: "Sessions of sweet silent thought," "my dear time's waste," "death's dateless night." These are the more remarkable in that the ideas they image are very abstract. . . .

Note, too, how this sort of poetic guidance of our associations transmutes the thought of a depression which is the main subject matter of the poem into something glorious and entrancing. "Death's dateless night" shows the way of this transformation most clearly. The idea is grief for his lost friends. But the great emptiness of death becomes under the poet's guidance the glory of a moonless and perhaps cloudless night under the changeless stars, the static symbol of eternity. . . .   •

As for the design of the poem, it is based on a contrast of thought and emotion between the sadness of the first three quatrains and the joy at the recollection of the friend in the final couplet. There is a sense of emotional gradation rising through the quatrains, and the couplet is expected as a climax and comes with the extra surprise of a contrasting joy. The joy is greater for the preceding sadness. . . .

Altogether the poem exhibits an exceptional capacity for pleasant stimulation and this increases with added discrimination. It is an exceptionally fine poem.

2. ... The details pointed out in the preceding account . . . are all aesthetically significant. But the [first analysis] puts the wrong emphasis upon them. . . . It is their vividness of quality that makes them important in the poem. . . .

What needs to be noted in all these details is their freedom from banality, their freshness which in general arises from stresses and conflicts in their contexts. The conflicts have to be so adjusted that, while they break through the dullness of habit and custom, they do not break out into practical action. . . .

The sadness of the theme is a case in point. This is an emotional fusion of suggested frustrations. The poet calls the conflicts out, "old woes," "dear time's waste," "precious friends" gone. The very intonation and rhythms of the phrases, the muffled vowels ("summon up remembrance"), and the wailing vowels and consonants further support the emotion. But the writer keeps it well below the threshold where it would become too painful and prompt a decisive and ends on a bright note, which by its contrast (a mode of conflict) makes its own contribution to vivid perception. We are prompted to read the poem immediately again. . . .

While we are on this point, observe that we have stumbled on the total fused quality, the unique quality, of the poem—name it how you will—world weariness, dejection, worry, but warmed with practical action such as closing the book. In fact, he takes no chances love in the specific manner Shakespeare makes you feel. . . .

Altogether . . . , we judge the poem exceptionally rich and vivid in quality.

3. ... Let us begin with the theme. The [second analysis] stated it well if somewhat emotionally. It is the feeling of a man in depression over adversity suddenly lifted at the thought of a dear friend. The pattern of the Shakespearean sonnet is obviously perfectly adapted to such a theme. The form might almost have suggested the theme.

The fitness of the imagery and the selections of sounds and rhythms have already been remarked on. . . . But the remarks were rather general and spotty. They missed the high degree of integration of all the imagery within itself and of all sound within itself and of each with each other that the poem contains. . . .

. . . Neither of the previous judgments noticed the inner ties

among all the main images of the poem. . . . They are all details
in the metaphor of a merchant's debts. . . . Consider "sessions,"
"summon," "old," "new," "dear," "waste," "unused," "precious,"
"date," "long since cancelled," "expense," "grievances," "heavily,"
"tell o'er," "account," "pay," "losses are restored." These images
springing from the metaphor are then all one connected image,
and from it like leaves from branches of a tree depend all the other
images of the poem. Moreover, notice how apt, how connected,
this legal and commercial image is with the theme of the poem.
From the misery of threatened bankruptcy all losses may be restored to the poor man if some one remaining piece of property
proves sound in value. . . .

. . . We cannot deny that the poem approaches very nearly to
its full capacity of aesthetic integration, or, in other words, its own
unique form of perfection.

4. . . . I now ask about the normality of the poem. How well
does it represent its culture? . . . How satisfying is it to a fully
developed highly discriminating man? . . . The first question need
not detain us, for this poem raises no serious problem of cultural
discrepancies. It is admired today probably very much as it was
admired in its own time. . . .

We need to consider carefully only the last and crucial question. And here no problem appears to present itself. The poem is
an expression of a normal emotional reaction to a frustrating situation. It depicts the instinctive attitude of grief in the recollection
of irretrievable loss, and the sudden comfort that comes in the
thought of love. The poem taps basic instincts and truthfully describes them as the normal man would exhibit them. We all recognize
ourselves in this sort of situation, and are elevated, so to speak, in
sharing in this expression of our own basic nature and capacities,
and, if we are under similar stress, we may experience catharsis.
It is a supremely good poem, in that sense of goodness . . . in which
the aesthetic and the moral come very close together. For it is a
poem that induces balance and adjustment of character in the
reader.

B

[The following abridged analysis by Samuel R. Levin considers
the sonnet from a linguistic point of view. For practical amateur

purposes, "syntagmatic" means "syntactic"; NP, VP, and C mean noun phrase, verb phrase, and conjunction; and "coupling" is Levin's term for the poetic phenomenon, described in his book, wherein equivalent meanings and/or sounds stand in equivalent syntactic, metrical, or rhyming positions.]

6.2 Constructionally, the entire sonnet consists of two conditional sentences . . . . Lines 1-2 constitute the first condition, lines 3-4—extended through lines 5-12—constitute the first conclusion; line 13 constitutes the second condition, line 14 the second conclusion. . . . These are parallel couplings which unify the poem in the first instance. The couplings may be described as follows: *when* of line 1 and *if* of line 13 are semantically equivalent and occur in equivalent syntagmatic positions; *then,* in its zero form, at the beginning of line 3 is semantically equivalent to and occurs in the same position as *then,* again in its zero form, at the beginning of line 14. . . .

In the clauses introduced by the respective *if-then*'s there are also a number of couplings. . . . The constructions underlying the lines in question may be represented in the following manner:

When − *to* − NP_1 (*the sessions*) − *of* − NP_2 (*sweet silent thought*)
NP_3 (*I*) − VP_1 (*summon up*) − NP_4 (*remembrance of things past*),
Then − NP_5 (*I*) − VP_2 (*sigh*) − NP_6 (*the lack of many a thing I sought*)
C − *with* − NP_7 (*old woes*) − NP_8 (*I*) − VP_3 (*new wail*) − NP_9 (*my dear time's waste*).
C − *if* − *the while* − NP_{10} (*I*) − VP_4 (*think*) − *on* − NP_{11} (*thee, dear friend*),
Then NP_{12} (*you*) − VP_5 (*restore*) − NP_{13} (*all losses*) − *C* − NP_{14} (*you*) − VP_6 (*end*) − NP_{15} (*sorrows*). . . .

Following are the couplings in these constructions; the natural equivalence is semantic, based either on similarity or antinomy; in the two *if*-clauses: $NP_3 \sim NP_{10}$, $VP_1 \sim VP_4$, $NP_4 \sim NP_{11}$; in the two *then*-clauses: $NP_5 \sim NP_{12}$, $VP_2 \sim VP_5$, $NP_6 \sim NP_{13}$ and, after the conjunctions, $NP_8 \sim NP_{14}$, $VP_3 \sim VP_6$, $NP_9 \sim NP_{15}$. . . .

6.5 The rhyme scheme of the poem is *abab, cdcd, efef, gg.* As we have seen . . . rhymes constitute couplings. The alternate rhymes of the first four lines occur with the first *if-then* sentence, and alternate rhymes occur with the amplification of this sentence through lines 5-12. The second *if-then* sentence (ll. 13-14) is accompanied by the immediate rhyme, *gg.* There is thus reinforcement of the syntagmatic structure by the rhyme structure. The fact that the sonnet employs the two types of rhyme and that the two immediate syntagmatic constituents correlate with these two types is largely responsible (along with the use of the adversative conjunction *but* of line 13) for the sense of juncture at the concluding couplet of the sonnet, and the sense of unity at its close.

6.6 In the first amplifying *then* clause (beginning with line 3), we find the following verbs, all semantically equivalent monosyllables, predicated of the subject *I*: *sigh, wail, drown (an eye), weep, moan,* and *grieve.* Inasmuch as these verbs are all predicated of the same subject, they occur in equivalent syntagmatic positions, in a comparable construction . . . and thus constitute a series of couplings. The fact that they all occur under the metrical stress renders them couplings on the conventional axis also. As objects of *sigh, wail,* and *moan,* we find *lack, waste,* and *expense,* the latter likewise constituting a series of couplings. . . .

6.9 . . . Other couplings could be described for this sonnet, but perhaps enough has already been done to indicate the integral and thoroughgoing role that these structures play in the poem's organization. Their major function is to unify the poem, this unity being due to the various and interlocking kinds of equivalence which lie behind couplings. But another result of the coupling principle as it is used in poetry is to make the poem memorable. It is frequently maintained, for instance, that rhyme is a mnemonic aid. Obviously, rhyme is such an aid because, having thought of one line in a rhymed piece, the possibilities at the end of the succeeding lines are restricted quite severely by the rhyme requirement. But couplings, by definition, impose similar restrictions at equivalent metrical and syntagmatic positions also. In a poem there are thus numerous points—syntagmatic, metrical, or rhyme— at which the mind is prompted to selection from among the stringently restricted subgroups of forms that are semantically and/or phonically equivalent to the form occurring in the preceding equivalent position. The unity and memorability of poetry are thus related, and find their common basis in coupling.

BIBLIOGRAPHY

Levin, S. R., *Linguistic Structures in Poetry,* 1962, pp. 52-58; Pepper, S. C., *The Basis of Criticism in the Arts,* 1945, pp. 115-27.

Let Me Not to the Marriage of True Minds

(Sonnet 116)

Let me not to the marriage of true minds
Admit impediments. Love is not love
Which alters when it alteration finds,
Or bends with the remover to remove.
O no, it is an ever fixed mark   5
That looks on tempests and is never shaken;
It is the star to every wandering bark,
Whose worth's unknown, although his height be taken.
Love's not Time's fool, though rosy lips and cheeks   9
Within his bending sickle's compass come;
Love alters not with his brief hours and weeks,
But bears it out even to the edge of doom.
  If this be error and upon me proved,
  I never writ, nor no man ever loved.   14

That Time of Year Thou Mayst in Me Behold

(Sonnet 73)

1 That time of year thou mayst in me behold
2 When yellow leaves, or none, or few, do hang
3 Upon those boughs which shake against the cold,
4 Bare ruined choirs, where late the sweet birds sang.
5 In me thou seest the twilight of such day   5
6 As after sunset fadeth in the west,
7 Which by and by black night doth take away,
8 Death's second self that seals up all in rest.
9 In me thou seest the glowing of such fire   9
10 That on the ashes of his youth doth lie,
11 As the death bed whereon it must expire,
12 Consumed with that which it was nourished by.
13 This thou perceivst, which makes thy love more strong,
14 To love that well which thou must leave ere long.   14

7 *bark*: ship.   8 *height be taken*: altitude be calculated.

Case

A

1. The primary theme is the speaker's appreciation of and desire for "thou's" devotion.

2. Structurally, the sonnet consists of four parts—three metaphorical quatrains modifying "this" (13) and an unadorned concluding couplet directly stating "thou's" love for the speaker.

3. At the same time that the speaker is calling attention to "thou's" devotion, he is subtly, perhaps unconsciously, asking for this devotion—by the doleful picture he paints of himself, by such an effect as the poignant, rhythmical uncertainty of line 2, by the very mention of death twice, and by an unexpected "*thou* must leave" when it is actually the speaker who is going to leave.

B

1. The primary theme is a contrast between the ravages of age and the vitality of youth.

2. The concluding couplet points a moral for the younger listener: since you see my situation as I grow old, you cling more vigorously to the youthful joys which you soon must put behind you.

3. The failings of old age are contrasted with happier youth in each quatrain by the symbols of winter vs. summer, night vs. day, and smoldering vs. burning.

Bibliography

Lumiansky, R. M., *Explicator,* 6 (June 1948), 55; Lynskey, W., *College English,* 5 (Feb. 1944), 244-45; Moore, C., *Explicator,* 8 (Oct. 1949), 2; Nolan, E. F., *Explicator,* 7 (Nov. 1948), 13; Ransom, J. C., *The New Criticism,* 1941, pp. 121-29; ———, *The World's Body,* 1937, pp. 297-98; Smith, H., *Elizabethan Poetry,* 1952, pp. 182-85; Thomas, W., and S. G. Brown, *Reading Poems,* 1941, pp. 744-48.

Th' Expense of Spirit in a Waste of Shame

(Sonnet 129)

1 Th'expense of spirit in a waste of shame
2 Is lust in action, and till action, lust
3 Is perjured, murderous, bloody, full of blame,
4 Savage, extreme, rude, cruel, not to trust,
5 Enjoyed no sooner but despised straight,
6 Past reason hunted, and no sooner had
7 Past reason hated, as a swallowed bait
8 On purpose laid to make the taker mad;
9 Mad in pursuit and in possession so,
10 Had, having, and in quest to have, extreme,
11 A bliss in proof, and [proved, a] very woe,
12 Before, a joy proposed; behind, a dream.
13   All this the world well knows, yet none knows well
14   To shun the heaven that leads men to this hell.

My Mistress' Eyes Are Nothing Like the Sun

(Sonnet 130)

My mistress' eyes are nothing like the sun,
Coral is far more red than her lips' red,
If snow be white, why then her breasts are dun,
If hairs be wires, black wires grow on her head.
I have seen roses damasked, red and white,
But no such roses see I in her cheeks,
And in some perfumes is there more delight
Than in the breath that from my mistress reeks.
I love to hear her speak, yet well I know
That music hath a far more pleasing sound;
I grant I never saw a goddess go:
My mistress, when she walks, treads on the ground.
    And yet, by heaven, I think my love as rare
    As any she belied with false compare.

---

1 *expense:* expenditure.   11 *proof:* experience. *proved, a:* accepted emendation for "proud and."

---

5 *damasked:* of mixed colors; variegated.   14 *she:* used as noun. *compare:* comparison.

Poor Soul, the Center of My Sinful Earth

(Sonnet 146)

Poor soul, the center of my sinful earth,
[Thrall to] these rebel powers that thee array,
Why dost thou pine within and suffer dearth,
Painting thy outward walls so costly gay?
Why so large cost, having so short a lease,   5
Dost thou upon thy fading mansion spend?
Shall worms, inheritors of this excess,
Eat up thy charge? Is this thy body's end?
Then, soul, live thou upon thy servant's loss,   9
And let that pine to aggravate thy store;
Buy terms divine in selling hours of dross;
Within be fed, without be rich no more.
　　So shalt thou feed on death, that feeds on men.
　　And death once dead, there's no more dying then.   14

2 *Thrall to:* usual emendation for an obvious error in the original printed text. *Thrall:* slave.　2 *array:* clothe (?).　8 *charge:* load.　10 *aggravate:* increase. 11 *terms:* periods of time.　11 *dross:* rubbish.　12 *without:* outside.

Critique

BEN BROWER: Perhaps the best beginning is to translate the poem into direct assertions in prose. The sonnet—and this is one of its most striking features—is dramatic in form; the poet is talking to his soul; one part of his consciousness is giving advice to another part. The argument is that the body and bodily pleasures, being transient and mortal, merit less attention than they ordinarily receive, or than they have received from the poet in the past. By a relative neglect of the body, therefore, and a concentration upon the soul which is immortal and partakes of divinity, mortality itself may be disregarded and even destroyed and spiritual strength may be achieved.

Yet such a prose analysis of the argument hardly begins to touch the poem. We must also look at the subtle shifts in emotional moods that give the sonnet its own poetic individuality. The tone at the beginning is reflective and even depressed. . . . There is a sharp change of tone, however, after the first two lines. . . . And in the succeeding questions the tone shifts steadily toward conviction that the course of the poet's life should and must be changed. As a result the final section of the poem moves on to assertion and action and closes in a key of affirmation far removed from the poignant, pitying doubt of the opening lines. This sonnet does not leave the reader in a quiet, single, simple frame of mind but carries him rapidly from one mood to another; it modulates from the minor to the major. Much of its richness comes from the various double meanings and overtones in the words and phrases; and in the main this complexity springs from the many fields of imagery which Shakespeare uses in order to realize his argument—architecture, real estate, money, inheritances. The metaphors derived from clothes and from eating give the sonnet a quality of robustness and sane humor throughout. . . .

JOHN CROWE RANSOM: But do you not find the imagery of the eating worms itself so excessive as to destroy any calm ethical judgments in the argument?

BEN: Gross and sensational it is, no doubt. And necessarily so. . . . Since the sonnet is in constant peril of turning into a flat moral lecture, Shakespeare cleverly manages to keep the argument from appearing priggish not only by using such emotional imagery but also by throwing most of it into the form of questions. The impression I get from the whole is that Shakespeare is being over-ingenious. He is writing with an air of great sophistication and worldly experience. . . .

DAN AARON: . . . I find it jaunty, full of a kind of super-wit. . . . It is positive and clever: Death may be hoodwinked and cheated out of its power only by the poet's resolved attitude toward the body. Yet the poem is forceful because it is genuinely dramatic: in spite of this central mood of jauntiness, the opponents are the worms, the flesh and the grave; therefore a certain grimness and irony are present.[1]

ELIZABETH DREW: I do not see, Dan, how you can call the tone

---

[1] *Edward Hubler:* . . . Surely it should be apparent to all men in their senses that although there is often wit in Shakespeare's seriousness, this is not a jaunty poem, that the poem is Christian, and that Shakespeare presents the Christianity without apology. The "opponents" are neither the worms nor the grave. The opponent is the inherent willfulness of the flesh, and the poem says that when sin is conquered death is conquered, for death has no power over the soul. . . .

of the whole poem jaunty and witty, nor where you, Ben, find this sane and robust humor.

BEN: In the imagery. Think how bloodless and highly serious the poem would be without its food and clothing!

DAN: And if the poem is not jaunty and witty and grim and ironical, what is it?

MISS DREW: It is plaintive, for one thing. Surely at the beginning Shakespeare is gentle with an almost paternal pity toward the soul's credulity. . . .

And now I come to something which I find hard to put in words and impossible to defend or demonstrate logically. It is the difference between the feeling of the whole poem and its argument. I do not believe that Shakespeare is making out a case for immortality except as a formal device. He convinces neither himself nor me. . . . Superficially I suppose we could call the doctrine of the poem Christian; it is conventional in its argument; it is almost sentimental in its doing away with the painful and the transient and the worthless, in its centering man's hope upon immortality and a system of future rewards and punishments. Yet in reading the poem I feel not a future but an immediate triumph over death. . . .

This feeling, for me, makes the last lines even more poignant than the opening; for Shakespeare's imaginative moving toward "terms divine," to him so tenuous, only increases the glory of the senses and of this world. . . . The individual life—not immortality, and not life in any one of its aspects—is in itself achievement and confirmation.

DONALD STAUFFER: You have said what I dimly felt, Elizabeth, so much better than I could that there's no need nor luck in my trying. I must take a different tack.

At the start I knew I liked the poem and was puzzled by it. I tried to ask myself why I liked it. Basically, I decided that my liking—of this poem or of any poem—sprang from moral agreement with the poet. I do not think that this is part of an esthetic judgment. But I find that in my case this conviction of the importance of the subject is a necessary preliminary to more purely esthetic pleasures in the form or manner or finality or perfection of the expression. I must be interested in *what* is made into a poem before I can wholly enjoy the making. . . .

Finally, I found that in spite of any theories I may try to hold about an absolute poem complete in itself, much of the richness of this sonnet came because I knew it was Shakespeare's, so that for me this poem carried in it the weight and associations of his other writings. . . .

MR. RANSOM: . . . Reading the poem with a vivid attention to the images, as I try to do, actually makes parts of it shocking. Lines seven, eight and thirteen are cannibalistic. . . .[2]

MISS DREW: I shall be afraid to go to sleep tonight, Mr. Ransom, if you don't stop frightening us with worms and cannibals. . . .

DAN: I wonder whether we have decided anything. Perhaps each of us simply created Shakespeare in his own image. . . .

MR. RANSOM: Actually, I feel that we have agreed on more points than one. Perhaps we might call such agreement: Shakespeare's sonnet.[3]

BIBLIOGRAPHY

Hubler, E., *The Sense of Shakespeare's Sonnets*, 1952, pp. 61-62; Stauffer, D., reconstruction of discussion by Reuben A. Brower, John Crowe Ransom, Daniel Aaron, and Elizabeth Drew, *American Scholar*, **12** (Winter 1943), 52-62.

Full Fathom Five Thy Father Lies

Full fathom five thy father lies.
Of his bones are coral made;
Those are pearls that were his eyes,
Nothing of him that doth fade
But doth suffer a sea-change   5
Into something rich, and strange.
Sea-nymphs hourly ring his knell.
                    Ding dong.
            Hark, now I hear them,
                Ding-dong bell.   10

[2] *Hubler:* . . . These remarks are the expression of a sensibility so intent upon itself that it disregards the poem, except to distort it. Animals that prey upon each other, or upon carrion, do not suggest cannibalism to a more disengaged intelligence.

[3] *Hubler:* . . . There is a reluctance to admit that Shakespeare means something; or, if a meaning is admitted, there is a refusal to view it simply. The criticism of this sonnet is on the whole a dismal record of the triumph of sophistication over sense.

Buick

As a sloop with a sweep of immaculate wing on her delicate spine
And a keel as steel as a root that holds in the sea as she leans,
Leaning and laughing, my warm-hearted beauty, you ride, you ride,
You tack on the curves with parabola speed and a kiss of goodbye,
Like a thoroughbred sloop, my new high-spirited spirit, my kiss.

As my foot suggests that you leap in the air with your hips of a girl,   6
My finger that praises your wheel and announces your voices of song,
Flouncing your skirts, you blueness of joy, you flirt of politeness,
You leap, you intelligence, essence of wheelness with silvery nose,
And your platinum clocks of excitement stir like the hairs of a fern.

But how alien you are from the booming belts of your birth and the
      smoke   11
Where you turned on the stinging lathes of Detroit and Lansing at
      night
And shrieked at the torch in your secret parts and the amorous tests,
But now with your eyes that enter the future of roads you forget;
You are all instinct with your phosphorous glow and your streaking
      hair.

And now when we stop it is not as the bird from the shell that I
      leave   16
Or the leathery pilot who steps from his bird with a sneer of delight,
And not as the ignorant beast do you squat and watch me depart,
But with exquisite breathing you smile, with satisfaction of love,
And I touch you again as you tick in the silence and settle in sleep.

As You Say: an Anti-Poem

As you say (not without sadness) poets don't see, they feel. And that's
  why people who have turned to feelers seem like poets. Why children
  seem poetic. Why when the sap rises in the adolescent heart the young
  write poetry. Why great catastrophes are stated in verse. Why lunatics
  are named for the moon. Yet poetry isn't feeling with the hands. A
  poem is not a kiss. Poems are what ideas feel like. Ideas on Sunday,
  thoughts on vacation.
Poets don't see, they feel. They are conductors of the senses of men, as
  teachers and preachers are the insulators. The poets go up and feel

the insulators. Now and again they feel the wrong thing and are
thrown through a wall by a million volt shock. All insulation makes
the poet anxious: clothes, straight jackets, iambic five. He pulls at the
seams like a boy whose trousers are cutting him in half. Poets think
along the electric currents. The words are constantly not making sense
when he reads what he reads. He flunks economics, logic, history.
Then he describes what it feels like to flunk economics, logic, history.
After that he feels better.

People say: it is sad to see a grown man feeling his way, sad to see a man
so naked, desireless of any defences. The people walk back in their
boxes and triple-lock the doors. When their children begin to read
poetry the parents watch them from the corner of their eye. It's only
a phase, they aver. Parents like the word "aver."

Ozymandias

I met a traveller from an antique land
Who said: Two vast and trunkless legs of stone
Stand in the desert. . . . Near them, on the sand,
Half sunk, a shattered visage lies, whose frown,
And wrinkled lip, and sneer of cold command,   5
Tell that its sculptor well those passions read
Which yet survive, stamped on these lifeless things,
The hand that mocked them, and the heart that fed:
And on the pedestal these words appear: .   9
'My name is Ozymandias, King of Kings:
Look on my works, ye Mighty, and despair!'
Nothing beside remains. Round the decay
Of that colossal wreck, boundless and bare
The lone and level sands stretch far away.   14

Ode to the West Wind

I

O wild West Wind, thou breath of Autumn's being,
Thou, from whose unseen presence the leaves dead
Are driven, like ghosts from an enchanter fleeing,

8: The hand of the sculptor that represented them, and the heart of the king
that produced them.

Yellow, and black, and pale, and hectic red,   4
Pestilence-stricken multitudes: O thou,
Who chariotest to their dark wintry bed

The wingèd seeds, where they lie cold and low,   7
Each like a corpse within its grave, until
Thine azure sister of the Spring shall blow

Her clarion o'er the dreaming earth, and fill   10
(Driving sweet buds like flocks to feed in air)
With living hues and odours plain and hill:

Wild Spirit, which are moving everywhere;   13
Destroyer and preserver; hear, oh hear!

II

Thou on whose stream, mid the steep sky's commotion,   15
Loose clouds like earth's decaying leaves are shed,
Shook from the tangled boughs of Heaven and Ocean,

Angels of rain and lightning: there are spread   18
On the blue surface of thine aëry surge,
Like the bright hair uplifted from the head

Of some fierce Maenad, even from the dim verge   21
Of the horizon to the zenith's height,
The locks of the approaching storm. Thou dirge

Of the dying year, to which this closing night   24
Will be the dome of a vast sepulchre,
Vaulted with all thy congregated might

Of vapours, from whose solid atmosphere   27
Black rain, and fire, and hail will burst: oh, hear!

III

Thou who didst waken from his summer dreams   29
The blue Mediterranean, where he lay,
Lulled by the coil of his crystalline streams,

Beside a pumice isle in Baiae's bay.   32
And saw in sleep old palaces and towers
Quivering within the wave's intenser day,

All overgrown with azure moss and flowers   35
So sweet, the sense faints picturing them! Thou
For whose path the Atlantic's level powers

4 *hectic:* feverish.   21 *Maenad:* nymph of Bacchus, god of wine.

Cleave themselves into chasms, while far below   38
The sea-blooms and the oozy woods which wear
The sapless foliage of the ocean, know

Thy voice, and suddenly grow gray with fear,   41
And tremble and despoil themselves: oh, hear!

IV

If I were a dead leaf thou mightest bear;   43
If I were a swift cloud to fly with thee;
A wave to pant beneath thy power, and share

The impulse of thy strength, only less free   46
Than thou, O uncontrollable! If even
I were as in my boyhood, and could be

The comrade of thy wanderings over Heaven,   49
As then, when to outstrip thy skiey speed
Scarce seemed a vision; I would ne'er have striven

As thus with thee in prayer in my sore need.   52
Oh, lift me as a wave, a leaf, a cloud!
I fall upon the thorns of life! I bleed!

A heavy weight of hours has chained and bowed   55
One too like thee: tameless, and swift, and proud.

V

Make me thy lyre, even as the forest is: 57
What if my leaves are falling like its own!
The tumult of thy mighty harmonies

Will take from both a deep, autumnal tone,   60
Sweet though in sadness. Be thou, Spirit fierce,
My spirit! Be thou me, impetuous one!

Drive my dead thoughts over the universe   63
Like withered leaves to quicken a new birth!
And, by the incantation of this verse,

Scatter, as from an unextinguished hearth   66
Ashes and sparks, my words among mankind!
Be through my lips to unawakened earth

The trumpet of a prophecy! O, Wind,   69
If Winter comes, can Spring be far behind?

Critique

1. On the most elementary level, the poem deals in the first three stanzas with the action of the West Wind upon the leaf, the cloud, and the wave. Through this action Shelley steps progressively toward an imaginative examination of the possibility of identifying himself with the wind, and what it stands for. . . . In stanza iv the identification is suggested, tentatively and provisionally through Nature, . . . and [it] culminates in stanza v . . . .

This identification represents, so to speak, the unity which the poem is to win from variety. The individual is to be merged with the general; Shelley is to become the instrument through which speaks the universal voice. . . .

The . . . structure, or problem of the "Ode" may also be defined as the "death and regeneration" contrast . . . . For the west wind is both destroyer and preserver . . . . This contrast, like the individual-general contrast earlier mentioned, needs and gets a poetic reconciliation, a unification concretely and emotionally satisfying. . . .

(R. H. Fogle)

2. . . . Shelley wants his reader to see the West Wind as a symbol of the forces of progress. That is what the poem *ought* to be about.

But is it? Is not the real subject of the poem (i) Shelley's delight in natural violence, (ii) Shelley's self-pity, (iii) Shelley's consciousness of failing inspiration? It is surely extremely significant that the Wind's destroyer-preserver rôle, so essential to the political argument, is lost sight of entirely in stanzas II and III. The minute structural parallelism of stanzas I-III presumes an identity of content in them. But in fact in stanzas II and III the Wind is conceived simply as an irresistible natural force. What it symbolizes is not political reform ˈbut the instinctive energies of the subconscious mind. Its contemplation restores Shelley to his boyhood (the typical Romantic reversion) . . . . And the altruism of stanza V is only on its surface. Essentially the ageing Shelley ('my leaves are falling') is demanding the restoration of his own adolescent ecstasies . . . . And the spring that is not far behind is less a prophecy of the Reform Bill than the personal consolation that a Romantic poet is offering himself. Like Wordsworth in his Ode, Shelley is *primarily* cheering himself up!   (F. W. Bateson)

3. . . . The poem's meaning turns upon the deliberate contrast between the fourth and fifth stanzas. In the fourth the poet pleads

for a negation of his human status; he wishes to be only an object for the wind, like leaf, cloud, wave. His despair here is like the despair of Job, who calls upon the wind to dissolve his substance. The final stanza recoils from this surrender, and cries out for a mutual relation with the wind. Yet even the Jobean fourth stanza is far removed from self-pity, modern critical opinion to the contrary. . . . These lines mix a Wordsworthian plangency for the hiding places of imaginative power with the accents of wrestling Jacob, who would not let the angel go until a divine blessing was bestowed. Yet this Jacob momentarily lets go in despair of his struggle and, as a mere natural object, falls back, out of the Spirit, and onto the thorns of life. Job, feeling his abandonment, cried out, "He hath cast me into the mire, and I am become like dust and ashes." A rhetorical critic could as justifiably, and as inaptly, accuse Job of self-pity, as he does Shelley. The *Ode to the West Wind*, like the *Book of Job*, is a religious poem, and the conventions of religious rhetoric apply equally to each work. . . .   (HAROLD BLOOM)

BIBLIOGRAPHY

Bateson, F. W., *English Poetry: A Critical Introduction*, 1950, pp. 215-16; Bloom, H., *The Visionary Company: A Reading of English Romantic Poetry*, 1961, pp. 292-93; Fogle, R. H., *ELH*, **15** (Sept. 1948), 220-24.

With How Sad Steps, O Moon, Thou Climbst the Skies

With how sad steps, O moon, thou climbst the skies,
　How silently, and with how wan a face!
　What, may it be that even in heavenly place
　That busy archer his sharp arrows tries?
Sure, if that long-with-love-acquainted eyes　　　　　5
　Can judge of love, thou feelst a lover's case;
　I read it in thy looks: thy languished grace
　To me, that feel the like, thy state descries.
Then, even of fellowship, O moon, tell me,　　　　　9
　Is constant love deemed there but want of wit?
　Are beauties there as proud as here they be?
Do they above love to be loved, and yet
　Those lovers scorn whom that love doth possess?
　Do they call virtue there ungratefulness?　　　　　14

10 *wit:* intelligence.

I Think Continually of Those Who Were Truly Great

I think continually of those who were truly great.
Who, from the womb, remembered the soul's history
Through corridors of light where the hours are suns,
Endless and singing. Whose lovely ambition
Was that their lips, still touched with fire,   5
Should tell of the Spirit, clothed from head to foot in song.
And who hoarded from the Spring branches
The desires falling across their bodies like blossoms.

What is precious, is never to forget   9
The essential delight of the blood drawn from ageless springs
Breaking through rocks in worlds before our earth.
Never to deny its pleasure in the morning simple light
Nor its grave evening demand for love.   13
Never to allow gradually the traffic to smother
With noise and fog, the flowering of the Spirit.

Near the snow, near the sun, in the highest fields,   16
See how these names are fêted by the waving grass
And by the streamers of white cloud
And whispers of wind in the listening sky.
The names of those who in their lives fought for life,   20
Who wore at their hearts the fire's centre.
Born of the sun, they travelled a short while toward the sun,
And left the vivid air signed with their honour.

Prothalamion

Calm was the day, and through the trembling air,
Sweet breathing Zephyrus did softly play
A gentle spirit, that lightly did delay
Hot Titan's beams, which then did glister fair;
When I whom sullen care,
Through discontent of my long fruitless stay
In princes' court, and expectation vain

Prothalamion: pre-marriage song, composed in honor of the prospective double
wedding of the two daughters of Edward Somerset, Earl of Worcester, describing a river trip which the two ladies made to see their fiancés at Essex House.
2 *Zephyrus:* West Wind.   4 *Titan's:* sun's.

Of idle hopes, which still do fly away,
Like empty shadows, did afflict my brain,
Walked forth to ease my pain   10
Along the shore of silver streaming Thames,
Whose rutty bank, the which his river hems,
Was painted all with variable flowers,
And all the meads adorned with dainty gems
Fit to deck maidens' bowers,
And crown their paramours
Against the bridal day, which is not long:
 Sweet Thames run softly, till I end my song.

There, in a meadow, by the river's side,   19
A flock of nymphs I chanced to espy,
All lovely daughters of the flood thereby,
With goodly greenish locks, all loose untied,
As each had been a bride.
And each one had a little wicker basket,
Made of fine twigs entrailed curiously,
In which they gathered flowers to fill their flasket:
And with fine fingers, cropt full feateously
The tender stalks on high.   28
Of every sort, which in that meadow grew,
They gathered some; the violet pallid blue,
The little daisy, that at evening closes,
The virgin lily, and the primrose true,
With store of vermeil roses,
To deck their bridegroom's posies
Against the bridal day, which was not long:
 Sweet Thames run softly, till I end my song.

With that, I saw two swans of goodly hue,   37
Come softly swimming down along the lee.
Two fairer birds I yet did never see:
The snow which doth the top of Pindus strew,
Did never whiter shew,
Nor Jove himself when he a swan would be
For love of Leda, whiter did appear;
Yet Leda was they say as white as he,
Yet not so white as these, nor nothing near;
So purely white they were,   46

14 *meads:* meadows.   15 *bowers:* boudoirs.   17 *Against:* toward.   *long:*
far off.   21 *flood thereby:* nearby river.   23 *As:* as if.   26 *flasket:* basket.
27 *feateously:* dexterously.   33 *vermeil:* bright red.

That even the gentle stream, the which them bare,
Seemed foul to them, and bade his billows spare
To wet their silken feathers, lest they might
Soil their fair plumes with water not so fair,
And mar their beauties bright,
That shone as heaven's light,
Against their bridal day, which was not long:
    Sweet Thames run softly, till I end my song.

Eftsoons the nymphs, which now had flowers their fill,   55
Ran all in haste to see that silver brood,
As they came floating on the crystal flood,
Whom when they saw, they stood amazed still,
Their wond'ring eyes to fill;
Them seem'd they never saw a sight so fair,
Of fowls so lovely, that they sure did deem
Them heavenly born, or to be that same pair
Which through the sky draw Venus' silver team;
For sure they did not seem   64
To be begot of any earthly seed,
But rather angels or of angels' breed;
Yet were they bred of Somer's-heat, they say,
In sweetest season, when each flower and weed
The earth did fresh array,
So fresh they seem'd as day,
Even as their bridal day, which was not long:
    Sweet Thames run softly, till I end my song.

Then forth they all out of their baskets drew   73
Great store of flowers, the honour of the field,
That to the sense did fragrant odours yield,
All which upon those goodly birds they threw,
And all the waves did strew,
That like old Peneus' waters they did seem,
When down along by pleasant Tempe's shore,
Scattered with flowers, through Thessaly they stream,
That they appear, through lilies' plenteous store,
Like a bride's chamber floor: 82
Two of those nymphs meanwhile, two garlands bound
Of freshest flowers which in that mead they found,
The which presenting all in trim array,
Their snowy foreheads there withal they crowned,

48 *to:* compared to.   55 *Eftsoons:* soon.   67 *Somer's-heat:* pun on Somerset
(Dodge).

Whil'st one did sing this lay,
Prepar'd against that day,
Against their bridal day, which was not long:
   Sweet Thames run softly, till I end my song.

Ye gentle birds, the world's fair ornament, 91
And heaven's glory, whom this happy hour
Doth lead unto your lovers' blissful bower,
Joy may you have, and gentle hearts' content
Of your loves' couplement:
And let fair Venus, that is queen of love,
With her heart-quelling son upon you smile,
Whose smile, they say, hath virtue to remove
All love's dislike, and friendship's faulty guile
Forever to assoil. 100
Let endless peace your steadfast hearts accord,
And blessed plenty wait upon your board,
And let your bed with pleasures chaste abound,
That fruitful issue may to you afford,
Which may your foes confound,
And make your joys redound,
Upon your bridal day, which is not long:
   Sweet Thames run softly, till I end my song.

So ended she; and all the rest around 109
To her redoubled that her undersong,
Which said their bridal day should not be long.
And gentle Echo from the neighbour ground,
Their accents did resound.
So forth those joyous birds did pass along,
Adown the lee, that to them murmured low,
As he would speak, but that he lacked a tongue
Yet did by signs his glad affection show,
Making his stream run slow. 118
And all the fowl which in his flood did dwell
Gan flock about these twain, that did excel
The rest, so far, as Cynthia doth shend
The lesser stars. So they, enranged well,
Did on those two attend,
And their best service lend,
Against their wedding day, which was not long:
   Sweet Thames run softly, till I end my song.

87 *lay:* song.   100 *assoil:* absolve.   121 *Cynthia:* Diana, goddess of the moon;
name also applied to Queen Elizabeth. *shend:* shame.

At length they all to merry London came,   127
To merry London, my most kindly nurse,
That to me gave this life's first native source:
Though from another place I take my name,
An house of ancient fame.
There when they came, whereas those bricky towers
The which on Thames' broad aged back do ride,
Where now the studious lawyers have their bowers,
There whilom wont the Templar Knights to bide,
Till they decayed through pride;   136
Next whereunto there stands a stately place.
Where oft I gained gifts and goodly grace
Of that great lord, which therein wont to dwell,
Whose want too well now feels my friendless case:
But Ah here fits not well
Old woes but joys, to tell
Against the bridal day, which is not long:
   Sweet Thames run softly, till I end my song.

Yet therein now doth lodge a noble peer,   145
Great England's glory and the world's wide wonder,
Whose dreadful name late through all Spain did thunder,
And Hercules' two pillars standing near,
Did make to quake and fear.
Fair branch of honour, flower of chivalry,
That fillest England with thy triumph's fame,
Joy have thou of thy noble victory,
And endless happiness of thine own name
That promiseth the same;   154
That through thy prowess and victorious arms,
Thy country may be freed from foreign harms:
And great Eliza's glorious name may ring
Through all the world, fill'd with thy wide alarms,
Which some brave muse may sing
To ages following,
Upon the bridal day, which is not long:
   Sweet Thames run softly, till I end my song.

132 *whereas:* where.   135 *whilom wont:* once used.   137-140: Essex House,
where Spenser had lived under the Earl of Leicester's patronage (Dodge).
140 *want:* absence.   145-147: The Earl of Essex, a patron of Spenser, had
recently returned from a successful Spanish attack (1596).   148 *Hercules'*
two pillars: adjacent tips of Spain and Africa.   153 *happiness . . . name:*
Essex's name was Devereux; pun on *heureux*, happy (Dodge).   157 *Eliza:*
Queen Elizabeth.   159 *brave muse:* fine poet.

From those high towers, this noble lord issuing,   163
Like radiant Hesper, when his golden hair
In th'ocean billows ho hath bathed fair,
Descended to the river's open viewing,
With a great train ensuing.
Above the rest were goodly to be seen
Two gentle knights of lovely face and feature,
Beseeming well the bower of any queen,
With gifts of wit and ornaments of nature,
Fit for so goodly stature: 172
That like the twins of Jove they seem'd in sight,
Which deck the baldrick of the heavens bright.
They two, forth pacing to the river's side
Received those two fair brides, their love's delight;
Which, at th'appointed tide,
Each one did make his bride,
Against their bridal day, which is not long:
Sweet Thames run softly, till I end my song.   180

Case

A

1. The poem is a highly pictorial song in praise of a forthcoming marriage among the nobility.

2. The structure of the poem consists of a number of colorful vignettes, usually composed of slowly moving figures: the poet pacing the shore, the nymphs gathering flowers, the swans, the nymphs paying homage, the swans and their entourage, the imposing Temple and Essex House, the glorious Essex, and the stately procession dominated by the bridegrooms.

3. The leisurely movement of the figures in the poem is reflected in the leisurely movement of the verse, a deliberateness to which the numerous caesuras and short lines contribute much.

4. Despite the pageant-like aspect of the structure, each scene points approvingly towards the approaching marriage—chiefly by

164 *Hesper:* evening star.   171 *wit:* intelligence.   173-174 *twins . . . bright:* Castor and Pollux, sons of Jove by Leda, became the constellation Gemini. 174 *baldrick:* belt.   177 *tide:* time.

means of the refrain, which skillfully seems to adapt itself to, and to conclude, the sense of each stanza, and which has a gentle singing and flowing quality that depends partially on its frequent repetition of *l*-, *n*-, and *s*-sounds.

5. Part of the praise of the prospective marriage is conveyed in terms of idealized natural beauty: the mythologized wind (1-3), sun (4), and swans (62-65); the highly-prized river (11), flowers (14), and swans (56); the nymphs themselves; the flowers that symbolize the modesty, purity, fidelity, and passion of the brides (30-33); and so on.

B

1. The real theme of the poem is the resolution of the poet's discontent with his society into a feeling of pride and satisfaction.

2. Stanza 1 stresses the discrepancy between the poet's "sullen care" and "discontent" at his treatment "In princes' court," and the natural beauty of the scene around him.

3. In Stanzas 2-8, the poet's sorrow is distracted by the beauty of nature, swans, and nymphs; by the brief reference to the unifying sovereign (121-22); and by the colorful atmosphere of the metropolis.

4. Although the personal note of disappointment momentarily returns (141-42), the poet suppresses it as being incongruent with the general harmony and happiness.

5. The resolving climax comes in the last two stanzas, whose unrestrained tributes to royal queen, national hero, and noble couples give a symbolic significance to the "Sweet Thames" that has interfused political, poetical, and sexual elements.

BIBLIOGRAPHY

Arms, G., *Explicator*, 1 (Mar. 1943), 36; Brooks, C., and R. P. Warren, *Understanding Poetry*, 1950 ed., companion *Manual*, pp. 42-43; Daiches, D., and W. Charvat, *Poems in English 1530-1940*, 1950, pp. 650-52; Woodward, D. H., *ELH*, 29 (Mar. 1962), 34-46.

Fable for Blackboard

Here is the grackle, people.
Here is the fox, folks.
The grackle sits in the bracken. The fox
    hopes.

Here are the fronds, friends,   4
that cover the fox.
The fronds get in a frenzy. The grackle
    looks.

Here are the ticks, tykes,   7
that live in the leaves, loves.
The fox is confounded,
and God is above.

In Waste Places

As a naked man I go
Through the desert, sore afraid;
Holding high my head, although
I'm as frightened as a maid.

The lion crouches there! I saw   5
In barren rocks his amber eye!
He parts the cactus with his paw!
He stares at me as I go by!

He would pad upon my trace   9
If he thought I was afraid!
If he knew my hardy face
Veils the terrors of a maid.

He rises in the night-time, and   13
He stretches forth! He snuffs the air!
He roars! He leaps along the sand!
He creeps! He watches everywhere!

His burning eyes, his eyes of bale   17
Through the darkness I can see!

17 *bale:* evil.

He lashes fiercely with his tail!
He makes again to spring at me!

I am the lion, and his lair!   21
I am the fear that frightens me!
I am the desert of despair!
And the night of agony!

Night or day, whate'er befall,   25
I must walk that desert land,
Until I dare my fear, and call
The lion out to lick my hand!

Sunday Morning

I

Complacencies of the peignoir, and late
Coffee and oranges in a sunny chair,
And the green freedom of a cockatoo
Upon a rug mingle to dissipate
The holy hush of ancient sacrifice.
She dreams a little, and she feels the dark   6
Encroachment of that old catastrophe,
As a calm darkens among water-lights.
The pungent oranges and bright, green wings
Seem things in some procession of the dead,
Winding across wide water, without sound.   11
The day is like wide water, without sound,
Stilled for the passing of her dreaming feet
Over the seas, to silent Palestine,
Dominion of the blood and sepulchre.

II

Why should she give her bounty to the dead?   16
What is divinity if it can come
Only in silent shadows and in dreams?
Shall she not find in comforts of the sun,
In pungent fruit and bright, green wings, or else
In any balm or beauty of the earth,   21

1 *peignoir:* dressing-gown.

Things to be cherished like the thought of heaven?
Divinity must live within herself:
Passions of rain, or moods in falling snow;
Grievings in loneliness, or unsubdued
Elations when the forest blooms; gusty   26
Emotions on wet roads on autumn nights;
All pleasures and all pains, remembering
The bough of summer and the winter branch.
These are the measures destined for her soul.

III

Jove in the clouds had his inhuman birth.   31
No mother suckled him, no sweet land gave
Large-mannered motions to his mythy mind.
He moved among us, as a muttering king,
Magnificent, would move among his hinds,
Until our blood, commingling, virginal,   36
With heaven, brought such requital to desire
The very hinds discerned it, in a star.
Shall our blood fail? Or shall it come to be
The blood of paradise? And shall the earth
Seem all of paradise that we shall know?   41
The sky will be much friendlier then than now,
A part of labor and a part of pain,
And next in glory to enduring love,
Not this dividing and indifferent blue.

IV

She says, "I am content when wakened birds,   46
Before they fly, test the reality
Of misty fields, by their sweet questionings;
But when the birds are gone, and their warm fields
Return no more, where, then, is paradise?"
There is not any haunt of prophecy,   51
Nor any old chimera of the grave,
Neither the golden underground, nor isle
Melodious, where spirits gat them home,
Nor visionary south, nor cloudy palm
Remote on heaven's hill, that has endured   56
As April's green endures; or will endure
Like her remembrance of awakened birds,

35 *hinds:* servants. 37 *requital:* repayment. 52 *chimera:* monster. 54 *gat:*
got.

Or her desire for June and evening, tipped
By the consummation of the swallow's wings.

V

She says, "But in contentment I still feel   61
The need of some imperishable bliss."
Death is the mother of beauty; hence from her,
Alone, shall come fulfilment to our dreams
And our desires. Although she strews the leaves
Of sure obliteration on our paths,   66
The path sick sorrow took, the many paths
Where triumph rang its brassy phrase, or love
Whispered a little out of tenderness,
She makes the willow shiver in the sun
For maidens who were wont to sit and gaze   71
Upon the grass, relinquished to their feet.
She causes boys to pile new plums and pears
On disregarded plate. The maidens taste
And stray impassioned in the littering leaves.

VI

Is there no change of death in paradise?   76
Does ripe fruit never fall? Or do the boughs
Hang always heavy in that perfect sky,
Unchanging, yet so like our perishing earth,
With rivers like our own that seek for seas
They never find, the same receding shores   81
That never touch with inarticulate pang?
Why set the pear upon those river-banks
Or spice the shores with odors of the plum?
Alas, that they should wear our colors there,
The silken weavings of our afternoons,   86
And pick the strings of our insipid lutes!
Death is the mother of beauty, mystical,
Within whose burning bosom we devise
Our earthly mothers waiting, sleeplessly.

VII

Supple and turbulent, a ring of men   91
Shall chant in orgy on a summer morn
Their boisterous devotion to the sun,
Not as a god, but as a god might be,

Naked among them, like a savage source.
Their chant shall be a chant of paradise,   96
Out of their blood, returning to the sky;
And in their chant shall enter, voice by voice,
The windy lake wherein their lord delights,
The trees, like serafin, and echoing hills,
That choir among themselves long afterward.   101
They shall know well the heavenly fellowship
Of men that perish and of summer morn.
And whence they came and whither they shall go
The dew upon their feet shall manifest.

VIII

She hears, upon that water without sound,   106
A voice that cries, "The tomb in Palestine
Is not the porch of spirits lingering.
It is the grave of Jesus, where he lay."
We live in an old chaos of the sun,
Or old dependency of day and night,   111
Or island solitude, unsponsored, free,
Of that wide water, inescapable.
Deer walk upon our mountains, and the quail
Whistle about us their spontaneous cries;
Sweet berries ripen in the wilderness;   116
And, in the isolation of the sky,
At evening, casual flocks of pigeons make
Ambiguous undulations as they sink,
Downward to darkness, on extended wings.

Anecdote of the Jar

I placed a jar in Tennessee,
And round it was, upon a hill.
It made the slovenly wilderness
Surround that hill.

The wilderness rose up to it,   5
And sprawled around, no longer wild.

100 *seraphin:* angels.

The jar was round upon the ground
And tall and of a port in air.

It took dominion everywhere.   9
The jar was gray and bare.
It did not give of bird or bush,
Like nothing else in Tennessee.

The Emperor of Ice-Cream

Call the roller of big cigars,
The muscular one, and bid him whip
In kitchen cups concupiscent curds.
Let the wenches dawdle in such dress
As they are used to wear, and let the boys   5
Bring flowers in last month's newspapers.
Let be be finale of seem.
The only emperor is the emperor of ice-cream.

Take from the dresser of deal,   9
Lacking the three glass knobs, that sheet
On which she embroidered fantails once
And spread it so as to cover her face.
If her horny feet protrude, they come   13
To show how cold she is, and dumb.
Let the lamp affix its beam.
The only emperor is the emperor of ice-cream.

Critique

1. ... The poem might be called Directions for a Funeral, with
Two Epitaphs. We have a corpse laid out in the bedroom and we
have people in the kitchen. The corpse is dead; then let the boys
bring flowers in last month's (who would use to-day's?) newspapers.
The corpse is dead; but let the wenches wear their everyday

3 *concupiscent:* lustful.   7 (a) "take whatever seems to be, as really being"
(Blackmur); (b) "let that which is put an end to that which seems" (Friar
and Brinnin); or (c) "let what is, be the grand finale of seeming" (Weiss).
9 *dresser of deal:* pine bureau.

clothes . . . . The conjunction of a muscular man whipping desirable desserts in the kitchen and the corpse protruding horny
feet, gains its effect because of its oddity—not of fact, but of expression: the light frivolous words and rapid meters. . . . Two ideas
or images about death—the living and the dead—have been associated, and are now permanently fused. . . .

The point is, that the oddity of association would not have its
effect without the couplets which conclude each stanza with the
pungency of good epitaphs. . . . "The only emperor is the emperor
of ice-cream," implies in both stanzas that the only power worth
heeding is the power of the moment, of what is passing, of the
flux. (R. P. BLACKMUR)

2. 'The Emperor of Ice-Cream,' one of Stevens's bitterest poems,
is an act of mordant revulsion against the brutality of death and
the self-deceptions of the ritualizing, aestheticizing mind itself. A
loved woman has died, and the poem calls ironically for an appropriate celebration. Let the life-force, or God, the muscular 'roller
of big cigars,' continue to whip up human passions . . . . 'Let be be
finale of seem,' he cries. For once let the supposedly transforming
imagination be still, and let us take things for what we so bleakly
see they are. There is no order except the one so childishly and
self-indulgently imposed by the imagination—an 'ice-cream' of the
mind, whipped up by that muscular deity who does not exist, 'the
emperor of ice-cream.' All this in the eight lines of the first stanza.
Then the horror and shock are expressed more directly; the concluding second stanza speaks of the dead woman outright. . . .
(M. L. ROSENTHAL)

3. . . . The way to treat death is to wear ordinary clothes, not
turbans or boots of fur. It is to whip up some ice cream in the
kitchen, not to be finical; it is to spread flowers, not to toll the bell
or ululate. . . . "Let be be finale of seem"—that is, away with the
panoply of empty conventional mourning and empty conventional
myths of death and afterlife. Let us accept being . . . .

The last battlement before us is the line, "The only emperor
is the emperor of ice-cream." . . . If we take the emperor to be life,
and the poet's whole sympathy to be with the living, then why does
the poem deal so precisely and deliberately with the corpse in the
second stanza? . . . On the other hand, if the emperor is to be
identified with death, why bring in the cigar-rolling, ice-cream-
mixing muscular man? . . .

I think we may reach a little nearer if we remember that the characteristics of ice cream are that it is tasty, transitory, and cold. Life may be tasty and perishable, but it is not cold. Death may be cold but scarcely transitory . . . . Whoever the emperor is, he is realer than the run-of-the-mill emperors, the kaiser and Erlkönige, and his domain seems to include both life and death. The coldness of ice-cream suggests the corpse, as its sweetness suggests life's concupiscence. Stevens has said that his only daughter had a superlative liking for ice-cream, and is reported to have said also that she asked him to write a poem about it. Whether she did or not, there is a child-like quality about the poem—its absence of taboo, its complete, simultaneous, unruffled acceptance of conventional contraries—party food and horny feet. The child examines both without distaste. Both are included in the imperial domain. Ice-cream then is death and life. (RICHARD ELLMANN)

4. . . . Mr. Max Herzberg . . . wrote to Mr. Wallace Stevens: "Possibly you have already seen the enclosed issue of *The Explicator,* in which two professional students of your poem . . . do their best to tell . . . what they think you meant to say. . . .

". . . It would interest readers . . . to know your views."

Mr. Stevens replied to Mr. Herzberg:

"Things that have their origin in the imagination or in the motions (poems) . . . very often take on a form that is ambiguous or uncertain. It is not possible to attach a single, rational meaning to such things without destroying the imaginative or emotional ambiguity or uncertainty that is inherent in them and that is why poets do not like to explain. That the meanings given by others are sometimes meanings not intended by the poet or that were never present in his mind does not impair them as meanings. . . .

(WALLACE STEVENS and EDITORS of *The Explicator*)

BIBLIOGRAPHY

Blackmur, R. P., *Hound and Horn,* **5** (Jan.-Mar. 1932), 231-32, and *Language as Gesture,* 1952, pp. 228-29; Ellmann, R., *Kenyon Review,* **19** (Winter 1957), 93-94; Herzberg, M., and W. Stevens, *Explicator,* **7** (Nov. 1948), 18, last paragraph edited by Stevens in letter, 11 Nov. 1953; Rosenthal, M., *The Modern Poets: A Critical Introduction,* 1960, pp. 129-30.

The Plot Against the Giant

FIRST GIRL

When this yokel comes maundering,
Whetting his hacker,
I shall run before him,
Diffusing the civilest odors
Out of geraniums and unsmelled flowers.
It will check him.

SECOND GIRL

I shall run before him,   7
Arching cloths besprinkled with colors
As small as fish-eggs.
The threads
Will abash him.

THIRD GIRL

Oh, la . . . le pauvre!   12
I shall run before him,
With a curious puffing.
He will bend his ear then.
I shall whisper
Heavenly labials in a world of gutturals.
It will undo him.

Why So Pale and Wan?

Why so pale and wan, fond lover?
    prithee why so pale?
Will, when looking well can't move her,
    looking ill prevail?
    prithee why so pale?

1 *maundering:* stumbling.   2 *hacker:* axe.   12: Oh, my . . . the poor fellow!
17 *labials . . . gutturals:* lip and throat sounds.

2 *prithee:* I pray thee.

Why so dull and mute, young sinner?   6
   prithee why so mute?
Will, when speaking well can't win her,
   saying nothing do 't?
   prithee why so mute?

Quit, quit for shame, this will not move,   11
   this cannot take her.
If of her self she will not love,
   nothing can make her:
   the devil take her.

A Description of the Morning

Now hardly here and there an Hackney-Coach
Appearing, show'd the Ruddy Morns Approach.
Now *Betty* from her Masters Bed had flown,
And softly stole to discompose her own.
The Slipshod Prentice from his Masters Door,   5
Had par'd the Dirt, and Sprinkled round the Floor.
Now *Moll* had whirl'd her Mop with dext'rous Airs,
Prepar'd to Scrub the Entry and the Stairs.
The Youth with Broomy Stumps began to trace
The Kennel-Edge, where Wheels had worn the Place   10
The Smallcoal-Man was heard with Cadence deep,
'Till drown'd in Shriller Notes of Chimney-Sweep,
Duns at his Lordships Gate began to meet,
And Brickdust *Moll* had Scream'd through half the Street.
The Turnkey now his Flock returning sees,   15
Duly let out a Nights to Steal for Fees.
The watchful Bailiffs take their silent Stands,
And School-Boys lag with Satchels in their Hands.

12 *take:* charm.

10 *Kennel:* gutter.   13 *Duns:* creditors.   15 *Turnkey:* jailer.   17 *Bailiffs:*
process-servers.

The Furniture of a Woman's Mind

A Set of Phrases learn't by Rote;
A Passion for a Scarlet-Coat;
When at Play to laugh, or cry,
Yet cannot tell the Reason why:
Never to hold her Tongue a Minute;   5
While all she prates has nothing in it.
Whole Hours can with a Coxcomb sit,
And take his Nonsense all for Wit:
Her Learning mounts to read a Song,
But, half the Words pronouncing wrong;   10
Has ev'ry Repartee in Store,
She spoke ten Thousand Times before.
Can ready Compliments supply
On all Occasions, cut and dry.
Such Hatred to a Parson's Gown,   15
The Sight will put her in a Swown.
For Conversation well endu'd;
She calls it witty to be rude;
And, placing Raillery in Railing,
Will tell aloud your greatest Failing;   20
Nor makes a Scruple to expose
Your bandy Leg, or crooked Nose.
Can, at her Morning Tea, run o'er
The Scandal of the Day before.
Improving hourly in her Skill,   25
To cheat and wrangle at Quadrille.

 In chusing Lace a Critick nice,   27
Knows to a Groat the lowest Price;
Can in her Female Clubs dispute
What Lining best the Silk will suit;
What Colours each Complexion match:
And where with Art to place a Patch.

 If chance a Mouse creeps in her Sight,   33
Can finely counterfeit a Fright;
So, sweetly screams if it comes near her,
She ravishes all Hearts to hear her.
Can dext'rously her Husband teize,

2 *Scarlet-Coat:* soldier. 7 *Coxcomb:* fool. 17 *endu'd:* endowed. 19 *Raillery:* banter. *Railing:* abuse. 26 *Quadrille:* card game. 32 *Patch:* to set off complexion.

By taking Fits whene'er she please: 38
By frequent Practice learns the Trick
At proper Seasons to be sick;
Thinks nothing gives one Airs so pretty;
At once creating Love and Pity.
If *Molly* happens to be careless,   43
And but neglects to warm her Hair-Lace,
She gets a Cold as sure as Death;
And vows she scarce can fetch her Breath.
Admires how modest Women can
Be so *robustious* like a Man.

   In Party, furious to her Power;   49
A bitter Whig, or Tory sow'r;
Her Arguments directly tend
Against the Side she would defend:
Will prove herself a Tory plain,
From Principles the Whigs maintain;   54
And, to defend the Whiggish Cause,
Her Topicks from the Tories draws.

   O yes! If any Man can find   57
More virtues in a Woman's Mind,
Let them be sent to Mrs. *Harding*;
She'll pay the Charges to a Farthing:
Take Notice, she has my Commission
To add them in the next Edition;   62
They may out-sell a better Thing;
So, Holla Boys; God save the King.

The Kraken

Below the thunders of the upper deep,
Far, far beneath in the abysmal sea,
His ancient, dreamless, uninvaded sleep
The Kraken sleepeth: faintest sunlights flee
About his shadowy sides; above him swell   5
Huge sponges of millennial growth and height;
And far away into the sickly light,

47 *Admires:* wonders.   59 *Mrs. Harding:* a printer (Williams).

Kraken: legendary sea-monster.   6 *millennial:* thousand-year.

From many a wondrous grot and secret cell
Unnumber'd and enormous polypi
Winnow with giant arms the slumbering green.   10
There hath he lain for ages, and will lie
Battening upon huge sea-worms in his sleep,
Until the latter fire shall heat the deep;
Then once by man and angels to be seen,
In roaring he shall rise and on the surface die.   15

Ulysses

It little profits that an idle king,
By this still hearth, among these barren crags,
Match'd with an aged wife, I mete and dole
Unequal laws unto a savage race,
That hoard, and sleep, and feed, and know not me.   5
I cannot rest from travel; I will drink
Life to the lees. All times I have enjoy'd
Greatly, have suffer'd greatly, both with those
That loved me, and alone; on shore, and when
Thro' scudding drifts the rainy Hyades   10
Vext the dim sea. I am become a name;
For always roaming with a hungry heart
Much have I seen and known,—cities of men
And manners, climates, councils, governments,
Myself not least, but honor'd of them all,—   15
And drunk delight of battle with my peers,
Far on the ringing plains of windy Troy.
I am a part of all that I have met;
Yet all experience is an arch wherethro'
Gleams that untravell'd world, whose margin fades   20
For ever and for ever when I move.
How dull it is to pause, to make an end,
To rust unburnish'd, not to shine in use!
As tho' to breathe were life! Life piled on life
Were all too little, and of one to me   25
Little remains; but every hour is saved
From that eternal silence, something more,
A bringer of new things; and vile it were

9 *polypi:* octopuses.

10 *Hyades:* stars supposed to indicate rain.

For some three suns to store and hoard myself,
And this gray spirit yearning in desire   30
To follow knowledge, like a sinking star,
Beyond the utmost bound of human thought.
   This is my son, mine own Telemachus,
To whom I leave the sceptre and the isle,—
Well-loved of me, discerning to fulfil   35
This labor, by slow prudence to make mild
A rugged people, and thro' soft degrees
Subdue them to the useful and the good.
Most blameless is he, centred in the sphere
Of common duties, decent not to fail   40
In offices of tenderness, and pay
Meet adoration to my household gods,
When I am gone. He works his work, I mine.
   There lies the port; the vessel puffs her sail;
There gloom the dark, broad seas. My mariners,   45
Souls that have toil'd, and wrought, and thought with me,—
That ever with a frolic welcome took
The thunder and the sunshine, and opposed
Free hearts, free foreheads—you and I are old;
Old age hath yet his honor and his toil.   50
Death closes all; but something ere the end,
Some work of noble note, may yet be done,
Not unbecoming men that strove with Gods.
The lights begin to twinkle from the rocks;
The long day wanes; the slow moon climbs; the deep   55
Moans round with many voices. Come, my friends,
'T is not too late to seek a newer world.
Push off, and sitting well in order smite
The sounding furrows; for my purpose holds
To sail beyond the sunset, and the baths   60
Of all the western stars, until I die.
It may be that the gulfs will wash us down;
It may be we shall touch the Happy Isles,
And see the great Achilles, whom we knew.
Though much is taken, much abides; and tho'   65
We are not now that strength which in old days
Moved earth and heaven, that which we are, we are,—
One equal temper of heroic hearts,
Made weak by time and fate, but strong in will
To strive, to seek, to find, and not to yield.   70

29 *suns:* years.

Case

A

1. The poem is primarily a dramatic address in which the legendary traveler Ulysses becomes a universal symbol of questing humanity.

2. The three structural sections of the poem correspond to three states of mind: (a) recollection of past search and struggle, (b) satisfaction of responsibility toward the obstructive present, and (c) exhortation to future inquiry into the unknown.

B

1. The poem is primarily a personal reverie merging romantic nostalgia, wanderlust, and desire for death.

2. Unable to retain the bright glories of war and its aftermath, and scornful of family, subjects, and royal responsibility, the aging Ulysses dreams of visiting "a newer world"—one which we recognize as being beyond this world.

BIBLIOGRAPHY

Basler, R. P., and W. Frost, *Explicator*, 4 (May 1946), 48; Baum, P. F., *Tennyson Sixty Years After*, 1948, pp. 299-303; Bush, D., *Mythology and the Romantic Tradition in English Poetry*, 1937, pp. 208-11; Chaisson, E. J., *University of Toronto Quarterly*, 23 (July 1954), 402-9; Langbaum, R., *The Poetry of Experience*, 1957, pp. 90-92; Marshall, G. O., *Explicator*, 21 (Feb. 1963), 50; Pettigrew, J., *Victorian Poetry*, 1 (Jan. 1963), 27-45; Roppen, R., *English Studies*, 40 (Apr. 1959), 77-90; Sonn, C. R., *Modern Philology*, 57 (Nov. 1959), 87-88; Stanford, W. B., *The Ulysses Theme*, 1954, pp. 202-5; Walcutt, C. C., *Explicator*, 4 (Feb. 1946), 28.

Tears, Idle Tears, I Know Not What They Mean

'Tears, idle tears, I know not what they mean,
Tears from the depth of some divine despair
Rise in the heart, and gather to the eyes,
In looking on the happy autumn-fields,
And thinking of the days that are no more.

'Fresh as the first beam glittering on a sail,   6
That brings our friends up from the underworld,
Sad as the last which reddens over one
That sinks with all we love below the verge;
So sad, so fresh, the days that are no more.

'Ah, sad and strange as in dark summer dawns   11
The earliest pipe of half-awaken'd birds
To dying ears, when unto dying eyes
The casement slowly grows a glimmering square;
So sad, so strange, the days that are no more.

'Dear as remember'd kisses after death,   16
And sweet as those by hopeless fancy feign'd
On lips that are for others; deep as love,
Deep as first love, and wild with all regret;
O Death in Life, the days that are no more!'

Critique

1. Since the subject of this poem is a feeling . . —indeed a feeling strong enough to produce tears, the poet is exposed to the charge of sentimental indulgence in emotion for its own sake. . . . Yet . . . the poem does not exhibit nostalgia for nostalgia's sake, but seeks to investigate, define, and present the specific qualities of an experience. Furthermore, this experience is universalized; the first person singular is never used . . . . Finally, the qualities of the experience are presented in a closely knit, highly functional pattern of organization evincing a high degree of artistic discipline. . . . (FRED H. STOCKING)

2. This first stanza, then, recapitulates the surprise and bewilderment in the speaker's own mind, and sets the problem which the succeeding stanzas are to analyze. . . .

In the second stanza we are not surprised to have the poet characterize the days that are no more as "sad," but there is some shock in hearing him apply to them the adjective "fresh." Again, the speaker does not pause to explain: the word "fresh" actually begins the stanza. Yet the adjective justifies itself [in the rest of the stanza]. . . .

The conjunction of the qualities of sadness and freshness is reinforced by the fact that the same basic symbol—the light on the
sails of a ship hull down—has been employed to suggest both qualities. With the third stanza, the process is carried one stage further:
the two qualities (with the variant of "strange" for "fresh") are ex-
plicitly linked together . . . .

That intensity [of the last stanza] . . . must grow out of a sense
of the apparent nearness and intimate presence of what is irrevocably
beyond reach: the days that are no more must be more than the
conventional "dear, dead days beyond recall." They must be beyond
recall, yet alive—tantalizingly vivid and near. It is only thus that
we can feel the speaker justified in calling them

> Dear as remember'd kisses after death,
> And sweet as those by hopeless fancy feign'd
> On lips that are for others. . . .

It is only thus that we can accept the culminating paradox of

> O Death in Life, the days that are no more.

(CLEANTH BROOKS)

3. . . . Are all these personal situations [in Stanzas 2-4] the stuff
out of which the days that are no more are composed—thus making
the poem one about personal love and sorrow? . . . Tennyson said
. . . "[The poem] was written in the yellowing autumntide at Tintern
Abbey, full for me of its bygone memories." The memories . . . seem
to link the poem with "In Memoriam" XIX, also said to have been
written at Tintern Abbey . . . , whose theme is Arthur Hallam's
burial at Clevedon close by. . . . Poems are not explained by the
circumstances that gave rise to them. But we are the less likely to
understand . . . poems if we decline to take note of their genesis. . . .

Dramatically the poem has its place in "The Princess" [a long
narrative poem of Tennyson]. It is one of the interspersed lyrics,
all of which embody useless, irrational or instinctive emotions, and
so oppose the active intellectualism of Princess Ida herself. . . .

(GRAHAM HOUGH)

BIBLIOGRAPHY

Brooks, C., *The Well Wrought Urn*, 1947, pp. 155-57; Hough, G.,
Hopkins Review, 4 (Spring 1951), 34-35; Stocking, F. H., *Explicator*, 5
(June 1947), 54.

Now Sleeps the Crimson Petal, Now the White

'Now sleeps the crimson petal, now the white;
Nor waves the cypress in the palace walk;
Nor winks the gold fin in the porphyry font.
The fire-fly wakens; waken thou with me.

'Now droops the milk-white peacock like a ghost,   5
And like a ghost she glimmers on to me.

'Now lies the Earth all Danaë to the stars,   7
And all thy heart lies open unto me.

'Now slides the silent meteor on, and leaves   9
A shining furrow, as thy thoughts in me.

'Now folds the lily all her sweetness up,   11
And slips into the bosom of the lake.
So fold thyself, my dearest, thou, and slip
Into my bosom and be lost in me.'

Come Down, O Maid, from Yonder Mountain Height

'Come down, O maid, from yonder mountain height:
What pleasure lives in height (the shepherd sang)
In height and cold, the splendour of the hills?
But cease to move so near the Heavens, and cease
To glide a sunbeam by the blasted Pine,   5
To sit a star upon the sparkling spire;
And come, for Love is of the valley, come,
For Love is of the valley, come thou down
And find him; by the happy threshold, he,
Or hand in hand with Plenty in the maize,   10
Or red with spirted purple of the vats,
Or foxlike in the vine; nor cares to walk
With Death and Morning on the silver horns,
Nor wilt thou snare him in the white ravine,
Nor find him dropt upon the firths of ice,   15
That huddling slant in furrow-cloven falls

3 *porphyry font:* fountain of purple stone.   7 *Danaë:* Zeus descended to her
as a shower of gold.

To roll the torrent out of dusky doors:
But follow; let the torrent dance thee down
To find him in the valley; let the wild
Lean-headed Eagles yelp alone, and leave   20
The monstrous ledges there to slope, and spill
Their thousand wreaths of dangling water-smoke,
That like a broken purpose waste in air:
So waste not thou; but come; for all the vales
Await thee; azure pillars of the hearth   25
Arise to thee; the children call, and I
Thy shepherd pipe, and sweet is every sound,
Sweeter thy voice, but every sound is sweet;
Myriads of rivulets hurrying thro' the lawn,
The moan of doves in immemorial elms,   30
And murmuring of innumerable bees.'

The Eagle
Fragment

He clasps the crag with crooked hands;
Close to the sun in lonely lands,
Ring'd with the azure world, he stands.

The wrinkled sea beneath him crawls;   4
He watches from his mountain walls,
And like a thunderbolt he falls.

Poem in October

It was my thirtieth year to heaven
Woke to my hearing from harbour and neighbour wood
    And the mussel pooled and the heron
            Priested shore
        The morning beckon
With water praying and call of seagull and rook   6
And the knock of sailing boats on the net webbed wall
        Myself to set foot
            That second
    In the still sleeping town and set forth.

My birthday began with the water-   11
Birds and the birds of the winged trees flying my name
   Above the farms and the white horses
      And I rose
     In rainy autumn
And walked abroad in a shower of all my days.   16
High tide and the heron divided when I took the road
   Over the border
     And the gates
Of the town closed as the town awoke.

A springful of larks in a rolling   21
Cloud and the roadside bushes brimming with whistling
   Blackbirds and the sun of October
     Summery
    On the hill's shoulder,
Here were fond climates and sweet singers suddenly   26
Come in the morning where I wandered and listened
   To the rain wringing
    Wind blow cold
In the wood faraway under me.

Pale rain over the dwindling harbour   31
And over the sea wet church the size of a snail
   With its horns through mist and the castle
     Brown as owls,
    But all the gardens
Of spring and summer were blooming in the tall tales   36
Beyond the border and under the lark full cloud.
   There could I marvel
    My birthday
Away but the weather turned around.

It turned away from the blithe country   41
And down the other air and the blue altered sky
   Streamed again a wonder of summer
     With apples
    Pears and red currants,
And I saw in the turning so clearly a child's   46
Forgotten mornings when he walked with his mother
   Through the parables
    Of sun light
And the legends of the green chapels

And the twice told fields of infancy   51
That his tears burned my cheeks and his heart moved in mine.
    There were the woods the river and sea
            Where a boy
        In the listening
Summertime of the dead whispered the truth of his joy   56
To the trees and the stones and the fish in the tide.
        And the mystery
            Sang alive
    Still in the water and singingbirds.

    And there could I marvel my birthday   61
Away but the weather turned around. And the true
    Joy of the long dead child sang burning
            In the sun.
        It was my thirtieth
Year to heaven stood there then in the summer noon   66
Though the town below lay leaved with October blood.
        O may my heart's truth
            Still be sung
    On this high hill in a year's turning.

In My Craft or Sullen Art

In my craft or sullen art
Exercised in the still night
When only the moon rages
And the lovers lie abed
With all their griefs in their arms,   5
I labour by singing light
Not for ambition or bread
Or the strut and trade of charms
On the ivory stages
But for the common wages   10
Of their most secret heart.
Not for the proud man apart
From the raging moon I write
On these spindrift pages
Not for the towering dead   15
With their nightingales and psalms

But for the lovers, their arms
Round the griefs of the ages,
Who pay no praise or wages
Nor heed my craft or art.   20

The Kingdom of God
'In No Strange Land'

O world invisible, we view thee,
O world intangible, we touch thee,
O world unknowable, we know thee,
Inapprehensible, we clutch thee!

Does the fish soar to find the ocean,   5
The eagle plunge to find the air—
That we ask of the stars in motion
If they have rumour of thee there?

Not where the wheeling systems darken,   9
And our benumbed conceiving soars!—
The drift of pinions, would we hearken,
Beats at our own clay-shuttered doors.

The angels keep their ancient places;—   13
Turn but a stone, and start a wing!
'Tis ye, 'tis your estrangèd faces,
That miss the many-splendoured thing.

But (when so sad thou canst not sadder)   17
Cry, and upon thy so sore loss
Shall shine the traffic of Jacob's ladder
Pitched betwixt Heaven and Charing Cross.

Yea, in the night, my Soul, my daughter,   21
Cry,—clinging Heaven by the hems;
And lo, Christ walking on the water
Not of Gennesareth, but Thames!

The Kingdom of God: "is within you" (Luke 17:21). *In No Strange Land:*
Moses said, "I have been a stranger in a strange land" (Exodus 2:22).   11
pinions: wings (of angels in 13).   15 *ye:* i.e., human beings.   19 *traffic of
Jacob's ladder:* angels Jacob saw (Genesis 28:12).   20 *Charing Cross:* land-
mark in busy part of London.

Go, Lovely Rose

Go, lovely rose,
Tell her that wastes her time and me
   That now she knows,
When I resemble her to thee,
   How sweet and fair she seems to be.

Tell her that's young,   6
And shuns to have her graces spied,
   That hadst thou sprung
In deserts where no men abide,
   Thou must have uncommended died.

Small is the worth   11
Of beauty from the light retir'd;
   Bid her come forth,
Suffer herself to be desir'd,
   And not blush so to be admir'd.

Then die, that she   16
The common fate of all things rare
   May read in thee,
How small a part of time they share
   That are so wondrous sweet and fair.

Call for the Robin Redbreast and the Wren

Call for the robin redbreast and the wren,
Since o'er shady groves they hover,
And with leaves and flowers do cover
The friendless bodies of unburied men.
Call unto his funeral dole   5
The ant, the field-mouse, and the mole
To rear him hillocks that shall keep him warm,
And, when gay tombs are robbed, sustain no harm.
But keep the wolf far thence, that's foe to men,
For with his nails he'll dig them up again.   10

Note: cf. Pound's "Envoi (1919)" (p. 232).

5 *dole:* lamentations.   8 *gay:* showy.

Out of the Cradle Endlessly Rocking

Out of the cradle endlessly rocking,
Out of the mocking-bird's throat, the musical shuttle,
Out of the Ninth-month midnight,
Over the sterile sands and the fields beyond, where the child leaving
    his bed wander'd alone, bareheaded, barefoot,
Down from the shower'd halo,   5
Up from the mystic play of shadows twining and twisting as if they
    were alive,
Out from the patches of briers and blackberries,
From the memories of the bird that chanted to me,
From your memories sad brother, from the fitful risings and fallings
    I heard,
From under the yellow half-moon late-risen and swollen as if with
    tears,   10
From those beginning notes of yearning and love there in the mist,
From the thousand responses of my heart never to cease,
From the myriad thence-arous'd words,
From the word stronger and more delicious than any,
From such as now they start the scene revisiting,   15
As a flock, twittering, rising, or overhead passing,
Borne hither, ere all eludes me, hurriedly,
A man, yet by these tears a little boy again,
Throwing myself on the sand, confronting the waves,
I, chanter of pains and joys, uniter of here and hereafter,   20
Taking all hints to use them, but swiftly leaping beyond them,
A reminiscence sing.

Once Paumanok,   23
When the lilac-scent was in the air and Fifth-month grass was growing,
Up this seashore in some briers,
Two feather'd guests from Alabama, two together,
And their nest, and four light-green eggs spotted with brown,
And every day the he-bird to and fro near at hand,   28
And every day the she-bird crouch'd on her nest, silent, with bright
    eyes.
And every day I, a curious boy, never too close, never disturbing them,
Cautiously peering, absorbing, translating.

2 *shuttle:* moving thread-holder in loom.   23 *Paumanok:* Indian name for
Long Island, N. Y.

Shine! shine! shine!   32
Pour down your warmth, great sun!
While we hask, we two together,

Two together!   35
Winds blow south, or winds blow north,
Day come white, or day come black,
Home, or rivers and mountains from home,
Singing all time, minding no time,
While we two keep together.

Till of a sudden,   41
May-be kill'd, unknown to her mate,
One forenoon that she-bird crouch'd not on the nest,
Nor return'd that afternoon, nor the next,
Nor ever appear'd again.

And thenceforward all summer in the sound of the sea,   46
And at night under the full of the moon in calmer weather,
Over the hoarse surging of the sea,
Or flitting from brier to brier by day,
I saw, I heard at intervals the remaining one, the he-bird,
The solitary guest from Alabama.

Blow! blow! blow!   52
Blow up sea-winds along Paumanok's shore;
I wait and I wait till you blow my mate to me.

Yes, when the stars glisten'd,   55
All night long on the prong of a moss-scallop'd stake,
Down almost amid the slapping waves,
Sat the lone singer, wonderful, causing tears.
He call'd on his mate,
He pour'd forth the meanings which I of all men know,   60

Yes, my brother, I know—
The rest might not, but I have treasured every note,
For more than once, dimly down to the beach gliding,
Silent, avoiding the moonbeams, blending myself with the shadows,
Recalling now the obscure shapes, the echoes, the sounds and sights
        after their sorts,   65
The white arms out in the breakers tirelessly tossing,

32, 52, 71: The italics indicate the bird's song.

I, with bare feet, a child, the wind wafting my hair,
Listen'd long and long.

Listen'd to keep, to sing, now translating the notes,
Following you my brother.

Soothe! soothe! soothe!   71
Close on its wave soothes the wave behind,
And again another behind embracing and lapping, every one close,
But my love soothes not me, not me.

Low hangs the moon, it rose late,   75
It is lagging—O I think it is heavy with love, with love.

O madly the sea pushes upon the land,   77
With love, with love.

O night! do I not see my love fluttering out among the breakers? 79
What is that little black thing I see there in the white?

Loud! loud! loud!   81
Loud I call to you, my love!
High and clear I shoot my voice over the waves,
Surely you must know who is here, is here,
You must know who I am, my love.

Low-hanging moon!   86
What is that dusky spot in your brown yellow?
O it is the shape, the shape of my mate!
O moon do not keep her from me any longer.

Land! land! O land!   90
Whichever way I turn, O I think you could give me my mate back
*   again if you only would,*
For I am almost sure I see her dimly whichever way I look.

O rising stars!   93
Perhaps the one I want so much will rise, will rise with some of you.

O throat! O trembling throat!   95
Sound clearer through the atmosphere!
Pierce the woods, the earth,
Somewhere listening to catch you must be the one I want.

Shake out carols!   99
Solitary here, the night's carols!
Carols of lonesome love! death's carols!
Carols under that lagging, yellow, waning moon!

O under that moon where she droops almost down into the sea!
O reckless despairing carols!

But soft! sink low!   105
Soft! let me just murmur,
And do you wait a moment, you husky-nois'd sea,
For somewhere I believe I heard my mate responding to me,
So faint, I must be still, be still to listen,
But not altogether still, for then she might not come immediately to me.

Hither my love!   111
Here I am! here!
With this just-sustain'd note I announce myself to you,
This gentle call is for you my love, for you.

Do not be decoy'd elsewhere: 115
That is the whistle of the wind, it is not my voice,
That is the fluttering, the fluttering of the spray,
Those are the shadows of leaves.

O darkness! O in vain!   119
O I am very sick and sorrowful.

O brown halo in the sky near the moon, drooping upon the sea!   121
O troubled reflection in the sea!

O throat! O throbbing heart!   123
And I singing uselessly, uselessly all the night.
O past! O happy life! O songs of joy!
In the air, in the woods, over fields,
Loved! loved! loved! loved! loved!
But my mate no more, no more with me!   128
We two together no more.

The aria sinking,   130
All else continuing, the stars shining,
The winds blowing, the notes of the bird continuous echoing,
With angry moans the fierce old mother incessantly moaning,
On the sands of Paumanok's shore gray and rustling,
The yellow half-moon enlarged, sagging down, drooping, the face of
       the sea almost touching,   135
The boy ecstatic, with his bare feet the waves, with his hair the
       atmosphere dallying,
The love in the heart long pent, now loose, now at last tumultuously
       bursting,
The aria's meaning, the ears, the soul, swiftly depositing,

The strange tears down the cheeks coursing,
The colloquy there, the trio, each uttering,   140
The undertone, the savage old mother incessantly crying,
To the boy's soul's questions sullenly timing, some drown'd secret
    hissing,
To the outsetting bard.

Demon or bird! (said the boy's soul)   144
Is it indeed toward your mate you sing? or is it really to me?
For I, that was a child, my tongue's use sleeping, now I have heard you,
Now in a moment I know what I am for, I awake,
And already a thousand singers, a thousand songs, clearer, louder and
    more sorrowful than yours,   148
A thousand warbling echoes have started to life within me, never to
    die.

O you singer solitary, singing by yourself, projecting me,   150
O solitary me listening, never more shall I cease perpetuating you,
Never more shall I escape, never more the reverberations,
Never more the cries of unsatisfied love be absent from me,
Never again leave me to be the peaceful child I was before what there
    in the night,
By the sea under the yellow and sagging moon,   155
The messenger there arous'd, the fire, the sweet hell within,
The unknown want, the destiny of me.

O give me the clew! (it lurks in the night here somewhere,)   158
O if I am to have so much, let me have more!

A word then, (for I will conquer it,)
The word final, superior to all,
Subtle, sent up—what is it?—I listen;
Are you whispering it, and have been all the time, you sea-waves?
is that it from your liquid rims and wet sands?

Whereto answering, the sea,   165
Delaying not, hurrying not,
Whisper'd me through the night, and very plainly before daybreak,
Lisp'd to me the low and delicious word death,
And again death, death, death, death,
Hissing melodious, neither like the bird nor like any arous'd child's
    heart,   170

144 *Demon:* spirit.

But edging near as privately for me rustling at my feet,
Creeping thence steadily up to my ears and laving me softly all over,
Death, death, death, death, death.

Which I do not forget,   174
But fuse the song of my dusky demon and brother,
That he sang to me in the moonlight on Paumanok's gray beach,
With the thousand responsive songs at random,
My own songs awaked from that hour,
And with them the key, the word up from the waves,   179
The word of the sweetest song and all songs,
That strong and delicious word which, creeping to my feet
(Or like some old crone rocking the cradle, swathed in sweet gar-
    ments, bending aside,)
The sea whispered me.

Case

A

1. The poem, whose original title was "A Child's Reminiscence,"
is primarily a poet's dramatic "reminiscence" (22) of a poignant
adolescent experience with love and death.

2. It is realistically divided into a large number of irregular
free-verse paragraphs that lack the formality of meter and rhyme.

3. In the first paragraph, which consists of a single sentence,
the poet furnishes the setting for the original incident by listing
its components in suspended and suspenseful prepositional phrases.

4. The narrative of 23-70 tells how a pair of mockingbirds
came north in spring, how the female disappeared, and how the
poet as a boy listened "all summer" (46) to the male's lamenting
song at night.

5. The narrative of 130-83 tells how the bird's love released the
boy's "love in the heart long pent" (136), a "sweet hell" (156)
of conflict which is resolved by the final understanding that death
ends all (168-73).

B

1. The poem, whose second title was "A Word out of the Sea,"
is primarily a philosophical reverie on nature.

2. The bird sings a song (indicated by italics) that symbolizes love, life, and the natural need for companionship (34-35, 76-79, 101, 127).

3. The sea sings a song that symbolizes birth, death, and the human interrelationship with nature (165-73).

4. Together they provide an understanding of nature's meaning, enabling the poet to be the "uniter of here and hereafter" (20).

5. The repetition, the parallel phrases, and the rolling rhythm of the lines help to give an impression of the cycle of nature.

C

1. The poem, whose final title was "Out of the Cradle Endlessly Rocking," is a revelation of an archetypal rebirth.

2. The first section (1-22) is a scene of involuntary return (18) to some birth (1-3) involving poetic expression (11-17), with a mysterious "undertone" (141) of death (4, 14, 20).

3. In the second section (23-129), the mockingbird's spring love and summer loss further involves images and symbols of birth (24, 27, 32-33, 72-78) and death (45, 101, 119, 128-29).

4. The triumphant third section clearly embodies the rebirth (146-49) of the boy out of the creative male singing bird (132, 150) and the "fierce old mother" (133, 141, 182).

5. The apparently illogical presence of death in this birth experience is accounted for by the unstated archetypal paradox that death—of the female bird and of the sea-mother's myriad waves (1, 46, 48, 57, 66, 133, 141, 160-83)—is necessary to produce creative life.

BIBLIOGRAPHY

Adams, R. P., *Tulane Studies in English*, **5** (1955), 138-40, 146-49; Allen, G. W., and C. T. Davis, *Walt Whitman's Poems*, 1955, pp. 158-59, 164-67; Cunningham, C. C., *Literature as a Fine Art*, 1941, pp. 176-85; Marks, A. H., *American Literature*, **23** (Mar. 1951), 110-11, 120-26; Miller, J. E., *A Critical Guide to Leaves of Grass*, 1957, pp. 104-10; Spitzer, L., *ELH*, **16** (Sept. 1949), 235-49; Walcutt, C. C., *College English*, **10** (Feb. 1949), 277-79; Warfel, H. R., *Tennessee Studies in Literature*, **3** (1958), 83-87; Whicher, S. E., *Explicator*, **5** (Feb. 1947), 28.

When I Heard the Learn'd Astronomer

When I heard the learn'd astronomer,
When the proofs, the figures, were ranged in columns before me,
When I was shown the charts and diagrams, to add, divide, and
measure them,
When I sitting heard the astronomer where he lectured with much
applause in the lecture-room,
How soon unaccountable I became tired and sick,   5
Till rising and gliding out I wander'd off by myself,
In the mystical moist night-air, and from time to time
Look'd up in perfect silence at the stars.

June Light

Your voice, with clear location of June days,
Called me—outside the window. You were there,
Light yet composed, as in the just soft stare
Of uncontested summer all things raise
Plainly their seeming into seamless air.

Then your love looked as simple and entire   6
As that picked pear you tossed me, and your face
As legible as pearskin's fleck and trace,
Which promise always wine, by mottled fire
More fatal fleshed than ever human grace.

And your gay gift—Oh when I saw it fall   11
Into my hands, through all that naïve light,
It seemed as blessed with truth and new delight
As must have been the first great gift of all.

The Death of a Toad

A toad the power mower caught,
Chewed and clipped of a leg, with a hobbling hop has got
To the garden verge, and sanctuaried him

14 *first great gift:* apple of the Tree of Knowledge in the Garden of Eden.

Under the cineraria leaves, in the shade
Of the ashen heartshaped leaves, in a dim,
    Low, and a final glade.

The rare original heartsblood goes,   7
Spends on the earthen hide, in the folds and wizenings, flows
    In the gutters of the banked and staring eyes. He lies
As still as if he would return to stone,
    And soundlessly attending, dies
        Toward some deep monotone,

Toward misted and ebullient seas   13
And cooling shores, toward lost Amphibia's emperies.
    Day dwindles, drowning, and at length is gone
In the wide and antique eyes, which still appear
    To watch, across the castrate lawn,
        The haggard daylight steer.

Two Voices in a Meadow

A Milkweed

Anonymous as cherubs
Over the crib of God,
White seeds are floating
Out of my burst pod.
What power had I   5
Before I learned to yield?
Shatter me, great wind:
I shall possess the field.

A Stone

As casual as cow-dung   9
Under the crib of God,
I lie where chance would have me,
Up to the ears in sod.
Why should I move? To move   13
Befits a light desire.
The sill of Heaven would founder,
Did such as I aspire.

13 *ebullient:* bubbling.

Junk

Huru Welandes
    worc ne geswiceð
monna ænigum
    ðara ðe Mimming can
heardne gehealdan.

WALDERE

An axe angles
    from my neighbor's ashcan;
It is hell's handiwork,
    the wood not hickory,
The flow of the grain   5
    not faithfully followed.
The shivered shaft
    rises from a shellheap
Of plastic playthings,
    paper plates,   10
And the sheer shards
    of shattered tumblers
That were not annealed
    for the time needful.
At the same curbside,   15
    a cast-off cabinet
Of wavily-warped
    unseasoned wood
Waits to be trundled
    in the trash-man's truck.   20
Haul them off! Hide them!
    The heart winces
For junk and gimcrack,
    for jerrybuilt things
And the men who make them   25
    for a little money,
Bartering pride
    like the bought boxer
Who pulls his punches,
    or the paid-off jockey   30
Who in the home stretch
    holds in his horse.

"The epigraph, taken from a fragmentary Anglo-Saxon poem, concerns the legendary smith Wayland, and may roughly be translated: 'Truly, Wayland's handiwork—the sword Mimming which he made—will never fail any man who knows how to use it bravely.' " (Wilbur).   13 *annealed*: baked.

Yet the things themselves

            in thoughtless honor

Have kept composure,   35

           like captives who would not

Talk under torture.

           Tossed from a tailgate

Where the dump displays

           its random dolmens,   40

Its black barrows

          and blazing valleys,

They shall waste in the weather

           toward what they were.

The sun shall glory   45

          in the glitter of glass-chips,

Foreseeing the salvage

          of the prisoned sand,

And the blistering paint

          peel off in patches,   50

That the good grain

          be discovered again.

Then burnt, bulldozed,

          they shall all be buried

To the depth of diamonds,   55

          in the making dark

Where halt Hephaestus

          keeps his hammer

And Wayland's work

          is worn away.   60

Lines

Composed a Few Miles Above Tintern Abbey, on Revisiting the Banks of the Wye During a Tour. July 13, 1798

Five years have past; five summers, with the length
Of five long winters! and again I hear
These waters, rolling from their mountain-springs

40 *dolmens:* stone monuments. 41 *barrows:* mounds. 57 *halt Hephaestus:* crippled Greek god of fire and smithy.

Tintern Abbey: well-known ruin in Western England.

With a soft inland murmur.—Once again
Do I behold these steep and lofty cliffs,   5
That on a wild secluded scene impress
Thoughts of more deep seclusion; and connect
The landscape with the quiet of the sky.
The day is come when I again repose
Here, under this dark sycamore, and view   10
These plots of cottage-ground, these orchard-tufts,
Which at this season, with their unripe fruits,
Are clad in one green hue, and lose themselves
'Mid groves and copses. Once again I see
These hedge-rows, hardly hedge-rows, little lines   15
Of sportive wood run wild: these pastoral farms,
Green to the very door; and wreaths of smoke
Sent up, in silence, from among the trees!
With some uncertain notice, as might seem
Of vagrant dwellers in the houseless woods,   20
Or of some Hermit's cave, where by his fire
The Hermit sits alone.
                              These beauteous forms,
Through a long absence, have not been to me
As is a landscape to a blind man's eye:
But oft, in lonely rooms, and 'mid the din   25
Of towns and cities, I have owed to them
In hours of weariness, sensations sweet,
Felt in the blood, and felt along the heart;
And passing even into my purer mind,
With tranquil restoration:—feelings too   30
Of unremembered pleasure: such, perhaps,
As have no slight or trivial influence
On that best portion of a good man's life,
His little, nameless, unremembered, acts
Of kindness and of love. Nor less, I trust,   35
To them I may have owed another gift,
Of aspect more sublime; that blessed mood
In which the burthen of the mystery,
In which the heavy and the weary weight
Of all this unintelligible world,   40
Is lightened:—that serene and blessed mood,
In which the affections gently lead us on,—
Until, the breath of this corporeal frame
And even the motion of our human blood

14 *copses:* thickets.   38 *burthen:* burden.   42 *affections:* feelings.

Almost suspended, we are laid asleep   45
In body, and become a living soul:
While with an eye made quiet by the power
Of harmony, and the deep power of joy,
We see into the life of things.
                              If this
Be but a vain belief, yet, oh! how oft—   50
In darkness and amid the many shapes
Of joyless daylight; when the fretful stir
Unprofitable, and the fever of the world,
Have hung upon the beatings of my heart—
How oft, in spirit, have I turned to thee   55
O sylvan Wye! thou wanderer thro' the woods,
How often has my spirit turned to thee!

    And now, with gleams of half-extinguished thought,
With many recognitions dim and faint,
And somewhat of a sad perplexity,   60
The picture of the mind revives again:
While here I stand, not only with the sense
Of present pleasure, but with pleasing thoughts
That in this moment there is life and food
For future years. And so I dare to hope,   65
Though changed, no doubt, from what I was when first
I came among these hills; when like a roe
I bounded o'er the mountains, by the sides
Of the deep rivers, and the lonely streams,
Wherever nature led: more like a man   70
Flying from something that he dreads than one
Who sought the thing he loved. For nature then
(The coarser pleasures of my boyish days,
And their glad animal movements all gone by)
To me was all in all.—I cannot paint   75
What then I was. The sounding cataract
Haunted me like a passion: the tall rock,
The mountain, and the deep and gloomy wood,
Their colours and their forms, were then to me
An appetite; a feeling and a love,   80
That had no need of a remoter charm,
By thought supplied, nor any interest
Unborrowed from the eye.—That time is past,
And all its aching joys are now no more,
And all its dizzy raptures. Not for this   85

Faint I, nor mourn nor murmur; other gifts
Have followed; for such loss, I would believe,
Abundant recompense. For I have learned
To look on nature, not as in the hour
Of thoughtless youth; but hearing oftentimes   90
The still, sad music of humanity,
Nor harsh nor grating, though of ample power
To chasten and subdue. And I have felt
A presence that disturbs me with the joy
Of elevated thoughts; a sense sublime   95
Of something far more deeply interfused,
Whose dwelling is the light of setting suns,
And the round ocean and the living air,
And the blue sky, and in the mind of man:
A motion and a spirit, that impels   100
All thinking things, all objects of all thought,
And rolls through all things. Therefore am I still
A lover of the meadows and the woods,
And mountains; and of all that we behold
From this green earth; of all the mighty world   105
Of eye, and ear,—both what they half create,
And what perceive; well pleased to recognise
In nature and the language of the sense
The anchor of my purest thoughts, the nurse,
The guide, the guardian of my heart, and soul   110
Of all my moral being.
                         Nor perchance,
If I were not thus taught, should I the more
Suffer my genial spirits to decay:
For thou art with me here upon the banks
Of this fair river; thou my dearest Friend,   115
My dear, dear Friend; and in thy voice I catch
The language of my former heart, and read
My former pleasures in the shooting lights
Of thy wild eyes. Oh! yet a little while
May I behold in thee what I was once,   120
My dear, dear Sister! and this prayer I make,
Knowing that Nature never did betray
The heart that loved her; 'tis her privilege,
Through all the years of this our life, to lead
From joy to joy: for she can so inform   125

108 *the sense:* the senses.   113 *genial:* vital.   115 *Friend:* the "sister" of 121,
Dorothy Wordsworth.

The mind that is within us, so impress
With quietness and beauty, and so feed
With lofty thoughts, that neither evil tongues,
Rash judgments, nor the sneers of selfish men,
Nor greetings where no kindness is, nor all   130
The dreary intercourse of daily life,
Shall e'er prevail against us, or disturb
Our cheerful faith, that all which we behold
Is full of blessings. Therefore let the moon
Shine on thee in thy solitary walk;   135
And let the misty mountain-winds be free
To blow against thee: and, in after years,
When these wild ecstasies shall be matured
Into a sober pleasure: when thy mind
Shall be a mansion for all lovely forms,   140
Thy memory be as a dwelling place
For all sweet sounds and harmonies; oh! then,
If solitude, or fear, or pain, or grief,
Should be thy portion, with what healing thoughts
Of tender joy wilt thou remember me,   145
And these my exhortations! Nor, perchance—
If I should be where I no more can hear
Thy voice, nor catch from thy wild eyes these gleams
Of past existence—wilt thou then forget
That on the banks of this delightful stream   150
We stood together; and that I, so long
A worshipper of Nature, hither came
Unwearied in that service: rather say
With warmer love—oh! with far deeper zeal
Of holier love. Nor wilt thou then forget,   155
That after many wanderings, many years
Of absence, these steep woods and lofty cliffs,
And this green pastoral landscape, were to me
More dear, both for themselves and for thy sake!

Case

A

1. The poem is a philosophical reverie, with a strong didactic
strain.

2. Section 1 (1-22) is concerned with a particular scene of Man in Nature, the preponderance of run-on lines and the exclusive use of masculine endings giving flow and vigor to the passage.

3. Section 2 (22-57) describes the threefold effects of Man's thoughtful awareness of Nature.

4. In Section 3 (58-111), the heart of the poem, the poet first reflects on a stage in the relationship when Nature overwhelms Man emotionally, in the midst of this reflection briefly calling up (73-74) an earlier stage, Man's purely physical enjoyment of Nature.

5. He then describes a third phase, in which Man finds primary value in a mysterious "sense sublime" of a "spirit" that "rolls through all things" (95-102).

6. Section 4 (111-59) further emphasizes the poet's faith in the healing power of Nature—an idea that has received earlier attention in the poem (e.g., 30, 109).

B

1. The poem is a dramatic monologue spoken by a thoughtful man, expressing a conflict between his doubt and faith in Nature.

2. The setting is given to the reader in specific detail in the title and in Section 1, and the speaker's audience is revealed in 114 ff.

3. In Section 2 the speaker says that recollections of his first visit have inspired and sustained him, yet he expresses some doubt in 49-50 and at the beginning of Section 3 (58-60).

4. Noting that five years ago his feeling for Nature was a physical reflex that required no thought, he wants to believe that "other gifts" have taken its place; by describing these gifts, he renews his faith (80-102).

5. Section 4 takes up—and ends the poem with—a point heretofore ignored: the way in which his sister's presence has an additional strengthening effect on the speaker's faith.

6. The total effect of the monologue is a resolution of conflict, a progress from apprehensiveness to renewed confidence.

Benziger, J., PMLA, 65 (Mar. 1950), 154-62; Bloom, H., The Visionary Company, 1961, pp. 127-36; Brooks, C., J. T. Purser, and R. P. Warren, An Approach to Literature, 1952 ed., pp. 403-4; Hartman, G. H., The Unmediated Vision, 1954, pp. 3-12.

A Slumber Did My Spirit Seal

A slumber did my spirit seal;
    I had no human fears:
She seemed a thing that could not feel
    The touch of earthly years.

No motion has she now, no force;   5
    She neither hears nor sees;
Rolled round in earth's diurnal course,
    With rocks, and stones, and trees.

Case

A

1. The tone of the poem is that of a lover lamenting his dead beloved.

2. Stanza 1 expresses his confidence in her youthful animation when she was alive.

3. Stanza 2 embodies his despairing sense of loss now that she is dead and underground.

B

1. The tone of the poem is that of a philosophical man detachedly commenting on a dead woman of his acquaintance.

2. In Stanza 1 he recalls how her qualities lulled his usual "human" feelings, how he thought of her more as a "thing" impervious to material pressures than as a human being.

3. In Stanza 2 he once again describes her as a thing, this time using impersonal scientific terms ("motion," "force," "diurnal") and speaking of her as now completely and literally subject to material pressures.

C

1. The tone of the poem is that of a human creature painfully coming to understand the relationship between man and nature.

2. Stanza 1 describes, in negative terms, his "spirit"'s insensitivity in the past.

7 *diurnal:* daily.

3. After the death of a friend, the speaker confidently accepts the eternal connection of human beings with other organic and inorganic substance.

BIBLIOGRAPHY

Bateson, F. W., *English Poetry: A Critical Introduction,* 1950, pp. 32-34; Brooks, C., *College English,* 9 (Feb. 1948), 235-37; Ferry, D., *The Limits of Mortality,* 1959, pp. 76-79; Henn, T., *The Apple and the Spectroscope,* 1951, pp. 35-37; Hirsch, E. D., *PMLA,* 75 (Sept. 1960), 471-72; Leavis, F. R., *Scrutiny,* 13 (Spring 1945), 53-55; Thomas, W., and S. G. Brown, *Reading Poems,* 1941, pp. 642-43.

I Wandered Lonely as a Cloud

I wandered lonely as a cloud
That floats on high o'er vales and hills,
When all at once I saw a crowd,
A host, of golden daffodils;   4
Beside the lake, beneath the trees,
Fluttering and dancing in the breeze.

Continuous as the stars that shine   7
And twinkle on the milky way,
They stretched in never-ending line
Along the margin of a bay: 10
Ten thousand saw I at a glance,
Tossing their heads in sprightly dance.

The waves beside them danced; but they   13
Out-did the sparkling waves in glee:
A poet could not but be gay,
In such a jocund company: 16
I gazed—and gazed—but little thought
What wealth the show to me had brought:

For oft, when on my couch I lie   19
In vacant or in pensive mood,
They flash upon that inward eye
Which is the bliss of solitude;   22
And then my heart with pleasure fills,
And dances with the daffodils.

Case

A

1. The poem recounts an uncomplicated experience—the delight of "A poet" in encountering natural beauty.

2. The simplicity of the experience is carried out in the diction, meter, and comparative lack of metaphor.

B

1. Although the poem seems uncomplicated, it actually embodies an emotional opposition.

2. This opposition is emphasized by the contrast between Nature (represented by the colorful, multitudinous, dynamic daffodils) and Man (represented by the colorless, single, passive human being), but both conflicts are resolved at the end of the poem.

BIBLIOGRAPHY

Greene, T. M., *The Arts and the Art of Criticism*, 1940, pp. 114-15; Pottle, F. A., *Yale Review*, **40** (Sept. 1950), 29-35.

Composed Upon Westminster Bridge, September 3, 1802

Earth has not anything to show more fair:
Dull would he be of soul who could pass by
A sight so touching in its majesty:
This City now doth, like a garment, wear   4
The beauty of the morning; silent, bare,
Ships, towers, domes, theatres, and temples lie
Open unto the fields, and to the sky;
All bright and glittering in the smokeless air.
Never did sun more beautifully steep   9
In his first splendour, valley, rock, or hill;
Ne'er saw I, never felt, a calm so deep!
The river glideth at his own sweet will:
Dear God! the very houses seem asleep;
And all that mighty heart is lying still!   14

9 *steep:* flood.

My Heart Leaps Up

My heart leaps up when I behold
  A rainbow in the sky:
So was it when my life began;
So is it now I am a man;
So be it when I shall grow old,   5
  Or let me die!
The Child is father of the Man;
And I could wish my days to be
Bound each to each by natural piety.

Ode

Intimations of Immortality from Recollections of Early Childhood

  The Child is father of the Man;
  And I could wish my days to be
  Bound each to each by natural piety.

I

There was a time when meadow, grove, and stream,
The earth, and every common sight,
    To me did seem
    Apparelled in celestial light,
The glory and the freshness of a dream.   5
It is not now as it hath been of yore;—
    Turn wheresoe'er I may,
    By night or day,
The things which I have seen I now can see no more.

II

    The Rainbow comes and goes,   10
    And lovely is the Rose,
    The Moon doth with delight
Look round her when the heavens are bare;
    Waters on a starry night   14
    Are beautiful and fair;

The Child . . . piety: see Wordsworth's "My Heart Leaps Up."

The sunshine is a glorious birth;
　But yet I know, where'er I go,
That there hath past away a glory from the earth.

III

Now, while the birds thus sing a joyous song,   19
　　And while the young lambs bound
　　　As to the tabor's sound,
To me alone there came a thought of grief:
A timely utterance gave that thought relief,
　　　And I again am strong: 24
The cataracts blow their trumpets from the steep;
No more shall grief of mine the season wrong;
I hear the Echoes through the mountains throng,
The Winds come to me from the fields of sleep,
　　　And all the earth is gay;   29
　　　　Land and sea
　　　Give themselves up to jollity,
　　　　And with the heart of May
　　　Doth every Beast keep holiday;—
　　　　Thou Child of Joy,   34
Shout round me, let me hear thy shouts, thou happy
　　　Shepherd-boy!

IV

Ye blessèd Creatures, I have heard the call   36
　　Ye to each other make; I see
The heavens laugh with you in your jubilee;
　　My heart is at your festival,
　　My head hath its coronal,
The fulness of your bliss, I feel—I feel it all.   41
　　　Oh evil day! if I were sullen
　　　While Earth herself is adorning,
　　　　This sweet May-morning,
　　　And the Children are culling
　　　　On every side,   46
　　In a thousand valleys far and wide,
　　Fresh flowers; while the sun shines warm,
And the Babe leaps up on his Mother's arm:—
　　I hear, I hear, with joy I hear!
　　—But there's a Tree, of many, one,   51

21 *tabor:* drum.   40 *coronal:* wreath.

A single Field which I have looked upon,
Both of them speak of something that is gone:
    The Pansy at my feet
    Doth the same tale repeat:
Whither is fled the visionary gleam?   56
Where is it now, the glory and the dream?

V

Our birth is but a sleep and a forgetting: 58
The Soul that rises with us, our life's Star,
    Hath had elsewhere its setting,
      And cometh from afar:
    Not in entire forgetfulness,
    And not in utter nakedness,   63
But trailing clouds of glory do we come
    From God, who is our home:
Heaven lies about us in our infancy!
Shades of the prison-house begin to close
    Upon the growing Boy,   68
      But He
Beholds the light, and whence it flows,
    He sees it in his joy;
The Youth, who daily farther from the east
    Must travel, still is Nature's Priest,   73
    And by the vision splendid
    Is on his way attended;
At length the Man perceives it die away,
And fade into the light of common day.

VI

Earth fills her lap with pleasures of her own;   78
Yearnings she hath in her own natural kind,
And, even with something of a Mother's mind,
    And no unworthy aim,
    The homely Nurse doth all she can   82
To make her Foster-child, her Inmate Man,
    Forget the glories he hath known,
And that imperial palace whence he came.

VII

Behold the Child among his new-born blisses,   86
A six years' Darling of a pigmy size!
See, where 'mid work of his own hand he lies,

Fretted by sallies of his mother's kisses,
With light upon him from his father's eyes!
See, at his feet, some little plan or chart,   91
Some fragment from his dream of human life,
Shaped by himself with newly-learned art;
    A wedding or a festival,
    A mourning or a funeral;
      And this hath now his heart,   96
    And unto this he frames his song:
      Then will he fit his tongue
To dialogues of business, love, or strife;
    But it will not be long
    Ere this be thrown aside,   101
    And with new joy and pride
The little Actor cons another part;
Filling from time to time his "humorous stage"
With all the Persons, down to palsied Age,
That Life brings with her in her equipage;   106
    As if his whole vocation
    Were endless imitation.

VIII

Thou, whose exterior semblance doth belie   109
    Thy Soul's immensity;
Thou best Philosopher, who yet dost keep
Thy heritage, thou Eye among the blind,
That, deaf and silent, read'st the eternal deep,
Haunted for ever by the eternal mind,—   114
    Mighty Prophet! Seer blest!
    On whom those truths do rest,
Which we are toiling all our lives to find,
In darkness lost, the darkness of the grave;
Thou, over whom thy Immortality   119
Broods like the Day, a Master o'er a Slave,
A Presence which is not to be put by;
Thou little Child, yet glorious in the might
Of heaven-born freedom on thy being's height,
Why with such earnest pains dost thou provoke   124
The years to bring the inevitable yoke,
Thus blindly with thy blessedness at strife?

89 *Fretted by sallies of:* covered by.   103 *cons:* learns.   104 *"humorous stage":*
cast of varied characters; the phrase is Samuel Daniel's (de Selincourt).   111
yet: still.

Full soon thy Soul shall have her earthly freight,
And custom lie upon thee with a weight,
Heavy as frost, and deep almost as life!

IX

O joy! that in our embers   130
Is something that doth live,
That nature yet remembers
What was so fugitive!
The thought of our past years in me doth breed
Perpetual benediction: not indeed   135
For that which is most worthy to be blest;
Delight and liberty, the simple creed
Of Childhood, whether busy or at rest,
With new-fledged hope still fluttering in his breast:—
Not for these I raise   140
The song of thanks and praise;
But for those obstinate questionings
Of sense and outward things,
Fallings from us, vanishings;
Blank misgivings of a Creature   145
Moving about in worlds not realised,
High instincts before which our mortal Nature
Did tremble like a guilty Thing surprised:
But for those first affections,
Those shadowy recollections,   150
Which, be they what they may,
Are yet the fountain light of all our day,
Are yet a master light of all our seeing;
Uphold us, cherish, and have power to make
Our noisy years seem moments in the being   155
Of the eternal Silence: truths that wake,
To perish never;
Which neither listlessness, nor mad endeavour,
Nor Man nor Boy,
Nor all that is at enmity with joy,   160
Can utterly abolish or destroy!
Hence in a season of calm weather
Though inland far we be,
Our Souls have sight of that immortal sea
Which brought us hither,   165
Can in a moment travel thither,

143 *sense:* the senses.   146 *realised:* made real.   149 *affections:* feelings.

And see the Children sport upon the shore,
And hear the mighty waters rolling evermore.

X

Then sing, ye Birds, sing, sing a joyous song!   169
  And let the young Lambs bound
  As to the tabor's sound!
We in thought will join your throng,
  Ye that pipe and ye that play,
  Ye that through your hearts to-day   174
  Feel the gladness of the May!
What though the radiance which was once so bright
Be now for ever taken from my sight,
  Though nothing can bring back the hour
Of splendour in the grass, of glory in the flower;   179
  We will grieve not, rather find
  Strength in what remains behind;
  In the primal sympathy
  Which having been must ever be;
  In the soothing thoughts that spring   184
  Out of human suffering;
  In the faith that looks through death,
In years that bring the philosophic mind.

XI

And O, ye Fountains, Meadows, Hills, and Groves, 188
Forebode not any severing of our loves!
Yet in my heart of hearts I feel your might;
I only have relinquished one delight
To live beneath your more habitual sway.
I love the Brooks which down their channels fret, 193
Even more than when I tripped lightly as they;
The innocent brightness of a new-born Day
  Is lovely yet;
The Clouds that gather round the setting sun
Do take a sober colouring from an eye   198
That hath kept watch o'er man's mortality;
Another race hath been, and other palms are won.
Thanks to the human heart by which we live,
Thanks to its tenderness, its joys, and fears,
To me the meanest flower that blows can give
Thoughts that do often lie too deep for tears.   204

190 *Yet:* still. 203 *blows:* blooms.

Case

A

1. The primary theme of the poem, as indicated by the title, is man's mortal intimations of immortality.

2. Stanzas 5-8 express the central concept of the poem, that of the immortal life of the soul, a life in which birth is but a mid-point.

3. Because the child has more lately left "God, who is our home" (65), he is still capable of perceiving the "celestial light" (4) which for mature man is replaced by "the light of common day" (77); over the child "Immortality / Broods like the Day" (119-20).

4. Despite the losses attendant upon maturity, it is the faint recollection of the childhood vision that provides the strongest evidence for future immortality (142 ff.).

5. The awareness especially is strong in those moments when "Our souls have sight of that immortal sea / Which brought us hither" (164-65), and in those moments when we feel "the faith that looks through death" (186), despite the reality of "man's mortality" (199).

6. The poet is, therefore, resigned to the loss of that more immediate contact with immortality which he had in childhood.

B

1. The primary theme is the gradual loss of childhood sensitivity and its replacement by other, lesser faculties—the substitution of the inglorious "philosophic mind" (187) for the glorious "visionary gleam" (56).

2. Stanzas 1 and 2 emphasize the poignant sense of loss that affects the poet's enjoyment of natural beauty; Stanzas 3 and 4 describe a partially successful attempt to recapture the perceptivity of childhood.

3. But the last seven lines of Stanza 4 revert to the original awareness of loss, with Stanzas 5-8 representing the poet's resentment at the growing insensitiveness.

4. In the last three stanzas the poet makes a brave attempt to console himself for the loss of "Delight and liberty" (137, 123, 191) by pointing to his "primal sympathy" (182), his "philosophic mind" (187), and his appreciation of nature's "sober coloring" (198).

5. But the fervent utterance of 178-79 indicates a deeper and more convincing pessimism.

6. That the poet unconsciously places a higher value on child-

hood than on maturity is partially proved by his frequent and consistent assignment of "joy" to the earlier stage (19, 34, 50, 71, 102, 160, 169).

C

1. The primary theme of the poem is the development and maturing of the "human heart" (201) from childhood to manhood.

2. The first two stanzas contrast the poet's mature view of earthly beauty with his vision, as a child, of a heavenly glory that impregnated the earth.

3. Stanzas 3 and 4 stress the boisterous, unreflective vigor of immaturity, as contrasted with a "thought of grief" (22), which recurs intermittently (42, 51-57).

4. The implicity meanings of the images of light (4, 10, 16, 56) are developed in Stanza 5: It is now apparent to the reader that the "celestial light" (4) must change into the mature "light of common day" (77).

5. Although Stanzas 6-8 embody the irony that the growing youth works actively to lose the innocent vision of childhood, Stanza 9 emphasizes the persistence of the light in the "embers" of maturity, which are still the "fountain light" and the "master light" of truth and understanding.

6. Having resolved the paradox, the poet returns in Stanza 10 to the scene described in 3, but no longer with thoughts of grief: although he has lost "the glory and the dream" (57) of childhood, in maturity he has gained a fundamental feeling of harmony with humanity and nature (182-end).

BIBLIOGRAPHY

Bateson, F. W., *English Poetry*, 1950, pp. 196-209; Bloom, H., *The Visionary Company*, 1961, pp. 166-73; Brooks, C., *Kenyon Review*, **8** (Winter 1946), 80-102; ———, *The Well Wrought Urn*, Harvest ed., n.d., pp. 124-50, 190, 213-14; ———, *Western Review*, **13** (Autumn 1948), 14-15; ———, and R. P. Warren, *Understanding Poetry*, 1950 ed., pp. 639-45; Darbishire, H., *The Poet Wordsworth*, 1950, pp. 64-74; Douglas, W. W., *Western Review*, **13** (Autumn 1948), 4-14; Knight, G. W., *University of Toronto Quarterly*, 1 (Apr. 1932), 216-35; ———, *The Starlit Dome*, 1941, pp. 37-41; Ransom, J. C., *Kenyon Review*, **12** (Summer 1950), 514-18; Raysor, T. M., *PMLA*, **69** (Sept. 1954), 861-75; Schneider, R. L., *Journal of English and Germanic Philology*, **54** (Oct. 1955), 625-33; Stauffer, D. A., *Kenyon Review*, **4** (Winter 1942), 133-44; Trilling, L., *English Institute Annual 1941*, 1942, pp. 1-28.

The Solitary Reaper

Behold her, single in the field,
Yon solitary Highland Lass!
Reaping and singing by herself;
Stop here, or gently pass!
Alone she cuts and binds the grain,   5
And sings a melancholy strain;
O listen! for the Vale profound
Is overflowing with the sound.

No Nightingale did ever chaunt   9
More welcome notes to weary bands
Of travellers in some shady haunt,
Among Arabian sands:
A voice so thrilling ne'er was heard   13
In spring-time from the Cuckoo-bird,
Breaking the silence of the seas
Among the farthest Hebrides.

Will no one tell me what she sings?—   17
Perhaps the plaintive numbers flow
For old, unhappy, far-off things,
And battles long ago:
Or is it some more humble lay,   21
Familiar matter of to-day?
Some natural sorrow, loss, or pain,
That has been, and may be again?

Whate'er the theme, the Maiden sang   25
As if her song could have no ending;
I saw her singing at her work,
And o'er the sickle bending:—
I listened, motionless and still;   29
And, as I mounted up the hill,
The music in my heart I bore,
Long after it was heard no more.

18 *numbers:* metrical lines.   21 *lay:* song.

The World Is Too Much with Us

The world is too much with us; late and soon,
Getting and spending, we lay waste our powers:
Little we see in Nature that is ours;
We have given our hearts away, a sordid boon!
This Sea that bares her bosom to the moon;   5
The winds that will be howling at all hours,
And are up-gathered now like sleeping flowers;
For this, for everything, we are out of tune;
It moves us not.—Great God! I'd rather be   9
A Pagan suckled in a creed outworn;
So might I, standing on this pleasant lea,
Have glimpses that would make me less forlorn;
Have sight of Proteus rising from the sea;
Or hear old Triton blow his wreathèd horn.   14

They Flee from Me

They flee from me that sometime did me seek
  With naked foot stalking in my chamber.
I have seen them gentle, tame, and meek,
  That now are wild, and do not remember   4
That sometime they put themselves in danger
To take bread at my hand; and now they range
Busily seeking with a continual change.

Thanked be fortune, it hath been otherwise   8
  Twenty times better; but once, in special,
  In thin array, after a pleasant guise,
When her loose gown from her shoulders did fall,
And she me caught in her arms long and small,   12
Therewith all so sweetly did me kiss,
And softly said: "Dear heart, how like you this?"

It was no dream: I lay broad waking   15
  But all is turned thorough my gentleness,
  Into a strange fashion of forsaking;

4 *boon:* gift.   11 *lea:* meadow.

10 *guise:* manner? masquerade?

And I have leave to go of her goodness:
And she also to use newfangleness;   19
But since that I so kindely am served,
I would fain know what she hath deserved.

My Lute, Awake

My lute, awake, perform the last
Labour that thou and I shall waste,
And end that I have now begun.
And when this song is sung and past,
My lute, be still, for I have done.   5
    As to be heard where ear is none,
As lead to grave in marble stone,
My song may pierce her heart as soon.
Should we then sigh, or sing, or moan?
No, no, my lute, for I have done.   10
    The rocks do not so cruelly
Repulse the waves continually,
As she my suit and affection;
So that I am past remedy,
Whereby my lute and I have done.   15
    Proud of the spoil that thou hast got
Of simple hearts, through love's shot;
By whom unkind thou hast them won,
Think not he hath his bow forgot,
Although my lute and I have done.   20
    Vengeance shall fall on thy disdain,
That makest but game on earnest pain.
Think not alone under the sun
Unquit to cause they lovers plain,
Although my lute and I have done.   25
    Perchance thee lie withered and old,
The winter nights that are so cold,
Plaining in vain unto the moon;
Thy wishes then dare not be told.
Care then who list, for I have done.   30
    And then may chance thee to repent
The time that thou hast lost and spent
To cause thy lovers sigh and swoon.

Then shalt thou know beauty but lent,
And wish and want as I have done.   35
   Now cease, my lute, this is the last
Labour that thou and I shall waste,
And ended is that we begun.
Now is this song both sung and past,
My lute, be still, for I have done.   40

The Magi

Now as at all times I can see in the mind's eye,
In their stiff, painted clothes, the pale unsatisfied ones
Appear and disappear in the blue depth of the sky
With all their ancient faces like rain-beaten stones,
And all their helms of silver hovering side by side,   5
And all their eyes still fixed, hoping to find once more,
Being by Calvary's turbulence unsatisfied,
The uncontrollable mystery on the bestial floor.

The Scholars

Bald heads forgetful of their sins,
Old, learned, respectable bald heads
Edit and annotate the lines
That young men, tossing on their beds,
Rhymed out in love's despair
To flatter beauty's ignorant ear.

All shuffle there; all cough in ink;   7
All wear the carpet with their shoes;
All think what other people think;
All know the man their neighbour knows.
Lord, what would they say
Did their Catullus walk that way?

The Magi: priests, the "wise men" at Christ's birth (Matthew 2).

12 *Catullus:* Roman poet of love and wit.

Leda and the Swan

A sudden blow: the great wings beating still
Above the staggering girl, her thighs caressed
By the dark webs, her nape caught in his bill,
He holds her helpless breast upon his breast.

How can those terrified vague fingers push   5
The feathered glory from her loosening thighs?
And how can body, laid in that white rush,
But feel the strange heart beating where it lies?

A shudder in the loins engenders there   9
The broken wall, the burning roof and tower
And Agamemnon dead.
                Being so caught up,
So mastered by the brute blood of the air,
Did she put on his knowledge with his power
Before the indifferent beak could let her drop?   14

Sailing to Byzantium

I

That is no country for old men. The young
In one another's arms, birds in the trees,
—Those dying generations—at their song,
The salmon-falls, the mackerel-crowded seas,
Fish, flesh, or fowl, commend all summer long   5
Whatever is begotten, born, and dies.
Caught in that sensual music all neglect
Monuments of unageing intellect.

II

An aged man is but a paltry thing,   9
A tattered coat upon a stick, unless

Leda and the Swan: Zeus as a swan made love to Leda, who bore Helen of Troy. Leda was also the mother of Clytemnestra, wife of Agamemon.

Byzantium: Constantinople, capital of the Eastern Roman Empire and of Eastern Christianity in the Middle Ages; home of highly abstract and symbolic art.   1 *That:* the country he has sailed from.

Soul clap its hands and sing, and louder sing
For every tatter in its mortal dress,
Nor is there singing school but studying   13
Monuments of its own magnificence;
And therefore I have sailed the seas and come
To the holy city of Byzantium.

III

O sages standing in God's holy fire   17
As in the gold mosaic of a wall,
Come from the holy fire, perne in a gyre,
And be the singing-masters of my soul.
Consume my heart away; sick with desire   21
And fastened to a dying animal
It knows not what it is; and gather me
Into the artifice of eternity.

IV

Once out of nature I shall never take   25
My bodily form from any natural thing,
But such a form as Grecian goldsmiths make
Of hammered gold and gold enameling
To keep a drowsy Emperor awake;   29
Or set upon a golden bough to sing
To lords and ladies of Byzantium
Of what is past, or passing, or to come.

Critique

1. In "Sailing to Byzantium" an old man faces the problem of old
age, of death, and of regeneration, and gives his decision. Old age,
he tells us, excludes a man from the sensual joys of youth; the
world appears to belong completely to the young, it is no place
for the old; indeed, an old man is scarcely a man at all—he is an
empty artifice, an effigy merely, of a man; he is a tattered coat

19 *perne in a gyre:* turn in a cone; see Yeats's elaborate system of history and
personality in *A Vision* (1938).   27-31: "I have read somewhere that in the
Emperor's palace at Byzantium was a tree made of gold and silver, and artificial birds that sang" (Yeats).

upon a stick. This would be very bad, except that the young also
are excluded from something; rapt in their sensuality, they are
ignorant utterly of the world of the spirit. Hence if old age frees
a man from sensual passion, he may rejoice in the liberation of
the soul; he is admitted into the realm of the spirit; and his rejoicing will increase according as he realizes the magnificence of
the soul. But the soul can best learn its own greatness from the
great works of art; hence he turns to those great works, but in turning to them, he finds that these are by no means mere effigies, or
monuments, but things which have souls also; these live in the
noblest element of God's fire, free from all corruption; hence he
prays for death, for release from his mortal body; and since the
insouled monuments exhibit the possibility of the soul's existence
in some other matter than flesh, he wishes reincarnation, not now
in a mortal body, but in the immortal and changeless embodiment
of art.   (ELDER OLSON)

2. The poem can be taken on a number of levels: as the transition
from sensual art to intellectual art; as the poet's new and brilliant
insight into the nature of the Byzantine imagination; as the poet's
coming to terms with age and death. . . .

"Sailing to Byzantium" . . . derives its direction from the poet's
own sense of loss and decay. The focus of the poem rests in the
reader's sense that the poet is in Ireland, *not* Byzantium. The appeal
to the sages of Byzantium is made in terms of the man whose soul
is "fastened to a dying animal."   (CLEANTH BROOKS)

3. A running analysis of Yeats's "Sailing to Byzantium" may show
how much of its beauty depends upon formal elements, how our
delight in it as poetry could not have been aroused apart from pure
architectonics. . . . Yeats writes it in four stanzas of *ottava rima,*
holding his thought closely parallel to the *a b a b a b c c* rhyme
scheme in the first two stanzas, counterpointing his sense rhythms
and pauses against the rhyme pattern more freely in the last two.
The first stanza represents the transient sensual existence of youth;
the second, the intellectual or spiritual life of old age; the third
identifies art with this unchanging wisdom of old age; the fourth
fuses the permanence of art with the transient energy of its raw
material, human life.

. . . The contrasting themes of permanence and transience are set
against each other by many cunning devices . . . .

. . . The first short sentence sets the poem as a debate between youth and age. . . . The themes of fluidity, of life, of music, are opposed in this stanza only by those stony monuments.

The second stanza catches up these images of sea, of music, and of stone. It is shaped by contrasting old age with "the young" of the first stanza . . . .

The third stanza intensifies the contrast between soul and body —fire and gold as opposed to water—as it turns more and more to the unchanging "monuments" of intellect and art . . . . It comes, too, almost as a formal incantation, an invocation to the sages . . . .

After such a prayer, which is not achieved by an easy renunciation of the "sensual music," nor by a denial of its values and its reality, the fusion of life and art in the image of the golden nightingale in the fourth stanza comes with a sense of resolution, of completeness, of rest. . . .

. . . Yeats is himself a great goldsmith. In this poem itself he has made a golden bird which, we may easily believe, will sing forever, because it has been taken "out of nature" and given "such a form as Grecian goldsmiths make." The dyingness and the desire, expressed through controlled form in the first three stanzas, are now over; tension has given way to fusion, expressed also through controlled form; and we have been gathered into the eternity of artifice.

(DONALD A. STAUFFER)

BIBLIOGRAPHY

Brooks, C., *Modern Poetry and the Tradition*, 1939, p. 192; Olson, E., in *The Permanence of Yeats*, ed. J. Hall and M. Steinmann, 1950, p. 290; Stauffer, D. A., *The Nature of Poetry*, 1946, pp. 243-46.

Among School Children

I

I walk through the long schoolroom questioning;
A kind old nun in a white hood replies;
The children learn to cipher and to sing,
To study reading-books and history,
To cut and sew, be neat in everything   5
In the best modern way—the children's eyes

In momentary wonder stare upon
A sixty-year-old smiling public man.

II

I dream of a Ledaean body, bent   9
Above a sinking fire, a tale that she
Told of a harsh reproof, or trivial event
That changed some childish day to tragedy—
Told, and it seemed that our two natures blent   13
Into a sphere from youthful sympathy,
Or else, to alter Plato's parable,
Into the yolk and white of the one shell.

III

And thinking of that fit of grief or rage   17
I look upon one child or t'other there
And wonder if she stood so at that age—
For even daughters of the swan can share
Something of every paddler's heritage—   21
And had that colour upon cheek or hair,
And thereupon my heart is driven wild:
She stands before me as a living child.

IV

Her present image floats into the mind—   25
Did Quattrocento finger fashion it
Hollow of cheek as though it drank the wind
And took a mess of shadows for its meat?
And I though never of Ledaean kind   29
Had pretty plumage once—enough of that,
Better to smile on all that smile, and show
There is a comfortable kind of old scarecrow.

V

What youthful mother a shape upon her lap   33
Honey of generation had betrayed,
And that must sleep, shriek, struggle to escape

9 *Ledaean:* Leda, loved by Zeus as a swan, was mother of Helen, Castor, and
Pollux. 26 *Quattrocento:* 15th-century Italian Renaissance. 34 *Honey of
generation:* "I have taken the 'honey of generation' from Porphyry's essay on
'The Cave of the Nymphs,' but find no warrant in Porphyry for considering it
the 'drug' that destroys the 'recollection' of prenatal freedom. He blamed a
cup of oblivion given in the zodiacal sign of Cancer" (Yeats).

As recollection or the drug decide,
Would think her son, did she but see that shape   37
With sixty or more winters on its head,
A compensation for the pang of his birth,
Or the uncertainty of his setting forth?

VI

Plato thought nature but a spume that plays   41
Upon a ghostly paradigm of things;
Solider Aristotle played the taws
Upon the bottom of a king of kings;
World-famous golden-thighed Pythagoras   45
Fingered upon a fiddle-stick or strings
What a star sang and careless Muses heard:
Old clothes upon old sticks to scare a bird.

VII

Both nuns and mothers worship images,   49
But those the candles light are not as those
That animate a mother's reveries,
But keep a marble or a bronze repose.
And yet they too break hearts—O Presences   53
That passion, piety or affection knows,
And that all heavenly glory symbolise—
O self-born mockers of man's enterprise;

VIII

Labour is blossoming or dancing where   57
The body is not bruised to pleasure soul,
Nor beauty born out of its own despair,
Nor blear-eyed wisdom out of midnight oil.
O chestnut-tree, great-rooted blossomer,   61
Are you the leaf, the blossom or the bole?
O body swayed to music, O brightening glance,
How can we know the dancer from the dance?

---

42 *paradigm:* pattern. 43 *taws:* whip. 44 *king of kings:* presumably his pupil Alexander. 45-46: The Greek philosophy Pythagoras, reputed to have a golden thigh, studied music and astronomy.

Long-Legged Fly

That civilisation may not sink,
Its great battle lost,
Quiet the dog, tether the pony
To a distant post;
Our master Caesar is in the tent   6
Where the maps are spread,
His eyes fixed upon nothing,
A hand under his head.
Like a long-legged fly upon the stream
His mind moves upon silence.

That the topless towers be burnt   11
And men recall that face,
Move most gently if move you must
In this lonely place.
She thinks, part woman, three parts a child,
That nobody looks; her feet   16
Practice a tinker shuffle
Picked up on a street.
Like a long-legged fly upon the stream
Her mind moves upon silence.

That girls at puberty may find   21
The first Adam in their thought,
Shut the door of the Pope's chapel,
Keep those children out.
There on that scaffolding reclines
Michael Angelo.   26
With no more sound than the mice make
His hand moves to and fro.
Like a long-legged fly upon the stream
His mind moves upon silence.

11-12: from Marlowe's *Doctor Faustus* (1604; scene 13, lines 18-19) on Helen "of Troy": "Was this the face that launched a thousand ships, / And burnt the topless towers of Ilium?"

Appendix A

Poetics: Rhythm, Rhyme, and Rhetoric

RHYTHM

Skillful readers often can understand roughly the rhythmic pattern in a poem by hearing it, but a complete analysis of the subtle changes is impossible, even for the best readers, without close study of the *metrics*—that is, of the patterns of *stressed* and *unstressed* words and syllables, and of pauses. These sounds and slight pauses move too fast for us to study and talk about them; we need a method of writing down for the eye the metrical effects which the ear assimilates automatically, so that we may take our time and rework our analysis until it satisfies us. This system is called *scansion*.

Along with stress and transition (*juncture*), linguists have recently emphasized the importance of *pitch* in our speech, and degrees of musical pitch obviously affect the stress and consequently the meaning of words in reading poetry aloud. But since pitch is not immediately involved in rhythm, and since it is difficult to represent on paper anyway, we omit discussion of it.

The smallest unit of rhythm with which we are concerned in scansion is the syllable, which consists of a vowel and its associated consonants. "Un-der" is a word of two syllables; "sy-ca-more" has three. If we are in doubt about the division of syllables in a word, we look it up in a dictionary.

Some syllables are by custom stressed more than others: In *un*-der and *sy*-ca-more the first syllable is stressed; in a-*gain* and re-*pose,* the second. Our normal pronunciation (or any dictionary) will tell us which syllable to stress. In scansion, we shall use the sign ∕ to indicate a stressed syllable and x to indicate an unstressed syllable:

∕ x   ∕ x x   x   ∕
un-der; sy-ca-more; re-pose. If we apply these marks to a line of poetry, it will look like this:

       x   ∕ x ∕   x   ∕ x ∕   x   ∕
    The day is come when I a-gain re-pose
                       ("Tintern Abbey," 9)

Our ear tells us that the line is rhythmical, and our marking of the

[334]

stressed and unstressed syllables makes the rhythm visible and therefore easier to talk about.

In the line above, we can see that the alternation of stressed and unstressed syllables is perfectly regular, that there are five of each, and that the series begins with an unstressed syllable. We can make this regularity clearer to the eye by inserting vertical strokes at intervals where the pattern repeats itself, either

(1)   x ı | x ı | x ı | x ı | x ı | or
(2)   x | ı x | ı x | ı x | ı x | ı

Notice that there is no difference in the sound of the line whether we make the divisions as in (1) or (2); the only difference is to our eyes as we work with the signs of scansion. But (1) is obviously superior to (2) because it makes a simpler, clearer pattern.

When we have put the vertical strokes at positions that make the rhythmic pattern of the poem clearest, we call the syllables between two strokes (or the stress-marks above the syllables) a *foot*. In (1), the foot is x ı, and is called an *iamb* or an *iambic foot*. (The names of metrical feet are cumbersome, but because they have been in use for centuries one must learn them in order to understand what other people mean when they discuss meter.)

> ı   x   ı   x   ı   x   ı   x
In a line like "Scratched his head and kept on thinking" ("Miniver Cheevy," 30) the foot division (3) ı x | ı x | ı x | ı x makes the regularity of the sound pattern clearer to the eye than would (4) ı | x ı | x ı | x ı | x. We call ı x a *trochee* or *trochaic* foot.

In many poems the rhythm is more complex—for example:

> x   x   ı   x   x   ı   x x   ı   x   x   ı
> If you have an-y strength in your thumb: like the bolt
>   ("Naming of Parts," 26)

The clearest foot division for this line is

(5)   x x ı | x x ı | x x ı | x x ı

This foot is an *anapest* or *anapestic foot*.

Another type is the *dactyl* or *dactylic foot—*ı x x :

> ı x   x | ı   x x | ı   x   x | ı
> an-y-one | lived in a | pret-ty how | town

(The last foot is, of course, incomplete.)

A kind of foot frequently mixed with other feet, although never as the predominant type in a whole poem, is the *spondee* or *spondaic foot*— ′ ′ :

$$\text{Five years} \mid \text{have past;} \mid \text{five sum-} \mid \text{mers, with} \mid \text{the length}$$

("Tintern Abbey," 1)

The first and third feet are spondees. The fourth foot (ˣ ˣ) is called a *pyrrhic* or *pyrrhic foot,* and like the spondee it occurs only as a substitute for other kinds of feet.

There are some thirty different kinds of feet in metrics, but for practical purposes in English verse, these six will suffice:

x ɪ *iamb* (*ic*)   x x ɪ *anapest* (*ic*)   x x *pyrrhic*
ɪ x *trochee* (*trochaic*)   ɪ x x *dactyl* (*ic*)   ɪ ɪ *spondee* (*spondaic*)

A line is called iambic if the predominant number of feet is iambic, trochaic if the predominant number is trochaic, and so on; but in any line of poetry, substitutions of other kinds of feet frequently occur. By such substitutions the poet can obtain variations that reinforce the meanings of the poem and keep the rhythm from becoming monotonous. As in ballroom dancing, it is the spontaneous and original variation on a fixed basic step that identifies the skilled artist.

Poems usually have a regular number of feet in a line—either the same number in each line, or a recurring pattern, such as four in the first, three in the next, then four, then three, or some other repetition. The terms for the number of feet in a line are:

one: *monometer*   four: *tetrameter*
two: *dimeter*   five: *pentameter*
three: *trimeter*   six: *hexameter*

Lines longer than six feet are not common in English poetry. In speaking of the rhythmic pattern of a line it is customary to use first the term for the kind of foot that predominates, followed by the number of feet in the line, as *iambic pentameter* (example 1, above), *anapestic tetrameter* (example 5), and so on.

In scanning a line of poetry, we must remember that we are trying to describe what the poem does, not tell it what it ought to do. It is a serious mistake to analyze the rhythm of a poem by first deciding what the pattern is, and then forcing every line into that pattern. For example, in the lines

> The day is come when I again repose
> Here, under this dark sycamore, and view

the first line is regular iambic pentameter. If we force this pattern on the second line it becomes

$$\text{Here, un-} \mid \text{der this} \mid \text{dark sy-} \mid \text{ca-more,} \mid \text{and view}$$

But this distorts the natural rhythm of the line. The meaning of the line demands

$$\text{Here, un-} \mid \text{der this} \mid \text{dark sy-} \mid \text{ca-more,} \mid \text{and view}$$

The fact that the first of these lines is regular iambic, but that the second has two spondaic, two pyrrhic, and only one iambic foot should not shock us. At this point our duty is to analyze the poem, not to pass laws for the poet. In fact, complete regularity of scansion is frequently a sign of a poet's inattention to opportunities for rhythmic subtleties. This is not to say that any irregularity is good, or that we are forbidden in the end to pass judgment on the rhythm of a poem. It is only to say that before we pass judgment we must understand, and that understanding requires, among other things, dispassionate analysis.

Therefore, the first step in scansion is to determine where the stresses naturally fall. Read each line aloud several times, and then mark the stressed syllables in the fashion that the meaning demands. Then mark the unstressed syllables. Finally divide the syllables into feet—into groups that make a predominant pattern evident.

An analysis of the meter of Wordsworth's "Tintern Abbey" might begin thus:

$$\text{Five years} \mid \text{have past;} \mid \text{five sum-} \mid \text{mers, with} \mid \text{the length}$$
$$\text{Of five} \mid \text{long win-} \mid \text{ters! and} \mid \text{a-gain} \mid \text{I hear}$$
$$\text{These wa-} \mid \text{ters rol-} \mid \text{ling from} \mid \text{their moun-} \mid \text{tain springs}$$
$$\text{With a} \mid \text{soft in-} \mid \text{land mur-} \mid \text{mur.—Once} \mid \text{a-gain}$$
$$\text{Do I} \mid \text{be-hold} \mid \text{these steep} \mid \text{and lof-} \mid \text{ty cliffs} \dots$$

Readers might differ by putting more stress on "These" in line 3, making the first foot a spondee, or by making the first foot of the fifth line a pyrrhic, or on other matters. But these would be minor differences. What the analysis has succeeded in doing is to put auditory rhythm into visible form, so that we can discuss its conversational tone, or its easy flow and vigor, or its dignity, and so on.

The discussion of rhythm in poetry has been concerned so far only with the pattern of stressed and unstressed syllables. Another important aspect is the *pause* (in juncture). Pauses can be of varying lengths, from the fullest stop that marks the end of a section of a poem to a faint hesitation, perhaps marked by a comma, or perhaps indicated only by the sense of the line. Pauses can be divided into two general types: first, those at the ends of lines—

> And now, with gleams of half-extinguished thought,
> With many recognitions dim and faint,
> And somewhat . . . .   ("Tintern Abbey," 58-60)

Such lines are called *end-stopped.* If there are no pauses at the ends of lines, as

> Five years have past; five summers, with the length
> Of five long winters! and again I hear
> These waters . . . ,

they are called *run-on* lines.

Secondly, pauses occur in the middle of a line, as, in the lines just above, after "past" and "winters." The pause within the line, or— if there are more than one—the one that is greater, is called a *caesura;* the lesser pauses, if any, are called secondary pauses. Often, of course, there is no pause within the line.

Pauses also occur in such a way that they can be treated in a metrical analysis as if they were syllables, and hence parts of the feet of a line. The foot in which such a pause occurs is called an incomplete or *imperfect foot* (although the term implies no condemnation). An example is the first foot in the second of these two lines:

> x   ′ | x   ′ | x ′ | x   ′
> And when | thy heart | began | to beat
> ′ | ′   ′ | ′   ′ | ′   ′
> What | dread hand? | & what | dread feet!
>   ("The Tyger," 11-12)

The imperfect foot *What* inserts a hesitation that effectively reinforces the feeling (and so the whole meaning) of the line. *Sprung*

rhythm, identified by Hopkins, uses an irregular number of syllables and pauses between regular stresses to give the impression
of emphatic speed.

   Free verse (which is not *blank verse,* that is, unrhyming iambic
pentameter) is poetry that uses neither a regular metrical pattern
nor regular line lengths; the basic unit tends to be the whole line
rather than the single foot. When it is successful it has a rhythm
of its own which eludes the usual techniques of metrical analysis:

```
x   /    /   x x  /   /   x x
A word then (for I will conquer it,)
x   /    / x   x / x x  x /
The word final, superior to all,
/  x   x   /    x  /  x   x / x
Subtle, sent up—what is it?—I listen;
x   /    /  x x  x   x   /    /  /   x  /    x   /   /
Are you whispering it, and have been all the time, you sea-waves?
```
               ("Out of the Cradle Endlessly Rocking," 160-63)

RHYME

   The deliberate repetition of sounds (*phonemes*) is, of course, one
of the characteristics that distinguishes poetry from prose. If we
consider Mother Goose rhymes, childhood chants like hop-scotch,
and football cheers, we recognize how basic is the pleasure we
derive from repeating single or grouped letters, whole words, and
parts of words. In versification the repetition of parts of words is
called rhyme. The repetition of single or grouped phonemes is
called *alliteration* (consonants at beginnings of words), *assonance*
(vowels with different consonants), and *consonance* (consonants
at ends of words with different vowels). Whole words that imitate
sounds are labeled *onomatopoetic* ("A tap at the pane, the quick
sharp scratch / . . . of a lighted match").

   Usually the term rhyme applies to the repetition of the same
sounds at the end of nearby lines, although words may rhyme within
the same line ("The guests are met, the feast is set" ["The Ancient
Mariner," 7]), a practice called *internal rhyme.* End-rhyme in
stressed syllables is *masculine, feminine* with unstressed. If the lines
of a poem rhyme in pairs (such as "To the Memory of Mr. Oldham")
we call these *couplets* and designate the rhyme as *a a* (for the first
two lines), *b b, c c,* and so on. If the first and third, and second
and fourth lines of a *quatrain* rhyme, we designate this as *a b a b;*
x indicates an unrhymed line.

When a poem, by means of rhyme and spacing on the page, puts lines together in groups, the groups are called *stanzas*. A frequently used stanza (found in "Sir Patrick Spence") is the *ballad stanza*, a succession of four-line groups in which lines 1 and 3 are tetrameter, 2 and 4 trimeter, and the rhyme scheme is *x a x a*.

Shelley's "Ode to the West Wind" is written in a stanza known as *terza rima*—that is, it rhymes *a b a, b c b, c d c,* and so on. *Rhyme royal* ("They Flee from Me") is a seven-line stanza of iambic pentameter, rhyming *a b a b b c c*. *Ottava rima* is an eight-line stanza of iambic pentameter, rhyming *a b a b a b c c* ("Sailing to Byzantium").

A complex stanza form is the *Spenserian* (so called because Edmund Spenser used it in *The Faerie Queene*). It is a nine-line stanza, the predominant foot iambic. The first eight lines are pentameter, and the ninth line is a hexameter (Alexandrine). The rhyme scheme is *a b a b b c b c c*. Keats's "Eve of St. Agnes" is in Spenserian stanzas.

The fourteen-line *sonnet* may be considered a stanza form, especially when the poet uses a series of them to develop one idea. Sonnets are traditionally called *Shakespearean* when they consist of three quatrains rhyming *a b a b, c d c d, e f e f* and a final *g g* couplet, and *Italian* or *Petrarchan* when they consist of an *octave* rhyming *a b b a, a b b a* and a *sestet* of various *c d e* combinations.

Unrhymed iambic pentameter, the most popular meter in English for long poems, is called *blank verse*. Wordsworth's "Tintern Abbey" is an example.

Frequently a long poem is divided into groups of lines according to sense only, with no repeated patterns of rhymes or even consistency in the number of lines in the group, as in Milton's "Lycidas." These groups, commonly called stanzas, are more descriptively termed *verse paragraphs*.

Although there must obviously be a close relationship between the sound of poetry and its sense, no one has been able to describe it absolutely, and even *prosodic* theory (*versification*) is highly controversial. It is possible that what is traditionally called the *euphony* (pleasant sounds) and *cacophony* (unpleasant sounds) of poetry has an absolute relation to the phonetic contrasts of "distinctive features" of certain phonemes—the "gravity" of back vowels versus the "acuteness" of front vowels, for example [see Roman Jakobson *et al.*, *Preliminaries to Speech Analysis*, M.I.T. Acoustics

Laboratory, 1952, and John Nist, *CE*, **23** (Jan. 1961), 291-95]. It is probably more helpful to analyze the sound and sense in more comprehensive linguistic terms, as with Samuel Levin's notion of "coupling," the poet's use of equivalent meanings and/or sounds in equivalent syntactic, metrical, or rhyming positions (see Levin's analysis of Shakespeare's "When to the sessions," pp. 250-52).

RHETORIC

A poet's manner of speaking, his *rhetoric* or *style,* depends of course on the meanings of his words as well as on repeated sounds, stresses, and spacings. These meanings are automatically absorbed in the grammatical syntax of the sentences the poet uses; these sentences may be profitably examined for recurrent patterns of word order, phrases, and clauses that emphasize meaning. Further, if the poet uses words describing the things around him—*concrete* objects and actions recognized through our sight, hearing, taste, touch, smell, and perception of motion—we call the words *images* or *imagery* ("And Marian's nose looks red and raw") and usually relish their quality of representing real things. More profound *abstract* feelings and concepts, however, are more difficult to define or describe, so that the poet cannot limit his vocabulary to sense-imagery. He must usually employ rhetorical *figures of speech,* terms of comparison and contrast: as Cleanth Brooks explains in *The Well Wrought Urn,* "the poet has to work by analogies." He may compare or contrast items directly by means of *similes* ("And like a thunderbolt he falls" or "My mistress' eyes are nothing like the sun"), or—more commonly in poetry because the figure is more subtle—indirectly by means of *metaphors* ("the emperor of ice-cream" or "Much have I travell'd in the realms of gold"). He may also use a kind of metaphor that vivifies concrete or abstract phenomena by the pretense of *personification* ("Love's not Time's fool").

A poet may, and usually does, operate on an even deeper figurative level. If he uses an image or a metaphor repeatedly or emphatically, it becomes a *symbol* referring to some feeling or concept too complex to be quickly identified or scientifically discussed. For example, in the first line of Blake's eight-line poem "The Sick Rose," we can be aware of the image "rose" and the personifying metaphor "sick": "O rose, thou art sick!" But by the time we reach the end of the poem and have felt the relation of the "invisible worm" to the rose, we may perceive the dying flower as a representation of mistreated love or sexual innocence or ephemeral beauty—something that actually exists only in the whole symbol itself and cannot be summed up exactly in any expository phrase. (Indeed, despite the symbolism, the rose and the worm manage to remain quite concrete.) When the poet connects a number of symbols into a sequence that is more interested in what the narrative stands for than in the narrative itself, he is said to produce an *allegory* (see "Riddle #29: The Moon and the Sun").

Finally, as Brooks and others have demonstrated, a poet may hold our attention forcibly and at the same time indicate the complexity of his subject by saying something rather surprising which he does not mean literally. This statement is usually called *irony* if the poet means something different from what his words actually say, as when Wyatt's forsaken lover in "They Flee from Me" notes that "I so kindly am served," or when Robinson is really talking about Miniver Cheevy's lack of action when he says that "Miniver thought, and thought, and thought, / And thought about it." When the figurative statement is strikingly unexpected, even to the point of appearing wrong, and yet is quite meaningful on reflection, it is called *paradox,* as when Donne *puns* on his name in telling God, "When thou hast done, thou hast not done," or when Hopkins tells the grieving child Margaret that "It is Margaret you mourn for." A further use of *paradox* is Brooks's notion that the situation and tone of most poems are *paradoxical* ("the language of poetry is the language of paradox") in that the poet is usually taking a fresh view of his subject that contrasts with the ordinary view, surprising us and forcing us to think poetically, in a special way that is quite illogical and unscientific. Thus we might call Frost's "Fire and Ice" paradoxical because the poet implies that "desire" and "hate," usually considered strong but personal emotions, could destroy the universe. Irony and paradox are plainly related to the exaggerated ways of speaking called *overstatement* (*hyperbole*) and *understatement.*

Poets have an additional set of *semantic* (embodying meaning) verbal tools to work with—words that refer to poetry, knowledge, and feelings already well known to educated readers. Thus many poets introduce brief *allusions* to historical or literary events ("Like Roland's ghost winding a silent horn") or use characters and crises from ancient *myth* as basis for new action, as in Tennyson's "Ulysses" or Housman's "Easter Hymn." Indeed, some critics and psychologists feel that literature is most successful when it embodies new representations of basic human and literary *archetypes,* those traditional characters, situations, and relationships that may concern (as Jung suggests) feelings common to every human psyche, like the son's need to displace the father that lies in the background of "Edward," or the sacrificial scapegoat lamb briefly contrasted with Blake's "Tyger," or the physical birth and emotional rebirth in "The Death of the Ball Turret Gunner." Formalized archetypes may be said to be present in literary *conventions,* or customary devices and patterns, which a poet imitates for his own purposes. Thus Milton's "Lycidas" discusses profound matters in the ancient Greek form of the *pastoral,* poetry in which surface life was simplified into that of shepherds. And thus all the many poems about dead persons, from "Lycidas" to "Danny Deever," follow the convention of the literary *elegy* of somehow eliciting the uniqueness of the deceased. Many poets, finally, are able to make meaningful reference beyond their immediate purposes by their *diction,* their selection of words from specialized vocabularies, or from levels of usage, or from established attitudes—as when Reed plays with the jargon of Army training in "Naming of Parts" or Roethke chooses terms from nature and animal life to evoke the special quality of the girl in "Elegy for Jane."

Beyond *figurative language,* there is in most poetry (as Brooks and Warren demonstrated) a *dramatic* element, even in non-narrative verse, a minimal amount of *plot,* of *conflict* and *resolution,* that can provide *structure* for a poem. There is not only the overt kind of story in a long piece like "The Rime of the Ancient Mariner," not only the *dramatic monologues* delivered by Browning's characters to persons in a specific *setting,* but also there is the faint, covert drama of even a two-line *Imagist* (a school of poets emphasizing images) poem like Pound's "In a Station of the Metro," where the speaker, the plot's *hero* or *protagonist,* after one line of implicit struggle to define what he sees, arrives at a triumphant *dénouement* in the second line.

As with all works of literary creation, every poem has a *tone,* the poet's way of speaking that partly expresses his underlying opinion of what he or his speaker is saying and his underlying opinion of his reader. Tone is easy to define when it is obvious:

extremely devout as in Poe's "To Helen" or extremely ironical as in Fearing's "Dirge." It is much more difficult to find proper adjectives for the implicit attitude of a more subtle modern piece, like Nemerov's "The Goose Fish" or the ancient quatrain "Western Wind." Similarly, it may be easy to sum up the *primary theme*—the total meaning, main idea, or governing concept—of a simple poem like "John Anderson, My Jo," but quite another problem to choose among the various possible *thematic* emphases of a Keats *ode* (see the cases).

Course Procedure and Study Sequences

COURSE PROCEDURE

1. The instructor should himself follow out the suggestions for using cases and critiques (Introduction) to determine how much he wishes the students to do for an assignment.

2. He should make sure that the students thoroughly understand the procedure and its aims before they do any assignments.

3. An instructor who wishes to guarantee the out-of-class preparation of his students can ask them to submit brief ("yes," "no," etc.) or extended (reasons for "yes," "no," etc.) written responses to all the points in a case or critique. If the teacher collects the completed forms at the beginning of class, he can be sure that his students have read the assigned poems carefully and have reacted to them, and that they are prepared for discussion, questions, or comments. The teacher may ignore the case completely in class, or he may take up as many points as he wishes; he may grade the papers or the performance of the class. He may also discover and deal with weak or recalcitrant students then instead of in the final examination. As a means for placing the burden of learning on the student, where it belongs, the case method is unique.

4. Any case or critique, or combination thereof, can serve as a quiz, an examination question, the basis for a short paper, or (with the critical references) the basis for a longer research paper, or as the unassigned basis for class discussion.

5. Any aspect of poetics discussed in Appendix A can be applied to any poem, including those with cases or critiques, for class discussion, outside papers, or testing.

6. The instructor may induce advanced critical thinking by assigning a poem and asking students to write original or research cases or critiques on it.

7. Instruction for students writing their own poems may be derived from the critique on haiku and from the appendix on poetics.

[1] Based on the first edition Introduction and *Teacher's Manual*.

STUDY SEQUENCES

1. *Clusters of Poems by Popular Poets*

Auden	Hardy (4)	Stevens (4)
Blake (9)	Hopkins (8)	Tennyson (6)
Browning (6)	Housman (5)	Wilbur (4)
Dickinson (8)	Keats (7)	Wordsworth (8)
Donne (7)	Robinson (5)	Yeats (6)
Frost (8)	Shakespeare (8)	

2. *National and Historical Groups*

American (71): Aiken, Booth, Ciardi (2), Cummings (2), DeSuze, Dickinson (8), Dugan, Eberhart (2), Eliot (3), Emerson, Fearing, Francis, Frost (8), Hall, Holmes, Jarrell, Kennedy, Levertov, Longfellow, MacLeish (3), Melville, Nash, Nemerov, Poe, Pound (3), Ransom (3), Robinson (5), Roethke (2), Shapiro (2), Starbuck, Stevens (4), Whitman (2), Wilbur (4) (*see also* American, Contemporary)

American, Contemporary (61): Aiken, Booth, Ciardi (2), Cummings (2), DeSuze, Dugan, Dickinson (8), Eberhart (2), Eliot (3), Fearing, Francis, Frost (8), Hall, Jarrell, Kennedy, Levertov, MacLeish (3), Nash, Nemerov, Ransom (3), Robinson (5), Roethke (2), Shapiro (2), Starbuck, Stevens (4), Wilbur (4)

Anglo-Saxon (2): Deor, Riddle #29

Biblical (1): Psalm 137

British (150): *see* Anglo-Saxon; British, Contemporary; Eighteenth Century; Elizabethan; Middle English; Pre-Elizabethan; Romantic; Seventeenth Century; Victorian

British, Contemporary (34): Auden (2), Betjeman, Bridges, de la Mare, Gunn, Hardy (4), Hopkins (8), Housman (5), Kipling, Reed, Spender, Stephens, Thomas (2), Yeats (6)

Eighteenth Century (7): Collins, Dryden, Gray, Pope (2), Swift (2)

Elizabethan (16): Campion, Daniel, Drayton, Marlowe, Nashe, Ralegh, Shakespeare (8), Sidney, Spenser

Japanese (4): Bashō, Chiyo, Issa, Moritake; *all under* Haiku

Middle English (1): Chaucer

Pre-Elizabethan (6): Ballads (3), Western Wind, Wyatt (2)

Romantic (35): Blake (9), Burns, Byron, Coleridge (3), Emerson, Keats (7), Poe, Shelley (2), Whitman (2), Wordsworth (8)

Seventeenth Century (23): Donne (7), Herbert (2), Herrick (2), Jonson (2), King, King James translators, Marvell (2), Milton (2), Suckling, Waller, Webster

Victorian (25): Arnold (3), Browning (6), Clough, Dodgson [Carroll], Holmes, Longfellow, Melville, Meredith (3), Rossetti, Tennyson (6), Thompson

3. *Types, Modes, and Subjects* (short titles)

Narrative Poems

Anonymous	Humpty-Dumpty	de la Mare	The Listeners
	Sir Patrick Spence	Dodgson	
	The Three Ravens	[Carroll]	Jabberwocky
Browning	Meeting at Night	Eliot	Sweeney among the
Chaucer	from Canterbury		Nightingales
	Tales		Journey of the Magi
Coleridge	The Rime of the An-	Frost	The Most of It
	cient Mariner	Keats	The Eve of St. Agnes
Cummings	anyone lived in a	Longfellow	Paul Revere's Ride
	pretty how town	Robinson	Mr. Flood's Party

Dramatic Monologues

Browning	My Last Duchess	Gunn	Jesus and His Mother
	Soliloquy of the	Hopkins	Spring and Fall
	Spanish Cloister	Marvell	To His Coy Mistress
	The Bishop Orders	Pope	Epistle to Miss
	His Tomb		Blount
Coleridge	The Rime of the An-	Pound	Sestina: Altaforte
	cient Mariner	Tennyson	Ulysses
Donne	The Canonization	Wordsworth	Tintern Abbey
	A Lecture upon the		
	Shadow		

Sonnets

Arnold	Shakespeare	Shakespeare	When to the Ses-
Daniel	Care-Charmer Sleep		sions
Donne	Death, Be Not Proud		Let Me Not to the
	Batter My Heart		Marriage
Drayton	Since There's No		That Time of Year
	Help		The Expense of
Frost	Design		Spirit
Hopkins	Spring		My Mistress' Eyes
	Thou Art Indeed Just		Poor Soul, the Cen-
	God's Grandeur		ter
	Felix Randal	Shelley	Ozymandias
	The Windhover	Sidney	With How Sad Steps
Keats	On First Looking into	Tennyson	Now Sleeps the
	Chapman's Homer		Crimson Petal
MacLeish	The End of the	Wilbur	June Light
	World	Wordsworth	Westminster Bridge
Meredith	Lucifer in Starlight		The World Is Too
Milton	When I Consider		Much with Us
Robinson	Cliff Klingenhagen	Yeats	Leda and the Swan

Poems of Praise

Arnold	Shakespeare	Jonson	Her Triumph
Blake	The Ecchoing Green	Keats	On First Looking into
	The Tyger		Chapman's Homer
Booth	Siasconset Song		Ode to a Nightingale
Bridges	A Passer-By		Ode on a Grecian
Browning	Home-Thoughts,		Urn
	from Abroad		Ode to Psyche
Campion	Rose-Cheeked Laura		Ode on Melancholy
Collins	Ode to Evening		To Autumn
Cummings	my father moved	Longfellow	Paul Revere's Ride
Dickinson	These Are the Days	Marvell	The Garden
	I Like to See It	Melville	The Portent
	The Brain Is Wider	Poe	To Helen
	A Route of Evanes-	Roethke	Elegy for Jane
	cence	Shapiro	Buick
Dryden	To the Memory of	Shelley	Ode to the West
	Mr. Oldham		Wind
Dugan	How We Heard the	Spender	I Think Continually
	Name	Spenser	Prothalamion
Herrick	Upon Julia's Clothes	Tennyson	The Eagle
Holmes	The Last Leaf	Wordsworth	Westminster Bridge
Hopkins	Spring		The Solitary Reaper
	God's Grandeur		
	Pied Beauty		
	The Windhover		

Poems of Humor and Satire

Auden	Law Like Love	Eliot	The Love Song of
Betjeman	In Westminster Ab-		J. Alfred Prufrock
	bey	Fearing	Dirge
Browning	Soliloquy of the	Frost	It Bids Pretty Fair
	Spanish Cloister	Nash	The Private Dining-
	The Bishop Orders		Room
	His Tomb	Pope	Epistle to Miss
Ciardi	In Place of a Curse		Blount
Clough	The Latest Deca-	Ralegh	The Nymph's Reply
	logue	Reed	Naming of Parts
Coleridge	On Donne's Poetry	Robinson	Miniver Cheevy
Cummings	anyone lived in a		Mr. Flood's Party
	pretty how town	Shakespeare	My Mistress' Eyes
Dickinson	Safe in Their Ala-	Shelley	Ozymandias
	baster Chambers	Swift	A Description of the
Dodgson	Jabberwocky		Morning
[Carroll]			The Furniture of a
Donne	Song		Woman's Mind
		Yeats	The Scholars

Poems of Character

Anonymous	Deor	Fearing	Dirge
Browning	My Last Duchess	Frost	Mending Wall
	Soliloquy of the	Holmes	The Last Leaf
	Spanish Cloister	Pound	Sestina: Altaforte
	The Bishop Orders	Robinson	Richard Cory
	His Tomb		Miniver Cheevy
Chaucer	from The Canter-		Mr. Flood's Party
	bury Tales	Roethke	My Papa's Waltz
Cummings	my father moved	Swift	The Furniture of a
Eliot	The Love Song of		Woman's Mind
	J. Alfred Prufrock	Tennyson	Ulysses

Poems about Love

Aiken	When Trout Swim Down	Keats	The Eve of St. Agnes
Anonymous	Western Wind	King	The Exequy
Auden	Law Like Love	Marvell	The Passionate Shep-
Blake	The Sick Rose		herd
Browning	Meeting at Night		To His Coy Mistress
	Never the Time and	Meredith	from Modern Love
	the Place	Nemerov	The Goose Fish
Burns	John Anderson, My	Ralegh	The Nymph's Reply
	Jo	Ransom	Winter Remembered
Campion	Rose-Cheeked Laura		The Equilibrists
Cummings	anyone lived in a	Robinson	Luke Havergal
	pretty how town	Shakespeare	When to the Ses-
Donne	Song		sions
	The Canonization		Let Me Not to the
	A Valediction		Marriage
	A Lecture upon the		That Time of Year
	Shadow		The Expense of
Drayton	Since There's No		Spirit
	Help		My Mistress' Eyes
Eberhart	'When Doris Danced'	Sidney	With How Sad Steps
Eliot	The Love Song of	Suckling	Why So Pale and
	J. Alfred Prufrock		Wan
Hardy	The Phantom Horse-	Tennyson	Now Sleeps the
	woman		Crimson Petal
	In Time of "The		Come Down, O Maid
	Breaking of Na-	Thomas	In My Craft or Sul-
	tions"		len Art
Jonson	On My First Son	Wilbur	June Light
	Her Triumph	Wyatt	They Flee from Me
			My Lute, Awake

Poems about Nature

Anonymous	Riddle #29	Meredith	The Wind on the Lyre
Bashō	Haiku		
Browning	Home-Thoughts, from the Sea	Moritake	Haiku
		Ransom	Winter Remembered
Ciardi	Two Egrets	Reed	Naming of Parts
Collins	Ode to Evening	Rossetti	The Woodspurge
Dickinson	These Are the Days	Shakespeare	When Icicles Hang
	A Route of Evanescence	Shelley	Ode to the West Wind
	Apparently with No Surprise	Starbuck	Fable for Blackboard
		Stephens	In Waste Places
Frost	After Apple-Picking	Stevens	Anecdote of the Jar
	Design	Tennyson	The Kraken
	Mending Wall		The Eagle
	Stopping by Woods	Thomas	Poem in October
	The Most of It	Waller	Go, Lovely Rose
Hall	The Sleeping Giant	Whitman	Out of the Cradle
Hardy	The Darkling Thrush		When I Heard the Learn'd Astronomer
	In Time of "The Breaking of Nations"		
		Wilbur	Two Voices in a Meadow
Herbert	Virtue		
Hopkins	Spring	Wordsworth	Tintern Abbey
	Spring and Fall		I Wandered Lonely as a Cloud
	God's Grandeur		My Heart Leaps Up
	Pied Beauty		Ode: Intimations of Immortality
	The Windhover		
Housman	Loveliest of Trees		The World Is Too Much with Us
Keats	Ode to a Nightingale		
	To Autumn		
Marvell	The Garden		

Poems about Art

Auden	Musée des Beaux Arts	Keats	On First Looking into Chapman's Homer
Campion	Rose-Cheeked Laura		Ode on a Grecian Urn
Coleridge	On Donne's Poetry		
	Kubla Khan		Ode to Psyche
Dryden	To the Memory of Mr. Oldham	Levertov	The Jacob's Ladder
		MacLeish	Ars Poetica
Francis	Pitcher	Meredith	The Wind on the Lyre
Gray	Elegy		
Housman	Terence, This Is Stupid Stuff	Milton	Lycidas
		Pound	Envoi (1919)

Poems about Art (continued)

Shakespeare	My Mistress' Eyes		The Emperor of Ice-Cream
Shapiro	Buick		
	As You Say: an Anti-Poem	Thomas	In My Craft or Sullen Art
Shelley	Ozymandias	Whitman	Out of the Cradle
	Ode to the West Wind	Yeats	The Scholars
Stevens	Anecdote of the Jar		Sailing to Byzantium
	The Plot against the Giant		Among School Children
			Long-Legged Fly

Poems about Ideas and Religion

Arnold	To Marguerite		A Lecture upon the Shadow
	Dover Beach		
Auden	Law Like Love		Batter My Heart
Betjeman	In Westminster Abbey	Eberhart	The Horse Chestnut Tree
Blake	The Lamb	Eliot	Sweeney among the Nightingales
	The Little Black Boy		
	The Chimney-Sweeper		Journey of the Magi
	The Sick Rose	Emerson	Days
	The Tyger	Frost	Mending Wall
	London		After Apple-Picking
	The Poison Tree		Fire and Ice
	And Did Those Feet		Design
Browning	Soliloquy of the Spanish Cloister	Gray	The Most of It
		Gray	Elegy
		Gunn	Jesus and His Mother
	The Bishop Orders His Tomb	Hardy	The Darkling Thrush
Ciardi	Two Egrets		In Time of "The Breaking of Nations"
	In Place of a Curse		
Clough	The Latest Decalogue		The Oxen
		Herbert	Virtue
Dickinson	The Soul Selects		The Collar
	The Brain Is Wider	Herrick	Another Grace for a Child
	Because I Could Not Stop		
		Hopkins	Spring
	Apparently with No Surprise		Spring and Fall
			Thou Art Indeed Just
Donne	The Canonization		God's Grandeur
	A Hymn to God the Father		Heaven-Haven
			Felix Randal
			Pied Beauty

Poems about Ideas and Religions (continued)

Housman	Terence, This Is Stupid Stuff	Stevens	Sunday Morning
	Easter Hymn		The Emperor of Ice-Cream
	I to My Perils	Thompson	The Kingdom of God
King James translators	Psalm 137	Wilbur	June Light
			Two Voices in a Meadow
MacLeish	You, Andrew Marvell	Wordsworth	Tintern Abbey
Meredith	Lucifer in Starlight		My Heart Leaps Up
Milton	Lycidas		Ode: Intimations of Immortality
	When I Consider		
Pope	from Essay on Man	Yeats	The Magi
Robinson	Cliff Klingenhagen		Leda and the Swan
Shakespeare	The Expense of Spirit		Among School Children
Starbuck	Fable for Blackboard		Long-Legged Fly

Poems about Death

Anonymous	The Three Ravens	King	The Exequy
	Edward	Kipling	Danny Deever
Chiyo	Haiku	MacLeish	The End of the World
DeSuze	Guitar Lament		
Dickinson	Safe in Their Alabaster Chambers	Melville	The Portent
		Milton	Lycidas
	Because I Could Not Stop	Nashe	Adieu, Farewell, Earth's Bliss
Donne	Death, Be Not Proud	Ransom	Bells for John Whitesides' Daughter
Dryden	To the Memory of Mr. Oldham	Robinson	Luke Havergal
Fearing	Dirge		Richard Cory
Frost	Design	Roethke	Elegy for Jane
	The Draft Horse	Shakespeare	That Time of Year
Gray	Elegy		Poor Soul, the Center
Issa	Haiku		
Hardy	The Phantom Horsewoman		Full Fathom Five
		Stevens	The Emperor of Ice-Cream
	The Darkling Thrush		
Hopkins	Spring and Fall	Tennyson	Tears, Idle Tears
	Felix Randal	Waller	Go, Lovely Rose
Housman	To an Athlete Dying Young	Webster	Call for the Robin Redbreast
Jarrell	The Death of the Ball Turret Gunner	Whitman	Out of the Cradle
		Wilbur	The Death of a Toad
		Wordsworth	A Slumber Did My Spirit Seal
Jonson	On My First Son		
Kennedy	Little Elegy		

BEST EDITIONS OF OLDER POETRY

Anonymous, "The Three Ravens," *Melismata,* T, Ravenscroft, ed. M. Leach, 1961. "Edward," "Sir Patrick Spence," *Reliques of Ancient English Poetry,* ed. T. Percy, 1765. Arnold, *Poetical Works,* eds. C. B. Tinker and H. F. Lowry, 1950. *The Complete Writings of William Blake,* ed. G. Keynes, 1957; *The Portable Blake,* ed. A. Kazin, 1946. *The Works of Robert Browning,* ed. F. G. Kenyon, 1912.*The Poetry of Robert Burns,* eds. W. E. Henley and T. F. Henderson, 1896–97. *The Poetical Works of Lord Byron,* ed. E. H. Coleridge, 1905. *Poetical Works (in Englsih) of Thomas Campion,* ed. P. Vivian, 1909. *The Text of The Canterbury Tales,* eds. J. M. Manly and E. Rickert, 1940. Clough, *Poems,* eds. H. F. Lowry et al., 1951. *The Poems of Samuel Taylor Coleridge,* ed. E. H. Coleridge, 1912. *The Poetical Works of Gray and Collins,* eds. C. Stone and A. L. Poole, 1917. Daniel, *Poems and A Defence of Ryme,* ed. A. C. Sprague, 1930. Dodgson, *The Annotated Alice,* ed. M. Gardner, 1960. Donne, *Poems,* ed. H. J. C. Grierson, 1929; *Divine Poems,* ed. H. L. Gardner, 1952. Drayton, *Poems,* ed. J. Buxton, 1953. Dryden, *Poems,* ed. J. Kinsley, 1958. *The Complete Works of Ralph Waldo Emerson,* ed. E. W. Emerson, 1903–4. *The Works of George Herbert,* ed. F. E. Hutchinson, 1941. Herrick, *Poetical Works,* ed. L. C. Martin, 1956. *The Complete Poetical Works of Oliver Wendell Holmes,* Cambridge Ed., 1887. *Ben Jonson,* eds. C. H. Herford and P. Simpson, 1925–52. *The Poetical Works and Other Writings of John Keats,* ed. H. Buxton Forman, 1938–39; *The Poems,* ed. E. de Selincourt, 1951; *Poetical Works,* ed. H. W. Garrod, 1958. King, *Poems,* ed. J. R. Baker, 1960. *Seventeenth-Century English Poetry,* ed. R. C. Bald, 1959. *The Works of Henry Wadsworth Longfellow,* ed. S. Longfellow, 1886–91; *Complete Works,* Craigie Ed., 1904. *The Works and Life of Christopher Marlowe,* ed. R. H. Case, 1955. Marvell, *Poems and Letters,* ed. H. M. Margoliouth, 1952. *Collected Poems of Herman Melville,* ed. H. P. Vincent, 1947. *The Poetical Works of George Meredith,* ed. G. M. Trevelyan, 1930. Milton, *Poetical Works,* ed. H. Darbishire, 1952–55. Nashe, *Works,* ed. R. B. McKerrow, 1958. *The Complete Works of Edgar Allan Poe,* Virginia Ed., 1902. Pope, *Minor Poems,* eds. N. Ault and J. Butt, 1954; *An Essay on Man,* ed. M. Mack, 1950. *The Poems of Sir Walter Ralegh,* ed. A. M. C. Latham, 1951. Rossetti, *Poems,* ed. O. Doughty, 1957. *A New Variorum Edition of Shakespeare,* eds. H. E. Rollins et al., 1871–1955. *The Complete Poetical Works of Percy Bysshe Shelley,* ed. T. Hutchinson, 1950. Sidney, *Silver Poets of the Sixteenth Century,* ed. G. W. Bullett, 1947. *The Works of Edmund Spenser,* eds. E. Greenlaw et al., 1943–47. Suckling, *Seventeenth-Century English Poetry,* ed. R. C. Bald, 1959. *The Poems of Jonathan Swift,* ed. H. Williams, 1937. *The Poetic and Dramatic Works of Alfred Lord Tennyson,* ed. W. J. Rolfe, Cambridge Ed., 1898; *The Works of Tennyson,* ed. H. Tennyson, 1908. *Poems of Francis Thompson,* ed. T. L. Connelly, 1941. Waller, *Seventeenth-Century English Poetry,* ed. R. C. Bald, 1959. *The Complete Works of John Webster,* ed. F. L. Lucas, 1927. *Whitman,* ed. E. Holloway, Inclusive Ed., 1924. *The Poetical Works of William Wordsworth,* ed. E. de Selincourt, 1940–49; *Poems in Two Volumes, 1807,* ed. H. Darbishire, 1952. Wyatt, *Collected Poems,* ed. K. Muir, 1950.

Index

Titles of poems, first lines when different from titles, and literary terms and types; for authors, see alphabetical contents.